Moral Imperative

Moral Imperative

1972, Combat Rescue, and the End of
America's War in Vietnam

DARREL D. WHITCOMB

UNIVERSITY PRESS OF KANSAS

Published by the University Press of Kansas (Lawrence, Kansas 66045), which was
organized by the Kansas Board of Regents and is operated and funded by Emporia
State University, Fort Hays State University, Kansas State University, Pittsburg State
University, the University of Kansas, and Wichita State University

Library of Congress Cataloging-in-Publication Data

Names: Whitcomb, Darrel D., 1947– author.
Title: Moral imperative : 1972, combat rescue, and the end of America's war in
Vietnam / Darrel D. Whitcomb.
Description: Lawrence : University Press of Kansas, [2020] | Series: Modern war
studies | Includes bibliographical references and index.
Identifiers: LCCN 2020013485
  ISBN 9780700630066 (paperback)
  ISBN 9780700630073 (epub)
Subjects: LCSH: Vietnam War, 1961–1975—Aerial operations, American. | Vietnam
War, 1961–1975—Search and rescue operations—Vietnam. | United States. Air
Force—Search and rescue operations—History—20th century. | United States.
Marine Corps—Search and rescue operations—History—20th century. | United
States. Navy—Search and rescue operations—History—20th century. | United
States. Army—Search and rescue operations—History—20th century. | Air America.
Classification: LCC DS558.8 .W47 2020 | DDC 959.704/348—dc23
LC record available at https://lccn.loc.gov/2020013485.

British Library Cataloguing-in-Publication Data is available.

Printed in the United States of America

10 9 8 7 6 5 4 3 2 1

This book is dedicated to the soldiers, marines, airmen, and civilians who answered the calls and conducted the rescue missions for those of us still in the fight in Southeast Asia in the violent year of 1972.

Aviators from many bases, often unknown to each other, formed up over a survivor to cooperate in a rescue mission, and valued that sense of purpose and mission.

Col. (ret) Bill Andrews, "To Fly and Fight: The Experience of American Airmen in Southeast Asia"

I like to visit with that noble brotherhood of men who know combat rescue, to recall with pride and satisfaction, a time when our entire focus was on duty, honor, and country. Our mission was noble in a war that was questionable. Yes, I like to stand again in the presence of men who went into harm's way to help their fellow airmen who were in peril of death or capture. We didn't get them all, but, by God, no one can say we didn't try.

Col. (ret) Baylor Haynes, personal papers

Those of us at the point of the spear have come to realize that instead of fighting for our country, we actually fight mainly for our buddies.

Col. (ret) Tom Yarborough, *Da Nang Diary: A Forward Air Controller's Gunsight View of Flying with SOG*

CONTENTS

PREFACE

We call it the Vietnam War. But that is a misnomer. In reality, the long war in which the United States was involved from the late 1950s through the mid-1970s was waged across the breadth and depth of Southeast Asia (SEA). Nobody knew that better than the airmen who flew across it on a daily basis, especially the aircrews of the rescue forces who were responsible for search and rescue (SAR) over that 1.1-million-square-mile expanse.[1] In fact, our experience in SEA was framed by rescue events, with the loss and eventual partial recovery of our first downed crew in Laos in March 1961 and the recovery of the crew of the SS *Mayaguez* and supporting US Marines at Koh Tang island, Cambodia, in May 1975.[2]

The history of SAR throughout the long war has been ably documented and chronicled by Dr. Earl Tilford in his seminal *Search and Rescue in Southeast Asia, 1961–1975* and George Galdorisi and Tom Phillips in their great work *Leave No Man Behind*.[3]

This work is a more tightly focused examination of our rescue efforts in 1972. It relies initially on Chris Hobson's *Vietnam Air Losses: United States Air Force, Navy and Marine Corps Fixed Wing Losses in Southeast Asia, 1961–1973*. His work provides a macro look at the losses we incurred throughout the year. However, as his title indicates, his work is limited in that it does not include rotary wing losses of any of our services and the private airline Air America. Hobson does reference rescue operations but only in a limited way. However, his data allows us to determine overall trends for shootdowns and chances of recovery throughout that turbulent year.

But the story of rescue goes beyond what are mostly documented US Air Force and Navy rescues. This project has uncovered a trove of rescue stories not even hinted at in Hobson's work. They are stories of soldiers cut off from their units, advisors trapped with allied forces, contract pilots ready to do rescues in Laos, special operators in Laos or Cambodia or North Vietnam or even in the hinterlands of South Vietnam. Their collected tales—in combination with the "conventional rescues"—present a larger message, one of national commitment to bring our men home from that war. While the return of our POWs was a stated national goal, the larger principle was not lost on the men still serving. And as the end of American operations in the war became clearly evident, nobody wanted to be the last guy lost or left behind. Therefore, our propensity to provide rescue, or at least the promise of rescue, was fundamental to the American soldiers, sailors, airmen, and marines still engaged in the war in 1972.

This work is presented chronologically. Chapter 1 covers the early years of the conflict and highlights how our rescue forces—for all of the services and Air America—were introduced, matured, and then evolved. This included the deployment/activation of four US Air Force rescue squadrons, eventually under the command of a rescue group, and the deployment and adaptation of new helicopters such as the HH-3 and HH-53 aircraft. These aircraft were modified to provide an inflight refueling capability, and C-130 aircraft were improved to serve as their tankers and also command and control aircraft. US Air Force and Navy A-1 aircraft were directed to provide dedicated escort protection and serve as on-scene commanders for recovery missions. Also, the US Navy deployed squadrons of U/SH-2 and SH-3 helicopters, which provided outstanding support to joint and allied forces from their ships in the Gulf of Tonkin and the South China Sea. Helicopter Combat Support Squadron (HC-7) became their key unit for rescue operations. Additionally, US Army and Marine helicopter units would routinely perform rescue operations as part of their standard operations. As our war effort matured, US Coast Guard aircrew members were deployed with the US Air Force squadrons for augmentation and cross-training. They would fly in some of the most harrowing rescue missions of the war. By the beginning of 1972, our total overall theater rescue capability was robust and mature.

Chapters 2 through 9 discuss our rescue operations during 1972 against the backdrop of our withdrawal from the war, our diplomatic efforts to achieve a lasting peace for us and our allies, and the major military operations and campaigns that exploded across the theater when the North Vietnamese launched a massive three-pronged invasion of South Vietnam. The North Vietnamese forces were modernized with tanks, artillery, and late-model antiaircraft artillery and surface-to-air missiles, both radar and infrared guided, and with all of the accouterments of decisive war supplied by the Soviet Union and China. Accordingly, the tempo and intensity of the war ratcheted up dramatically.

After several years of direct participation in the war, the United States was withdrawing its forces. Most major US Army and Marine ground and supporting units had been withdrawn. US air and naval power was covering our retreat, although our air units were also steadily dwindling. But they would join with the forces of South Vietnam to staunch the invasion, through several dramatic air campaigns, eventually leading to a peace treaty and our nation's exit from Vietnam.

Integral to the remaining US forces were the rescue units. While also shrinking in number, they responded to downed aircrews in most regions of the theater where our air, sea, and ground combat operations ranged from counterinsurgency and interdiction to close air support for conventional units and strategic bombing of the enemy's heartland. The rescue forces utilized their equipment and personnel to the maximum of their capabilities and conducted or attempted to conduct SAR missions whenever and wherever they occurred. However, as enemy threats to recovery forces increased throughout the theater, some areas became just too dangerous for recovery forces to operate, at least in daytime and visual flight conditions. As a countertactic, the US Air Force developed a limited night recovery system for its HH-53 helicopters. Additionally, the US Air Force also began utilizing newly developed laser and loran technology that had direct applicability to rescue. During the year, the air force retired its venerable A-1s and replaced them with A-7s, a new and more capable aircraft, certainly, but not as well attuned to the rescue mission. The men of rescue exploited their new technology to its limits and experienced successes and failures.

Chapter 10 offers a compilation of macro numbers concerning our rescue operations and discusses the larger themes concerning our overall rescue motivations, operations, strengths, and weaknesses. The postscript draws a brief connection to our rescue operations today and shows how current operations are a result of the lessons hard learned from those violent days of 1972.

In the narrative, numerous specific rescue operations are discussed, some briefly, some in great detail. However, the story does not address every aircraft shot down during the year. There are two reasons for this: First, many aircraft losses did not generate a rescue effort. Second, in some instances, there is not enough information about the event to script a coherent and informative narrative. Disappointing but true.

ACKNOWLEDGMENTS

The writing of any book is really a journey, and this effort has certainly created its own trail of heroes who facilitated the effort. Special thank yous go out to Rebecca Kammerer, Aviation Technical Library at Fort Rucker, Alabama; Tim Brown and his associates at the Air Force Special Operations Command History Office, Hurlburt Field, Florida; Charles O'Connell, Maranda Gilmore, Archie Difante, Sly Jackson, and associates at the Air Force Historical Research Agency, Maxwell AFB, Alabama; the Jolly Green Association; the Southeast Asia Forward Air Controllers Association; the A-1 Skyraider Association; the Vietnam Helicopter Pilots Association; Dr. Tom Allen, Paul Oelkrug, and Patrizia Nava at the Special Collections and Archives Division, Eugene McDermott Library, University of Texas at Dallas; Lyman Reid and Martin Gedra at the National Archives, Suitland, Maryland; and Fred Allison at the US Marine Corps University.

I had an opportunity to travel to Edward AFB, California, where I visited the History Office of the Air Force Test Center. Jeannine Geiger, the archives specialist, and Darrell Shiplett in the Technical Research Library graciously helped me find several test reports concerning HH-53 development during the Vietnam War.

I had a chance to spend some special time with Merle Pribbenow. He is retired from the Central Intelligence Agency and translates North Vietnamese military unit histories into English. He was able to provide me with extracts from several that were highly germane to this work. I thank him profusely for his beyond-generous help and guidance.

My fellow SEA vets Tom Phillips and Bob LaPointe served as a navy helicopter pilot and an air force pararescueman, respectively. Both have done extensive research and writing about the Vietnam War and were more than generous in sharing their time, insight, perspectives, experiences, and works with me on this project.

I offer a special thank you to Ron Milam. He served as an enlisted sailor in US Navy rescue squadrons. He has collected voluminous data on their operations in Southeast Asia and graciously shared his data trove with me. It is an important and fascinating part of the overall rescue story, and I sincerely thank him for his generosity.

Let me also express my appreciation to Carol Stovall for her review and editing of this work. Carol, your kindness is humbly acknowledged and deeply appreciated.

I extend a special thank you to Carolyn Oredugba at the US Air Force Public Affairs office for shepherding my manuscript through the necessary security and policy review process.

The publications team at the University Press of Kansas is a great group and has been most helpful in steering me through the publication process. Special thank yous go out to Joyce Harrison, Colin Tripp, Michael Kehoe, Hannah Coleman, and the other technicians who guided me along this journey.

I am especially thankful to all of the veterans of that war who stood for interviews and reviewed the document: Dale Stovall, Jerry Shipman, Rick Simmon, Tom Green, Jim Harding, Ron Smith, Byron Hukee, Rich Finn, Jeff Colbath, Mike Moore, Larry McCaskill, Nguyen Van Kiet, and so many others. Your words are the key to and essence of the story. All of you—us— were deeply affected by the war. Some loved it and some hated it. But all of us were changed irrevocably by that experience when we were the beautiful young men of summer.

To Howie Pierson, Charlie Yates, Larry Norman, Harrold "H" Ownby, Greg "Growth" Wilson, Chuck Hines, Briggs Diuguid, Tim Carey, Bill Carruthers, and Duke Findley—I love you and miss you so. Thank you all for helping me to write it right. And let us never forget those who have yet to return—for they are the real heroes.

To Tou Xiong Ly, a valiant Hmong pilot who, like most of the Hmong pilots, flew until he died. I shared combat with you over the jungle-covered and endless mountains of northern Laos and humbly thank you for saving my life.

And lastly, to my wife, Christine. None of this could have happened without your support, encouragement, and discerning eye. You are the love and joy of my life and eternity.

CHAPTER ONE

A LONG WAR THE NEED FOR, BUILDUP, AND EVOLUTION OF RESCUE FORCES

The story of rescue in 1972 started long before that eventful year. In fact, the rescue story is interwoven with the development and flow of the conflict in its many dimensions.

Unlike World War II or Korea, no single event clearly defines the beginning of US involvement in Southeast Asia (SEA). Instead, the origins of American involvement are imbedded in the ethnic and nationalist tensions that roiled the region after World War II. The United States supported France as it tried to reestablish its colonial control over the countries of the region that had been seized by Japanese forces and deployed a small military assistance and advisory group (MAAG) to Vietnam in 1950. In 1953, France granted independence to Laos and Cambodia. However, France's forces were defeated by Vietnamese communist forces at Dien Bien Phu in 1954. The Geneva Accord of 1954 formally ended the war. It codified the separation of Vietnam into two separate countries: the north, with a communist government supported by the Soviet Union and China, and the south, with a weak democracy supported by the United States and other Western powers. When the French departed Vietnam in 1957, the US MAAG took over the entire training and assistance effort. In parallel, the United States supported the formation of the Southeast Asia Treaty Organization (SEATO) to guarantee the security of Cambodia, Laos, and South Vietnam from communist aggression.[1]

Laos

While Laos was not physically divided like Vietnam, in reality the nation was contested between communist and pro-Western factions. This devolved into a bitter civil war, complicated by the fact that in 1959 the communist leaders in North Vietnam had adopted a resolution to reunite both Vietnams under their control and were beginning to use southern Laos as a conduit to move supplies and forces into South Vietnam. President

Dwight Eisenhower and his administration were deeply concerned about affairs in Laos and dispatched a small military team to the US embassy in Vientiane, Laos, to observe the civil war and the developing North Vietnamese actions. As the situation worsened, in December 1960 President Eisenhower directed the activation of Joint Task Force (JTF) -116, a US Air Force, Army, and Marine team, which could move forward into Thailand and be prepared to enter Laos. However, both sides in the Laotian conflict began peace talks, and President Eisenhower did not deploy the task force.[2]

The previous November, Senator John Kennedy of Massachusetts had been elected president of the United States. President Eisenhower briefed him on the current status of events in Laos. He told Kennedy, "If Laos should fall to the communists, then it would be just a question of time until South Vietnam, Cambodia, Thailand and Burma would collapse." The next day, Kennedy took the oath as the thirty-fifth president of the United States.[3]

The new president and his advisors considered the growing crises in SEA. They had listened carefully when the premier of the Soviet Union, Nikita Khrushchev, declared that Moscow would support "wars of national liberation" and "help the peoples striving for their independence," through the overthrow of pro-Western governments. Kennedy and his team knew that the Soviet Union was involved in the Laotian civil war, where communist forces were encroaching on northeastern Laos.[4]

In March 1961, President Kennedy ordered elements of JTF-116 consisting of US Army and Marine forces moved to Udorn Royal Thai Air Force Base (RTAFB), located in northern Thailand, just a few miles from the Mekong River and Laos, as a show of American resolve. They began to arrive on the twenty-first. Two days later, a US Air Force C-47, carrying eight American airmen and soldiers assigned to the US embassy in Laos, was shot down while on a reconnaissance mission over the Plain of Jars region of northern Laos. One man was able to bail out of the stricken aircraft. The others were killed in the crash. The Thirteenth Air Force had general responsibility for rescue in the area, but no recovery forces had been moved into Thailand. The survivor was taken prisoner by Laotian communist forces and released through diplomatic channels in 1962.[5]

One of the units attached to JTF-116 was Marine Air Base Squadron 16 (MABS-16) from Okinawa, which deployed with 455 marines and sailors, with instructions to be prepared to support 80 "other" personnel as part of Operation Millpond. Those "other" personnel were employees of a private airline named Air America, on contract to the US government. Derived from a company earlier known as Civil Air Transport, it had long

Air America H-34 1965. (Courtesy Joe Guilmartin family)

experience in Asia. Air America provided logistical air support to friendly Laotian forces as they battled with the opposing forces. It flew a collection of older fixed-wing transports and had a year previously been given four H-34s to provide direct logistical support to the Laotian army. At one point, the helicopters had been used to extract US advisors with a Laotian unit that was being overrun by communist forces. Other US elements were working with the Laotian army air force, but its development was constrained by cultural, financial, and logistical problems and increasing demands for Air America's services.[6]

As part of Millpond, MABS-16 was directed to transfer sixteen more H-34 helicopters from USMC to Air America ownership. They could be used to provide direct support for indigenous forces being recruited in the area or for search and rescue (SAR) missions. The need was present as the USAF began supporting Thai-flown RT-33s conducting reconnaissance missions. They also deployed to Thai bases a force of sixteen A-26 light bombers for possible strike missions (also as part of Millpond) and some F-100s to provide air defense.[7]

However, Kennedy decided not to order the JTF-116 ground combat elements into Laos. In an effort to defuse tensions building in Laos, Kennedy and the Soviet leader, Nikita Khrushchev, agreed to call for a cease-fire in the country and an international conference to forge a solution to the Laotian problem. The Geneva Conference on Laos started on 16 May 1961 and lasted fourteen months. The warring factions generally honored the cease-fire, and in the end, in the Geneva Accords of 1962, formally known as the Protocol on the Neutrality of Laos, declared Laos a neutral country to be ruled by a coalition government and required the removal of all foreign military forces. US forces left—the North Vietnamese forces did not. The civil war would go on but at a lower level of intensity. However, the actual "neutrality" of the country would exist only in the eyes of the beholder, and Laos would later be the scene of much heavy fighting. However, since the agreement forbade any US forces in Laos, any US activity there would be under the control of the US ambassador and his "country team."[8]

Regardless, Air America was still in place and flying throughout Laos. Its pilots were developing an intimate knowledge of the topography of the country, the location of enemy forces—especially antiaircraft artillery (AAA) units—and the ebb and flow of war in Laos. Additionally, many pilots were former military and understood the importance of SAR as well as the fundamental procedures for accomplishing recoveries. The H-34 helicopters were slow, but they were equipped with radios fully compatible with US fighter aircraft, to include auxiliary receivers for the emergency "Guard" frequency. This small force of helicopters and experienced crews with its inherent capabilities would soon serve as a SAR force in waiting.

South Vietnam

In June 1961, deeply concerned by Soviet actions around the globe in general, President Kennedy signed National Security Action Memorandum 56, which directed the US military forces to develop counterinsurgency forces capable of resisting the inroads of such Soviet-backed forces. He was also aware that the Soviet Union was already supplying the North Vietnamese with arms, equipment, and supplies. He reviewed a report written by Brig. Gen. Edward Lansdale, USAF, that warned that South Vietnam was being overwhelmed by an insurgency force of fifteen thousand fighters, with equipment and supplies from North Vietnam. Kennedy concluded that South Vietnam afforded a more favorable battleground in what appeared to be a worldwide battle against communist aggression and decided to provide increased military support to South Vietnam.[9] Throughout the rest of

the year, US Army, Air Force, Marine, and Navy ground and aviation elements began to deploy to South Vietnam. Ostensibly, they were being sent
to "advise and assist" the South Vietnamese forces. However, they would be
facing the same enemy guns, and the companies of US Army and Marine
helicopters employing the new tactic of air mobility, as well as the US Air
Force A-1, A-26, and AT-28 attack aircraft and C-123 tactical transports and
almost 3,200 soldiers, sailors, airmen, and marines would be at risk of in-
jury and loss. Regardless, very quickly, they were in the thick of the fight.[10]

These initial deployments were semicovert and did not include any res-
cue forces. By November 1962, the USAF element had lost four C-123s, a
C-47, two AT-28s, and a U-10. All "recovery" efforts were, at best, ad hoc. To
establish some form of rescue presence, the commander of the Pacific Air
Rescue Center (PARC) sent three officers and two enlisted men to Saigon,
South Vietnam, to establish a search and rescue center within the growing
USAF Air Operations Center at Tan Son Nhut Air Base on the edge of the
city. The small team arrived to find nothing but an empty room. By 1 April
1963, they had a functioning facility and were designated the Search and
Rescue Coordination Center (SARCC), with a mission to "control and coordinate search and rescue operations." However, they had no operational
control over anything except themselves and had to rely on units in the field
for any operational support.[11]

Later that year, the SARCC team helped script a Joint Vietnamese and
US Search and Rescue Agreement. It defined responsibilities and policies
for mutual coordination and control of SAR efforts within South Vietnam.
It dictated that South Vietnam was responsible for its own civil SAR and
for rescue of its own forces. SAR for US forces was the responsibility of
the commander of the recently activated US Military Assistance Command Vietnam (MACV) and the commander Second Air Division, which
controlled all USAF assets in country. US Army and Marine helicopters
were routinely conducting intra-unit recoveries as part of their assigned
missions but were not always released by their commanders for SARCC
tasking. This deficiency was illustrated on 8 October 1962, when an AT-28
crashed near the Laotian border west of Da Nang. The resulting rescue
effort required the forward deployment of a SARCC officer to serve as the
on-scene commander (OSC) and coordination with USMC helicopters (two
of which were shot down themselves), Vietnamese infantry, US Army helicopters, and a special forces team. Several days of effort were fruitless, and
the bodies of the two crewmembers were never found. This and other comparable failures indicated that a specialized recovery force was needed.[12]

Arriving at the SARCC in mid-1963, Maj. Alan Saunders conducted a study of rescue operations to date. It detailed rescue efforts to date, identified deficiencies, and determined that the tactical unit helicopter crews had no formal rescue training. Saunders completed his study in September and submitted it to the Second Air Division commander, Maj. Gen. Rollen Anthis, who approved it and began coordinating with his superior commands. This caused interservice bickering all the way up the chain of command until in May 1964, the Joint Chiefs of Staff resolved the issue by assigning the rescue mission in SEA to the air force. USAF planners had anticipated such an outcome, and rescue equipment and airmen would shortly arrive in SEA.[13]

Laos

In Laos, the Geneva Accords did not end the fighting. In the spring of 1964, the communist Pathet Lao and North Vietnamese Army (NVA) forces drove out Laotian loyalist forces from the strategic Plain of Jars in north central Laos. The Royal Lao government requested more military aid, including aircraft capable of conducting air strikes. The USAF dispatched four AT-28Ds to Udorn RTAFB in northern Thailand to train Laotian pilots to perform close air support and interdiction. There, the deployed Detachment 6 of the First Air Commando Wing from Hurlburt Field, Florida, was creating a large training, operations, and logistics center to directly support Laotian or Thai forces. It was called Waterpump. Seven Air America pilots were also trained to fly the aircraft so that they could escort their H-34s on resupply or SAR missions, or if directed, strike missions.[14]

Additionally, President Lyndon Johnson directed the dispatch of USAF F-100s and RF-101s to South Vietnam and Thailand, while four US Navy aircraft carriers, USS *Bon Homme Richard*, USS *Constellation*, USS *Kitty Hawk*, and USS *Ticonderoga*, were on station in the Gulf of Tonkin (GOT) as part of Task Force 77 (TF-77). In support of the Royal Laotian forces within a program code named Yankee Team, USAF RF-101s and Navy RF-8s were dispatched to perform reconnaissance of attacking forces. On 6 June, an RF-8 off the *Kitty Hawk* was downed by AAA east of the Plain of Jars, and the pilot, Lt. Charles Klusmann, ejected. Air America aircraft responded to his mayday call and initiated a rescue operation. The four AT-28s at Waterpump launched with Air America pilots flying them. However, before they could arrive, Klusmann was taken prisoner by Pathet Lao troops. Fortunately, he was able to escape three months later and made it to a friendly village, where an Air America helicopter picked him up and returned him to US control.[15]

On 7 June, an F-8 escorting another reconnaissance mission was mortally damaged by AAA and the pilot, Commander Doyle Lynn, ejected. Again, Air America crews diverted to initiate a SAR operation. However, they were not able to determine his location. The next morning, an Air America C-7 crew picked up his beacon signal and H-34s were dispatched to search for Lynn. When he heard them approaching, he fired a flare and was rescued. The next day, President Johnson authorized USAF F-100s to strike AAA sites in northern Laos, and air missions steadily escalated.[16]

On 15 June, representatives of Air America met with senior Air Force leaders from Second Air Division to review SAR operations in Laos. At that meeting, Air America assumed responsibility for SAR operations for the Plain of Jars region of Laos during all Yankee Team missions, while the Air Force would be responsible for SAR in the rest of Laos, subject to the rules of engagement established by the US embassy in Laos. At the time, the air force was finalizing plans to deploy rescue assets to the theater. To meet the Laotian requirement, two HH-43Bs, crews, and support teams would be sent to a new base being opened in northeast Thailand, Nakhon Phanom (NKP) RTAFB, just a few miles from the Mekong River. NKP overlooked Mu Gia Pass, one of the key entry points for the Ho Chi Minh trail that North Vietnamese forces were using to move supplies and troops to the battlefields in South Vietnam, just 90 miles farther east. Additionally, two HU-16s would be dispatched to Udorn RTAFB, 110 miles west of NKP, to serve as airborne rescue control ships, and two more HU-16s would fly into Da Nang Air Base to perform recovery duties in the GOT. Since strike operations were also now being contemplated against enemy positions in southern Laos along the expanding Ho Chi Minh trail, arrangements were made to have US Marine H-34s sit alert at the small airfield at Khe Sanh in northern South Vietnam just a few miles from the Laotian border. By the end of June, the HH-43s were on alert at NKP. However, they had only a 140-mile range of action. Consequently, Air America still had to be prepared to conduct rescue operations. Over the last year, they had lost several H-34s, and they requested four more from the DOD. Their request was approved. As the enemy threat in Laos increased, F-100 units in Thailand were authorized to strike enemy AAA facilities in Laos, and the AT-28s were more frequently scrambled to support the Air America helicopters on rescue operations. However, the US ambassador in Laos still retained authority over all rescue missions in that country.[17]

In August 1964, US Navy ships engaged North Vietnamese patrol boats in the Gulf of Tonkin incident. In response, President Johnson directed the

HH-43s arrive at NKP in 1964. (Courtesy John Christianson)

execution of Operation Pierce Arrow. On 5 August, sixty-four strike aircraft from the USS *Ticonderoga* and USS *Constellation* struck four North Vietnamese torpedo boat bases and a fuel storage depot near Vinh in southern North Vietnam. An A-1 and an A-4 were shot down. The A-1 pilot was killed, and the A-4 pilot, Lt. Everett Alvarez, became the first POW captured by the North Vietnamese. He would not be the last. Pierce Arrow was a harbinger of what was to come in less than a year.[18]

North Vietnam Prepares

North Vietnam's military leader, General Vo Nguyen Giap, realized that his country was not prepared for what appeared to be the looming US onslaught. Working with Ho Chi Minh, he reached out to the Soviet Union and China to request large shipments of AAA, the newly developed SA-2 air defense missiles, and MiG fighters to protect his homeland. Both nations complied, and soon North Vietnamese personnel were training in both countries to operate the AAA, missiles, and MiGs, and the equipment and supplies began to arrive in North Vietnam. Accordingly, the North Vietnamese Air Defense Service began to expand and started culling the military ranks and colleges for personnel with the necessary technical skills to maintain and operate the sophisticated equipment.[19]

The shootdown of Lt. Everett Alvarez also made General Giap realize that his nation had to be prepared to capture the airmen who would be flying the aircraft that his nation had to defend against. He sent a directive to all provinces that they were to have militia teams organized and trained to respond whenever and wherever an enemy aircraft was shot down. Their mantra was:

When the enemy comes, we will know it.

When the enemy arrives, we will destroy him.

Our personnel are resolved to shoot down enemy aircraft and to capture enemy pilots on the first day of battle.[20]

Over the next year, North Vietnam would receive hundreds of 12.7mm, 14.5mm, 23mm, 37mm, 57mm, 85mm, and 100mm antiaircraft guns, some with radar guidance; SA-2 radar-guided missiles; and thirty-six MiG-17s. The 228B Missile Regiment was formed, and its Sixty-Third and Sixty-Fourth Missile Battalions were activated and deployed around the Hanoi-Haiphong region. The AAA weapons were dispersed throughout the nation, and militias formed for immediate action. They were "ready to move out to capture any sky-pirates who were shot down."[21]

American Expansion of Forces

Subsequent to Operation Pierce Arrow, President Johnson authorized two hundred thousand more US troops for the war and the movement of more USAF fighter squadrons with F-102s, F-100s, F-105s, and F-4s to Thailand and South Vietnam, with commanders contemplating missions against North Vietnam. This dramatically increased the demand for USAF rescue because the conflict was potentially spreading throughout the area, and the number of potential "customers" was also rapidly increasing. HH-43 detachments at several US and Pacific bases received orders to prepare their aircraft, crews, and support personnel for deployment to SEA. They were transported by C-124s to Bien Hoa and Da Nang Air Bases in South Vietnam and to the detachments at Udorn RTAFB and Nakhon Phanom RTAFB in Thailand. Additionally, the USAF arranged with Kaman, the maker of the HH-43, for aircraft upgrades, including armor plating, self-sealing fuel tanks, auxiliary fuel tanks, more powerful engines, better radios, a machine gun mount, and a 217-foot hoist cable with a jungle penetrator, to make the aircraft more combat ready. This would be the HH-43F model. On arrival in Thailand, the Air America crews gave the airmen green paint to cover their hot orange "rescue" colors on the aircraft. None of the USAF crews had any combat experience, and they listened intently as the Air America guys tried to prepare them for flying over the mountainous jungles of Laos and possibly North Vietnam. By November, HH-43s were on alert at four SEA bases and two forward locations.[22]

In November, another SAR occurred that showed how much rescue operations had evolved in the last year. An F-100 was shot down while escorting a Yankee Team mission near Ban Senphan, Laos. The Air America Operations Center in Vientiane was notified, and Air America diverted a C-123 into the area to act as the airborne controller until an HU-16 from Udorn could take over. They requested the services of US Navy A-1s for AAA suppression and helicopter escort. The HH-43s from NKP were directed to take off and fly to the area. This was the first combat mission for HH-43s. The A-1s met them and escorted them into the area. However, the survivor could not be located, and the HH-43s returned to NKP. Regardless, the HU-16s on station directed thirteen F-105s, eight F-100s, six A-1s, and a pair of Air America H-34s in a focused effort to find and recover the pilot. Darkness forced them to cease their efforts. Undeterred, the HU-16s were overhead the next morning at sunrise, looking for the pilot. They put in more F-105s until they sighted the pilot's parachute. The F-105s then destroyed a gun site just fifty yards away, and the HU-16 called NKP for the HH-43s. Unfortunately, they were weathered in. Instead, two Air America H-34s escorted by four AT-28s flown by Air America pilots flew out to do the pickup. Arriving over the survivor, the copilot of the H-34 went down on the hoist to assist and discovered that the F-100 pilot was dead, apparently killed when he landed in the sharp, jagged karst. It was quite a team effort, and most of the individual skill exhibited that day had been learned in just the last few months.[23]

The buildup of Air Force rescue assets continued as more HH-43s flowed into the theater. Yet everybody realized that even the improved HH-43F was barely sufficient for the needs of the theater. It would suffice for the local base rescue (LBR) and short-range recoveries. But for the longer-range missions and missions against formidable enemy defenses, something better was needed.

Laos—Operation Barrel Roll

On 14 December 1964, USAF fighter units were ordered to begin a daily and continuous air campaign against targets in northern Laos. This operation was called Barrel Roll. It would continue for eight years as USAF, US Navy, and US Marine units would support Laotian forces in their struggles against the invading North Vietnamese and their Pathet Lao allies. Air America was always in the middle of the battles because those were occurring in and around their operating areas. To direct the fighters when they worked directly in close proximity to Laotian troops, the USAF assigned a small team of enlisted combat controllers. To facilitate their mission, they would occasionally fly in the back seat of Laotian or Air America observation aircraft and function as forward air controllers (FACs). This operation continued until 1967, when they were replaced with experienced USAF volunteer FACs from the Tactical Air Support Squadrons in South Vietnam and Thailand. These FACs began using the call sign Raven with a numerical suffix based on the Laotian Military Region in which they were working, that is, 11, 25, 31, 42, and so on. They would patrol the skies of Laos until February 1973.[24]

The first USAF aircraft lost in Barrel Roll were an F-105 and F-100 downed on 13 January 1965. An Air America C-123 was in the vicinity to provide SAR support. The crew had immediate contact with two Air America H-34s and was able to quickly call them in for the recoveries of both men.[25]

In South Vietnam, the war continued to escalate. In response to increased troop deployments, Viet Cong guerrillas attacked several US bases in December and January, causing President Johnson to order retaliatory strikes in the southern part of North Vietnam on 7 February. The strikes were flown by forty-nine aircraft from the USS *Coral Sea*, USS *Hancock*, and USS *Ranger*. One A-4 was lost and the pilot was killed. When the Viet Cong retaliated with another terrorist attack, a second strike was directed, and ninety-nine aircraft, US Navy with USAF and Vietnamese Air Force (VNAF) added, struck more targets in North Vietnam. Additionally, the fighter units in South Vietnam were now authorized to begin missions in direct support of South Vietnamese units.[26]

Frustrated that his efforts thus far had not forced the North Vietnamese to staunch their support for the Viet Cong in the south, President Johnson ordered his military forces to begin a sustained bombing campaign against North Vietnam. The campaign was called Rolling Thunder. It was directed at an initial list of ninety-four targets designated by the Joint Chiefs of Staff but ultimately expanded well beyond that.

North Vietnam—Rolling Thunder

The Rolling Thunder campaign started on 2 March 1965. Its stated objectives were to boost the morale of South Vietnamese leaders; persuade the North Vietnamese leaders to cease their support for the insurgency in the South; destroy the North's transportation system, industrial base, and air defenses; and halt the flow of men and materiel to the south. A force of forty-four F-105s, forty F-100s, seven RF-101s, twenty B-57s, and nineteen VNAF A-1s struck targets just north of the Demilitarized Zone (DMZ) that separated the two Vietnams. Enemy AAA sites shot down three F-105s and two F-100s. Rescue assets were ready. HH-43s on alert forward at Quang Tri and an HU-16 on orbit over the GOT were about to score several firsts. One pilot ejected into the gulf and was picked up by an HU-16—a first for these aircraft, but successful because of a timely intervention by a flight of navy A-1s, which dealt with several North Vietnamese boats that tried to interfere. Another was picked up by an HH-43 crew in North Vietnam, the first USAF rescue from that country, and no small feat for an HH-43. A third pilot made it into Laos before ejecting and being recovered by another HH-43 crew at night as supporting fighters dropped flares, another first for the rescue forces. The fourth made it into Thailand before ejecting and was picked up by locals near the town of Roi Et. The fifth pilot, 1st Lt. Hayden Lockhart, landed in North Vietnam and became the first USAF member captured by the North Vietnamese. He would be released in 1973.[27]

About two weeks later, the HH-43s sitting alert at Quang Tri, South Vietnam, launched to recover two marines downed in an O-1 spotter aircraft ten miles north of Da Nang. In the process, one of the HH-43s was shot down, another first. The second crew was able to recover them and the bodies of the two marines. The HH-43s and HU-16s were doing their best. But the rapidly expanding arena of combat in SEA was clearly taxing them to the limits. The fighting was about to further expand, but for the men of rescue, help was on the way.[28]

The US Navy carriers in TF-77 joined the Rolling Thunder campaign on 15 March when strike flights from the USS *Ranger* hit targets east of Hanoi. One A-1 was lost when the pilot flew into the gulf. Eleven days later, a larger force of seventy aircraft off the USS *Coral Sea* and USS *Hancock* struck several targets along the coastal area of North Vietnam. Three aircraft were lost, with two pilots being rescued by an HH-43 and the third crash-landing near Da Nang. On 29 March, a comparable package returned to several of the same targets, and three more aircraft were shot down. After being hit, all the pilots turned to head out over the water. One man was recovered by a US Navy submarine, the USS *Charr*, off Haiphong. Another was rescued at sea by an HU-16.[29]

Laos—Steel Tiger

USAF units in Thailand were now bombing in northern Laos and North Vietnam on a daily basis. On 3 April, that effort expanded into southern Laos, as Operation Steel Tiger was initiated to interdict the growing Ho Chi Minh trail, which entered Laos through the Mu Gia and Ban Karai Passes and extended down to several entry points into South Vietnam and

Cambodia. There, the attack aircraft would work with USAF FACs from Da Nang and Pleiku in South Vietnam and from Udorn and then NKP RTAFB in Thailand.

That same day, both USAF and US Navy strike flights hit targets in the Thanh Hoa area of North Vietnam. Two aircraft were downed, with one pilot killed and another taken as a POW. Ominously, the flights were also attacked for the first time by North Vietnamese fighters, in this case, MiG-17s. The war was entering a new phase where air-to-air combat was going to become another factor to consider by the strike flights and the rescue forces.[30]

On 24 July, an SA-2 missile fired by a battery with a joint Soviet–North Vietnamese crew downed an F-4 from Ubon RTAFB, Thailand, about forty miles northeast of Hanoi. This was the first loss to an SA-2. The F-4 crew of Capt. Roscoe Fobair and Capt. Richard Keirn ejected. Both were immediately captured by the local militia before any rescue attempt could even be launched. However, only Keirn was confirmed as a POW, and he was held until 1973. Fobair's remains were returned in 1998. This was Keirn's second experience as a POW. In September 1944, he had been shot down in a B-17 over Germany and had spent nine months in Stalag Luft I.[31]

US Navy Rescue

With the initiation of now sustained combat and rescue operations in the theater, the US naval forces realized that they also needed to address the issue of rescue capability. Their initial effort consisted of the placement of diesel submarines in the GOT. The rescue on 29 March by the USS *Charr*, the immediate fruit of that endeavor, reckoned back to the great results of the use of submarines to form the "Lifeguard League," which rescued thousands of allied airmen and seamen during World War II. The submarines were in the GOT from March through December 1965. They were eventually replaced by ship-based US Navy UH-2 "Clementine" and later SH-3 "Big Mother" helicopters, which could forward base aboard a variety of ships. The navy began a North SAR in the northern GOT and a South SAR in the GOT just north of the DMZ, both of which could move closer to the target areas and dramatically reduce response time. Several different helicopter squadrons provided aircraft and crews for this operation but with no unit specifically designated for rescue. Navy rescue operations were also tied into the theater rescue capability through a command node aboard whatever ship was serving as the TF-77 flagship and the SARCC in Saigon, which was renamed the Joint Search and Rescue Coordination Center (JSARCC) when naval personnel were assigned to augment that facility.

Of course, US Navy ships could conduct rescues as they did for two downed aviators on 13 August, when both made it into the GOT before ejecting. However, the first US Navy helicopter rescue came on 13 September, when a navy helicopter picked up an USAF F-100 pilot in the water east of Nha Trang, South Vietnam. The first North SAR recovery occurred on 20 September, when an A-4 was shot down and the pilot ejected thirty-five miles inland. A UH-2 from the USS *Galveston*, escorted by two A-1s, flew in and picked him up. These two events demonstrated that another sorely needed vital asset had been added to the overall theater rescue capability. By that point, seventy-four navy aircraft had been lost in the war, and seven personnel had been rescued by HU-16s, four by USAF HH-43s, two by Air America, and two by the destroyers.[32]

New USAF Helicopters and Escorts
The efficacy of the US Navy A-1s as rescue escort aircraft was obvious to all. However, they were needed for strike operations in North Vietnam. The Seventh Air Force (AF) began rotating A-1s from the 602nd Air Commando Squadron (ACS), located initially at Bien Hoa Air Base, South Vietnam, to Udorn for rescue support on a temporary duty (TDY) basis. However, the Seventh AF planners accepted the operational necessity, and by the end of 1966, the 602nd was permanently stationed at Udorn. They were better at providing escort than the AT-28s located across the runway at the Waterpump detachment. Additionally, they were called on to provide strike support to Laotian loyalist forces, and they performed yeoman duty in that role, much to the delight of the US ambassador to Laos.[33]

On 30 June 1965, the Thirty-Eighth Air Rescue Squadron (ARSq) was activated at Tan Son Nhut Air Base, South Vietnam, to command and control all of the rescue detachments that were being activated in the theater. Eventually, they would command ten detachments and operate the JSARCC.[34]

A month later, two Sikorsky CH-3Cs arrived at NKP to supplement the HH-43 detachment. These larger helicopters were stronger and faster than the HH-43s, with a longer range and some armor protection. They could fly higher to avoid the ever-increasing enemy antiaircraft guns. Adorned in a mottled coat of camouflage paint, the aircraft were quickly dubbed the "Jolly Green Giants" after the character used to advertise canned vegetables back in the United States.

In September, two new HH-3E helicopters arrived and assumed rescue duties at Udorn. The CH-3s from NKP joined them. As more HH-3s arrived, some were also stationed at Da Nang. The HH-3E aircraft were specifically optimized for rescue. They had external fuel tanks and an added internal tank for extended range, one thousand pounds of armor plating arrayed around critical parts of the aircraft, shatterproof canopies, a hydraulic hoist with 240-foot steel cable for pulling personnel up out of the dense triple-canopy jungle, and more powerful engines that allowed the helicopters to climb up to twelve thousand feet to avoid antiaircraft guns. Additionally, they were modified with mounts for machine guns, and later miniguns, for self-defense. The pararescue jumpers (PJs) and flight engineers were trained to fire the guns.[35]

However, the HH-43s were still on alert for combat recoveries. On 20 September, two were scrambled from NKP to recover an F-105 pilot downed near Vinh, North Vietnam. The helicopters rendezvoused with two A-1s who had located the survivor and were covering him. No enemy action was noted, and the lead helicopter went into a hover over the survivor and lowered the jungle penetrator. It was a trap. Enemy forces surrounding the area raked the aircraft with heavy fire, and the helicopter crashed near the F-105 pilot. As the A-1s attacked the enemy forces, the second helicopter tried to enter the area but was driven away when it too was badly damaged by the fire. The F-105 pilot and three airmen from the HH-43 were captured. They were released in 1973. The fourth man on the helicopter crew evaded west through Laos until captured by Laotian communist forces. Imprisoned, he escaped and evaded until June 1966, when he was killed by a Laotian villager. On 21 September, the HH-43s were rerolled for rescues in more benign areas and local base rescue, and the CH-3s and the HH-3Es were solely placed on call for missions into high-threat areas.[36]

The the HH-3s were quickly put to use. In a big strike package into North Vietnam on 5 November, an F-105, Oak 01, was downed by a recently introduced SA-2 radar-guided missile. A wingman reported that he had seen the pilot eject, but the lateness of the day and the weather precluded an immediate effort. The next morning, two Udorn A-1s using the call sign of Sandys 11 and 12 (the first use of that call sign) launched to find him. They were escorted initially by an HC-54, now performing the airborne mission commander (AMC) role since the HU-16s had been transferred to Da Nang to do the water recoveries. Additionally, two of the new CH-3s on alert at a forward location at Lima Site (LS) 36 near Na Khang, Laos, launched. One CH-3 had an engine problem and returned. The other, Jolly Green 85, proceeded toward the rescue area.

In the massive three-day rescue effort, two of the A-1s, Jolly Green 85, and a US Navy UH-2 were shot down. One man from Jolly Green 85 and the UH-2 crew were recovered; all of the rest were either killed or captured. SARs in North Vietnam could be dangerous events.[37]

As 1965 drew to a close, the air campaigns in SEA intensified. US Navy SAR forces were now in place aboard the ships. An aircraft carrier with the newer and bigger SH-3 helicopters would be in the GOT for the duration of Rolling Thunder. This was a vital reinforcement because losses to enemy AAA, SA-2s, and MiGs rose faster than the growth in aircrew recovery capability. From 1962 through 30 June 1965, 71 USAF aircraft were shot down. From 1 July to 31 December 1965, the USAF lost 112. The USAF rescue forces logged 29 combat saves in the first half of 1965 and 93 in the second half. In country, US Army helicopters were credited with the rescue of 238 individuals from all services, and civilians. In part because of their role in rescue escort, especially in North Vietnam, the A-1s were rapidly acquiring the highest overall loss rate of any airplane in SEA.[38]

USAF Rescue Reorganization

On 1 January 1966, the rescue units went through a name change when the Air Rescue Service (ARS), which owned all USAF rescue aircraft and units, was redesignated the Aerospace Rescue and Recovery Service (ARRS), reflecting the assignment of the worldwide requirement for recovery of space hardware for the National Aeronautics and Space Administration. All rescue units would also be so renamed.

Eight days later, the USAF activated the Thirty-Seventh Aerospace Rescue and Recovery Squadron (ARRSq) at Da Nang Air Base, South Vietnam, and assigned all fixed-wing rescue aircraft in SEA and the HH-3s to it. Essentially, it was responsible for the combat recovery of personnel in North Vietnam, Laos, and the GOT. The ARRSq owned all of the HH-43s and now focused on the local base rescue mission for all USAF bases. Increasingly, though, it was also being used in South Vietnam to support US Army operations. On one such mission on 7 March 1966, an Air Force PJ, A1C William Pitsenbarger, was lowered to the ground to provide medical support to an engaged army company and organize the wounded for evacuation. In the ensuing battle, enemy forces overran the unit and killed Pitsenbarger. The unit suffered 80 percent casualties. For his actions that day, the young airman was awarded the Air Force Cross, which was later upgraded to the Medal of Honor.[39]

Concurrent with the activation of the Thirty-Seventh ARRSq, the Third Aerospace Rescue and Recovery Group (ARRG) was activated and deployed to Tan Son Nhut Air Base, to command and control all USAF rescue units and operations in the theater and operate the JSARCC. The recovery forces continued to receive more HH-3E aircraft, building to a projected force of thirty-two of the newer aircraft to be split between Da Nang and Udorn to replace the HH-43s as the combat recovery aircraft.

Theater War

As the rescue units were being reorganized, the air campaigns continued unabated and aircraft were being shot down in every part of the theater, straining the rescue forces. On 14 March 1966, a USAF F-4C was shot down thirty miles south of Thanh Hoa, and the crew ejected into the GOT about a mile offshore. The orbiting USAF HU-16 from the Thirty-Eighth ARRSq immediately diverted for the recovery and discovered that enemy boats were attempting to capture the crew. The HU-16 landed and attempted to move close to the survivors. The PJ jumped into the water to recover them as the other HU-16 crewmembers used their personal weapons to try to fend off the approaching boats. However, a mortar round from one of the boats hit the aircraft, damaging it and setting it on fire. Fortunately, a US Navy SH-3 and UH-2 had also responded and joined the fight. They were able to recover the two F-4 crewmembers and four of the HU-16 crewmembers. Tragically, two were killed in the action. This event showed the vulnerability of the HU-16 in combat operations. Within eighteen months, they would be removed from the theater, having rescued forty-seven airmen from the GOT. [40]

Two months later, on 10 May, an F-105 was shot down fifteen miles west of Yen Bai, North Vietnam. An HH-3 was scrambled out of LS-36 and picked him up within two hours in what was the deepest rescue in North Vietnam to date. In fact, throughout the conflict, rescues this far north would be very problematic and very rare. An hour after the Yen Bai rescue, another HH-3 scrambled out of LS-36 to recover another F-105 pilot, who had been shot down near Sam Neua in northern Laos. The HH-3s were paying off. [41]

The Joint Personnel Recovery Center

As air operations continued to expand across the theater, the Pacific Air Forces (PACAF) commander, Gen. Hunter Harris, was concerned about the increasing number of combat crewmembers who were being shot down and not rescued. He was aware of the USAF rescue growth plans but wanted another approach to the problem. In May 1966, he contacted Col. Harry "Heinie" Aderholt, USAF, and proposed that he develop a post-SAR operation to focus on what could be done for downed or evading airmen not rescued. He also wanted Aderholt to determine how to conduct efforts to liberate POWs. Aderholt studied the problem and recommended that Military Assistance Command, Studies and Observations Group (MACSOG), with its broad mission statement, theater authorities, and considerable operational and intelligence assets, should undertake the missions and so recommended. MACSOG had been established in January 1964 as a joint task force, combining the skills of unconventional warfare specialists from the US Army, Navy, Air Force, and Marines, and was specifically focused on operations outside of South Vietnam. MACSOG was given operational control of some of the finest air and ground special operations forces in the world, highly experienced men who were trained to work in diverse and challenging environments across international borders. Given the access that the new command had to theater-wide intelligence from a variety of sources, it was natural that it would become involved in the recovery of missing personnel.[42]

The usual turf fights ensued among the various services, but on 17 September, the Joint Personnel Recovery Center (JPRC) was activated as a separate staff division of MACSOG and given the then-classified designation of SOG Ops-80 and the code name of "Bright Light." Aderholt was designated as the first director. He had a small staff consisting of a USAF major, an army major, and three enlisted men. They provided a focal point for all intelligence information relating to detained or missing personnel in SEA. The information was used to plan and conduct recovery operations for downed airmen in evadee or escapee status and US or allied POWs. However, SOG Ops-80 had no operational control over any combat units. Aderholt and his team could advise and recommend on recovery possibilities, but they could not order their execution. That had to be done through the service component commanders and considered in comparison to all other mission requirements.[43]

On 12 September 1966, an F-105 was shot down thirty-five miles northwest of Vinh. The pilot was quickly captured. However, American commanders were not aware of his capture, and based upon information that indicated that he was evading, the JPRC (in place but not yet formally activated) recommended a recovery effort. This was its first effort. A MACSOG team was inserted but did not find the pilot.[44]

On 12 October 1966, a US Navy A-1 was shot down thirty miles southwest of Thanh Hoa. The pilot, Lt. Robert Woods, was able to make an emergency call, but a responding US Navy SH-3 was driven off by enemy fire. Woods evaded for two days until he was captured. Unaware of his status, the JPRC recommended a recovery effort with a MACSOG team.

A twelve-man team of army special forces and Nung tribesmen was flown out to the USS *Intrepid* and then inserted at the crash site by two SH-3s. After searching for four hours, the team was engaged by North Vietnamese troops. The two SH-3s returned and extracted the team. However, one of the helicopters was badly damaged and four members aboard were injured. The crew had to ditch the aircraft in the gulf, and all personnel were then rescued by the USS *Henley*.[45]

The JPRC was slow to start and a latecomer to the war. But it did provide another and unique recovery asset for American operations in Southeast Asia.

HC-130s—Inflight Refueling and Airborne Mission Commander

The new HH-3Es were in-flight refuelable, and the Air Rescue and Recovery Service conceptualized, procured, and modified HC-130s to refuel them. In the summer of 1966, the first of eleven HC-130s arrived at Udorn to replace the HC-54s as airborne mission commander (AMC) aircraft in addition to their refueling role. They would be another key piece on the rescue armada. When three more arrived, the aircraft and personnel became the initial cadre for the Thirty-Ninth ARRSq, which was also assigned to the Third ARRG.[46]

Initially, these HC-130s used the call sign Crown. Later, though, they would adopt King as their call sign. They had a full suite of radios and could contact just about any command center or tactical aircraft in the theater. Their aircraft would begin maintaining an orbit 24/7 over Laos and were easily contactable on the Guard emergency frequency. All of their crewmembers were career rescue personnel, and each cockpit crew was task-organized to support SARs. The aircraft commander actually served as the AMC. He would monitor Guard and other tactical frequencies and was usually the first to respond to a mayday call. During a SAR, the co-pilot generally talked to the airborne battlefield command and control craft (ABCCC) to coordinate fighter and tanker support. The navigator would talk to the Jolly Greens and Sandys. The radio operator maintained all communication links to the JSARCC in Saigon and, later in the war, the two local rescue coordination centers (RCCs), now established at Udorn RTAFB, Thailand, and Son Tra, South Vietnam. The flight engineer would "fly" the aircraft with the autopilot and keep it in its assigned orbit. They could also refuel the rescue helicopters when required and coordinated their rendezvous with an onboard radar.[47]

Not to be outdone, the US Navy helicopter units operating in the GOT also developed an in-flight refueling procedure. However, their helicopters were not optimized or equipped to refuel from an HC-130. Instead, they developed a method to refuel from ships while underway. In this procedure, called helicopter in-flight refueling (HIFR), the helicopters hovered next to a moving ship. A fuel line was passed to the helicopter crew. They attached it to the helicopter fuel tank(s) and received the necessary fill. It was a crude system but very effective—and sporty, especially at night.[48]

A New USAF Helicopter

Accumulating rescue after-action reports were suggesting that the new HH-3s needed more onboard firepower and better hover capability at the higher elevations in the mountainous areas of Laos. Such reports generated deep concern among the rescue commanders that the HH-3 was not up to the evolving task in SEA. Major Baylor Haynes, the Thirty-Seventh ARRSq detachment commander at Udorn, noted in a comprehensive field study that even though the HH-3 was the best recovery aircraft then available, it still had its shortcomings. While in-flight refueling gave it the range it needed, the steady increase of enemy antiaircraft guns put the aircraft at high risk in increasingly more areas. Additionally, studies showed that the longer an airman was on the ground, the worse were his odds of being rescued. Speed was life! A faster, more heavily protected and armed helicopter was needed.

Haynes also suggested that a night rescue capability would be extremely useful. Some night rescues had been attempted. But they consisted of helicopters and fixed-wing escort aircraft dropping flares so that the crews could execute standard daylight procedures for a recovery. Haynes was aware of some developmental work being done with infrared sensors, low light level television, and light-intensification systems and suggested that those technologies would possibly be useful in addressing the challenge. However, until such developmental breakthroughs existed, the only option extant was to plan for a sunrise recovery effort, further exposing the survivor(s) to capture.[49]

Combat Aircrew Recovery Aircraft

Aware of Haynes's suggestions, in the spring of 1967, the Third ARRG commander, Col. Albert Lovelady, directed his staff to analyze rescue operations in SEA to date. Maj. John McLeaish and Maj. John Silvis carried out the project. Their detailed and exhaustive report was chockablock full of data and analysis. It included a requirement for a new combat aircrew recovery aircraft (CARA).

However, the document had a larger purpose. It noted that the increasingly sophisticated and heavy antiaircraft defensive arrays being steadily deployed around Hanoi, at the coastal regions of North Vietnam, and near the DMZ in the south seriously challenged rescue in those areas. It declared: "The single most important parameter to successful combat aircrew recovery is to minimize the time from bailout to recovery, i.e., speed of reaction. CARA must be able to penetrate the most highly defended areas day or night, since this is where most aircrew are downed. Lastly, CARA must be able to survive in [the] pick-up area."[50]

The report suggested that CARA needed to have several specific capabilities:

1. Utilization of electronic countermeasures (ECM) to penetrate and operate in high-threat areas.
2. Better aircraft armor and onboard weapons for dealing with AAA and the close-in fight in the hover recovery phase.
3. Multi-engined for redundancy and safety. Effectiveness at slow speed and hover over sloped and jungle terrain.
4. Capability to carry auxiliary fuel tanks and refuel in flight.
5. Onboard advanced integrated avionics, secure communications capability with all SAR participants, and advanced navigational systems allowing precision navigation over a vast area.
6. Operations at night and in low-visibility conditions. Provide quick recovery response under all conditions. Night and low-visibility operations would also negate the capability of visually aimed weapons to shoot down low and slow helicopters.[51]

The Seventh Air Force staff submitted the requirement to Pacific Air Forces (PACAF). The specification for a night and low-visibility capability was submitted as a stand-alone requirement as SEA operational requirement (SEAOR) #114 dated 3 April 1967.[52]

The PACAF commander, Gen. John Ryan, concurred and asked that the requirement be expeditiously addressed.[53] Air Staff planners, though, concluded that the procurement of CARA, a completely new aircraft, would have necessitated a long and costly development and certification process. They also rejected any consideration for converting the HH-3s for this mission, determining that the HH-3s were already performing at maximum capability.[54]

Having seen the success that the USMC was having with the new heavy-lift CH-53As, the Air Staff concluded that this machine could be procured as an off-the-shelf replacement and modified for the rescue mission to include the avionics developed to enable night and all-weather recovery operations, thus satisfying the requirements of SEAOR #114.[55]

When the USAF contracted to buy an initial batch of eight HH-53B aircraft for rescue duties, Sikorsky loaned two CH-53As built for the USMC to the USAF and delivered them to the Forty-Eighth ARRSq at Eglin Air Force Base, Florida, for initial operational test and evaluation (IOT&E) and to train the first cadre of aircrews. Over the next eight years, the USAF would procure a total of fifty-two HH-53B/C aircraft and twenty CH-53C helicopters for special operations use.[56]

The JRCC and the RCCs

While these equipment and training developments were ongoing in the United States, the Third ARRG continued to expand its operations. Its main command center was the JSARCC (later redesignated the Joint Rescue Coordination Center [JRCC], call sign Joker)—located with the Seventh AF Tactical Air Command Center at Tan Son Nhut Air Base, near Saigon. In late 1967, it created two rescue coordination centers (RCCs) to assist in directing missions over the broad expanse of SEA. These two centers were at Son Tra, South Vietnam, and Udorn RTAFB, Thailand, respectively designated Operating Location 1 and 2 (OL-1, -2, later changed to -A and -B, and also respectively using the call signs of Queen and Jack). This was a change to allow better management of events across such a wide area. Generally, the JSARCC/JRCC controlled missions in Cambodia and South Vietnam up to about Pleiku. OL-1 handled missions in the rest of South Vietnam, the lower section of North Vietnam, and the eastern section of southern Laos. OL-2 handled missions in the remaining areas of Laos and most of North Vietnam. They were also tied in with the US Navy TF-77, which would handle SAR in the Gulf of Tonkin and up to five miles inland (very loosely interpreted)—referred to as "Feet Dry" operations—and the Bangkok SAR Sector RCC, which handled civil SAR in that region.[57]

Navy Rescue—"The Orphans of Seventh Fleet"

Navy rescue forces were in some disarray. Since the beginning of sustained air operations in the theater, several different US Navy aircraft carriers had done tours in TF-77. Each had helicopter units assigned and aboard that performed SAR. Helicopter Combat Support Squadron One (HC-1), covered most of the deployments with support from five other helicopter squadrons. To simplify overall helicopter operations, on 1 September 1967, HC-1 was broken up into three squadrons, HC-3, HC-5, and HC-7. Each had specific duties assigned to it, with HC-7 designated to be the primary SAR recovery unit for TF-77. It took control of all UH-2 and, later, HH-3A SAR detachments in the fleet. This change enabled it to focus on SAR and develop a "corporate memory" of SAR techniques, procedures, training, and organization.[58]

HC-7 was an interesting unit. Nicknamed the "Sea Devils," it was initially "based" at Naval Air Facility Atsugi, Japan, and later Naval Air Station Imperial Beach, California. However, its aircraft and most personnel were aboard the ships assigned to TF-77. They were organized into two detachments, one equipped with UH-2 aircraft and another equipped with SH/HH-3A aircraft. They were also supported by a large maintenance detachment located at Naval Air Facility Cubi Point, Philippines. As the various ships would join and then depart TF-77, the sailors, equipment, and aircraft of HC-7 would "cross-deck," that is, transfer from ship to ship. Since, unlike other sailors, they did not have a permanent base or ship to which they were assigned, they collected the moniker of "the orphans of Seventh Fleet," which they carried as a badge of honor.[59]

Rescue swimmers were assigned to the unit. These enlisted sailors were SERE (survival, evasion, resistance, and escape) trained and were experts in first aid and weapons—including the various machine guns carried on the helicopters—and were expert swimmers in any conditions day or night. They flew aboard the HC-7 helicopters or other USN or USMC helicopters being used for SAR alert. Also, they had to be very adaptive since the helos could rescue personnel at sea or on land. On one rescue, the swimmer was preparing for a land rescue when the rescue crew realized that the survivor was actually out in the water. The tactical situation changed so fast that the swimmer had no time to get his swim suit on. So, he jumped naked. The survivor had stopped talking on the radio as he thought the North Vietnamese were sending a helo to capture him. But, when he saw the red-headed naked swimmer—well, he knew he was saved.

One HC-7 enlisted member, Ron Milam, described their general modus for recoveries:

> SAR alerts varied in time, and being near the helo to respond when notified was necessary. Alert times were 15 and sometimes, 5 minutes. Crewmen slept in the helos to be ready to launch.
> En route, each crewman would prepare for feet DRY—with guns loaded and tested. We would provide the pilot and co-pilot M-16s and extra magazines.

We had to find the rescuee—small item to find in the OCEAN. We were very concerned when shore batteries were hitting close. Our rule was—"Fly no lower than the highest column of exploding ordnance."
Once the rescue swimmer was deployed, the helo would depart the immediate area of rescue. It would drop a SMOKE, to create a diversionary target for the North Vietnamese artillery. Below, the swimmer would prepare the survivor, check for injuries, and signal the helo to come in for pick-up. The first crewman in the helo would direct the helo pilot over the swimmer and/or the survivor and then toss the pre-rolled cable and hook to them. After they were hooked to the hoist line, the first crewman would instruct the pilot to begin forward flight—not a gentle operation! Exploding ordnance would require expeditious execution. The swimmer and survivor would be hoisted up on the FLY. The helo could certainly divert to the nearest ship for more substantial medical aid. SHOCK was a common rescue response and had to be anticipated. After the rescue was complete, the swimmer would keep the name tag of the rescue as a squadron trophy.[60]

The helicopter crews and rescue swimmers of HC-7 provided a critical rescue capability in the GOT. Every crewmember who flew over North Vietnam knew that "Feet Wet" was a valid and immediate rescue option.

A Night Recovery

Night rescue was a challenge. While the Air Force preferred first-light operations and addressed night recovery capability through evolving technology, the US Navy saw the advantages of night operations because the darkness limited the effect of visually aimed AAA guns, the main killer of aircraft. Throughout the conflict, they tried to develop valid night tactics. On 20 June 1968, a US Navy F-4 was shot down by an SA-2 missile twenty miles north of Vinh. Both men ejected and hid in dense foliage. As darkness settled over the area, an HC-7 UH-2 Clementine, flown by Lt. Clyde Lassen and crew, launched from the USS *Preble*. Using the darkness as cover, they flew to the burning wreckage of the F-4 and using the burning wreckage as a reference point, began to search for the two survivors as fighter aircraft dropped illumination flares, which made it possible for the helicopter pilots to hover just above the trees. The two survivors had moved to an open area, and Lassen and crew spotted them and landed to pick them up as their gunner fired at enemy troops pursuing the survivors. When they were aboard, Lassen took off and dodged more AAA through the darkness.

HC-7 cross-deck repositioning. (HC-7 History Collection, contributed by Carl Guenst)

They landed on the USS *Jouett*, with only five minutes of fuel remaining. The rescue showed the efficacy of using the cloak of night to negate visually guided AAA. Lieutenant Lassen was awarded the Medal of Honor for his actions on this mission.[61]

HH-53 Helicopters

The ARRS received the first HH-53B in June 1967. The aircraft and the second production model were loaded aboard the USS *Card*, an old escort aircraft carrier, for transport to Southeast Asia.

When the aircraft arrived at Udorn RTAFB, Thailand, Lt. Col. James Dixon was designated the HH-53B detachment commander. He certified that the first crews were ready for combat, and the HH-53Bs, quickly nicknamed the "Super Jolly Greens," began to augment the HH-3s sitting alert for rescue missions. Their initial use was limited, as maintenance crews had to work through some preliminary equipment challenges, and several aircrew members needed to qualify for in-flight refueling. Immediately, though, all participants could see that the HH-53 was indeed a major advancement over the HH-3.

As the USAF was accepting completed aircraft, it dispatched four more HH-53Bs to Udorn. Colonel Dixon put HH-53s and crews on alert at Udorn and NKP and even dispatched them to secure remote locations in northern Laos, such as Lima Site 98 near the Plain of Jars. In an evolutionary development, Dixon also put the HH-53Bs into orbits over Laos with newly received HC-130 tankers, where they could periodically refuel for several hours, remaining instantly on call for a recovery so that reaction and recovery times could be reduced as much as possible. If available, A-1s would orbit with them.

On 23 October 1967, a Udorn HH-53B commanded by Capt. Russ Cayler was scrambled to recover an F-105 pilot who had bailed out over Thailand. One month and two days later, the HH-53s logged their first combat rescue when Cayler and his crew scrambled off of the alert pad at Lima Site 98 in northern Laos to rescue the crew of an Air America H-34 that had gone down fifty miles northeast of their location.[62]

MACSOG/JPRC

On 14 January 1968, an EB-66 from Korat RTAFB, Thailand, was shot down by a MiG-21 forty miles west of Thanh Hoa. All seven crewmembers ejected or bailed out. Voice contact was established with four crewmembers, but poor weather precluded a rescue attempt that day. The next morning, a USAF HH-3E launched from LS-36 in Laos and proceeded to the area. However, just after crossing the border into North Vietnam, the helicopter crashed, but the crew escaped. Two more HH-3Es launched from LS-36. Again, the helicopters could not accomplish any recoveries because of the weather, and one aircraft was damaged by AAA. Two days later, two USAF HH-3Es were able to get through the weather to recover the downed HH-3 crew and three of the EB-66 crewmembers. Subsequently, the JPRC began planning a Bright Light recovery effort but terminated it when it was determined that terrain and enemy forces made such an attempt unfeasible. None of these efforts staged out of a Laotian airfield were cleared through the US ambassador to Laos, William Sullivan. He was furious and sent a blistering message to MACV reminding them that he ran the war in Laos and that he worked directly for the president.[63] On 11 December 1968, an RF-4C was downed at night along a segment of the Ho Chi Minh trail in southern Laos. The pilot ejected and reported that his backseater had also ejected, although he had no further contact with him. The next morning, A-1s escorted in an HH-3E who picked up the pilot. The JPRC alerted a Bright Light team at NKP for a recovery effort for the remaining man. However, an indigenous road watch team was in the area and searched fruitlessly for the second man, who was never recovered. Subsequently, Ambassador Sullivan in Vientiane forbade the Bright Light effort for the backseater.[64]

The Fortieth ARRSq

On 18 March 1968, the Fortieth ARRSq was activated at Udorn and assumed control of the six HH-53Bs. Lieutenant Colonel Dixon was assigned as the commander. He was notified that within the year, the unit would be receiving at least three newer HH-53C aircraft with more powerful engines. Dixon directed the Fortieth to establish a forward operating location (FOL) at Ubon Air Base in southeast Thailand for possible use in southern Laos.[65]

As the Fortieth ARRSq crews continued to fly missions, they were rapidly becoming a highly combat-experienced squadron. The HH-53B crews, their ever-present escort A-1 "Sandys," the HC-130 tankers, which also served as command and control aircraft, and forward air controllers (FACs) were melding into a cohesive team.

In early June 1968, crews from the Fortieth responded with unit HH-3s to the shootdown of a USN A-7, call sign Streetcar 304. The pilot was alive and located a few miles southwest of Tchepone on the Ho Chi Minh trail in central Laos. For forty hours, an armada of helicopters and support aircraft made several attempts to rescue the survivor. In the melee, an A-1 was shot down and that pilot taken prisoner. The effort became a battle, as successive shifts of recovery and support aircraft fought to rescue the A-7 pilot. They were supported by forty-four F-4s and forty-two F-105s that relentlessly pummeled the enemy guns. Almost mind-boggling at the time, that mission would soon be dwarfed many times over as the number of SAR missions continued to increase and the enemy fought tenaciously to oppose them. Many would become much more than SAR. They were horrific battles, dances of death for the purposes of facilitating a rescue. No quarter was asked, and no quarter was given.[66]

Army and USMC "Rescue"

As US Army and Marine units deployed to Vietnam, they brought with them thousands of helicopters. These aircraft were organized into air cavalry units, aerial rocket artillery units, air assault units, Medevac units, signal units, and more. They were all over South Vietnam. But the army and marines did not have designated rescue units. However, the aviators would not hesitate to respond to calls for help from any US or allied personnel. Their service tactical doctrine recognized this natural capability and designated SAR as a collateral function for the aviation units. When they operated, they always had at least a generic SAR plan, and it could be utilized at a moment's notice to recover anybody who had become isolated and needed recovery.[67]

This phenomenon was on display on 12 September 1968. Captain Ron Fogleman, USAF, was flying an F-100 on a close air support mission in the Mekong Delta region of South Vietnam. His aircraft was mortally damaged by ground fire. He ejected and landed in a mangrove swamp. A US Army AH-1 from the "Delta Devils" of the 235th Aerial Weapons Company, working in the area, heard his emergency call and quickly diverted to his location. The crew landed and directed Fogleman to open a storage bay door on the left side of the helicopter and "hang on" while they lifted him out of the area. The ubiquitous presence of US Army and USMC helicopters across Vietnam, all equipped with UHF radios and auxiliary Guard receivers, provided its own rescue capability that saved countless soldiers, sailors, marines, and airmen during the war. These numbers have never been recorded.[68] Said the great aviation pioneer, Igor Sikorsky, "It would be right to say that the helicopter's role in saving lives represents one of the most glorious pages in the history of human flight."[69]

Pave Star to Pave Imp

As 1968 ended, USAF rescue commanders took stock of their accomplishments. Blessedly, no HH-53s had been shot down; however, many had been damaged by the enemy guns. Their efforts had led to the recovery of one hundred personnel, seventy-nine in noncombat conditions and twenty-one in combat. The HH-53s were performing well, although they too were power-limited at the higher elevations. All recognized the need for a true night and all-weather capability that could be used in combat conditions as specified in SEAOR #114, subsequently changed to Seventh Air Force Combat Required Operational Capability 11–70 (CROC 11–70). Efforts were underway with Sikorsky Aircraft Corporation to develop just such a capability.[70]

In 1967, Sikorsky was awarded a contract to develop onboard avionics with off-the-shelf technology to satisfy CROC 11–70. The project was named Pave Star, and USAF engineers estimated that eight HH-53s could be equipped with a fully tested system by early 1969.[71]

Sikorsky engineers, working with the Norden Division of United Aircraft Corporation, developed a prototype kit that would provide the HH-53 with a night operations system.[72] The new systems would rely on the onboard TACAN and Doppler navigational systems for overall navigation and could conceptually be supplemented with a terrain following radar (TFR).

However, the program was plagued with problems. Increasingly, it became clear that the program would require quite a bit of elemental development work because the Pave Star system would require more than 60 new components and 200-plus electronic interfaces and basic modifications to the HH-53. Pave Star was canceled and all remaining funds redirected to the Aeronautical Systems Division of the Air Force Systems Command that was concurrently developing a limited night recovery system (LNRS) under the program Pave Imp, which called for the installation of a Doppler navigation system and a hover coupler system. The requirement was adopted by the Military Airlift Command (MAC), which owned the ARRS, as MAC Required Operational Capability (ROC) 19–70.[73]

Rolling Thunder Ends

Bowing to domestic political pressure in 1968, President Lyndon Johnson began reducing the Rolling Thunder operations. On 31 March, they were limited to 20 degrees North, then on 1 April, 19 degrees North, and finally on 1 November all operations except reconnaissance missions and escorting fighters to protect them were stopped. The cost of the three-and-one-half-year campaign was staggering in terms of aircraft and personnel lost:

Fixed-Wing Total Losses	1,314
Killed in Action	1,009
POWs	243
Combat Rescues	276
Failed Rescues	95
Rescue Aircraft Losses	45
Rescue Crew Losses	27
Rescue Crew POWs	10[74]

The end of Rolling Thunder did not presage the end of the war. There was still much hard fighting to be done, and rescue was busier than ever.

A New President

Four days after President Johnson stopped bombing North Vietnam, Richard Nixon was elected president of the United States, pledging to secure an honorable peace in the war and bring American troops home. Upon assuming office, Nixon maintained the bombing halt against North Vietnam. However, as American troops in Vietnam peaked at 536,100, he began to make plans to withdraw them, announcing the return of the first contingent of 25,000 that summer. He also agreed to a request from General Creighton

Abrams, the commander of MACV, to secretly begin bombing NVA forces in Cambodia with B-52s. The first missions occurred in March.[75]

In parallel with his bombing halt, President Johnson had also agreed to begin meeting with North Vietnamese representatives in Paris to explore a diplomatic solution to the war. President Nixon continued that initiative. Meetings were held in Paris, but these sessions quickly devolved into propaganda vehicles for both sides. Nixon directed his assistant for national security affairs, Henry Kissinger, to hold secret talks with the North Vietnamese government, whose delegation was led by Politburo member Le Duc Tho. In a more private setting the two could hold frank discussions and begin to consider a path to a diplomatic conclusion to the war.[76]

Laos—Commando Hunt

As noted, limited numbers of reconnaissance flights continued to operate over North Vietnam to observe their military activities. These flights were escorted by fighter aircraft armed and authorized to provide "protective reaction" to any North Vietnamese air defenses that might threaten the reconnaissance aircraft. However, the bulk of US tactical airpower was now focused on staunching the flow of supplies from North Vietnam into South Vietnam along the Ho Chi Minh trail complex in Laos and Cambodia. In fact, President Nixon increased the number of fighters and bombers in the theater while withdrawing ground forces. US air power would provide top cover for the ground forces as they withdrew from the war. This operation, called Commando Hunt, would continue until 1973. North Vietnam responded to this shift in focus and began moving AAA guns to protect the trail complex. Consequently, SARs began to increase in Laos and the western regions of South Vietnam. The rescue forces with their HH-3s, new HH-53s, and HC-130 aircraft were paired with an A-1 fleet that provided protection and navigational support for the vulnerable helicopters. All fighter crews knew how to contact SAR forces, and the ubiquitous FACs flying O-1, O-2, and newly introduced OV-10 aircraft were available across most of the theater to initiate SARs and serve as initial OSCs. All US military aircraft in the theater had UHF Guard frequency auxiliary receivers on their UHF radios, which meant that they could instantaneously communicate with any other aircraft in an emergency. This frequency was also installed in all survival radios. This expedient facilitated countless rescues.[77]

In the summer of 1969, the USAF rescue force peaked with a fleet of seventy-one dedicated rescue aircraft operating in four squadrons under the Third ARRG and at locations throughout South Vietnam and Thailand.

Additionally, HC-7 was dispersed aboard ships throughout the GOT. South Vietnam was still home to thousands of US Army and USMC helicopters, which would always respond to requests for help. And in Laos, the aircrews of Air America stood ready to do the same.[78]

The POWs

Aware that US POWs being held by the North Vietnamese were being badly treated and even tortured, President Nixon began speaking out about these atrocities, and he held meetings with POW families and support organizations to publicize the status of the POWs. In response, the North Vietnamese began allowing the POWs to receive more package deliveries and to more regularly send and receive mail. Most POWs were shot-down airmen who had been trained in covert communications techniques. They began sending hidden messages to family members, who shared them with military intelligence services. Many contained terse descriptions of ongoing torture and lists of POWs being held. In return, the intelligence services were able to send messages to the POWs through return mail, creating a slow but effective de facto communications system with the POWs. Mail was also carried to and from the POWs by various "peace" delegations that visited the camps—the participants unaware of the covert role they were playing. Up until the end of 1969, 100 families had received 600 letters. During 1970, the families of 330 POWs received more than 3,000 letters. In a few instances, the information that the POWs sent had direct operational value, such as one letter that included the phrase "REQMANORSAREPKMTBAVI." US intelligence sources determined that this message translated to "Request man or SAR east peak Mt Ba Vi." Consulting current maps of North Vietnam, analysts at the Defense Intelligence Agency determined that there was an active POW camp at a place called Son Tay, about twenty-two miles northwest of Hanoi, and so notified the national command authorities.[79]

HH-53Cs

The last of the HH-53Bs and then the improved HH-53Cs continued to flow into the theater through 1969 and 1970 until the Fortieth ARRSq had received a total of six Bs and eight Cs. The Thirty-Seventh ARRSq at Da Nang received eight HH-53Cs. The two squadrons relinquished their HH-3s as the larger HH-53s arrived. The HH-3s were reassigned to other rescue units worldwide.[80]

On 17 January 1969, an F-4, Stormy 02, was shot down in the dangerous

Tchepone area of central Laos. It was serving as a Fast FAC, reflecting the fact that the enemy AAA and SAM forces had gotten so large and effective that O-2s and OV-10s could not survive, and fighter assets like F-100s, F-4s, and A-4s had to be used to FAC in those areas. The downing of Stormy 02 reflected that reality, and the subsequent rescue effort dwarfed any rescue to date. The almost-three-day event involved 264 aircraft, each playing a critical role to bring out the downed airmen. Two A-1s, an O-2, and an HH-53 (the first lost in the war) were shot down. The amount of weapons tonnage expended was staggering. In-flight refueling was now almost routine. It played a key role as the helicopters logged fourteen refuelings, taking a total of 40,200 pounds of fuel from the HC-130s.[81]

As the year 1969 progressed, the battle pace for the rescue forces remained steady; missions of desperation and, sometimes, life-or-death dilemmas shattered endless periods of tedious alert. Additionally, the HH-53s were continuously called on to perform military and civil medevacs, heavy lifts, and civic actions operations. In December, they mounted another massive rescue effort to recover the crew of Boxer 22, an F-4 crew shot down just below Mu Gia Pass in Laos. The rescue effort lasted more than fifty hours. In the process, fourteen pickup attempts were made before only the weapons systems operator (WSO), Capt. "Woody" Bergeron, was rescued. Twelve helicopters and five A-1s were damaged in the effort, and one PJ was killed. The operation was supported by 366 other strike and suppression sorties, another horrendous battle against well-equipped enemy units determined to defeat the effort, and the largest SAR effort to date.[82]

The new year of 1970 started ominously for the rescue forces when on 28 January 1970, an HH-53B and crew from the Fortieth ARRSq were lost in North Vietnam. They were one of four helicopters launched to recover an F-105G crew of two shot down north of Mu Gia Pass in North Vietnam while escorting an RF-4C on a protective reaction mission. Two of the helicopters were in an orbit over Laos refueling from an HC-130 when two MiG-21s attacked Jolly Green 71, its wingman, and escort A-1s. No MiG combat air patrol (MiGCAP) USAF fighters were available, and a heat-seeking missile from one of the MiG-21s hit and destroyed the Jolly Green. There were no survivors, mute testimony that vulnerable aircraft like rescue helicopters and HC-130 tankers could not operate without air superiority. It was a tragic and egregious mistake.[83]

To readily locate and communicate with isolated personnel, the HH-53s were also equipped with the standard ultrahigh frequency (UHF) radios used by all US military aircraft. They could also be tuned to the same frequencies programmed into the survival radios. The HH-53 UHF radios included a "direction finder" capability that allowed them to receive steering guidance from voice or beeper communication from a survivor's radio. However, these auxiliary systems were notoriously finicky and too often unreliable. In November, the Third ARRG forwarded an operational requirement for an "electronic location finder" (ELF) to replace this built-in device on the helicopters. The Military Airlift Command (MAC), published MAC ROC 27–70 to address this requirement on a worldwide basis. The ROC generated a requirement for an ELF that would provide a terminal location to within ten feet at close ranges and would operate covertly and under jungle canopies without significant degradation, day and night and any weather conditions.[84]

Cambodia

In March 1970, after more than two hundred thousand American troops had been withdrawn from Vietnam, Prince Sihanouk, the leader of Cambodia, was overthrown by a military junta led by General Lon Nol, who was very supportive of South Vietnam. In response, NVA forces already in large sections of eastern Cambodia began to strike against his government. He asked President Nixon for assistance. The president responded by ordering forty-two thousand US military forces with forty-eight thousand ARVN troops to attack into the NVA sanctuaries. These moves were assisted by tactical air strikes in direct support of ground forces and a short series of air strikes against southern North Vietnam. During the entire operation in Cambodia, eight fighter or FAC aircraft were shot down. Eight crewmembers were killed, and five were rescued by US Army ground teams or helicopters. FAC, fighter, and gunship operations would continue to support allied forces and conduct interdiction missions over Cambodia until 15 August 1973. In support of this operation, the president also directed air strikes against targets just above the DMZ in North Vietnam. This was the first bombing there since the end of Rolling Thunder and took the NVA by surprise. It overwhelmed their air defenses, and only one aircraft, a USAF F-4, was downed. Both crewmembers were rescued by an HH-3 from the Thirty-Seventh ARRSq.[85]

Joint Personnel Recovery Center

The troops inside the Joint Personnel Recovery Center (JPRC) at MAC-SOG monitored all shootdowns and loss reports. When they saw an opportunity for a possible recovery, they developed the case and provided the information to the concerned command for action. On 15 April 1970, a US Army UH-1 was shot down near the Laotian border west of Dak To. Reconnaissance Team (RT) Montana was dispatched aboard two more UH-1s to recover the crew and passengers. As they arrived over the evaders, the two helicopters were taken under fire, and both were damaged. However, the evaders were picked up. Both helicopters then had to land at the Dak Seang Special Forces Camp, itself under fire, until several more UH-1s could arrive and pick up all survivors and several wounded members of RT Montana.[86]

On 21 March 1970, a USMC UH-1 was supporting a MACSOG insertion in Laos, about forty-five miles southwest of Hue, when it was shot down. Three crewmembers were killed. The copilot, 1st Lt. Larry Parsons, escaped and evaded for nineteen days before a helicopter on another MACSOG mission spotted him in an open field as he waved his map and picked him up. He had suffered third-degree burns to his arms and legs.[87]

Son Tay

In mid-November, the Fortieth ARRSq received an unusual order to stand down for a few days, ostensibly to spend additional time doing maintenance on the hard-flown helicopters. The directive also stipulated that the unit would have five aircraft ready to go on 20 November. Late that evening, several C-130s arrived from Takhli RTAFB, Thailand. They disgorged a small force of US Army and Air Force personnel, who then transferred to the ready HH-53s and also an HH-3. That force and several accompanying HC-130 tankers took off just a few minutes before midnight and turned northeast. They were headed for the POW camp near the village of Son Tay in North Vietnam, about twenty-two miles northwest of Hanoi. They would combine with A-1s, MC-130s, and other strike and support elements departing other airfields and even aircraft carriers in the Gulf of Tonkin in an effort to recover the estimated seventy-five US and allied POWs being held there.[88]

Arriving at the camp, the raiders and support aircraft overwhelmed the guards and quickly searched the cells as support aircraft swarmed above to distract the North Vietnamese air defenses. Unfortunately, the prisoners had been moved out of the camp, apparently, just a few days before. The mission was a failure in that it did not bring back any POWs. However, it did force the North Vietnamese to collect all prisoners into larger groups, where they received better care. This improved morale, as did the prisoners' inevitable discovery of the rescue effort. Remembered Maj. Richard Smith,

USAF, one of the earlier Son Tay prisoners, "We were absolutely elated when we heard of the raid. . . . It was the single most significant event in terms of our POW life. . . . It brought us together. . . . It reinforced the belief that the US would go to any length to see that we were returned."[89]

Such consolidation allowed the POWs to use the skills that they had learned in survival school to communicate more with one another and share the information and now even communications gear that they were receiving from their families through their letters and packages. Remembered one POW, "We had communications with everyone who had been shot down up to that point. And more information was being sent back to the US and being steadily collected and analyzed by the military intelligence agencies."[90]

Even though no prisoners were returned, from the perspective of the rescue crews and support personnel, the mission was quite successful. The helicopters and crews performed magnificently. Undoubtedly, there were tactical advantages to operating at night doing rescue or whatever else those heavy-lift helicopters were needed to do.

All and all, except for the two terrible losses, SAR activity in 1970 was much less intense than in previous years. For the year, the HH-53s logged fifty-four combat and twenty-three noncombat saves.[91]

1971

The new year started as several before it had in SEA. Third ARRG helicopters sat alert at Da Nang, Udorn, NKP, Ubon, Bien Hoa, and intermittently at Dong Ha and Pleiku in South Vietnam and several sites in Laos, depending on operational requirements. Most alert aircraft were now HH-53s, as they were steadily replacing the HH-3Es. Jolly Greens also maintained orbits over Laos and occasionally off the coast of North Vietnam when reconnaissance aircraft were operating there. Most helicopters and crews were ready from first light to last light. Unit aircraft were launched for several SARs in Laos, with the majority occurring near Tchepone, Laos, where South Vietnamese forces tried to cut the Ho Chi Minh trail in February and March.[92]

Into Laos

This operation was called Lam Son 719. The number of American troops in Vietnam had been shrunk to less than three hundred thousand, and their use on the ground outside of South Vietnam had been forbidden by congressional action. The MACV commander, Gen. Creighton Abrams, worked with his South Vietnamese counterpart to shape an attack with ARVN forces to achieve this objective. It was directly supported with hundreds of US Army helicopters and massive US air support. Between 8 February and 24 March, the ARVN forces were able to penetrate all the way to Tchepone in central Laos. However, the North Vietnamese commanders knew that if the ARVN prevailed, the war was lost. Consequently, they threw an overwhelming force into their counterattack and drove the ARVN back into South Vietnam. During this operation, six USAF and one USN strike aircraft were downed and six crewmembers were killed. Five were saved by USAF rescue helicopters.[93]

One of the rescue operations caused a bit of controversy. On 25 February, Gunfighter 44, an F-4 from Da Nang, was hit while providing close air support to an ARVN unit at Fire Support Base 31, a key ARVN location in Laos. The pilot did not eject. However, the WSO got out. An O-2 FAC supporting the ARVN units in the area and directing the air strike diverted from that mission to initiate the SAR for the downed airman. When he did so, direct air support for the besieged ARVN unit stopped, giving the NVA forces a critical advantage. US Army aviation units in the area tried to pick up the WSO but were driven off by intense enemy fire. After several more air strikes, a USAF HH-53 slipped in and picked up the WSO. However, the ARVN base was overrun. ARVN commanders later complained that the FAC's action had diverted tactical air at the worst possible time and had directly contributed to the fall of the base. Whether or not the actions of the FACs led to the loss of the position is undeterminable. All FACs were qualified to initiate and direct SARs and did feel a stronger allegiance to their fellow American airmen than they did to the ARVN forces on the ground. This issue of a SAR interfering with a ground battle would reappear in a much more serious way a year later.[94]

Another dramatic rescue occurred during this battle. On 5 March, 120 US Army helicopters began shuttle lifting a massive force of ARVN soldiers into Laos. Within this huge gaggle, three aircraft were designated to serve as rescue and recovery aircraft, and each carried a three-man maintenance crew. One of the recovery craft, Witchdoctor 05, from the 174th Assault Helicopter Company, was about fifteen miles into Laos and serving as the "low" bird at 50 feet above the ground when it was hit with several rounds of 12.7 mm fire. The pilot was able to put the aircraft down in the trees, and all seven soldiers escaped unscathed with every weapon that they could grab: pistols, rifles, an M-60 machine gun, and survival radios.

Over the next two days, several attempts were made to recover the troops. As USAF FACs orbited overhead, army helicopters and Jolly Greens were driven away by the AAA, and an A-1 was shot down. That pilot was recovered by one of the Jolly Greens. Regardless, USAF FACs and AC-130 gunships stayed overhead, striking any enemy forces that approached until an ARVN "Hoc Bao" force was inserted to extract the soldiers. The FACs watched as a flight of F-4s laid down a smoke screen to partly hide a team of recovery and attack helicopters from the 2/17 Cavalry as they swooped in and extracted the seven members of Witchdoctor 05 and the entire Hoc Bao extraction team.[95]

On 24 March 1971, as the very last ARVN units were crossing the border back into South Vietnam, Covey 231, 1st Lt. Jack Butcher, an OV-10 FAC from the Twentieth Tactical Air Support Squadron (TASS), was flying over the Ho Chi Minh trail when AAA destroyed his aircraft. He ejected and was quickly captured by North Vietnamese troops. Five days later, he escaped but was recaptured. Five days after his recapture, he escaped again and evaded until recaptured. This time, the NVA troops securely bound him and assured him that if he tried to escape again, he would be killed. Then they moved him north to Hanoi.

The JPRC intelligence cell monitored the message traffic generated by his escapades and recommended a Bright Light effort to recover him. MACSOG teams were flown to NKP for insertion by the CH-53s of the Twenty-First Special Operations Squadron (SOS) and escort by A-1s from the First SOS. They found signs of Butcher and conducted a wider search, but after seven hours found no hard evidence that he was still alive and free, and they were extracted by the CH-53s. The JPRC maintained a close watch over the area until determining that Butcher was under North Vietnamese control and being moved to Hanoi.[96]

Overall, Lam Son 719 was a partial success. Great quantities of supplies had been destroyed and NVA units had been decimated. But the flow of supplies was not reduced for any length of time. The South Vietnamese showed a lack of leadership and inability to mount such a large-scale operation. Additionally, owing to poor security procedures—a journalist spy had access to the South Vietnamese General Staff—the North Vietnamese were aware of the pending operation and able to take effective measures to defend against it.[97]

Politburo Planning

The North Vietnamese postmortem was much more sanguine. Their losses were high but were worth the cost of defending their key logistics line.

Their leaders concluded that the ARVN could not stand up to the North Vietnamese forces. In this, they saw strategic possibilities, perhaps even suggesting an opportunity for a strategic offensive in 1972. On 14 May, the North Vietnamese Politburo directed the Central Military Party Committee and the General Staff to prepare a plan for offensive operations that would defeat the South Vietnamese military, drive out the Americans, and unify the nation under their control. The subsequent plan called for an all-out attack with fifteen of the army's sixteen divisions in three theaters. The main attack would be made out of Cambodia through An Loc, to threaten Saigon. Another attack would come out of northeast Cambodia and attempt to cut South Vietnam in half. A third attack, coming out of Laos south of the DMZ, would seize Quang Tri and threaten Hue. NVA forces in northern Laos would support this attack with strong efforts in late 1971 to destroy Laotian forces and seize territory in the PDJ area as a way to draw off American air power.[98]

The Politburo approved the plan, directing that the operation was to begin in the spring of 1972. Party first secretary Le Duan then flew to Moscow to acquire agreements to receive a massive infusion of Soviet equipment, to include ten battalions of SA-2s, hundreds of tanks, armored personnel carriers, artillery, thousands of trucks, and required logistical support. It would take over 350 shiploads to carry it all. At the same time, the army, using lessons hard learned in Lam Son 719, began to transform itself from a light infantry force into a modern heavy mechanized force. Draft calls were expanded (to ages sixteen to thirty-five) and 150,000 more Vietnamese were ordered into national service. General Giap posted a proclamation to the men of Vietnam: "In order to fulfill the goals of Chairman Ho Chi Minh, all young men must fight. . . . A costly battle is ahead. Much sacrifice and heartache will precede our victory. . . . The Armed Forces must be increased. All youths, regardless of past deferments, must serve. . . . Victory is in sight."[99]

The 559th Transportation Group, which ran and maintained the Ho Chi Minh trail, was directed to upgrade its roads for heavier traffic and to build new heavily camouflaged routes for the southern movement of the soon-to-arrive units. In anticipation of a strong American air power response, the air defenses along the trail were strengthened and the 377th Air Defense Division, equipped with various AAA guns and SA-2 missile batteries, prepared to enter the route system to protect the traversing units as they moved south. Additionally, NVA units worked with Laotian Pathet Lao forces to push further to the west in southern Laos near Muong Phine and Saravane as further protection for the Ho Chi Minh trail complex.[100]

Rescue Changes, Modifications, and Unit Inactivations

In July, the Fortieth ARRSq moved to NKP. This allowed the unit to consolidate its operation at one base and placed it ninety miles closer to the Ho Chi Minh trail, the arena of most of its rescues. It also maintained an FOL at Ubon RTAFB for better coverage of southern Laos. The 602nd SOS was inactivated and its A-1s assigned to the First SOS also at NKP.[101]

With the demise of the Pave Star program in 1970, remaining hopes for a night and adverse-weather recovery system to satisfy the original SEAOR #114 requirement rested with the LNRS—Pave Imp. Two HH-53Bs in the states and six HH-53Cs scheduled to be shipped to Thailand would be modified for field testing.

MAC and the ARRS conducted the initial testing at Eglin AFB in late 1970. The aircraft in Thailand would be tested after they arrived. All participants realized that this would only partially fulfill the requirement initially stated in SEAOR #114.[102]

Testing at Eglin identified numerous problems with onboard systems interface and larger logistical support challenges. The field test was conducted by the crews of the Fortieth and extended into early 1971. The Fortieth commander, Lt. Col. John Morse, wrote up a final report. It stated: "The present configuration of the Pave Imp, HH-53 helicopter will not support the theater commander's requirement for a night, all weather rescue vehicle. . . . However, the system should continue to be utilized to the fullest extent possible within the limits of capabilities."[103]

The Seventh Air Force commander concurred that it was the best technology available. Two HH-53Cs equipped with the LNRS would stand ready on forty-five-minute alert at NKP or Ubon.[104] However, all parties realized clearly now that the LNRS had to have an improved navigational system, a flight director, a computer interface system, and TFR that allowed "blind" flying.[105]

The commander of the Third ARRG, Col. Warner Britton, was also worried about the increasing enemy threat posed by radar-controlled SAMs and antiaircraft guns. He forwarded a request to Seventh Air Force for radar homing and warning (RHAW) systems for the HH-53s so that the crews would receive visual and aural warnings when enemy radars were painting (detecting and tracking) or targeting them. The first conversion kits would arrive in May 1972, and by September all HH-53s in SEA had working RHAW gear.[106]

During 1971, the rescue force drew down with the inactivation of the Thirty-Eighth ARRSq. Its HH-43 detachments remained in place, but were assigned to the Thirty-Seventh and Fortieth ARRSqs, and still focused on local base rescue.[107]

The Thirty-Seventh ARRSq, still at Da Nang, supported an FOL at Bien Hoa Air Base, just north of Saigon, with helicopters and crews for possible use in the southern regions of the theater.

The "Rescue" Wing

With the transfer of the Fortieth ARRSq to NKP, the base had become a center for SAR activities. The First SOS was there with its A-1s. Additionally, the base was the home station for the Twenty-Third TASS, a FAC squadron, which flew OV-10s and provided coverage for the northern part of the Ho Chi Minh trail and northern Laos. Their radio call sign was Nail, and the Nail FACs were well versed in SAR tactics. Additionally, their squadron had just gone through a technological upgrade. Fifteen of their aircraft were being modified with a first-generation laser system called Pave Spot, which allowed them to guide laser guided bombs. The aircraft also received a loran navigational system, which was tied into the Pave Spot system and could read out the coordinates of the target being illuminated. These modified aircraft were referred to as "Pave Nails." The FACs had figured out that this system could be useful on SAR missions and were working more and more with the crews from the Fortieth ARRSq and the First SOS. In fact, the young officers would gather in one of the squadron hooch bars and discuss tactics by feeding off one another's ideas. They also formed a very strong relationship with the intelligence section of Task Force Alpha, which closely monitored and analyzed the activities along the Ho Chi Minh trail and could be very helpful by providing near real-time intelligence during SARs. It was a very fertile environment.[108]

On 16 December, an F-4 from the 366th Tactical Fighter Wing (TFW) at Da Nang, Gunfighter 82, while escorting an RF-4, was shot down by an SA-2 at about 2230 local time, just north of Mu Gia Pass. Nail 13, a Pave Nail OV-10, diverted into the area, and the backseater, Capt. Rick Atchison, was able to locate the infrared strobes of both survivors with the Pave Spot system. Nail 13 acted as the on-scene commander until four A-1s and two Jolly Greens could enter the area at first light to recover both men. This was the first use of the Pave Spot system to detect infrared strobes, another useful tactic for the rescue forces.[109]

Two days later, three F-4s from Udorn were shot down in a series of air-to-air engagements with MiG-21s in northern Laos. Two crews were captured, but a third crew awaited rescue. Two A-1s, Sandys 03 and 04, were scrambled to the area. Pave Nail OV-10s were also dispatched to the area to locate the survivors and plot their locations with their Pave Spot–loran systems. As F-4s provided top cover from more MiGs, a Pave Nail OV-10 flown by Capt. Ian Cooke and Capt. Bob Wikstrom flew into the area and located both survivors with their system. However, bad weather and darkness prevented a rescue in the mountainous terrain until the next morning. Pave Nail OV-10s stayed over the survivors through the night. At one point, a follow-on Pave Nail flown by 1st Lt. Bill Henderson and Capt. Bob DeWerff was attacked by a MiG-21, which fired two Atoll missiles at them, luckily without effect. They were replaced by another Pave Nail flown by 1st Lt. Dale Holmlund and 1st Lt. John Bush, who used their loran system to direct the release of area-denial ordnance around the survivors to prevent their capture by enemy forces.

Two HH-53s and two A-1s flown by Capt. Randy Jayne and Capt. Ron Smith were dispatched for a first light recovery. Smith was in the Sandy upgrade program, and this was his second SAR. However, the weather in the valleys precluded a pickup attempt, and BLU-52, an effective incapacitant dust, had been dropped too close to the survivors. The helicopter crew had to prepare to execute the necessary procedures to work around this area-denial weapon. Back at NKP, crews from the three squadrons got three-dimensional maps from the intelligence section and plotted the location of the survivors as determined by the Pave Nails. They designed an approach to the survivor's locations that could be flown by the Pave Nail OV-10s to guide the A-1s and Jolly Greens through the weather. The intelligence section at Task Force Alpha again provided timely and critical enemy information, which helped the recovery forces avoid considerable threats. Cooke and Wikstrom led the task force down through the weather under a one-hundred-foot ceiling. However, the rotor wash of the Jolly Greens disturbed the area-denial ordnance dropped previously, and the task force had to depart. Later in the day, the weather broke up a bit and the procedure was repeated to successfully recover both men as the enemy troops were moving in on them.[110]

Soon, these procedures were codified and coordinated with more precise intelligence to further heighten their effectiveness. For the Sandy, Jolly Green, and Nail crews, these missions showed that the new LNRS, Pave Spot, and loran systems, while clearly recognized as limited tools, could still be used in unforeseen ways to effect successful recoveries, even when facing stiff enemy opposition. The evolving technology was a clear advancement of capabilities, especially when it was combined with eager and smart young operators who would push the technology well beyond intended uses and limits. It was testimony to the inventiveness and creativity of young aircrews from the various squadrons who were able and willing to take it into battle.

All of this was captured by the NKP wing commander, Col. Jack Robinson, who wrote directly to the Seventh Air Force commander, now Gen. John Lavelle, of these amazing events:

> Recent introduction of sophisticated navigation and ordnance delivery systems designed for IFR conditions . . . have major implications for USAF rescue capabilities.
>
> The PAVENAIL can lead the helicopter directly over the survivor and provide a zero reference for the Jolly's Doppler navigation system. This technique permitted the rescue of Ashcan 01[A] . . . in IFR conditions, and the PAVE IMP instrumentation proved invaluable in this situation.
>
> TFA sensor monitoring provided real-time targeting of traffic attempting to move through the route structure into the survivor's location.[111]

Subsequently, throughout the tumultuous campaigns to come, this combination of evolving technology with creative and savvy young airmen would be utilized numerous times to recover downed US and allied airmen across the breadth and depth of Southeast Asia.

General Lavelle was heartened by the report. He had taken command of Seventh Air Force in August and was aware that the leadership of North Vietnam had decided to launch a general military offensive in 1972 to "win a decisive victory . . . and force the US imperialists to end the war by negotiating from a position of defeat." He also saw the intelligence estimates that indicated that the North Vietnamese were prepared to utilize up to fourteen of their fifteen divisions. Lavelle also knew that those forces would be heavily defended by massive AAA and SA-2 missiles and supported by increased MiG activity into northern Laos and southern North Vietnam. He intended to meet this force head on, and that was going to generate lots of business for his SAR forces.[112]

However, the year was still not over for the men of rescue. Intelligence sources had been tracking the heavy movement of men and materiel down the Ho Chi Minh trail for the past two months and the stockpiling of massive quantities of supplies just north of the DMZ. To preempt them, President Richard Nixon directed a five-day campaign of about one thousand USAF and US Navy strike sorties against this buildup. Unfortunately, bad weather caused by the northeast monsoon limited its effectiveness. The

North Vietnamese air defenses were very active, with AAA batteries firing thousands of rounds and SA-2 sites launching forty-five missiles. The USAF lost an F-4 with both crewmembers killed, and the navy lost an F-4 and an A-6. The crew of the F-4 were quickly captured, the first navy guys taken by North Vietnam since Rolling Thunder. The A-6 pilot was also killed, but the BN ejected and landed in the GOT, not far from an enemy-controlled island. Navy A-7s protected him from Vietnamese boats and guns on the island, as two HH-3As from HC-7 stationed on the USS *Denver* arrived. One searched vainly for the pilot while the other spotted the BNO and picked him up. The pilot's body was never recovered.[113]

The Seventh Air Force was still conducting reconnaissance flights over North Vietnam—the holdover from the Rolling Thunder campaign. Such flights were still being escorted by strike flights in case enemy air defenses fired on the aircraft or activated their SAM radars. When this occurred, the escorts could attack the sites and supporting elements. General Lavelle received guidance from Secretary of Defense Melvin Laird and the JCS chairman, Admiral Thomas Moorer, to be very liberal in his use of these "protective reaction strikes" under existing rules of engagement. Lavelle was aware that the North Vietnamese had just modified the tactics for their SA-2 missiles, which allowed them to utilize their large area search and AAA radars to provide tracking data to the targeting radars of individual SAM sites. The larger radars were not detectable by the radar warning systems on American aircraft. This tactical modification by the North Vietnamese enabled the SAM sites to launch missiles without initial tracking signals, thus greatly reducing their electrical emissions. The practical result of this modification was to reduce the warning time that crews of targeted aircraft would receive through their radar warning receivers and to make them more vulnerable to being shot down. Lavelle was very concerned about this modification. He knew that North Vietnamese radars were always on, and this justified the strike aircraft to drop their ordnance. He began liberally and aggressively directing "protective reaction" strikes against the major logistical sites in southern North Vietnam that were being prepared for the planned invasion. These strikes would continue into the new year.[114]

The threat to allied aircraft was also increasing in Laos. As the NVA forces began to move through the main passes at Mu Gia, Ban Karai, and Ban Ravine, the NVA moved SA-2 missile batteries and multicaliber AAA batteries around those locations. MiG-21s were also more active in that area, and SAC restricted B-52 operations in those zones. In Saigon, General

Southeast Asia, 1972. (Author photo)

Abrams was very concerned about this restriction because the B-52s were one of his most effective weapons against the advancing NVA units. Concerned about SAC's overly cautious actions, he stated, "If too great a reluctance to risk losses becomes the dominant psychology in SEA, it should be a matter of highest concern. Such a psychology is infectious and could have widespread impact." Regardless, SAC controlled those bombers, and their guidance stood. Clearly, now the limitation of American losses was an overriding concern. This put a further added premium on rescue.[115]

Rescue Statistics

Since the end of Rolling Thunder, USAF, Navy, and Marine aerial forces had suffered the following losses:

Fixed-Wing Total Losses	875
Killed in Action	405
POWs	19
Combat Rescues	183
Failed Rescues	33
Rescue Aircraft Losses	78
Rescue Crew Losses	27
Rescue Crew POWs	13[116]

Rescue was not free. It carried its own "butcher's bill."

As 1971 ended, US Navy rescue was in place. Residual US Army aviation units were still traversing South Vietnam. Air America crews were still plying their trade across Laos. MACSOG still had their capabilities and were eager to help. The Third ARRG with its Thirty-Seventh, Thirty-Ninth, and Fortieth ARRSq stood prepared to respond to downed airmen across the span of the theater with their HH-53s and LNRS aircraft, some now also modified with electronic location finders (ELF) to home in on survivor radios, follow-on plans for radar homing and warning receivers to alert them to enemy activity, flare dispensers to protect them from heat-seeking missiles, and first-generation night vision goggles to facilitate night flying.[117] All tactical aircraft were equipped with UHF radios with Guard receivers. Fighter pilots and FACs knew how to initiate and conduct a SAR. In mass, the combat aviators of the US forces in SEA were ready and able to meet the enemy head-on and to provide top cover for our ground forces as the nation withdrew from Vietnam. The rescue forces were their guardian angels. That was a part of the American way of war.

CHAPTER TWO

JANUARY–MARCH DRAWDOWN BUT

CONTINUED BATTLE

We are going to do everything we can to protect our people. . . .
The only assistance we're going to give the South Vietnamese is
air.

General Creighton Abrams, quoted in Col. (ret) Darrel
Whitcomb, *The Rescue of Bat 21*

Southeast Asia, 0001L, 1 January 1972

As planned and organized, Jolly Green HH-53s and Sandy A-1s on alert at Nakhon Phanom RTAFB (NKP), Ubon, and Da Nang greeted the new year. One
King HC-130 was airborne and orbiting over central Laos. The controllers in
the Joint Rescue Coordination Center (JRCC) were busy. Captain Elsberry was
the senior controller on duty, working a downed F-4 from Ubon RTAFB. The
aircraft, Owl 02, flown by Maj. Bill Duggan and Capt. Fred Sutter, was a night
fast forward air controller (FAC) and had gone down just south of Mu Gia
Pass. Nail FACs from NKP flying the Pave Nail OV-10s and other Owl FACs
searched for the survivors but never made voice contact. General Lavelle was
briefed on the incident. Concerned that Owl 02 might have been shot down by
an SA-2, he directed that F-105Gs maintain a cap over the scene and ordered
the Nails out of the area. Just five days earlier, a Nail FAC had been shot down
and captured near Ban Karai Pass, thirty miles south, and Lavelle felt that the
OV-10s were just too vulnerable along the border, especially at night. A visual
and listening watch was maintained in the area for the crew of Owl 02 for several days, but all efforts were in vain, and no recovery forces were committed.
Neither man ever returned. It was an inauspicious beginning for the year.[1]

Residual US Forces

As the year began, approximately 156,000 American soldiers, sailors, coast
guardsmen, marines, and airmen remained in South Vietnam. President

Nixon announced that another 70,000 would be returned by 1 May. Some of the designated US Air Force units were slated to move to Thailand. But all knew that America's role in the war was steadily waning, and some questioned the necessity of it all. To many, the incessant bombing along the Ho Chi Minh trail just seemed like a huge waste of resources and people. President Nixon kept a wary eye on the secret negotiations between Kissinger and Le Duc Tho in Paris. However, the two sides were at an impasse over the fundamental issues of the conflict: the status of two Vietnams, the long-term role of the United States as the guarantor of South Vietnam, the removal of combat forces from the region, the return of POWs, and all within the larger context of peace and stability in the entire Southeast Asia region. Nixon was scheduled to travel to Beijing and Moscow during 1972 to suggest that a reduction of support for North Vietnam would be very beneficial to overall world peace and stability. He acutely felt his countrymen's desire to withdraw from this war. However, he wanted to honor America's national commitment to South Vietnam and also Cambodia and Laos. He spoke of "Peace with honor." That rang hollow with those actually doing the fighting in this last year. Nobody wanted to be the last guy lost, although all knew that if they were downed or trapped by enemy forces, their buddies would come for them. When all other causes fade, soldiers would always fight for their compatriots. That was what the rescue forces represented.[2]

Not included in those macro numbers were also a varying number of men afloat aboard the ships of TF-77, which had assigned to it three aircraft carriers, USS *Enterprise*, USS *Constellation*, and USS *Coral Sea*. They carried almost two hundred strike/support aircraft and a rescue squadron, and a rotational number of ships that could provide ship-to-shore gunfire support. However, the navy's riverine forces, TF-117, so effective in the delta region of South Vietnam, were being reduced and withdrawn, and the Alpha Platoon of SEAL Team One was being transferred to Okinawa but could be recalled to Vietnam if needed. Their premier light strike unit VA(L)-4, "Black Ponies," equipped with OV-10s, was slated for inactivation at the end of March, and its cohort, HA(L)-3 Helicopter Attack Squadron, "Seawolves," equipped with UH-1s, was slated for a similar fate later in the year.[3]

HC-7 was still with the fleet. Led by Cdr. John Woolam, its two detachments with their UH-2 and HH-3A aircraft were scattered out on several ships. However, they too were designated for a troop reduction, with their five-ship UH-2 detachment slated to inactivate and return to the contiguous United States (CONUS) on 31 March. But the ten HH-3A "Big Mothers" and their crews were ready for action. The squadron had now been afloat in Southeast Asia (SEA) for almost four and one-half years, the longest of any unit in the US Navy. And they were now, certainly, the repository of knowledge and experience of navy SAR capability.[4]

US Air Force strength in the theater was still significant, with 280 fighter and strike aircraft, 28 AC-119/AC-130 gunships, and 52 B-52s, at six bases in South Vietnam and Thailand. This included the 42 pilots and 26 A-1s of the First Special Operations Squadron (SOS) at NKP. This squadron was the last of the USAF A-1s squadrons that had been active in SEA since 1963. Their mission was to "provide direct and close air support to allied forces in SEA and to accomplish such missions as directed by higher headquarters." Throughout the war, they had provided direct support to indigenous forces in Laos and were a favorite asset of US ambassadors in Laos, who fought fiercely to keep them in the theater and supporting our allies in Laos. They interdicted enemy supplies and trucks on the Ho Chi Minh trail and escorted special operations helicopters for the infiltration and exfiltration of small special forces/Military Assistance Command, Studies and Observations Group (MACSOG) performing highly specialized missions. And they still had to cover the Sandy tasking and were slowly recovering from the hard flying that they had logged in December.[5]

The pilots of the First SOS were drawn from across the Air Force. Primarily, the older pilots were former air defense or tactical fighter pilots. But over half of the squadron was younger airmen, many on their second flying tour after duty as instructor pilots, or even recent graduates from flight training. The unit was commanded by Lt. Col. Martin Barbena. He focused on flight operations and liked to fly a lot. However, he flew strike missions, not the SARs. He let the younger airmen do that, serving instead as a SAR coordinator when his squadron was involved in intense and challenging rescues.[6]

This considerable force was backed up with another thirty-one B-52s at Anderson AFB, Guam, and twenty-four rotational C-130s and a varying number of KC-135s based in Thailand. Three FAC squadrons, the Twentieth, Twenty-First, and Twenty-Second Tactical Air Support Squadron (TASS), still patrolled the skies of South Vietnam, Cambodia, and Laos in their O-2s and OV-10s. From Thailand, the Twenty-Third TASS still provided coverage over northern Laos, the Ho Chi Minh trail, and northern Cambodia with its OV-10s and Pave Nail OV-10s. In Laos, the Raven FACs still covertly operated with about twenty individuals working with indigenous forces in northern and southern Laos. Including its rescue units, overall, the US Air Force still had about eight hundred aircraft operating in Southeast Asia. And its Twentieth and Twenty-First Special Operations Squadrons, equipped with CH-53Cs and UH-1Ns, respectively, could also conduct recovery missions if needed.[7]

The big US Marine ground and aviation combat units had returned to their home stations in Japan, Hawaii, and the continental United States. Residual forces totaled about 500. This comprised several groups: the 156 men of Company E, Marine Security Guard Battalion, who guarded the US embassy in Saigon and the US consulate in Da Nang; 195 marines of the First Air and Naval Gunfire Liaison Company (ANGLICO), which had sub-units throughout South Vietnam to coordinate air and fire support with US and allied ground forces; 68 marines assigned to the Marine Advisory Unit of the Naval Advisory Group who worked directly as advisors down to the battalion level with Vietnamese Marine Corps units; a 20-marine advisory team at Da Nang who ran the Marine Tactical Data Control Center; and 107 disparate marines who worked on various staffs with Vietnamese Army or Navy headquarters or the Military Assistance Command Vietnam (MACV) staff. Additionally, Marine All-Weather Attack Squadron (VMA[AW]) 224 was aboard the USS *Coral Sea* with its A-6 aircraft, crews, and support team.[8]

The members of the First ANGLICO were spread out across Vietnam and engaged daily with the tactical units to which they were assigned. They were especially busy supporting Army of the Republic of Vietnam (ARVN) units in the Delta region. They also supported Australian and Korean units and had several teams operating within the area of operations of the Third ARVN Division on outposts in the far north of South Vietnam, just below the DMZ. These teams could sense and see the activities of the North Vietnamese Army (NVA) elements operating in the area and what appeared to be activities to support offensive action. Daily, they conducted fire missions, utilizing US Navy ships off shore and ARVN artillery batteries in the area. Their commander, Lt. Col. D'Wayne Gray, called them the "disaster preventers."[9]

However, there were still combat marine elements in the region. The Third Marine Amphibious Force in the western Pacific held a responsive posture in the US Navy Seventh Fleet. It maintained the Thirty-First Marine Amphibious Unit (MAU), which included a battalion landing team, an aviation element, and a support element. This unit was at sea, and always within 120 hours of South Vietnam. Additionally, it served as the lead element of a marine amphibious brigade, drawn from the larger Fleet Marine

Force Pacific. These elements regularly exercised throughout the southwest Pacific and were in a high state of readiness.[10]

The US Army forces had been greatly reduced, and that process was continuing. During this period, the aviation units in particular would stand down on average ten aircraft a day. But some significant combat power still remained. The Third Brigade of the First Cavalry Division was still operating in the Saigon area with the Second Squadron 11 Armored Cavalry Regiment, and the 196th Light Infantry Brigade was still operating in the Da Nang area. Each had aviation assets assigned. Additionally, each military region (MR) of South Vietnam had an aviation group from the First Combat Aviation Brigade assigned. However, the alignment and assignment of units was constantly changing. The medevac helicopter units so designated were attached to residual medial commands in each military region.

MR-1 Eleventh Combat Aviation Group
Sixty-Second Aviation Company
D Troop Seventeenth Cavalry (D/17 Cavalry)
142nd Transportation Company
237th Medical Detachment—Helicopter Ambulance (MDHA)
571st MDHA
196th Light Infantry Brigade
F Troop Eighth Cavalry (F/8 Cavalry)

MR-2 Seventeenth Combat Aviation Group
120th Assault Helicopter Company (AHC)
361st Aerial Weapons Company
H Troop Seventeenth Cavalry (H/17 Cavalry)
Eagle Combat Aviation Battalion (Provisional)
180th Assault Support Helicopter Company (ASHC)
H Troop Tenth Cavalry (H/10 Cavalry)
Sixtieth AHC
129th AHC
Fifty-Seventh AHC
201st Aviation Company
604th Transportation Company
247th MDHA

MR-3 Twelfth Combat Aviation Group
F Troop, Fourth Cavalry (F/4 Cavalry)
Fifty-Ninth Aviation Company

Command Aircraft Company
388th Transportation Company
Fifty-Seventh MDHA
159th MDHA
Third Brigade/First Cavalry Division
229th Aviation Battalion
F Troop Ninth Cavalry (F/9 Cavalry)
F Battery Seventy-Ninth Artillery (F/79 Artillery)
362nd Aviation Company
F Battery Seventy-Seventh Artillery (F/77 Artillery)
Air Ambulance Platoon, Fifteenth Medical Battalion

MR-4 164th Combat Aviation Group
188th Aviation Company
C Troop Sixteenth Cavalry (C/16 Cavalry)
611th Transportation Company[11]

All army aviation units carried as one of their capabilities the ability to perform SAR. It was a doctrinally assigned mission and something that was part of their planning process for all missions. All of these assets were potential recovery platforms for shot-down airmen or other personnel who needed to be rescued.[12]

However, as the US role in the war was winding down, a larger percentage of our remaining troops were serving as advisors with ARVN units down to the regimental level and territorial forces, generally in five-man teams. Beyond the marine advisors, there were an estimated 5,400 army, air force, and navy personnel serving with Vietnamese units all over the country. Their role was to serve in a liaison capacity, monitoring the status of South Vietnamese units and staffs and coordinating direct US material assistance and combat support—especially air support. This was very challenging work because these individuals were almost always junior in rank to the officer with whom they were working, and in most cases they lacked the vast experience of their Vietnamese advisees. When in the field with their units, they could be at risk, and when available, army aviation units were assigned to be on call to evacuate them if necessary. In extremis, they could call also upon the services of the USAF rescue units.[13]

The South Vietnamese forces were at peak strength. They had recovered and rearmed since the Lam Son 719 battle. The ARVN (including militias and regional/popular forces) had almost one million soldiers, well-equipped and receiving heavy artillery and M-48 heavy tanks. Their navy had 43,000 sailors and 1,680 ships and boats. The Vietnamese Air Force (VNAF) had 40,000 airmen and more than 1,000 aircraft, including A-1s, A-37s, AC-47s, and F-5s. The Vietnamese Marine Corps had 15,000 marines. By 1972, the combined armed forces of South Vietnam were one of the largest militaries in the world.[14]

The Enemy

Enemy forces, consisting of the North Vietnamese Army and its allies, numbered 96,000 troops in Laos, 63,000 in Cambodia, and 201,000 in South Vietnam. Intelligence sources indicated that enemy forces had more than ninety antiaircraft artillery (AAA) guns of all calibers in northern Laos and more than five hundred in Steel Tiger along the Ho Chi Minh trail. Additionally, they had moved SA-2 missile sites up along the Laos–North Vietnam border and were attempting to engage aircraft that penetrated that area. There were also indications that the NVA had moved some SA-2 batteries into Laos as far south as Tchepone. In Cambodia and South Vietnam, enemy forces would engage allied aircraft with small arms and automatic weapons and a few 23mm and 37mm AAA guns in the triborder area.[15]

As the new year began, NVA-led enemy forces were attacking in Laos to put pressure on loyalist forces near Luang Prabang and the Plain of Jars (PDJ) area, especially along the Skyline Ridge area just above Long Chieng, the key location for Air America operations in that region and one of the main bases for the Hmong forces led by Laotian Maj. Gen. Vang Pao. He and his forces had been fighting for years against Pathet Lao and North Vietnamese forces in a series of savage campaigns to control this strategic sector of the country.[16]

In southern Laos, Royal Laotian forces were active in operations along the western periphery of the Ho Chi Minh trail as NVA forces pushed to extend their security zone around and over the trail area and prevent the Laotians from taking any offensive action against the trail complex. They would also draw off US air strikes from the trail. Daily, US Air Force Raven FACs were flying direct support for the Hmong and Royal Laotian forces in the north and south.

Along the trail, the NVA were building new roads and improving the older structure while utilizing deception to protect the road structure and supply depots and emplacing the added guns and SA-2s. In Cambodia, their forces and allies were striking the Khmer Army as widely as possible to weaken them and the government and possibly cause its downfall. They were also protecting their base areas along the South Vietnam border and the northeast corner of the country.[17]

Main Attack

The NVA's plans for the upcoming invasions were well advanced and being carried out. However, analysis showed that American interdiction efforts along the Ho Chi Minh trail had been more effective than anticipated. This put the primary attack plan against Saigon at risk. But stockpiles were more robust in the DMZ area. Consequently, the Politburo shifted the main attack axis to the attack south of the DMZ, explaining, "We could mass our forces, centralize command, and provide adequate logistics for a massive, extended operation."[18]

The NVA had learned the hard way about the awesomeness of US air power and clearly understood that if they shot down one of our aircraft, fellow forces would attempt to rescue the airmen. In fact, the NVA appreciated all of the things that could be done with helicopters, especially general troop transport, insertion of commando units, and the rescue of downed airmen or any isolated troops. They had carefully studied our tactics and considered any US helicopter as a threat. As a countertactic, they had issued instructions to their troops on how to shoot down helicopters. "In attacking aircraft of this type [helicopters], we must aim right at the cockpit compartment where the pilot sits in the nose of the helicopter—and open fire. It contains the controls for the mechanical systems and a fuel tank." The instructions further pointed out that "[another area] is the hump on the back of the aircraft under the main rotor. That area also contains very complex machinery."[19]

The instructions for dealing with downed pilots were more detailed and had evolved since the beginning of the conflict. They explained that the Americans would use smoke bombs, tear gas, and different types of cluster bomb units (CBUs) to protect downed flyers. They discussed the makeup of a rescue task force with the A-1s, and then the recovery helicopters. They provided instructions on how to build a trap to lure in the helicopters so that they could be ambushed. An article from *Quan doi Nhan Dan*, a soldier's magazine, laid it all out:

> To capture pilots, we must disperse from our position in many directions and quickly and tightly encircle them. . . . After capturing pilots, they must be stripped of radio transmitters, weapons, and documents, and immediately taken from the area under guard. . . . The pilot's radio and signal flares can be used to lure enemy aircraft into the ambush sites. The element on the outer perimeter fires at the A-1s. The one on the inner perimeter must conceal itself and suddenly open fire when the [helicopter] hovers and drops the rope ladder to rescue the pilot.[20]

Over the previous decade, the North Vietnamese troops and their Viet Cong brethren had had plenty of opportunities to practice and perfect these techniques.

Commando Hunt VII

Since its initiation in 1968, the Commando Hunt series of operations had been focused on interdiction in Steel Tiger only. In this iteration, it was the overall air campaign plan for the theater. Priority was given to interdicting enemy supplies and forces moving into all theaters so as to make the efforts of the NVA more difficult and costly. A maximum of 10,000 fighter and 700 gunship sorties per month was authorized. And increasingly the aerial forces of South Vietnam, Cambodia, and Laos were providing another 1,600 sorties to support the campaign.

The US assets could be directed as necessary against the trail or diverted to friendly forces in contact with enemy units. On a daily basis, strike flights out of Thailand or South Vietnam or off the aircraft carriers in the Gulf of Tonkin (GOT) would hit targets in any of these areas. Given the indications that the NVA were preparing to attack into South Vietnam, US forces were being dispatched into North Vietnam on operations such as Proud Deep and protective reaction strikes when NVA air defenses fired on reconnaissance aircraft flying over North Vietnam. In the first quarter of 1972, many regions of SEA were very hostile for US and allied aircraft. It was a dangerous time.[21]

Rescue Operations

The men of rescue were ready. With lessons well learned over the last nine years, they sat alert at NKP, Da Nang, or Ubon, or on orbit over mountainous jungle, or on the fantail of a ship in the GOT waiting for the call in their HH-43s, HH-53s, HC-130s, or HH-3As. They had been briefed on the projected enemy offensive. They knew what to expect.

Although they were not as heralded as the larger HH-53 rescue helicopters, the US Air Force still had nineteen of the older HH-43s still serving as local base rescue vehicles at eight bases in South Vietnam and Thailand. And occasionally they would be forward placed at austere locations to support specific operations. They could still perform SAR in their local area, but generally supported crash response teams and occasionally served as medevac vehicles for patients needing transfer base to base. On 2 January, the on-call HH-43 at Phan Rang Air Base, SVN, Pedro 21, was scrambled to carry a soldier stricken with an acute appendicitis to the hospital at Cam

Ranh Air Base. The detachment was credited with a noncombat save. In Southeast Asia, rescue came in many forms, and operations such as these were an almost daily occurrence.[22]

At about the same time, a critical situation was developing in Laos. A MACSOG indigenous team providing overwatch of the Ho Chi Minh trail reported that they were trapped and needed an immediate extraction. They were located about twenty miles east of Attopu. A CH-53 from the Twenty-First SOS at NKP had tried to extract the team but had been badly damaged, and escorting A-1s were almost out of ordnance. The on-scene commander (OSC), Mike 92, an O-2 FAC, contacted the orbiting King HC-130 and requested rescue support. As Sandy A-1s scrambled from Ubon and two HH-53s took off from Da Nang, Mike 92 directed several flights of F-4s and VNAF A-1s against enemy forces trying to surround the team. When Mike 92 had to depart for fuel, he was replaced by Mike 79, who worked several flights of VNAF A-37s. One of the HH-53s was damaged by enemy fire. As they held, a Vietnamese H-34 "Kingbee," dashed in and recovered three of the team members. The fourth man was declared missing.[23]

More Action in Laos

At midday on 20 January, King 21, an HC-130 orbiting in Laos, monitored a mayday call from an Air America aircraft, Porter 445. The pilot stated that his aircraft had been mortally damaged by enemy AAA and he was going down in a valley about seventy miles northeast of Vientiane. King 21 immediately diverted to his location while alerting the Sandys and Jollys at NKP. Air America Operations then informed King 21 that the pilot had survived the crash and had joined up with five Laotian troops, and the group was evading to an open area. They had a survival radio. An Air America helicopter, call sign Papa Foxtrot Hotel, diverted into the area and assumed OSC duties. At NKP, Jollys 62 and 56 were launched and proceeded north, followed thirty minutes later by Sandys 03 and 04. However, the crew of Papa Foxtrot Hotel determined that the rescue area was relatively quiet, and they landed to pick up the Air America Porter pilot. Another Air America helicopter, Hotel 15, arrived, picked up the other five Laotian troops, and delivered them to friendly control.[24]

About four hours later, an RF-4C, call sign Bullwhip 26, from the Fourteenth Tactical Reconnaissance Squadron (TRS) Udorn RTAFB, Thailand, was shot down by NVA AAA on a reconnaissance mission south of the Ban Ban Valley in Northern Laos, about fifty miles north of where the recovery operation for the Air America pilot had occurred earlier that morning.

Nail 12, a Pave Nail OV-10 from the Twenty-Third TASS flown by Capt. Bob Willis and 1st Lt. Mark Clark heard the emergency calls, proceeded into the area, and made voice contact with the survivors, Maj. Bob Mock, and 1st Lt. John Stiles. The crew of Nail 12 determined the locations of both survivors with their Pave Spot and loran systems and passed them to King 22, who was orbiting over Laos. The Fortieth Aerospace Rescue and Recovery Service (ARRS) and First SOS at NKP, Thailand, were directed to launch their alert HH-53s and A-1s. However, before they could arrive, King 22 contacted Air America Operations and were informed that some Air America helicopters were in the area and readily available. Once again, Air America helicopter Papa Foxtrot Hotel, now crewed by John Fonberg, William Phillips, and Bob Noble, was able to reach the scene and recover Stiles. Almost simultaneously, another Air America helicopter, call sign 13 Foxtrot, used its jungle penetrator to pick-up Mock. Both helicopters flew to a forward airfield in Laos and transferred their survivors to an Air America C-123, which then flew the survivors back to Udorn. When briefed on the recovery, General Lavelle sent a "hearty well done," to Udorn Air America Operations. Once again, the ubiquitous presence of the Air America aircraft had provided a quick pickup capability that prevented the capture of an American aircrew.[25]

At about the same time, Stormy 04, an F-4 Fast FAC from Da Nang, flown by Capt. C. Davis and Capt. R. Venables, was shot down while attacking a truck convoy on the ever-dangerous route 9 in Laos where the Lam Son 719 incursion had taken place one year prior. The controllers at OL-A heard Stormy 04's emergency call on guard and immediately scrambled the Sandys and Jolly Green 71 flown by Lt. Col. Bill Harris and crew, and 66 flown by Maj. Reg Murray and crew from the Thirty-Seventh Aerospace Rescue and Recovery Squadron (ARRSq) at Da Nang. They were reinforced with two more Sandys from NKP. However, before they could arrive in the area, a US Army UH-1 from D Troop of the Seventeenth Cavalry, which had been searching for enemy units in the Khe Sanh area, had dashed into Laos with an AH-1 escort and had recovered Davis and Venables.

A few minutes later, another US Army UH-1 was shot down near Khe Sanh, and six survivors were recovered by another UH-1 in the formation. That UH-1 then landed at the Quang Tri Airfield. Jolly 71 landed next to them and then transported the severely burned survivors to Hue for emergency medical care.[26]

On 29 January, USAF 1st Lt. Bob Kain, Raven 52, was flying a mission in a T-28 north of Paksane, Laos, about eighty miles east of Vientiane,

Capt. Bob Kain as a Raven FAC. (Courtesy Bob Kain)

when his recently remanufactured engine experienced a runaway propeller, causing it to overspeed and fail. He quickly called Cricket, the airborne battlefield command and control craft (ABCCC), reporting his dilemma and general position as the aircraft began to descend. He was not near a useable airfield, so he glided toward the nearest friendly position and used his newly installed "Yankee" extraction system to eject. King 26 heard his emergency calls and launched Sandys 01, Capt. Ron Smith, and 02, and Jolly Greens 62 and 32 from NKP.

Landing in a bamboo patch, Kain took out his survival radio and made voice contact with Ron Smith. Moments later, an Air America H-34, Hotel 29, arrived and came to a hover over Kain. The helicopter had been shuttling loads in the local area and had heard the emergency calls and then seen the burning wreckage of the aircraft. The pilot flew to the smoke, spotted Kain's parachute, and hovered until his loadmaster spotted the survivor and then lowered the hoist cable with a horse collar attached. Kain strapped in and then enjoyed the view as he was raised up and out of the bamboo, and the helicopter pilot turned to head southwest. He flew to the airfield at Paksane, dropped Kain off with the Raven's profuse thanks, and resumed his shuttle missions. One of the Jolly Greens landed at Paksane and took Kain to Udorn. There, Kain was debriefed by the commander of Detachment 1 of the Fifty-Sixth Special Operations Wing (SOW), which ran the T-28 school and maintenance center. The detachment also administratively handled the pilots assigned to the Raven program. Coincidentally, a team of technicians from Stanley Aviation, which built the Yankee extraction system, was at Udorn, modifying the T-28s there with their system. They seized Kain and received from him a thorough debrief of his experiences in riding and surviving a true operational test of their extraction system. He filled them with data, expecting payoff at the Udorn Officer's Club later in the evening. However, when the debrief was over, Kain was directed to take a U-17 aircraft and fly back to Vientiane. He did so, and his boss there gave him the next day off. They celebrated his experiences that evening in proper fashion.

His recovery was another manifestation of the value of the ubiquitous presence of Air America helicopters all over Laos. Unless they were on orbit or flying in the local area, the US Air Force Jolly Greens could not respond as quickly as the Air America aircraft, all equipped with UHF radios and Guard receivers and all ready to help at a moment's notice.[27]

Two days later, another Raven FAC, further north in Laos, found himself in similar straits. Raven 11, Capt. Mike Kelly, USAF, took off from Luang Prabang, Laos, in an O-1 on a visual reconnaissance mission for NVA elements. He had found an enemy 122mm rocket launch site and directed a flight of Laotian T-28s to bomb it when his O-1 was peppered with multiple rounds of small-caliber fire. Several rounds stuck the engine, causing it to fail. He attempted to glide away from the area. As he lost altitude, he spotted a small open field in a karst valley and put the aircraft down in it. The left wing sheared off and the aircraft rolled on its left side. As the aircraft came to a stop, Mike smelled gas, and he and his Hmong backseater scrambled out of the cockpit and began moving up a karst hill. Kelly took out his URC-64 survival radio, only to discover that its antenna was broken. Fortunately, he was also carrying a second radio, and he used it to call on the Guard frequency, reporting that he was down and providing a general description of his area.

He was only a few miles from the Luang Prabang Airport, and aircraft there heard his calls. Fellow Raven Maj. Mike Cox launched in a T-28 to provide support. Bill Collier was piloting an Air America helicopter and approaching the airport when he heard Mike's calls on the Guard frequency.

He could tell that Mike was northeast. He turned in that direction and began to recognize the terrain features that Kelly was calling out. Kelly then heard the helicopter and vectored him in to their location. Collier brought the helicopter to a hover over the two men and dropped his hoist to recover the Hmong troop and then Kelly. He flew the two men back to Luang Prabang, where Kelly discovered that he had broken his left arm. Later, Kelly wanted to find Collier to thank him and give him a bottle of booze for his efforts. Kelly was told by the Air America chief pilot in Luang Prabang that the names of the Air America pilot and crewmembers were classified. It took Kelly thirty-three years to deliver that bottle.[28]

On 10 February, Seafox 01, an F-4 Fast FAC from the 388th Tactical Fighter Wing (TFW), Korat RTAFB, Thailand, flown by Capt. John Murphy and 1st Lt. Tom Dobson, was downed by AAA near a segment of the Ho Chi Minh trail in southern Laos just at sunset. Both men ejected and descended into the jungle below. Murphy landed on a steep slope just below a peak. Neither man made an initial emergency call, but they did make contact with each other and reported enemy forces in the area. Pizza 20, a B-52, heard the beepers and chatter on Guard frequency, and the crew made voice contact with both Murphy and Dobson. Spectre 10 diverted from its mission to serve as initial OSC. Operating Location Alpha (OL-A) at Son Tra, SVN, took control of the mission. Initially, they tried to make contact with US Army helicopters still operating along the SVN/Laos border to request that they make a quick recovery attempt before dark. However, that effort was not successful. They contacted King 24 and directed them to assume airborne mission commander (AMC) for a night recovery effort.

The controllers at JRCC then intervened. Sensing an opportunity to utilize the limited night recovery system (LNRS) capability of the HH-53s of the Fortieth ARRSq, they directed the alert LNRS-equipped Jolly Greens 52 and 53 at Ubon to launch. They then also directed that control of the SAR effort be shifted to OL-B at Udorn because that center could better coordinate with the assets necessary for a night recovery.

OL-B directed the Twenty-Third TASS to launch Pave Nail OV-10s to serve as the OSC and use their Pave Spot–loran systems to precisely locate the survivors and kill AAA that might endanger the recovery effort. Jolly Greens 30 and 32, both LNRS-equipped, were also launched to support the effort. Two more King aircraft, 27 and 23, were launched. King 27 would directly provide tanker support for the Jolly Greens, and King 23 would replace King 24 as AMC.

Nail 55 was the first Pave Nail FAC to arrive in the SAR area. The crew contacted, located, and authenticated both survivors and also locked their locations into their navigation system. Then, they led Jolly Greens 52 and 53 into the area so that they could determine if a recovery was possible with the LNRS system. Nail 43, another Pave Nail OV-10, replaced Nail 55, and Jolly Greens 30 and 32 entered the recovery area. Spectre 08 orbited overhead to provide firepower support if necessary; however, the area appeared to be relatively benign. Nail 43 led the two Jolly Greens over the pilot's position so that they could lock in the position in their Doppler navigation system. The flashing strobe of one of the survivors was spotted, but it was not enough of a steady reference for the Jolly Green crews to utilize the LNRS system. Jolly Green 32 made several attempts. However, the Jolly crews could not spot the survivors, who were under jungle canopy and on uneven rising terrain three hundred feet below a ridgeline. They found that searching with night vision goggles and the low light television (LLTV) on the aircraft was very challenging. At one point, they spotted a small light and began to move toward it. However, it was not near the reported positions of the survivors, and the Jolly Green pilots, anticipating an enemy trap, aborted the run in. Jolly Green 30 did attempt to hover fifty feet above Murphy. But the hover coupler system failed and both helicopters had to abort their attempts to recover the survivors with the LNRS system. Murphy remembered that

> I had the Jolly Green almost right on top of me, perhaps no more than 10–15 feet to one side. I jumped up and moved to the top of the hill, but did not get there before the Jolly Green moved on out. I was of course disappointed, but I totally understood—the Jolly Green really hung it out there, one extremely brave crew. If I could see [them], so could anyone else in the area.[29]

King 25 then took over as the AMC and began coordinating for a first-light conventional recovery. Four A-1s, Sandys 01, 02, 03, 04, were launched from NKP. Jolly Greens 64 and 67 from the Thirty-Seventh ARRSq, accompanied by Sandys 07 and 08, launched out of Da Nang. Arriving at the survivors' locations at about 0715L, Sandy 01 took over as the OSC. He made contact with the survivors and validated their positions with the departing FAC. Not detecting any significant threat in the immediate area, he directed Sandys 07 and 08 to lead Jolly Green 32 in for the recovery of both survivors, which was accomplished with no further problems. All forces then returned to their respective bases.[30]

As noted, the JRCC took a direct hand in this mission, because they saw it as an opportunity to operationally validate the capabilities of the

LNRS system. Afterward, the Third Aerospace Rescue and Recovery Group (ARRG) commander, Col. Cy Muirhead, directed that the LNRS crews be interviewed in depth. Debriefs indicated that the crews derived a great deal of training in their attempts to utilize the system for a recovery under the cover of darkness. They collected many lessons learned that helped define what the LNRS system could and could not do. They refined procedures for working with the Pave Nail OV-10s and the integration of crew usage of night vision goggles, LLTV, and the auto pilot, hover coupler, and Doppler navigational system. They also identified mechanical problems that led to equipment modifications. Muirhead concluded that the remaining problem that limited the system as configured was the inability to precisely locate the survivors. The OV-10 Pave Nails could do this with their Pave Spot–loran combination. However, the LNRS Jolly Greens had no way to utilize that information because they had not been given loran navigation systems. Instead, they had to be led to a survivor's general location by the A-1s and then perform a visual search. Then they still needed a signal from the survivors themselves to facilitate the recovery.[31]

This revelation about the efficacy of potential loran utilization made Colonel Muirhead and others realize that a serious opportunity to improve rescue capability was being missed. De facto, the Jolly Green's "navigation systems" were the Sandys. The A-1 pilots would locate the survivors and visually lead the Jollys in for the recovery. Under General Lavelle's, and later General Vogt's, direction, F-4s and RF-4s were being equipped with loran and had developed procedures for leading strikes and bombing in bad weather on loran coordinates. For targeting purposes, the entire theater was eventually mapped for loran coordinates to facilitate bad-weather targeting. Possibly, this system could have been used for SAR purposes, although there were problems with loran reception in the Hanoi area. However, there is no record that it was ever considered for rescue missions other than the contributions of the Pave Nail crews or that the HH-53s were ever considered for modification with loran receivers. Some of the HH-53s had been modified with Doppler navigation systems. However, tests showed that the Dopplers needed constant update from "known locations" based on old maps, and the combination of TACAN and Dopplers could provide five-mile accuracy at a range of one hundred miles. Bottom line: the crews did not trust them and some did not even know how to program them or understand that they had to be frequently updated to have any accuracy at all. Most of the Jolly pilots were more than happy to rely in the A-1s to take them where they needed to go.[32]

Reinforcements

Both MACV and Seventh Air Force (AF) closely monitored the steady buildup of enemy equipment and supplies north of the DMZ and Laos. They were aware that near Bat Lake just above the DMZ the North Vietnamese had established a huge storage area that was full of T-54 tanks, long-range 130mm artillery, and possibly AT-3 antitank missiles and SA-7 heat-seeking antiaircraft missiles. The JCS directed an F-4 squadron to deploy from Clark Air Base, Philippines, to Da Nang and Udorn, Thailand. They also ordered eight more B-52s to deploy to Thailand and twenty-nine more to Anderson Air Base, Guam, and directed a fourth aircraft carrier, the USS *Kitty Hawk,* to join TF-77. Additionally, all budget restrictions on sorties were lifted, giving General Creighton Abrams added air-power capability to disrupt the building North Vietnamese invasion.[33]

To support air operations command and control over northern Laos and western North Vietnam, the USAF also deployed a task force of EC-121T aircraft that used the call sign Disco. These large aircraft were equipped with radar, which provided an early warning capability of MiG activity in those areas. The controllers onboard radioed guidance for fighter crews against enemy fighters and utilized several electronic upgrades that gave them special capabilities to detect and track the MiGs. Disco also provided navigational support to any aircraft flying over the poorly charted northeast sectors of Laos and western areas of North Vietnam. The A-1s and HH-53s learned to rely on Disco for navigation and early warning support in this area. This early warning capability was linked to the Red Crown facility stationed aboard one of the US Navy ships in the Gulf of Tonkin and, when available, E-1B Tracer aircraft launched from the aircraft carriers of TF-77. Together, these assets provided a general early warning capability for US forces operating over North Vietnam.[34]

Rescue Operations Theater Wide

On 16/17 February, USAF and Navy strike flights flew 173 sorties against targets in the Bat Lake area. They destroyed an estimated eight 130mm field guns, five 85mm field guns, twenty trucks, two SA-2 missile launchers, twenty-four weapons/ammo storage facilities, and an unknown number of AAA sites. On the first day, Musket 01, an F-4 Fast FAC from Ubon RTAFB, flown by Capt. Bill Schwertfeger and 1st Lt. Ralph Galati, was shot down by an SA-2 missile just north of the DMZ in the vicinity of Bat Lake. A Covey FAC working just south of the DMZ had brief voice contact with Galati. In response, Sandy 07, Capt. Don Whaylen, and Sandy 08, 1st Lt. Randy Scott, were launched from Da Nang. As they approached the DMZ, they were engaged with heavy AAA of multiple calibers, and several SA-2 missiles, one of which detonated an estimated 150 yards in front of Sandy 08. The two pilots orbited for about thirty minutes. However, when no radio contact could be established with either crewmember, the effort was terminated and they returned to Da Nang. A few days later, intelligence reported that both men had become prisoners. They were released in March 1973.[35]

The second day, an F-105G from Korat, Junior 02, was shot down by an SA-2 in the same area. The pilot, Capt. James Cutter, and electronic warfare officer (EWO), Capt. Ken Fraser, were quickly captured. Unaware of their fate, a USAF F-4 from Udorn, Falcon 74, flown by Maj. Robert Irwin and Capt. Ed Hawley, assumed OSC and began to organize a SAR effort. It was shot down by AAA. Hawley ejected and was quickly captured. Irwin did not eject from the aircraft. Sandys 03 and 04 launched from Da Nang and headed north. A US Navy HH-3A from HC-7 launched and approached the coastline. However, the area was just too dangerous. The surface-to-air missile (SAM) sites were active, and AAA fire was observed at several locations. Lacking any contact with survivors, the controllers at Queen advised the Sandys to return to Da Nang and the helicopter to return to its ship. The netted radars that General Lavelle was so concerned about were apparently having an effect. The three survivors were released in March 1973. Irwin's remains were returned in 1989.[36]

At almost the same time, Sun Dog 12, 1st Lt. Richard Christy, an O-2 FAC assigned to the Twenty-First TASS, took off from Tan Son Nhut Air Base to support allied ground forces in Cambodia. He had a USAF airman interpreter, S.Sgt. William Silva, with him, just new to the unit and very inexperienced. They were working with a Cambodian unit, Hotel-05, when they spotted enemy forces and requested fighter support. Two USAF A-37s were directed to rendezvous with him thirty miles west of Phnom Penh. However, while orbiting over the target area, the O-2 was hit by several rounds of AAA, which damaged the front engine and killed Christy. Silva took control of the aircraft and tried to fly away. He made an emergency call on his VHF-AM radio, but no other aircraft in the area were monitoring that frequency. When the front engine quit, the airplane began to descend, and Silva bailed out about 2,500 feet above the ground. As he swung in his parachute, he watched the airplane crash. He landed on a river bank, took out his survival radio, and made a mayday call on Guard frequency. The A-37 flight leader, Hawk 03, heard him and reported through command channels that Sun Dog 12 was down with at least one survivor. Rustic 16, Capt. Doug Aitken, an OV-10

FAC assigned to the Twenty-Third TASS and based at Ubon Air Base, also heard the emergency calls and diverted to support the SAR. It took him about twenty minutes to arrive overhead, and he became the initial OSC.

Orbiting further north, King 21 also heard the calls and also headed for the SAR area to serve as AMC. When the Seventh AF TACC apprised the JRCC of the downed aircraft, their controllers directed the alert A-1s, Sandy 05, Capt. Jim Clevenger, and Sandy 06, 1st Lt. Joe Seitz, and HH-53s at Ubon to launch and head south toward Phnom Penh. While waiting for the rescue forces, Aitken had his interpreter speak with the ground commander while he quizzed Silva for ground references so that he could determine Silva's location. At one point, he was contacted by a flight of US Army helicopters working along the South Vietnam–Cambodian border sixty to ninety miles away, who then flew over and joined the search. However, King 21 announced that the Sandys and Jollys were coming to conduct the recovery. Low on fuel, Aitken passed OSC to Rustic 03, Lt. Col. Ray Stratton, and diverted to the airport at Phnom Penh, landing on fumes. The Sandys arrived and Captain Clevenger assumed OSC. He authenticated the survivor, and after determining that the area was relatively quiet, he cleared Jolly Green 57, flown by Maj. Fred Hartstein and crew, to make the pickup. As they came to a hover fifty feet above the survivor, the flight mechanic tried to lower the penetrator. However, the hoist motor failed and he had to use the emergency override to lower it. While he did, the pararescue jumpers (PJs) used their miniguns to return fire from enemy troops in the area. When Silva was onboard, the crew departed the area and flew to Tan Son Nhut Air Base, South Vietnam.[37]

Subsequently, elements of the Khmer Army found the wreckage of Sun Dog 02 and recovered the body of Lieutenant Christy. With full military honors presented by them and the Khmer Air Force, he was returned to American control at the Phnom Penh Airport, loaded aboard an USAF C-47, and flown back to Tan Son Nhut. The US air attaché responded to this kind gesture with a letter: "These profound expressions of sentiment and honor shown by the Khmer Air Force to a fallen American Pilot will long be remembered and treasured."[38]

On 18 February, as residual strikes were being conducted against targets just above the DMZ, an F-4 from the USS *Constellation*, Silverkite 207, was severely damaged by NVA AAA. The crew of Lt. Bruce Rowe and LTJG D. Spence were able to fly back to the ship. However, while they maneuvered for landing, the aircraft went out of control and the crew ejected. Spence was picked up by an escort ship, but Rowe was never found.[39]

On 20 February, aviation elements from the F Troop/Fourth Cavalry (F/4) were conducting a reconnaissance mission near Cu Chi, South Vietnam, when one of their OH-6 helicopters with three crewmembers, Centaur 16, was shot down. The Sun Dog Alpha Command Center in MR-3 notified the Seventh AF TACC, Blue Chip, who directly notified the JRCC. They scrambled Sandys 07 and 08 from Da Nang and Jolly Greens 60 and 61 from Ubon, both at least an hour and a half away. Much closer, Capt. Ron Radcliffe, Centaur 14, was leading another air cavalry team and immediately diverted to conduct a recovery operation. Within five minutes, he was overhead the crash site and marked it with smoke flares. He was able to see that one crewmember was still alive, but the other two were nonresponsive. He identified enemy 12.7mm positions and directed supporting AH-1s as they destroyed them. His actions drew enemy fire, and his gunners killed an estimated ten enemy troops and destroyed a machine gun site before his OH-6 was damaged by the enemy fire. He diverted to a safe area, unloaded his two gunners, determined that his helicopter was still capable of flying, and then returned to the crash site. Two medevac UH-1s attempted to land to recover the survivors but were driven away by enemy fire. When an ARVN recondo team inserted to secure the site, Radcliffe landed to recover the sole survivor, and then brought in another UH-1 to recover the two bodies. Radcliffe stayed over the crash site until the ARVN team was safely extracted. Returning to his base, Radcliffe discovered that his helicopter had sustained twenty-nine hits.[40]

A few days later, F/4 Cavalry was notified that they would be redeploying. Unlike most other units, though, they would not be going back to the United States. They would be moving north to the big US Army base near Hue, for duty in MR-1, and were expected to be in place by early April.[41]

In the late afternoon of 2 March, Covey 219, an OV-10 FAC from the Twentieth TASS, Capt. Mahlon Long, was hit by AAA while working a southern section of the Ho Chi Minh trail near Saravane, Laos. He attempted to divert into the airfield at Pakse but had to eject about thirty-five miles northeast of the airfield. King 22 heard his "Mayday" and called OL-B, Jack, to initiate SAR procedures as Covey 233 took over as the OSC. Jolly Greens 57 and 56 were airborne on a training flight to qualify a new Jolly pilot, Capt. Dale Stovall, as an aircraft commander. Hearing the mayday calls, his instructor pilot, Capt. Bob Paul, declared that he was qualified and the check ride was over so that they could divert for the SAR. Paul also declared, "I've got the aircraft, you are back to copilot for this rescue."[42]

Additionally, Sandy 01, Capt. Ron Smith—a newly qualified Sandy lead, and Sandy 02, Capt. John Lackey, with Jolly Greens 50 and 32, also took off from NKP. They arrived over the survivor and took over as OSC. Sandys 05 and 06 took off from Ubon for support if necessary. After trolling the area for threats, Smith laid down a smoke screen and Captain Paul brought Jolly 57 in over a ridge to recover the survivor. When he was onboard, they began an egress to the west. However, they were surprised by several 23mm AAA sites, which shot at the lumbering helicopters. As the Sandys attacked the guns, Paul turned back to the east over a ridge and climbed to altitude to avoid the sites and rising thunderstorms. Stovall learned a lot on that mission. He noted later, "I didn't know the intel for the area. . . . Never again did I fly somewhere and not know where the guns were." It was a sobering beginning to his combat tour.[43]

Fratricide

The next day was a quiet one for the US rescue forces because no allied aircraft were shot down. However, a significant event did occur in the southern part of North Vietnam. In preparation for the upcoming offensive, additional forces were moving south and were protected by the Sixty-Third Missile Battalion of the 236th Air Defense Missile Regiment, equipped with SA-2s and located near Vinh. When its troops detected an unidentified aircraft flying south from the Hanoi area, they shot it down. Unfortunately, it was a North Vietnamese Li-2, the Soviet version of the American C-47. All aboard were killed, including the crew of six and sixteen members of the headquarters element of the 921st Fighter Regiment, forward deploying to an airfield in the area. Those killed included Maj. Le Trong Huyen, the deputy commander, who had been credited with shooting down four US aircraft. There is no such a thing as a "friendly" surface-to-air missile.[44]

Rescue at Sea

On 6 March, Big Mother 64, one of the HC-7 HH-3As flown by Lt. Cdr. William Barnes and crew, was on orbit at its assigned SAR location east of Vinh, when it returned to the USS *Chicago* for refueling. As it was approaching the stern of the ship, the crew was notified that a sailor had fallen off the ship and needed to be rescued. Barnes immediately discontinued his approach and repositioned to the left of the ship to recover the man. A Vietnamese junk was beginning to approach the area. However, Barnes came to a hover over the sailor and the interloper turned away. When the man was safely aboard, Barnes landed aboard the USS *Chicago* to disgorge the survivor and take on fuel for return to their assigned SAR orbit.[45]

Ho Chi Minh Trail

On 8 March, while conducting a strike on the trail just west of the DMZ, an A-4, Garfish 502, from the USS *Hancock*, flown by Cdr. George Fenzl, was hit and severely damaged by NVA AAA. He was able to fly out of the area and head toward Da Nang. However, when his engine flamed out, he ejected about fifteen miles northwest of the airbase. When notified, Jolly Green 21, flown by Capt. "Bo" Johnson and crew, and Jolly Green 64, flown by Lt. Cdr. Jay Crowe (Coast Guard exchange officer) and crew, from the Thirty-Seventh ARRSq scrambled for the recovery. Arriving in the area, they found a US Army helicopter orbiting Fenzl, who had hurt his legs and was tangled in the trees. He was on a steep slope, and the army helicopter crew could not pick him up. Jolly Green 21 hovered over the survivor and one of its PJs, T.Sgt. Al Avery, went down to assist the survivor. Both men were then recovered uneventfully.[46]

Ten days later, another crew did not have it quite so easy. On 18 March Nail 31, a Pave Nail OV-10 from the Twenty-Third TASS, flown by 1st Lt. Dave Breskman and Capt. Steve Boretsky, was shot down by AAA over the "Catcher's Mitt," a prominent series of river bends crossed by a heavily traveled section of the Ho Chi Minh trail, about thirty-five miles north of where Covey 219 had been recently hit. The "Mitt," as it was affectionately known by the FACs, was an area full of storage depots and bivouac areas, all protected by multiple 12.7mm, 14.5mm, 23mm, 37mm, and 57mm guns. It was one of the most heavily defended areas in Laos.

When Breskman arrived on the ground, he encountered an NVA soldier. Dave shot him with his pistol and took his AK-47 and ammunition. Boretsky took out his survival radio and contacted another FAC Nail 15, Capt. Bob Humphrey, who was working another section of the Ho Chi Minh trail not far to the north. Humphrey saw the parachutes of the two survivors and diverted to help. He became the OSC and was able to determine the location of each of the survivors. King 21 had monitored the emergency and quickly notified OL-B at Udorn, who launched Sandys 01, 02, 03, and 04 and Jolly Greens 32 and 53. Unbeknownst to all, the two airmen were actually down in the midst of the command and control liaison center that was coordinating the movement of enemy units and supplies through that section of the Ho Chi Minh trail.

Time was of the essence. King 21 also determined that an Air America H-34 helicopter, Hotel 70, was flying from Udorn RTAFB to Pakse. They contacted the crew, and the aircraft commander, Ben Van Etten, stated that he would be glad to help after quickly refueling at Savannakhet.

As the Sandys arrived over the Catcher's Mitt, Sandy 01, Capt. Mike Faas, received a situation brief from Humphrey, who also pointed out the positions of the survivors. Then Faas took over as the OSC and began trolling the area for enemy guns. Now refueled and airborne, Ben Van Etten contacted him and offered his services. Faas told him to head to the Catcher's Mitt, about forty miles to the east, to pick up the two downed airmen. Van Etten acknowledged and headed east. As he approached the area, through the haze, he could see that the A-1s were delivering ordnance and he could hear Faas talking to the survivors. Van Etten called Faas and told him that he was close. Faas told him to hold to the west because the Jolly Greens were fifteen minutes out and would be the primary recovery aircraft. That was fine with Van Etten and his crew.

Then the enemy gunners spotted Faas's A-1 and riddled it with multiple rounds. He announced that his aircraft had been hit and he was going to have to eject. King 21 notified the controllers at OL-B, and all realized that this was going to a bloody SAR. Ben Van Etten's response was more immediate. He quickly tuned his UHF radio to the automatic direction finder (ADF) position and got an immediate steer to Sandy 01's emergency calls. As he turned to pursue the flaming A-1, he queried his copilot and flight mechanic, who told him to press on for the recovery as they crossed the open road segment. Another Air America H-34, crewed by Bill Johnson and Dave Ankerberg, called and offered their help. Van Etten told them to stay well west of the road and stand by.

Visibility in the haze was barely a mile, but Van Etten spotted the burning wreckage. Faas landed in a tree, which trapped his parachute. He was dangling about fifty feet above the ground. He took out his survival radio and announced that he was okay and could hear the approaching helicopter. Van Etten saw his parachute caught up in a tree with Faas swinging below. The flight mechanic lowered the penetrator, but Faas could not reach it. Van Etten backed the helicopter away as Faas climbed down the tree. Van Etten and crew began to hear incoming ground fire as the other A-1s made passes above on approaching enemy forces. They hovered over to a more open area, and Faas ran over and got on the penetrator. As they began to climb out, they could hear more ground fire directed at their aircraft. Then Van Etten noticed that the fuel low-level light was on steady, indicting that they had maybe ten minutes of fuel left. As the flight mechanic pulled Faas through the door, Van Etten told King 21 that they had Faas safely aboard and were heading out of the area. King advised them not to cross the road because of the threat. They had no extra fuel to maneuver and just headed west as fast as their helicopter would go. Fortunately, that road segment was quiet. They found a peaceful field and landed next to Bill Johnson's helicopter, which was carrying a barrel of fuel, and transferred the fifty-five gallons into their aircraft. Now refueled, they flew to the Pakse airport, and an Air America C-7 delivered Captain Faas back to NKP. Within two hours, the crew of Hotel 70 was engaged heli-lifting an assault element into a fight up on the Bolovens Plateau. That was what Air America pilots did.[47]

With the shootdown of Sandy 01, OSC passed to Sandy 05, Maj. Don Milner, as the rescue forces realized that the recovery of the Nail 31 crew was going to be a major battle. They spent the afternoon attacking enemy positions and AAA guns in the area, until Milner's aircraft was hit and seriously damaged and he had to return to NKP. At that point, the most experienced A-1 pilot on scene was Smoke 43, Capt. Randy Jayne, and he became the OSC. All types of ordnance were dropped, including cluster bombs, area denial ordnance, and tear gas, in an effort to destroy the guns and deny the enemy the ability to close in around the survivors. By 1900L, as the sun was setting, the A-1s led in Jolly 32 for a recovery attempt behind a wall of obscurant smoke. However, the AAA was just too heavy, and they had to abort. As the Jollys departed, strike aircraft delivered more ordnance in an effort to destroy more AAA.

King 22 took over as the AMC and FACs remained overhead throughout the night and continued to put in air strikes on enemy forces to prepare for the resumption of rescue operations the next day. Some consideration was given to attempting a recovery with the LNRS aircraft. But the use of chemical weapons and problems with the location of Captain Boretsky, who was moving and having radio problems, obviated that course of action. Instead, the controllers at OL-B and the aircrews at NKP were planning for a classic first-light recovery.

The next morning, King 21 reassumed AMC, and Jolly Greens 32 and 63 were airborne out of NKP by 0530L. They were followed fifteen minutes later by Sandys 01, 02, 03, and 04, and an hour later, Jolly Greens 30 and 61. Unfortunately, Jolly Green 63 and Sandys 03 and 04 had maintenance problems and had to return to NKP. They were replaced by Jolly Green 56 and Sandys 05 and 06 from Ubon. Arriving over the Catcher's Mitt, they discovered that the enemy gunners were still very active and had probably been resupplied during the night. Two hours later, Sandys 07 and 08 from Da Nang joined the effort. The task force again engaged the enemy forces in an attempt to sterilize the area enough to permit a Jolly Green to make the recoveries. As the OSC, Sandy 01, Capt. John Lackey, directed the A-1s and flights of fighters as they destroyed an estimated thirty enemy positions. When he reached bingo fuel, he was replaced as the OSC by Sandy 09, Capt. Ron Smith. At about 1000L, Smith decided that the area was safe enough to allow a pickup. He directed Jolly Green 61, flown by Maj. Ken Ernest and crew, to make the effort just above the trees to stay below the larger caliber guns. Smith ordered Sandy 07 to use smoke rockets to mark the ingress route for the helicopter and then with Sandy 08 escort him on his run in, picking up Breskman and then Boretsky. When everyone was ready, he called for the force to execute the mission. As the Jolly Green initiated his run, Breskman popped his smoke marker and the helicopter flew directly to a hover over him. One of the PJs came down on the hoist and brought Breskman out. Boretsky was about one hundred meters away, and Jolly Green 61 hovered over to his position, where again a PJ inserted to help bring him up on the hoist. As the survivor entered the helicopter door, Ernest began his exit from the area and returned to NKP with two very happy survivors. Throughout this epic battle, one A-1 had been lost and five more were damaged. It was a tough fight. Captain Ron Smith almost ran out of fuel and had to land at Savannakhet to take on enough gas to make it back to NKP.[48]

The participation of Capt. John Lackey in this mission was accidental. He was scheduled to return to the United States on 18 March and was sitting in the passenger terminal at base operations when he heard that a nasty SAR had just started and the First SOS was launching aircraft to support it. He walked down to the squadron to see what was going on and encountered Capt. Buck Buchanan, who was the squadron scheduler and was scrambling to line up pilots for the SAR. John was a qualified and experienced A-1 Sandy lead and asked if he could be of help. Buchanan checked with Maj. Jim Harding, the squadron operations officer, and since John had not actually left the squadron yet and was qualified to fly the mission, he could be used. Accordingly, he was Sandy 01 the next day—with Capt. Buck Buchanan on his wing. And for his efforts on that brutal second day, Capt. John Lackey was awarded the Air Force Cross.[49]

General Lavelle and the Protective Reaction Missions

Interspersed within all of the missions being directed at North Vietnam were twenty-eight missions that were carried out under the authority of "protective reaction." General Lavelle liked to closely monitor these missions and even listened in on their radio chatter. On one strike against a North Vietnamese airfield, the flight lead reported the strike results and then added that there was no enemy reaction. Lavelle responded, "We cannot report 'no reaction,'" based on his understanding that since the enemy radars were now all netted together, the enemy was always reacting to US strike flights. Dutifully, the flight lead reported that there had been enemy reaction, on the standardized after-action reports, thus justifying the strike under the current rules of engagement. Other crews did the same. General Lavelle also briefed this to his deputy for operations, Maj. Gen. Alton Slay, who called the commander of the 432nd Tactical Reconnaissance Wing at Udorn Air Base, Thailand, Col. Charles Gabriel, and briefed him on the reporting procedure.[50]

At Udorn, Sgt. Lonnie Franks, an intelligence specialist who debriefed the crews, discovered the altered report procedure and confirmed it with his supervisors. He subsequently wrote a letter to Senator Harold Hughes from his home state of Iowa, explaining the falsification of the battle reports. Hughes passed the letter through channels to the Air Force chief of staff, General John Ryan. He immediately dispatched his inspector general, Lt. Gen. Louis Wilson to Saigon. There, he met with all parties, who talked to him freely. When Wilson reported his findings to Ryan, he summoned Lavelle to Washington. Lavelle arrived on 26 March and reported directly to General Ryan. He admitted that a limited number of strikes had been conducted as "protective reaction," and that he had ordered that crews could not report "no reaction." General Ryan told him that his actions were unacceptable and had placed his aircrews and support personnel in a situation where they had to falsify reports. He also told Lavelle that he could either be reassigned as a major general or retired. Lavelle chose the latter.[51]

Lieutenant General Marvin McNickle, the commander of Thirteenth Air Force, was appointed as acting commander of Seventh Air Force, and Maj. Gen. Winton Marshall, the deputy commander of Seventh Air Force, ran the day-to-day operations until a new commander could be selected and dispatched to assume command. However, Marshall was aghast at this turn of events. He saw what the enemy was doing and believed that Seventh Air Force was taking prudent steps to blunt the enemy's expected offensive. And the news of the relief of General Lavelle quickly spread through the combat units. The airmen did not know all of the details behind the story. But they did know that Lavelle had been sending them against an enemy that was openly planning to attack and was modifying tactics to shoot down more allied aircraft. The general was clearly trying to support our allies and protect his airmen. That made a lot of sense to those still flying and fighting in this war. One of the Udorn pilots, 1st Lt. Bill Dalecky, remembered:

The sense was that . . . [it was] an artificial limitation that was being done for a political reason and it was limiting extremely what we had to do. This [ground fire reporting] was the solution. . . . I don't think that anybody ever had a real sense that people were concerned about it. . . . Everyone felt a sense of collective frustration at not being able to fly, to really get at the North Vietnamese. . . . There were fairly regular intel reports about the large amount of supplies being built up. It was obviously in preparation for [the invasion] . . . there was a collective sense that . . . lives were going to be at stake. . . . All this material is going to be used to kill Americans and South Vietnamese.[52]

Another young Udorn fighter pilot, 1st Lt. Marty Cavato, explained that the bar talk was all about the protective reaction procedures and how one guy on each strike would be briefed to call out ground fire at some point. They could see that they were hitting valid and vital targets and were doing great damage to the enemy units that were preparing to invade South Vietnam. It all made tactical sense. Concerning General Lavelle, Cavato was more emphatic: "The General got fired because he was protecting his troops." His firing bred a lot of bitterness among the guys who had to fly the missions.[53]

The War Goes On
On 27 March, the OL-A at Son Tra launched Jolly Greens 52 and 62 when it received a report of a downed Jolly Green aircraft in northeastern Cambodia. Jolly Greens 60 and 61 had departed NKP earlier to rendezvous with Jolly Green 64, which had departed Da Nang and was en route to NKP via Cambodia. At one point, the other two crews lost sight of Jolly Green 61. When the Jolly 61 crew did not respond to a radio check, the two crews began a visual search and spotted a large fire with black smoke. They swiftly realized that it was Jolly Green 61, HH-53C #68–10365. The crews of Jolly Greens 60 and 64 tried to hover over the wreckage but were driven away by enemy ground fire. Both sustained damage to their aircraft. When Jolly Greens 52 and 62 arrived and could find no survivors, they escorted 60 and 64 to friendly fields and then returned to the crash site. Eventually, a PJ was able to descend to the crash site but was unable to search it in any detail because of the lingering fire. When a search was finally conducted, no survivors or remains were found. Instead, the searcher discovered that the cockpit and cabin had been reduced to ashes. Sandy 05, Capt. George Throckmorton, and Sandy 06, 1st Lt. Byron Hukee, were launched out of

Ubon to support the search. They trolled the area for enemy response but encountered none and orbited above until the ground search was complete. It was a tragic loss for the rescue community.[54]

As the NVA forces continued to move south through the trail complex, they were accompanied by the 377th Air Defense Division. Since entering Laos, its gunners had been observing the actions of the allied aircraft that were constantly pummeling them day and night. They greatly feared the AC-130 gunships, labeling them the "Thug," because they just seemed to never go away and were very good and finding and destroying trucks and materiel. However, the NVA commanders had begun to notice that the AC-130s flew common flight patterns, and they could be exploited. They wanted to destroy the AC-130s, knowing that such victories would be great morale enhancers for their troops. They would soon experience success.[55]

The next evening, disaster struck the USAF forces in Thailand. An AC-130 gunship, Spectre 13, from the Sixteenth SOS based at Ubon RTAFB, Thailand, was patrolling the Ho Chi Minh trail near the deadly crossroads at Tchepone when it was engaged and destroyed by an SA-2 missile about twenty miles north of where Nail 31 was downed. The explosion was seen by several other aircraft and FACs, and other Spectres rushed into the area to search for survivors and initiate recovery operations. The orbiting King aircraft was also aware of the downing and immediately coordinated with the JRCC and OL-B to alert the SAR forces at NKP and support aircraft from throughout the theater. However, there were no survivors, just burning wreckage. The next day FACs and fighters swarmed central Laos attacking anything that even remotely looked like it might be part of an SA-2 site, as the Sixteenth SOS held a memorial service for its lost members.[56]

Two nights later, 30/31 March, another Sixteenth SOS AC-130 modified to carry a 105mm side-firing howitzer, Spectre 22, was performing a strike mission along the Ho Chi Minh trail and had destroyed several trucks when it was hit and severely damaged by 57mm AAA, north of the Bolovens Plateau in southern Laos. The crew made a mayday call, which was heard by just about everybody else, and turned toward Ubon. The aircraft commander, Capt. Waylon Fulk, initially declared, "Everybody is cleared out on your own" over the intercom system, and one gunner and the copilot bailed out. Fulk then was able to control the aircraft and directed everybody to hang on as he tried to fly further away from the Ho Chi Minh trail. They travelled about thirty more miles before the rest of the crew bailed out of the dying aircraft. Redbird 13, a B-57 crew, reported multiple beeper and voice contacts with crewmembers. King 27 launched to assume AMC duties, and

Nail FACs diverted into the area to begin searching for the crewmembers, quickly realizing that all fifteen persons aboard (thirteen USAF and two US Army) had bailed out and were spread out in two groups, one group of two near a major road segment and thirteen in a more remote area about thirty miles away. Nail 39, a Pave Nail OV-10 flown by Capt. Pete Morelli and 1st Lt. Vic Gedris, began determining positions with their Pave Spot–loran system and coordinated this process with Spectre 20 and 21, who had joined in and were using their sensor systems to search for survivors and deal with any enemy forces who might be in the area. The clustered thirteen survivors were in a relatively benign region, while the first two were closer to the main road segment and the guns that had shot down the aircraft. They would have to be dealt with separately. Nail 49, another Pave Nail OV-10, crewed by Capt. Dan Gibson and Capt. Rick Atchison, arrived overhead and became OSC for those two survivors.

Needless to say, such a dramatic event was generating a huge amount of communications. To bring order to the chaos, King 27 developed a communications plan so that the FACs, Sandys, Jolly Greens, and survivors could converse as necessary to facilitate the individual recoveries. Regardless, it was a cacophonous night as all participants worked through the unusual challenges and got the job done.

At NKP, the Twenty-Third TASS set up a schedule to ensure that Nail FACs were being dispatched for continuous OSC coverage. OL-B conferred with the Fortieth ARRS, and they decided that the terrain in the area was not conducive to LNRS recoveries. Instead, a first-light conventional effort was planned. Consequently, the First SOS launched eight A-1s, led by Maj. Jim Harding. The Fortieth ARRS launched two flights of helicopters from NKP, Jolly Greens 53 and 62, and a few minutes later, Jolly Greens 60 and 64. Jolly Green 63 was also launched from Ubon. Arriving in the area, Sandys 01, 02 05, and 06 began working the pickup of the first two survivors and Sandys 03, 04, 07, and 08 worked with the larger group. When the helicopters arrived in the recovery area, Raven 10 and Raven 40, both flying O-1s, joined the gaggle of aircraft over the larger group. They helped point out each survivor as Jolly Green 53, flown by Maj. Ken Ernest and crew, recovered two personnel; Jolly Green 62, flown by Maj. Fred Hartstein and crew, recovered one; Jolly Green 60, flown by Capt. Dale Stovall and crew, recovered eight; and Jolly Green 63, flown by Maj. David Daus, recovered two.

As the SAR was ongoing, King 27 also contacted Air America Operations and requested support from their helicopters in the area. Bruce Jachens, an H-34 pilot stationed at Savannakhet, was told that he was needed for the SAR effort. Operations out of Savannakhet required only one pilot, so he discussed the effort with his Filipino flight mechanic and they decided to go. They took off using the call sign Hotel 59, and King directed them to rendezvous with another Air America H-34, flown by Allen Cates, Chuck Frady, and Jim Nakamoto, using the call sign of Hotel 45. Together they headed to the recovery area, discovering that flying formation at night was a challenge and certainly something that they were not normally required to do. En route, Hotel 59 experienced a battery fire, which the flight mechanic extinguished. Normally, such an emergency would cause the flight crew to divert to the nearest airport. However, this was a rescue and Jachens was not turning back.

The two Air America helicopters were directed to head toward the two remaining survivors farther north and close to the road. The FACs and Sandys there had put in some air strikes on enemy forces in the area, and it was still dangerous. As they flew in, Hotel 59 and Hotel 45 established contact with the two survivors and proceeded directly to their locations, which were about one hundred yards apart. Hotel 45 went in first and picked up the copilot as Hotel 59 stood off as back up. As Hotel 45 lifted off with their survivor, Hotel 59 dashed in to recover the last man, one of the AC-130 gunners. Unfortunately, he was on uneven sloped terrain, and Jachens had to hold a difficult hover as his flight mechanic lowered the collar to the gunner. However, looking up at an unmarked helicopter being flown by two men in civilian clothes, and one of them Asian in appearance, the survivor seemed to hesitate. Jachens knew that there were enemy forces in the immediate area and was not going to wait much longer when the gunner came to his senses and put the collar around him. The flight mechanic winched him in as Jachens turned to depart the area. Above, two of the A-1s, led by Jim Harding, laid down a smoke screen to hide the helicopter from the NVA gunners along the trail. As they were departing, Jachens asked his mechanic how the survivor was doing. The response was not encouraging. Jachens handed him a tuna sandwich made for the crew as their flight lunch. "Welcome to Air America," he said with a smile. They flew to a small airfield near Pakse. There, one of the Jolly Greens was waiting to pick up the two survivors and return them to Ubon. The two Air America crews then returned to regular operations. The recovery of the fifteen crewmembers of the Spectre 22 was complete.[57]

However, the destruction of the two AC-130s was a great victory for the NVA 377th Air Defense Division. Seventh Air Force placed a restricted area over the center of the Ho Chi Minh trail, pulling the gunships off of that vital sector—a tremendous operational advantage for the NVA forces flowing south. Noted in the 377th Division history for that time period: "Just one hour when the AC-130s did not operate over our choke-points was both precious and rare. This time, we got 15 days or 360 hours. During this time a great many truck convoys were able to transit the entry points to carry their supplies to the front lines."[58]

Late in the month, Capt. Ron Smith at the First SOS replaced Capt. Randy Jayne as the Sandy SAR briefer for the theater. As such, he was tasked with traveling to other units and briefing their aircrews on current SAR procedures. Smith's first trip was out to the USS *Coral Sea*, where he gave his briefing to their combat aviators. One of the squadrons that he visited there was the USMC VMFA (AW) 224, an A-6 equipped all-weather attack squadron. Sitting in his audience was Maj. Clyde Smith, who in about two weeks would be the single survivor in the midst of one of the First SOS's biggest and most challenging rescues in Laos.[59]

These rescues are just a few of so many, yet representative of how diverse rescues were geographically and in terms of complexity and ferocity. Each was its own battle in place and time to recover our airmen and soldiers.

Looking at this portion of Commando Hunt in 1972, the shootdowns recorded in Chris Hobson's *Vietnam Air Losses* present an interesting picture.

Aircraft Lost: USAF—21, USN—10		
Results:	29 KIA/40%	
	5 POW/7%	
	39 recovered/53%	
	AirAm helis 5	Army helis 2
	USAF helis 20	USN helis 6
	Unknown 6[60]	

But Hobson's data is limited to fixed-wing losses and does not include US Army fixed-wing and rotary-wing losses, most allied losses, and losses recorded by special programs like the Ravens in Laos. Accordingly, shoot downs like Raven 11, Jolly Green 61, Centaur 16, and the UH-1 lost in the Stormy 04 recovery recorded above are not in these numbers and have to be accounted for anecdotally. Yet Hobson's numbers do indicate that over 50 percent of downed airmen were recovered during this period, and by a variety of recovery assets available across the theater. The SARs cited during this period show the variety and complexity of SARs occurring across the breadth of SEA and the multitudinous challenges that they presented.

As March was ending, tectonic events were occurring. While the crew of Spectre 22 was being recovered, the whole pace of the war was changing as NVA regular forces, mechanized infantry, armor, artillery, engineer, air defense weapons, and more were pouring across the DMZ and out of Laos and Cambodia. It was the long-expected North Vietnamese offensive. Commando Hunt was terminated as the mighty force of US air power was about to be unleashed on the invaders.

Undoubtedly, US air power had savagely wounded the invading NVA forces in the run-up to the invasion. American intelligence calculated that in the effort, our forces had destroyed 4,727 trucks and damaged another 5,882, and the AC-130s had accounted for 70 percent of the damage. Overall US estimates indicated that only 16 percent of shipped supplies actually reached the fighting forces in South Vietnam. NVA records show a different tale. They indicate that they had 4,228 trucks destroyed, about 58 percent of their truck fleet, and that 2,450 support troops were killed. However, their records show that only 10 percent of their supplies were attrited in the passage. Which side's analysis was more correct would be determined by the performance of the NVA units in the coming battles.[61]

CHAPTER THREE

APRIL INVASION AND

REINFORCEMENT

Air America, special ground teams, clandestine operations, frogmen, aircraft carriers, tanks . . . there is no limitation on the tactics or concepts to be employed to effect a rescue.

Lieutenant Colonel Bill Harris, commander, Thirty-Seventh Aerospace Rescue and Recovery Squadron, End of Tour Report

MR-1, the DMZ to Quang Tri

North Vietnam labeled this assault the Nguyen Hue Offensive, named for a Vietnamese leader who in 1789 led their armies in the defeat of a Chinese occupying force and ended one thousand years of Chinese rule. Now their national army would drive out the latest invaders and reunify the nation under their control. As planned, their divisions, newly reorganized as mechanized formations, were supported by a sizable array of air defense weapons from antiaircraft artillery (AAA) to SA-2s, and even the newly introduced SA-7 missiles were prepared to fight the Americans for control of the skies. Together, the three offensives were intended to carry out the Politburo's plans and embarrass President Nixon as he approached reelection in November.[1]

In MR-1, the enemy's military objectives were the capture of Quang Tri and Hue and the destruction of ARVN forces. The 308th Division, North Vietnamese Army (NVA), with supporting armor and artillery regiments, initiated their attack on 30 March at high noon with a massive artillery barrage and then a direct frontal attack through the DMZ. This area was defended by the Third Division, Army of the Republic of Vietnam (ARVN), which was reinforced with a brigade of South Vietnamese marines, an armored brigade, and several ranger groups. These forces were arrayed in a series of forward bases—a ten-mile strip running west to east above the small city of Dong Ha.

NVA artillery pulverized the bases, destroying the South Vietnamese artillery and forcing the ARVN soldiers there to retreat. The forward air controllers (FACs) of the Twentieth Tactical Air Support Squadron (TASS) at Da Nang tried to provide air support, but the weather was unrelenting, with thick low clouds and rain. And nobody wanted to be flying around in that muck, especially when and where NVA radars were operating.

At one base, Alpha 2, a five-man USMC team from the First Air and Naval Gunfire Liaison Company (ANGLICO), led by 1st Lt. David Bruggeman, directly supported the ARVN units by directing naval gunfire from US Navy ships offshore and coordinating air support when it could get in through the horrible weather. By the morning of 1 April, it appeared that the NVA was getting ready to launch an all-out infantry assault against Alpha 2, and Bruggeman radioed the Third ARVN Division headquarters requesting that he and his team be evacuated by helicopter. The commander of Team 155, the advisory team for the Third ARVN Division, was Col. Don Metcalf. He had just directed that all US advisors from the forward units be evacuated, and he approved the ANGLICO team extraction. A UH-1 flown by Warrant Officers Ben Nielson and Robert Sheridan and two supporting AH-1s from F Troop of the Eighth Cavalry (F/8) were dispatched to recover them. The helicopters had to fight their way in to the landing strip at Alpha 2. As the UH-1 was landing, Bruggeman was hit by artillery shrapnel and grievously wounded. Three of his marines carried him to the helicopter. However, a fifth marine, Cpl. James Worth, could not be found. Nobody knew what had happened to him, and a quick search was unsuccessful. As the incoming artillery increased in intensity, the helicopter took off. They flew directly to the nearest medical facility, but it was too late, and Bruggeman died en route.[2]

The attack of the 308th NVA Division was supported by the 304th and 324B NVA Divisions, which attacked out of Laos. Concurrently with the actions of the 308th, they initiated attacks against a series of South Vietnamese outposts along ridges about fifteen miles west of Quang Tri. These positions were manned by South Vietnamese marines of the 147th Brigade, Vietnamese Marine Corps (VNMC), and their USMC battalion advisors. Attacking under low clouds and rain, which made air support and even FAC overwatch almost impossible, the enemy was able to drive the defenders out of these positions. Unfortunately, two US Army specialists manning a radio intelligence bunker were killed when an NVA artillery round impacted their position and destroyed it. Their bodies were never recovered. As the South Vietnamese units retreated to the east, their advisors were able to evade with them. US Army helicopters from F/8 Cavalry were available to extract the advisors, but the advisors decided to stay with their units as a morale-saving gesture. By 1 April, they had evaded to the main base at Mai Loc.[3]

On the evening of 1 April, the Third ARVN Division commander, Brig. Gen. Vu Van Giai, directed that all of his northern units would fall back and establish a defensive line along the Mieu Giang River, which flowed through Dong Ha and drained into the Gulf of Tonkin (GOT). The next morning, 2 April, his units had pulled back and were consolidating their positions as the skies cleared and both FACs and strike aircraft could attack the advancing enemy units. In the early afternoon, an O-2, Mike 81, 1st Lt. Richard Abbot, was hit by NVA AAA while orbiting over the water east of the mouth of the Cua Viet River. He bailed out and another FAC, Bully 14, initiated a SAR for him. Jolly Greens 65 and 67, and two A-1s, Sandys 07 and 08, from the First Special Operations Squadron (SOS) operating location at Da Nang Air Base, South Vietnam, were launched to support the effort. However, within thirty minutes, a small boat from the USS *Hamner* picked up Abbot, and the Sandys and Jollys just held off the coast as a standby force in case Colonel Metcalf at the Third ARVN Division decided to evacuate his Team 155 advisors.[4]

Ten miles west of Dong Ha, the Third ARVN Division held a key firebase called Camp Carroll. It was the main base for the Fifty-Sixth Infantry Regiment and twenty-two pieces of artillery and perhaps was the key location on the entire defensive line. Two US Army advisors, Lt. Col. Bill Camper and Maj. Joe Brown, were assigned to the regiment, and they were working hard to provide all the support that they could for the soldiers to hold out against the invading forces. However, as Mike 81 was being picked up, the ARVN commander of the Fifty-Sixth Regiment was making arrangements with NVA forces in the area to surrender Camp Carroll and his unit to them. Camper tried to intercede because he knew that such a move would rip a hole in the entire South Vietnamese defensive line. But his efforts were rebuffed, and as the South Vietnamese soldiers prepared to surrender to the enemy forces, he and Brown escaped through the perimeter wire and called frantically for a helicopter pickup. A US Army CH-47 of the Sixty-Second Aviation Company, Coachman 05, was diverted from a supply run and turned north to proceed to Carroll. Two AH-1s from F/8 also heard the call and proceeded to escort Coachman 05. They were needed because NVA troops spotted Camper and Brown and attempted to intervene. The gunners on the two AH-1s and Coachman were busy engaging the enemy as the CH-47 landed. The two Americans plus about thirty Vietnamese boarded before the crew lifted off and headed south. One entire battalion also went through the wire and escaped, and over the next month, more than one thousand members of the Fifty-Sixth Regiment returned to friendly control. As Camper flew away from Camp Carroll, he could see white flags blossoming all over the base.

However, Camper and Brown's ordeal was not yet over. Coachman 05 had been badly damaged in the rescue, and the crew had to land it in friendly territory on a main highway. They were able to contact other helicopters, which then landed and picked up the two advisors and delivered them to the division headquarters. Camper could also hear the radio calls from other units that, because of the loss of Carroll, would now have to evacuate their exposed positions.[5]

While these events were playing out, some reinforcements were on the way. F/4 Cavalry was moving up from MR-2. The preponderance of the unit would arrive at Phu Bai by sundown on 3 April and was prepared to begin combat operations the next morning. They flew their orientation flights with the soldiers from F/8 Cavalry, who greatly appreciated the help. Soon, their formations of two OH-6s, one or two UH-1s, and two AH-1s would fully engage against the invading NVA forces.[6]

The Centaurs of F/4 Cavalry would quickly be called upon to engage. Dramatic events were also occurring at Dong Ha. There, a key north-south highway, QL-1, crossed the Mieu Giang River. As Carroll was falling, NVA units began to approach the key bridge over the river with a strong force of tanks and mechanized infantry. A combined task force of ARVN M-48 tanks and the VNMC Third Battalion was in place to stop them from crossing. In the midst of this battle, Capt. John Ripley, USMC advisor to the VNMC battalion, placed a heavy charge on the main bridge and blew it up. As he did that, a flight of VNAF A-1s attacked the NVA forces on the north bank and claimed the destruction of twenty-nine tanks and vehicles. One of the A-1s was struck by enemy AAA and the pilot ejected. The marines scrambled to rescue him, but the winds out of the south carried him north of the river and he was captured. The stout defense mounted by the joint force of South Vietnamese soldiers and marines at Dong Ha kept the NVA forces from crossing. Instead, they turned west to try to cross four miles upriver at Cam Lo, where there was another small bridge and some shallow fording points. Captain Ripley contacted the US Navy ships out on the gun line and had them bombard the enemy columns.[7]

The Saga of Bat 21

As the weather continued to improve, more air strikes were going in to staunch the NVA invasion. "Copper" Cell, a flight of three B-52s, was entering the area to strike a regimental column moving to exploit the gap in the South Vietnamese lines created by the fall of Camp Carroll. It was escorted by a flight of two F-105G aircraft to protect the flight from SA-2s, a flight of two F-4Es to protect it from any NVA MiGs that might be foolish enough to attack it, and an EB-66E with powerful electronic jammers as further protection against the SA-2 missile batteries. Additionally, the flight was escorted by an EB-66C, which was equipped to collect signals data on any radar sites that might engage the gaggle of aircraft. Such data could be used to determine the location of the surface-to-air missile (SAM) sites so that they could be destroyed. The two EB-66s were from the Forty-Second Tactical Electronic Warfare Squadron based at Korat RTAFB, Thailand. Their call signs were Bat 22 and Bat 21, respectively.

As the flight of aircraft entered the area from the southwest at about 1700 local time, they were being tracked by North Vietnamese area radars and by SA-2 sites near Khe Sanh and in the DMZ. The controllers at the various sites were sharing their tracking information. The B-52s activated their onboard jamming, and Bat 22 joined that effort as the two F-105Gs launched missiles against radar sites. Salvos of SA-2 missiles were fired at the aircraft, all of which missed. Then a third site to the northwest engaged and fired three more missiles. One missile detonated directly below Bat 21. The damage was mortal, and the aircraft nosed over toward the ground. Only one man of the crew of six, the fifty-three-year-old navigator, Lt. Col. Iceal Hambleton, was able to eject. Since he was the second man on the crew manifest, his personal call sign would be Bat 21Bravo. A few miles away, another flight of F-4s, led by Maj. Jim Kempton, saw the explosion and ejection. He reported it to King 21, who had flown into the area a few hours prior to cover the Mike 81 SAR and had remained. The King crew dutifully passed the notification to the JRCC in Saigon. So began perhaps the most consequential SAR of the entire war.[8]

The North Vietnamese air defense forces in the area were part of the 236B Regiment of the 365th Air Defense Division assigned to protect the invading combat units. Their Sixty-Fourth Missile Battalion was equipped with SA-2 missiles. The 236's history report for this period states:

At 1545 [Hanoi time—one hour earlier than Saigon time] hours on 2 April, the 365th Air Defense Division alerted its subordinate units that many B-52 cells had been detected approaching from western Route 9 [Laos]. The division ordered the 236B and 274th Regiments to engage and destroy B-52s in the western Route 9 sector. . . . The 236B Regiment commander quickly ordered his 62nd and 64th Battalions to mass their fire to destroy a B-52 cell approaching to bomb the Tan Lam-Dau Mau-Ta Con [Khe Sanh] area. The B-52 jamming was very powerful, so both battalions decided to use the three-point method. The two battalions fired a total of five missiles at a B-52 target at an altitude of eight kilometers. The B-52 caught fire and crashed in the area of Cam Tien Village, Cam Lo District. The 64th Battalion was given credit for shooting down one B-52.[9]

That claimed B-52 was actually Bat 21.[10]

To the Rescue

Orbiting below this air battle was an O-2 flown by 1st Lt. Bill Jankowski. He saw the missiles climb skyward but did not see the actual explosion. Hanging in his parachute above, Hambleton, now using the personal call sign of Bat 21Bravo, contacted the "FAC O-2" and asked him to rock his wings. When Jankowski did, Hambleton told him that he had him in sight. Only then did Jankowski realize that Hambleton was above him. Jankowski circled the descending aviator, at one point, even considering trying to fly by and "grab" the survivor before he landed. When Hambleton reached the ground, Jankowski noted his location. He was just north of the small bridge at Cam Lo and in the midst of one of the biggest battles in the entire Vietnam War.[11]

Jankowski called for help on the Guard frequency. He was answered by the pilots of a UH-1 and an AH-1 from F/8—Blue Ghosts 39 and 28. He asked them to try an immediate pickup. They attempted to fly into the area, but Blue Ghost 28 was badly shot up. He headed east and crashed on the beach, where Jolly Green 67 picked up the two crewmembers. Blue Ghost 39 crossed the Mieu Giang River and was also shot down. Three crewmembers were killed, and one was captured. The two Sandy A-1s that had launched for Mike 81 also joined Jankowski. However, low clouds were moving back in, and there were just too many guns for the Jolly Greens to try another pickup as the day was ending. Hambleton was in the middle of the battle, and any attempt to rescue him was going to require a major effort.

Throughout the night, FACs remained on station to "babysit" Bat 21Bravo. The Twenty-Third TASS at NKP dispatched Pave Nail OV-10s to use their Pave Spot system to try to facilitate a rescue and plot key locations for loran-guided bomb strikes. To facilitate the operations of the SAR forces in the midst of the larger battle, controllers within the JRCC declared a no-fire zone of twenty-seven kilometers around Bat 21Bravo's position. This restriction was passed to the ground commanders, who deeply resented so much being done for the American airmen while Vietnamese troops were dying in the larger battle. It was a replay of the resentment generated by the SARs in the Lam Son 719 battle a year earlier. It was reinforced by the inclination of the senior American commanders to evacuate their advisors from the Vietnamese units when they were in heavy combat. Some advisors refused to go, sensing that their ARVN counterparts would respect them only if they fully shared the risk of combat. Such an evacuation was a sensitive issue—it made sense to the Americans but was anathema to the Vietnamese.[12]

The next day, 3 April, another team of two Sandy A-1s tried to lead in two Jolly Greens for two separate pickup attempts. The first attempt was flown by Lt. Cdr. Jay Crowe and crew. Crowe was a Coast Guard exchange pilot. Since 1967, the US Coast Guard had been providing experienced crewmembers to fly HH-3s, HH-53s, and HC-130s with the USAF rescue units to share their rescue experience and cross-training. In fact, Crowe was one of the most experienced pilots in the Thirty-Seventh ARRSq, and he and his crew were able to bring their helicopter close to Hambleton before they were driven away by the heavy enemy fire. He remembered, "In the most exciting 90 seconds of my life, we descended, saw tanks, tracked vehicles, troops, took 40 hits and climbed back into the clouds," before diverting their now badly damaged helicopter to the US Army base at Hue/Phu Bai.[13] Lieutenant Colonel Bill Harris, the Thirty-Seventh ARRSq commander, led the next attempt. He and his crew tried an approach from a more northerly sector. However, the result was the same. He also took his damaged aircraft to Hue/Phu Bai.[14]

One of the Pave Nail OV-10s, Nail 38, was also shot down by an SA-2, and the two crewmembers, Nail 38Alpha, Capt. Bill Henderson, and Nail 38Bravo, 1st Lt. Mark Clark, ejected just two kilometers from Hambleton and were also evading. Nail 22, Capt. Arnie Franklin, quickly diverted to cover Nail 38 and take over as the OSC for this devolving mess. He was flying another Pave Nail aircraft and was able to quickly get a loran location for Clark. Again, helicopters from F/8 tried to make quick recoveries but were either shot up or shot down in the process. Fortunately, all crewmembers were recovered. That night, Henderson was captured and sent north.

Once again, the 236B SAM Regiment claimed credit for the shootdown. Its history states: "On 3 April, from its Me Tre launch site, the 64th Missile Battalion, stretching its fire forward to support our attacking infantry formations, shot down one OV-10 and two F-4s."[15] No F-4s were lost at that time and place. That OV-10 was Nail 38.

On 4 April, the Sandys and Jollys launched and prepared for another rescue effort. Numerous air strikes were directed against enemy forces in an attempt to dampen the threat, and in the process eight A-1s were damaged, two severely, and one would never fly again. Meetings were held at Da Nang and Saigon to consider other courses of action. They discussed using the Fulton recovery system but discarded it because the recovery MC-130 would be far too vulnerable in such a high-threat area. The limited night recovery system (LNRS) aircraft of the Fortieth ARRSq were considered but then ruled out, also because of the threat. Colonel Cy Muirhead flew a night mission in a OH-6 with Capt. Hugh Mills to see if it could feasibly serve in the ongoing effort. He also requested that Mills and a small support team be deployed to Phu Bai airfield for possible use. The next day, the weather was very bad, with low ceilings and limited visibility. Aircraft dropped bombs with their loran navigation systems and delivered several loads of BLU-52 chemical incapacitants around the survivors to protect them from ground forces. At one point, Nail 22, Capt. Arnie Franklin was again the OSC and directed a flight of F-4s that dropped BLU-52. Unfortunately, in briefing the fighters for their drop, Franklin inadvertently gave them Clark's loran location instead of the enemy locations, and Clark was doused with the powder. The result was predictable. However, it also protected him from enemy forces in the area. Later, he and Franklin had a colorful conversation about that.[16]

One of the crewmembers who dropped those weapons that day, 1st Lt. Ted Sienicki, later reported:

> We were directed by a Nail FAC . . . and I did see his OV-10 wing dip out of the clouds. The Quang Tri TACAN was out of commission, and we were screaming in below 400' under thick overcast, which obscured a lot of light. Thousands of tracers were visible in the dim light, forming an X that we were flying through. It was my personal record for seeing airborne bullets, and I could not believe our aircraft had no holes upon return.[17]

Unfortunately, this action would be repeated the next day when Capt. Bill Begert, an O-2 Covey FAC, was serving as OSC and had to deal with the same terrible weather. With great difficulty, he was able to direct another flight of F-4s to deliver another load of BLU-52 around Clark, because large numbers of enemy troops were seen in that area. Once again, Clark was doused with the nasty power. Begert tried to contact him on his survival radio, but Clark did not answer. Concerned that the strike had harmed Clark, Begert extended his time on station by another hour and was dangerously low on fuel, especially considering that most airfields in the area were fogged in.

His only option was to return to Da Nang and utilize their ground control radar for a precision approach to one of their runways. When he arrived in the Da Nang area, his fuel gauges were just about at zero. Checking in with the radar controllers, he was notified that he was eighteenth in the landing pattern. He declared "emergency fuel" and was moved up to twelfth. When he finally had a chance to make an approach, he never saw the runway. His fuel gauges were now reading zero. While vectoring for a second approach he decided that if he did not see the runway this time, he would head east out over the bay and bail out. Fortunately, his next approach brought him right over the runway. However, he could not see it through the fog. Instead of going around and bailing out, he continued to descend through the fog and spotted the runway. The landing was uneventful. Remembered Begert, many years later, "Somehow I had enough fuel to taxi in without the engines quitting. My airplane took a few bullet holes in the wings that day, but my trusty O-2 got me home despite my poor judgement." Seems that the enemy forces were not the only thing that the combat aircrews had to worry about in the skies of Southeast Asia.[18]

Ground Battle and Reinforcements

Surrounding the SAR effort, the ground battle continued, although the NVA units seemed to be pausing to consolidate their gains to date and resupply their units. US aerial units attacked their convoys wherever they were found. Reacting to the invasion overall, General Abrams and his air commanders requested authority to attack targets in North Vietnam. President Nixon authorized Military Assistance Command Vietnam (MACV) to initiate Operation Freedom Train, an interdiction campaign directed at North Vietnam up to twenty degrees north. The withdrawal of US ground forces continued. However, Nixon authorized the reinforcement of aerial combat units in Thailand and at Da Nang.

In Operation Constant Guard I, the USAF deployed three F-4 squadrons, an EB-66 squadron, an F-105G squadron, and fifty-four more B-52s, which deployed to Andersen AFB, Guam. Additionally, the Twentieth TASS at Da Nang was reinforced with twelve O-2 FACs from the Twenty-Second TASS, which had moved to Hawaii in 1971. To increase SAR capability in South Vietnam, the Third ARRG coordinated the deployment of six HH-3s from the Philippines to Tan Son Nhut, and HC-130s from Clark Air Base, Philippines, to cover the SAR orbit off the coast near the DMZ. Three USMC F-4 squadrons, a detachment of EA-6 electronic-jamming aircraft, and a detachment of TA-4s for target spotting deployed to Da Nang, all as part of marine aircraft group (MAG) 15. The US Navy deployed the USS *Midway* and USS *Saratoga* to join TF-77. HC-7 also deployed 138 officers and men and four more HH-3A helicopters to support its operations in the GOT and also the repair facility in the Philippines. This provided the squadron with eleven HH-3As and two SH-3As, enabling them to have four Big Mothers on alert at all times.[19]

Jolly Green 67

For the ongoing SAR operations, the rescue forces at Da Nang were reinforced with extra HH-53s and A-1s from NKP. On 6 April, the weather over the area was mostly clear, and US and VNAF FACs directed strikes throughout the area to support both the SAR and the ARVN forces along their defensive line. At 3:15 p.m., Capt. Fred Boli, flying as Sandy 01, took off with Sandy 02, 1st Lt. Bob Carlsen, and Sandys 05 and 06, and proceeded to the Dong Ha area. Sandys 03 and 04 would join later. They were followed by Jolly Greens 67 and 60 and two more Jollys from NKP. The gaggle of aircraft rendezvoused southeast of Quang Tri. Sandys 01 and 02 proceeded to the survivor's location to determine if a pickup was feasible. Sandy 01 assumed OSC from Bilk 11, Capt. Harold Icke, who had been there for the last three hours. Sandys 01 and 02 trolled the area looking for enemy forces while Bilk 11 and Nail 59, who was also in the area, watched for enemy reaction. When all seemed quiet, Boli briefed the recovery plan to all participants. Sandy 02 would lead Jolly 67 in to Hambleton for a pickup with Sandys 05 and 06 as escort. If all remained quiet, Jolly 67 could also pick up Clark. Sandys 03 and 04 had just joined the effort, and Boli instructed them to use their smoke bombs to build a wall of smoke behind which Jolly 67 could approach the survivor's area. When all were ready, Boli ordered the operation to proceed. Dutifully, Sandy 02, Lieutenant Carlsen, led Jolly 67 into the recovery area. As they crossed the river, the enemy gunners opened up on them, focusing on the helicopter. As they approached a hover, somebody on Jolly Green 67 said on the radio, "I'm hit—they got a fuel line!"

Simultaneously, the lumbering helicopter began to turn to the right to an exit heading of southeast. The Sandys responded as best they could to cover the stricken aircraft. But the Jolly crews continued their turn to a heading of southwest, which took them back over enemy units. Everybody yelled at them to "turn south," but somebody on the Jolly Green was holding down his transmit button, which blocked the frequency. Boli and Carlsen saw something streak up from the ground behind the helicopter and strike it in the tail section. They watched flames appear along the top of the fuselage

Jolly Green 67 burning. (Courtesy Gary Ferentchek)

as the main rotor blades disintegrated. The helicopter then rolled to the left and crashed in a field about a mile south of Clark. It exploded and violently burned. Boli and Carlsen orbited over the wreckage and searched in vain for the crew. The fuselage appeared intact, but the fire was all-consuming. There were no survivors, and no determination of what had shot down Jolly Green 67.

Boli ordered the aircraft back to the rendezvous point. Everybody had an opinion to offer. They still had three more helicopters, and the A-1s still had some ordnance. But the burning wreckage of Jolly Green 67 and the experiences of the earlier Jolly Greens and the helicopters of F/8 indicated that the airspace over the survivors was just too dangerous for any more helicopters. Boli ordered the rescue force back to Da Nang. There were some who disagreed with his decision, but it was his decision to make. The battle continued, but another Sandy pilot, Capt. Bob Burke, noted, "There are times and circumstances when rescue by helicopter is impossible."[20]

Decisions

As the battles were raging across Vietnam, President Nixon and his key leaders were reviewing the most recent developments and considering bolder actions. He directed Maj. Gen. Al Haig, his assistant national security advisor, to work with military planners to design an air campaign against North Vietnam, looking at all military targets and even the possibility of mining all harbors. Its scope and implementation would be determined by the effectiveness of the North Vietnamese offensive to seriously erode South Vietnam's ability to defend its nation, and, if necessary, was to start no later than 8 May.[21]

The next day, more meetings were held at Da Nang and Saigon about Bat 21Bravo and Nail 38Bravo. The OH-6 and LNRS options were considered and discarded as too dangerous. The First SOS commander, Lieutenant Colonel Barbena, was at Da Nang. He was not Sandy qualified but was serving as a SARCO, liaising between his unit and the command centers at Queen and Joker. He decided to swap out his crews. Captain Boli departed and went to Saigon to brief the commanders there on the rescue events. There, General Creighton Abrams, when briefed on the ongoing saga of Bat 21Bravo and Nail 38Bravo, forbade any more attempts to pick up these men by helicopter.[22]

The other pilots departed for NKP. They were replaced by Capt. Ron Smith, 1st Lt. Lance Smith, Maj. Zeke Encinas, and 1st Lt. Joe Seitz as the efforts to recover the two downed airmen continued. Fellow First SOS pilot Capt. Bob Burke briefed the new arrivals on the current situation including the directive from General Abrams. He also told them that they were reasonably sure the NVA were monitoring the radio frequencies. For the purposes of area orientation, the Sandys planned to fly a fake pickup with the Jollys. This would allow the new arrivals to orient to the area, locate the survivors, and test the theory that the NVA were monitoring their communications.

The Sandys took off from Da Nang. Two Jollys launched and held out over the water with instructions not to cross the beach regardless of what happened and to make all their transmissions to the Sandys on their VHF-AM radios. With their UHF radios, the Sandys made quick calls to the survivors, positive in tone, just to make sure that they were still there and not in any immediate danger. As the Sandys approached the Dong Ha area, Captain Smith made several calls to the Jollys on VHF-AM stating that if they did not get any ground fire, they would call for another pickup attempt. The Sandys then used their VHF-FM radios to transmit among themselves, figuring that the NVA, if monitoring, would not be able to correlate what was being said on different radios in different frequency bands. Doing this, the Sandys were able to familiarize themselves with the area and the locations of the survivors. While orbiting the area at three thousand feet, they did not observe any AAA. After several minutes, Smith announced on the VHF-AM radio that the Sandys were returning to base, adding for his wingmen, "Safe up your weapons and let's go home." On *that same radio*, he also told the survivors to hold on, while they figured out what to do, and within thirty seconds all four Sandys were taking ground fire from several places in the SAR area. They then knew for sure the NVA were monitoring the VHF-AM radio frequencies and had to assume that they were also monitoring the UHF frequencies being used with the survivors. They also discovered that the enemy would most likely shoot at them when they believed that the Sandys would not or could not return fire. Ron Smith and his fellow A-1 pilots were clever guys.[23]

Later that day, another OV-10, Covey 282, was shot down by an SA-2 about five miles north of Dong Ha. The two crewmembers, Covey 282Alpha, 1st Lt. Bruce Walker, and Covey 282Bravo, USMC 1st Lt. Larry Potts, ejected. However, only Walker made contact with his fellow airmen on his survival radio. Potts's status was unknown. Several other FACs working in the area attempted to locate the two men and initiate a SAR operation. However, the SA-2s were shooting at everybody, and the small vulnerable FAC aircraft were forced out of the area. Some other way would have to be developed to get them out. Fortunately, there were men in the Military Assistance Command, Vietnam, Studies and Observations Group (MACSOG) who could do those kinds of things.[24]

The North Vietnamese air defense forces in the area also claimed credit for this shoot down, noting cryptically in their after-action report, "64th Battalion, located at its Me Tre firing position, shot down one enemy OV-10 while providing fire support for our forward troop formations."[25]

Freedom Train

As the rescue force was gathering for the Bat 21Bravo/Nail 38Bravo rescue attempt on 6 April, US Navy forces were striking targets in southern North Vietnam as part of Operation Freedom Train. A flight of two A-7s off the USS *Kitty Hawk* was performing road reconnaissance for enemy trucks near Dong Hoi when an SA-2 battery fired several missiles at them. One struck and seriously damaged the flight leader, Chippy 415, flown by Cdr. Mace Gilfry. He was able to turn his aircraft out to sea before he ejected about three miles offshore. His wingman contacted the recovery forces of HC-7. Big Mother 60, an HH-60A, flown by Lt. Frank Lockett and crew, had just completed an in-flight refueling off the USS *Ouellet* and responded to the call. As they approached Gilfry, the survivor told them that enemy rounds were hitting all around his location. Lockett dropped his rescue swimmer to help Gilfry and made an orbit of the area in an attempt to draw off the enemy fire. He then returned and picked up the two men. When they were safely aboard, he flew to the USS *Sterett* to drop them off.[26]

Two days later on, another Freedom Train strike, several flights of F-4s took off from Da Nang and struck the SAM sites in the DMZ area. As they were doing so, a VNAF O-1 and A-1 were literally blown out of the sky by SA-2s. There were no survivors. The missile batteries also fired at three cells of B-52s, damaging one aircraft, which had to divert into Da Nang. The SAMs had to be eliminated so that allied aircraft could interdict the NVA forces in the area and directly support the South Vietnamese forces. The US Navy ships on the gun line supported this effort with direct fire from their five- and eight-inch guns.[27]

As the SAM sits were being devastated, the Sandys were busy talking to the FACs and the Jolly crews to develop some recovery options. Based on guidance that he had received from Queen, Lieutenant Colonel Barbena forbade his pilots to fly any more missions in the SAR effort. Regardless, Capt. Ron Smith brainstormed with the FACs and Jolly crews and conjured up an idea to move the survivors to areas more amenable to facilitate a successful recovery—possibly utilizing the Mieu Giang River, which ran east–west through that area. All agreed that this would require developing an evasion plan for each individual and then communicating this plan to them on frequencies known to be monitored by the enemy forces. They contacted Hambleton's and Clark's squadrons for useful personal information. Smith thought that they had a viable plan. He decided to do something with their ideas. Believing that anything that he passed through Queen to the JRCC would be disregarded, he decided to call directly to the Joint Personnel Recovery Center (JPRC) at MACSOG. However, any detailed discussion of such methods would be classified. Smith went to the communications squadron at Da Nang and asked to talk on a top secret phone line. The airmen there informed him that they did not have a top secret line but did have a secret line. He used it to call the JPRC. His call was taken by the director of the JPRC, Lt. Col. Andy Andersen, USMC. Smith laid out his general plan. Andersen told him that he was about to depart for Da Nang and would talk with him when he arrived. When Lieutenant Colonel Barbena found out what Smith had done, he was livid. He told Smith that if he ever went out of the chain of command like that again, he would be court-martialed. But the wheels were turning.[28]

Three days later, two more fleet aircraft carriers, the USS *Midway* and USS *Saratoga*, joined Task Force 77, as the air armada continued to grow.

Ho Chi Minh Trail

As Freedom Train was being prosecuted, air operations were still being conducted along the Ho Chi Minh trail as supplies were flowing to the attacks that were building in the Central Highlands and in MR-3. On 4 April, a QU-22, Vampire 46, took off from NKP. The single-engine aircraft was assigned to the 554th Reconnaissance Squadron (RS) and was equipped with communications gear that received signals from the sensors seeded along the trail and retransmitted them to the collection center at Task Force Alpha, also located at NKP. While on its orbit over south central Laos, the aircraft experienced an engine failure and the pilot bailed out. He landed near Dong Hene, Laos, a relatively peaceful area. Nail 12, Capt. Bob Willis, served as OSC, and he quickly located the survivor. Jolly Green 62 was on a training flight in the NKP area and diverted to recover the survivor. However, the helicopter crew diverted back into NKP when the machine developed an engine problem. Fortunately, Air America helicopter H-59 quickly responded and was vectored to the survivor by Willis. They picked up the pilot and took him to Savannakhet, where Jolly Green 52 picked him up and returned him to NKP. These events raised serious questions about the efficacy of the QU-22, a modified Beech Bonanza, for this combat mission.[29]

On the afternoon of 9 April, an F-4 Fast FAC, Musket 01, from Ubon RTAFB, flown by Capt. W. Banks and Capt. M. Jacobs, was shot down while searching for targets along Route 23 northwest of the Catcher's Mitt where the Nail 31 SAR had occurred just a few weeks prior. Nail 81, Capt. Hal Mischler, diverted to serve as OSC, quickly made radio contact with both crewmembers and determined their general locations. Two A-1s, Sandy 01, Capt. Bob Burke, and Sandy 02, 1st Lt. Rick Fossum, two HH-53s, Jolly Greens 53 and 52, launched out of NKP. King 22 also proceeded into the area and determined that three Air America H-34 helicopters were available and on alert at Savannakhet. One of them, H-15, launched and headed to the recovery site. However, Jacobs was badly injured, and the single pilot aboard could not provide medical support. Consequently, when the Jollys arrived, Jolly Green 53, flown by Maj. Dave Daus and crew, recovered both survivors and took them to NKP. They had only been on the ground in Laos for about two hours and fifteen minutes.[30]

Just a few hours later, the rescue forces at NKP were alerted for another

SAR in Laos. Just after sunset, Bengal 505, an USMC A-6 from Marine All-Weather Attack Squadron (VMA[AW]) 224 aboard the USS *Coral Sea*, was shot down while attacking a convoy of trucks just west of the DMZ. That night, an RF-4, Cosmic 24, heard a beeper and made voice contact with the pilot, Maj. Clyde Smith. He stated that he did not know the status of his bombardier/navigator, 1st Lt. Scott Ketchie. Nail 12, Capt. Bob Willis and Capt. Lynn Steincamp, located the pilot the next morning. However, the area was bristling with NVA AAA guns. Their OV-10 was hit, and they had to depart the area. For the next three days, rescue forces worked the area in an attempt to beat down the enemy guns so that an HH-53 could slip in and pick up Smith. Nail FACs directed flight after flight of USAF and US Navy strike aircraft as they attacked the NVA forces in the area.

At one point, consideration was given to direct Major Smith to evade to a safer area, but the large number of enemy forces in the area just made that too dangerous. Major Jim Harding flew several missions as Sandy 01 with a force of up to six A-1s. Finally, on 13 April, the combined force of A-1s with supporting FACs and strike flights were able to lay down a smoke screen and dampen the NVA AAA enough for Jolly Green 32, flown by Capt. Bennie Orrell and crew, to slip in and recover Major Smith. As the helicopter came to a hover for the pickup, enemy soldiers could be seen firing at them from all directions. The A-1s were constantly attacking the enemy forces. All gunners on the Jolly were firing, and one airman was wounded. When he could reach it, Smith quickly attached himself to the jungle penetrator and called for extraction. When he was on board, Orrell turned to the exit heading, and the A-1s kept up their withering fire as the Jolly Green climbed away and headed for NKP. Maj. Jim Harding and Capt. Bennie Orrell were awarded the Air Force Cross for this mission.[31]

More Efforts at Dong Ha

As these actions played out in Laos, Bat 21Bravo, Nail 38Bravo, and Covey 282Alpha evaded behind the front lines of the invading NVA. FACs maintained contact with them, and the rescue centers updated their status and kept commanders up to date on how they were doing. One person in particular who monitored their status was Lt. Col. Andy Andersen, USMC, director of the JPRC within MACSOG, who as such saw all of the operational reports and intelligence data on their situations. However, the JPRC had been ordered to cease operations on 31 March and inactivate on 30 April. Assigned personnel were being transferred to other MACV branches.

Seizing the moment, Andersen gathered his remaining troops and had them develop some options for recovering the three evading airmen in the Dong Ha area. Intuitively, he knew that such an operation was feasible, and he wanted to send his troops off with a big win. However, instead of taking his ideas to the MACSOG commander, he went out of his chain of command and on 8 April visited Seventh AF vice commander Winton Marshall, who held a meeting with him and Col. Cy Muirhead from the Third ARRG. After reviewing the current situation and intelligence, Andersen presented a plan to place a small commando-type team along the Mieu Giang River and have the survivors float down to a collection point. It is not clear whether Andersen had received his call from Capt. Ron Smith before or after he met with Marshall, but that call was certainly fortuitous because it showed how the different elements of rescue were thinking and working toward a common goal. Marshall liked the plan and said he would support it. Marshall also briefed Gen. John Vogt, who had just arrived to assume command of Seventh AF, and General Abrams, who was concerned that assets being used in the SAR were not available for the larger battle but otherwise did not object. He even allowed some B-52 missions to be used in the effort.

Andersen had the mission. He quickly did some internal coordination within MACSOG and obtained the use of a team of Vietnamese sea commandos based in MR-1. The next morning, he was flown to Da Nang on General Marshall's T-39. There he met with the sea commandos and quickly realized that he needed an American intermediary to work with them. He called back down to MACSOG headquarters and procured the services of Lt. Tom Norris, a US Navy SEAL, who had plenty of experience working with the sea commandos. He was immediately flown to Da Nang and linked up with Andersen. There, they built their team and developed their overall plan. They would use the Mieu Giang River as their avenue of approach and retreat. Bat 21Bravo and Nail 38Bravo would be given verbal messages over their survival radios, instructing them to move to the river. Since the radios were nonsecure, the messages had to be in a form of code that only they would understand. This was what Capt. Ron Smith and some of the FACs had been working on, and Andersen was more than happy to avail himself of their efforts.

Ron Smith had received from Hambleton's and Clark's unit's data from their personal backgrounds to create such messages. Clark had grown up in Idaho, and Hambleton was an avid golfer, and these salient facts were used to craft their messages, which were then radioed to them by FACs. Ron Smith remembered how they crafted the messages:

We convinced Lt. Col. Andersen that using sports terms, people, and places would be the best way to go since the survivors were tired and we wanted to use terms they would easily understand and remember. The deciding factor was Bat 21s love of golf, and the thinking was that he would remember things about golf even though he was exhausted. We also knew that he had lived in the Tucson area and was familiar with the golf courses both on DM AFB and in Tucson. We decided the FAC would tell him we wanted him to play a round of golf—that we wanted him to play the front 9 holes of golf going from the Tucson country club to the DM AFB golf course (due south). After figuring out what the FAC was telling him, he asked if there were any hazards on this course. The FAC—he told Bat 21 that there were many "sand traps" on the front 9 holes, and the back 9 were full of water hazards, but that he would be able to meet the rest of his foursome at the 19th hole. For Mark Clark it didn't work so well, but again the FAC figured out what to say to get the message across. In sticking with the sports theme, we told the FAC to try telling him to "make like Don Schollander" (he was the 1968 swimming champ in the Olympics). We did not use Esther Williams figuring that Mark was too young to know who she was. Unfortunately, Mark drew a blank with Don Schollander. Again, the FAC used his head. He told Mark to "make like the guy named Charlie on the TV commercial who is always trying to better himself in order to get caught." Mark immediately knew that he was talking about Charlie the Tuna without ever identifying that Charlie was a fish.[32]

Bruce Walker was a tougher problem because he had farther to travel to the river. In his case, he would need to be dropped a detailed plan in a container. This could be done by aircraft, probably an A-1.[33]

On the morning of 10 April, Andersen's team moved up to Quang Tri. They met with the Third ARVN Division commander, who promised his support while also adding that he thought they were crazy. They then moved up to the front lines just west of Dong Ha and set up their operation in an old French concrete bunker guarded by a platoon of infantry and one tank. The sector was relatively quiet, but the larger battle ranged all around them. Hambleton had been given his evasion instructions of several individual segments and was already moving. US Navy ships off the coast fired artillery flares to give him some light for his journey. That night, Norris and five of the commandos moved down to the river. Andersen called Clark and told him to begin moving. He floated down the river, and Norris and his team recovered

Nail 38Bravo, 1st Lt. Mark Clark returning to NKP. (Courtesy Mark Clark)

him. During the day, as the team rested, their position was bombarded by NVA artillery. Andersen and several of the commandos were wounded and had to be evacuated. That night Norris went further up the river looking for Hambleton. However, two of his remaining commandos balked at continuing, and he had to abort. The next day, Norris requested resupply and determined to go upriver that night and find Hambleton. One commando, Petty Officer Nguyen Van Kiet, agreed to go with him. Hambleton was in dire straits. He was exhausted, hungry, and thirsty. Captain Ron Smith and Maj. Zeke Encinas both dropped "Madden" supply bundles (with water, food, batteries for the radio, and maps) for him, but he was too weak to recover either one. Norris and Kiet used a canoe, and after dark, they proceeded as far as the Cam Lo Bridge before doubling back and finding Hambleton.[34]

The Sandys were not part of this operation. While Norris and Kiet were executing the recovery, Capt. Ron Smith and his team were being scrambled for a different mission. Just after midnight, they were directed to launch and fly north off the coast of North Vietnam, to a hold point east of Vinh. They were to be there in case any aircraft were shot down from a planned B-52 raid near that city. No Jollys were launched with them, and they surmised that US Navy helicopters would be available if needed. The four A-1s duly took off into the dark night and stayed below a thousand-foot ceiling to remain in clear air. Only Sandy 04 had an operable TACAN. Ron Smith flew headings and times to best arrive at the designated hold point, just a dark spot east of Vinh. En route, they flew over ships of Task Force (TF-) 77 and could only assume that the navy knew who they were and what they were doing. At the designated time, they watched for, but did not see, any bombs exploding. In fact, the B-52 strike had been cancelled. They returned to Da Nang.[35]

West of Dong Ha, Norris and Kiet and their survivor were in a bit of trouble. Coming back down the river, they were accosted by enemy soldiers and needed help. Bilk 11, Capt. Harold Icke, was overhead. He directed a flight of A-4s that provided some immediate firepower. At Da Nang, Ron Smith and flight had just landed and refueled their aircraft. They were scrambled again and headed north to Dong Ha, where they provided cover for the recovery team and survivor to make it back those last few hundred meters to the safety of the ARVN position.[36]

Andersen received medical attention for his wounds and then returned to Dong Ha. There, he and Norris planned to move their operation to a small island in the Cua Viet River and focus on recovering Walker. He had been unable to move south because of the enemy forces in the area. Again, Capt. Ron Smith was involved in developing the evasion plan. He explained:

We got permission to drop him a survival kit . . . "Madden Kit." Inside would be water, food, new batteries for the radio, and maps. . . . We spent time at the Danang wing intel making maps to put into the kits. We color coded each map individually with magic markers and an individual numbered coordinate system within the colored areas. This way when [the survivor] got a map, there was a number on the map, and we could match it to the only other map like it that we had, and could tell him in the clear where he was (by color and number/coordinate), and where we wanted him to go (if he could go).[37]

On 14 April, Ron Smith again led his flight over Bruce Walker's location. He and Major Encinas both dropped Madden kits as the others delivered ordnance, effectively masking the delivery. Walker found the second kit and was ecstatic. The FAC began using the grid system. Initially, they tried to move him west and then south, but the enemy forces were just too numerous. Instead, they began moving him east, intending to place him along a canal or maybe even the coast so that Andersen and his team could recover the young pilot.[38]

Unfortunately, in the early hours of 18 April, Walker encountered some locals who reported his presence to the hamlet VC cadre. They chased him and by morning had him surrounded in a rice paddy. He made contact with another Bilk FAC, 1st Lt. Mickey Fain, who tried to put in an air strike to support him. But the enemy soldiers were able to kill Walker, and his body was never recovered. The Bat 21 episode was over, but it was a mostly successful and rewarding ending for the men who quietly served in and with the JPRC.[39]

For his efforts in the Bat 21Bravo/Nail 38Bravo/Covey 282Alpha effort, Lt. Tom Norris was awarded the Medal of Honor, and Petty Officer Nguyen Van Kiet was awarded the Navy Cross.[40]

The Battle for MR-1 Continues

By 14 April, battle lines had stabilized in the Dong Ha area. The commander of the Third ARVN Division directed his units to conduct limited offensive operations, but they made little headway. Both US and VNAF FACs were overhead and supported the operations with air strikes, but little was gained. That afternoon, as Andersen and his team were preparing for the attempt to recover First Lieutenant Walker, a US Navy F-4 off the USS *Kitty Hawk*, Linfield 203, was working with Covey 244 when it crashed one mile west of Bat 21Bravo's hiding place. The FAC saw the aircraft get hit by AAA and did not see either crewmember eject before the aircraft exploded on impact. US Army helicopters did respond to his calls for help, but there were no signs of survivors.[41]

The next day, another OV-10 FAC, Covey 299, was hit and seriously damaged by AAA while on a mission to adjust gunfire for the ships on the naval gun line. The pilot, Capt. James Harrison, decided to crash-land on the beach instead of ejecting. The area was under friendly control. Fortunately, Jolly Greens from the 37th ARRSq were holding in an orbit offshore and were able to quickly pick up him and his USMC backseater.[42]

On 27 April, intelligence sources indicated that the NVA units in the area were organizing for a major attack focused on capturing Quang Tri. Pilots were reporting that missiles were being fired that seemed to be guiding on their aircraft. Intelligence sources confirmed that NVA units had been equipped with heat-seeking SA-7 "Strella" missiles. These weapons could be very dangerous for slower, low-flying aircraft, both fixed and rotary wing.[43] The next morning, NVA attacks forced all South Vietnamese units out of the area around Dong Ha. As the friendly forces retreated south, NVA heavy artillery bombarded them with deadly fire. The ARVN units consolidated around Quang Tri, as four NVA divisions focused on the city.

The next day, as they were supporting the withdrawal of the ARVN forces from the Quang Tri area, F/4 Cavalry had one of their OH-6s shot down. An assault team led by Capt. Ron Radcliffe, Centaur 14, spotted a force of NVA tanks. Radcliffe directed his AH-1s to destroy them. As they were engaging the tanks with their rockets, Radcliffe hovered over one of the tanks and his gunner dropped a thermite grenade through an open turret. The tank burned furiously. A few minutes later, one of the AH-1s was shot down. Radcliffe flew to the burning helicopter. He could see that the pilot was dead, but the aircraft commander was alive and out of the aircraft. Radcliffe landed twenty feet away and his crew chief dismounted to retrieve the survivor. Seeing that the soldier was having trouble carrying the injured man, Radcliffe then hovered his aircraft to within ten feet of the burning gunship to expedite the recovery of the two soldiers so that they could depart. For his actions that day, Capt. Ron Radcliffe was awarded the Distinguished Service Cross.[44]

Two days later, a VNAF A-37, Scorpion 115, was shot down nine miles south of Quang Tri by what was suspected to be one of the new SA-7 missiles. Sandy 07, 1st Lt. Bob Herklotz, and Sandy 08 launched from Da Nang to serve as the OSC. They made voice contact with the pilot and located him. Coachman 22, a UH-1 from the Sixty-Second Aviation Company, was in the area and diverted to pick up the pilot. They spotted his parachute and began their approach. Enemy forces were swarming over the area and shot down Coachman 22. Another UH-1, Red Hawk 06 (the commander of the Eleventh Combat Aviation Group), landed and picked up the crew of Coachman 22. However, as they lifted off, they were also shot down. Above, the A-1s tried to suppress the enemy fire, but it was overwhelming. Several more army helicopters joined what was now a fully raging battle. Two more UH-1s, Coachman 508 and Bluestar 33, both landed and between them recovered all of the downed US Army crewmen. Several were seriously wounded, and the helicopters headed for Camp Evans, which had a field hospital.

The pilot of Scorpion 115 was still on the ground and was moving away from the enemy units, now pursuing him. He reported that he had been shot in the abdomen. The Sandys continued to work the area and put in several strike flights. Two VNAF UH-1s, Eagles 16 and 17, arrived to support the operations. They landed and searched the area for twenty minutes but could not find the survivor. When the Sandys had to depart, FACs maintained a watch through the night for the pilot. However, he was not heard from again, and the next morning, intelligence sources reported that he had been captured.[45]

The South Vietnamese units fought valiantly to hold Quang Tri as the civilian population fled south. However, the NVA forces were unrelenting, and by 30 April all South Vietnamese units had evacuated south and east of the Thach Han River just west of Quang Tri. As the civilians fled south along Route QL-1, the main road to Hue, they mixed in with military traffic. The NVA set up their heavy 130mm artillery west of the city and shelled the highway, killing an estimated two thousand civilians.[46]

Noted an MACV assessment of the fighting in MR-1, "In a month of the severest conventional fighting yet seen in the Vietnam conflict, the North Vietnamese destroyed the new South Vietnamese 3rd Division, routed other defending forces, and captured most of Quang Tri Province including the capital, Quang Tri City." More ominously, the NVA forces were now poised to roll on toward the ancient national capital of Hue.[47]

Going North

As the Battle for Quang Tri was raging, other actions were ongoing throughout the theater. On 9 April, a force of twelve B-52s, accompanied by numerous support aircraft, struck a railroad yard and petroleum, oil, and lubricants (POL) storage area near Vinh in southern North Vietnam. They were engaged by SA-2 missile batteries. The aircraft commander of Aqua 02, Capt. Ken Curry, remembered that after they had released their bombs:

> I began rolling into a 45-degree bank to the right . . . we were all seeing missiles in the air and by plan, were now not remaining in a normal formation. . . . A bright flash and huge explosion severely jolted our aircraft. . . . Next, I went to "Guard" frequency and transmitted "MAYDAY, MAYDAY, MAYDAY, Aqua 02 is hit." . . . Turning right to take us over water . . . I turned to the south and decided that Danang South Vietnam was the closest airfield.[48]

The North Vietnamese leadership noted that this was the first use of B-52s against their nation since October 1968. In the United States, some congressional leaders saw this as a dangerous escalation of the war. The Senate Foreign Relations Committee voted out a resolution cutting off all funds for the war after 31 December 1972. President Nixon was undeterred and called for further attacks. On 16 April, in Operation Freedom Porch Bravo, flights of USAF and USN aircraft struck targets in the Hanoi/ Haiphong area for the first time in four years. The USAF aircraft included a package of 17 B-52s. NVA air defenses blacked the sky with AAA and launched more than 250 SA-2s. In this melee, only one aircraft was lost, an F-105G shot down while attacking one of the SAM sites. Both men were killed in the action. In this same attack, a US Navy A-7E from the USS *Coral Sea* was also mortally hit. The pilot, Cdr. Dave Moss, was able to fly out to sea and eject. He was picked up by a destroyer positioned twenty miles off the coast just for this purpose.[49]

Initially, the North Vietnamese did not realize that B-52s were involved in this raid. However, poststrike analysis by their engineers determined that the bomb damage patterns indicated much larger bomb loads that could be delivered only by B-52s. This set off alarm bells among the air defense forces, which had been moving more and more SA-2 batteries to the south. They realized that President Nixon would use the bombers in the capital region and began to make plans for a more robust defense of that key area. As the offensive unfolded, they also sent personnel south to observe and analyze the operations of their batteries, especially against the B-52s. They carefully analyzed engagements such as the one with Aqua 02 and modified their tactics accordingly.[50]

A few days later, the North Vietnamese Air Force and Air Defense Command convened a military-political conference to develop the military tasks to be accomplished during the coming phase of operations. After studying their successes and failures to date, they issued a common mission statement for actions through the rest of 1972:

> Strive to exploit to the highest degree the combined strength of all of our
>   Service's forces
> Shoot down many enemy aircraft
> Capture enemy pilots
> Restrict the operations of enemy air forces
> Make the most vigorous contribution to the defense of our rear area
> *Protect supply lines and lines of communication*
> *Protect the combat formations of our combined forces on the battlefields*
> *Provide solid defense to our key strategic areas.*[51]

Strangely, senior USAF leaders had a different reaction to these first raids. Noted one SAC general, "Night strikes were completely feasible even in the most heavily defended region of Haiphong and Hanoi. Also, we learned that the support package that we provided, plus the internal capability of the B-52 was perfectly adequate and effective." The results of the adjustments made by the NVA compared to the smugness of USAF leadership would become starkly evident in about eight months.[52]

Rescuing a Ship

In the early morning hours of 16 April as the strike aircraft were approaching Hanoi, Big Mother 62, an HH-3A flown by Lt. Ron Abler and crew, was launched off the USS *Worden* to be on station as the primary SAR aircraft in the Hanoi-Haiphong area. The *Worden* was a guided missile frigate, equipped with several radars, electric countermeasure equipment, and surface-to-air missiles, which provided coverage for American strike aircraft operating in the Hanoi area. The *Worden* and similar ships frequently served as "lily pads" for the SAR helicopters of HC-7 and provided overwatch and early warning for the helicopter crews, too. As Big Mother 62 assumed their assigned position, the crew heard a faint call on the Guard frequency. It was somebody on the *Worden*, stating that the bridge of the ship had been hit by some kind of projectile, and the ship was badly damaged with many wounded. The ship was just eight miles south of the first sea buoy for Haiphong. Just prior to the explosion, the *Worden* crew had spotted several fishing boats in the near vicinity and had indications that enemy radars were tracking the ship. Additionally, one of the gun mounts had spotted what appeared to be patrol boats and had opened fire on them. They suspected that they had been hit by enemy fire.[53]

The captain was in quarters but was alerted. He immediately returned to the bridge and found that all fourteen sailors on the bridge had been wounded, one fatally. He quickly formed another watch crew and turned the ship to a heading of 180 degrees to escape the danger.

On their assigned SAR station, Abler and crew immediately turned back to the ship. In fact, the communications system on the ship had been seriously damaged, and its crew could talk only to the Big Mother crew, who immediately notified other ships in the area of the crisis aboard the *Worden*. Big Mother then maintained an orbit over the ship and acted as communications relay as the fleet began to mobilize to aid the stricken ship. At one point, the Big Mother crew was notified by the bridge on the USS *Tripoli* that enemy speedboats were attempting to attack the *Worden*. A flight of A-7s was diverted to assist, and the Big Mother crew directed them in their attack on the patrol boats, which either disabled them or drove them away. Big Mother landed aboard the USS *Tripoli* to refuel and take on a medical team. When the *Worden* was able to allow a helicopter landing, Abler and crew landed on the ship, delivered the medical team, and loaded up with wounded personnel. Stated the after-action report: "The injured men put the [helicopter] 800 lbs over maximum allowable gross weight, but the critical circumstances dictated the launch." When the status of the ship was stabilized and secure, it

USS Worden *(DLG18). (US Navy photo)*

was pulled off the line and sent for repairs. Once again, Big Mother 62 cross-decked to another ship and returned to its SAR duties.[54]

Postmortem investigation of the damage to the USS *Worden* indicated that the event was an act of fratricide. Stated the HC-7 history for that period:

> The facts were pieced together after missile remnants found on the *Worden* were studied . . . and found to have United States markings. It was determined that two AGM-45 Shrikes were fired at the cruiser by an Air Force F-105G *Wild Weasel*. The incident was a result of several factors, number one being a lack of communication between the Air Force and the Navy. The junior service failed to inform anyone that they planned to have a *Wild Weasel* on call off Snake Island, just in case one of the SA-2 radars came up. On the other hand, the *Worden* was found to be ten miles north of its scheduled position. When the ship's commanding officer lit off his radars ahead of schedule, the F-105G crew fired at what it thought was a legitimate target.[55]

Years later, Warrant Officer Four John Dill, a retired navy electronics technician, offered another explanation for this debacle. He had spoken with another sailor who had been aboard the *Worden* that night and explained:

A junior Fire Control Technician, working on one of the two forward SPG-55 Terrier missile illuminators, went to "Radiate" without telling anyone. This, he was clearly not supposed to do. Using a "steer" from the air search radar, he found an aircraft coming off the beach in the vicinity of Haiphong, and began tracking it. (It proved to be a USAF jet . . .). Once he had a solid track, the young [technician] went to "lock" on his system, and the target's [USAF aircraft] RHAW gear & on-board defensive systems became <u>very</u> concerned and functioned as designed.[56]

Regardless of the facts to this tragedy, in April 1972 the skies in and around Hanoi were a very dangerous place for foe and friend alike.

Theater Rescues

On 20 April, Cosmic 16, an RF-4 from the 432nd Tactical Reconnaissance Wing (TRW) at Udorn RTAFB, was hit by an SA-2 as it photographed a major supply depot five miles west of Dong Hoi. The pilot, Maj. Ed Elias, turned west in an attempt to land at NKP. However, Elias lost control of the aircraft, and he and his WSO, 1st Lt. Woody Clark, ejected twenty miles southeast of Mu Gia Pass in North Vietnam. Each evaded separately, and they had intermittent radio contact. Elias was captured. Clark was wounded but able to evade pursuing NVA troops. Unaware of Elias's status, Clark continued to try to contact him with his survival radio. Several aircraft flying over that area the next day heard snippets of his calls and his emergency beeper. However, nobody was able to make voice contact with Clark. Clark's squadron, the Fourteenth Tactical Reconnaissance Squadron (TRS) stationed at Udorn, launched several support recce sorties for the SAR, including missions flown by his roommate, Capt. Brian DeLuca.[57]

On 21 April, Utah 02, an F-4 from the 334th Tactical Fighter Squadron (TFS) flown by Capt. Doug Brown and Capt. Larry Peters, who had recently deployed to the war from Seymour Johnson AFB, North Carolina, was hit by an SA-2 missile on a strike mission near Than Hoa. The crew flew out over the water before ejecting just a mile off Hon Me Island. Big Mother 61, flown by Lt. Frank Pinegar and crew, launched off of the USS *Denver* and proceeded to pick up both men as support aircraft attacked enemy guns on the island and mainland.[58]

On 22 April, Vampire 50, another QU-22 from the 554th RS, took off from NKP for patrol duties over the Ho Chi Minh trail. Just after sunset, the aircraft encountered a thunderstorm and sustained severe structural damage. The pilot bailed out about ten miles northwest of the Catcher's

Mitt. Nail 28, a Pave Nail OV-10 flown by Capt. Jennings Pewthers and 1st Lt. Bill Barron, heard his emergency call and assumed OSC duties. They used their Pave Nail system to search for and precisely locate the survivor. Then they were contacted by Air America helicopter Hotel 63, a Hotel 34 out of Savannakhet who volunteered to help. Pewthers rendezvoused with the helicopter and led him quickly and directly to the survivor for a successful pickup. A Jolly Green did launch out of NKP. He followed the Air America helicopter back to Savannakhet, picked up the QU 22 pilot, and returned him to NKP.[59]

On 23 April, an F-4, Dobby 03, from the 366th Tactical Fighter Wing (TFW) at Da Nang, flown by Maj. Charles Hall and 1st Lt. Lee Boughner, was severely damaged by SA-2 missile, and the crew bailed out off the coast of Dong Hoi. King 25 diverted to serve as the AMC. Sandys 07 and 08 launched out of Da Nang and joined with two Jolly Greens on orbit near the DMZ. However, one of the Big Mothers of HC-7 was on orbit off the coast of Dong Hoi. Their crew spotted the two parachutes and proceeded to recover both men. The augmentation of the HC-7 was paying off.[60]

Cosmic 16

As the men of Dobby 03 were being rescued, a flight of F-4s made voice contact with Cosmic 16Bravo, 1st Lt. Woody Clark. When his status was confirmed, the SAR forces rapidly mobilized at NKP and put together a plan to recover him. The commander of the Twenty-Third TASS, Lt. Col. Lachlan Macleay, took a personal role in this mission and was intimately involved in the planning, even flying some of the support sorties himself.

To reach the survivor, the force would have to cross the Ho Chi Minh trail between Mu Gia Pass and Ban Karai Pass, a very dangerous area of Laos. Additionally, the NVA airfield at Khe Phat, just twelve miles from Clark's position, was active with four MiG 17s on site, and the netted SAM sites in the Dong Hoi area were a threat to all. Detailed planning was necessary to integrate all of the assets necessary to protect the SAR force. During this period, heavy strike packages were being sent into North Vietnam, which limited assets for the SAR effort. Additionally, low clouds and fog restricted operations near Dong Hoi for two days.

Daily, aircraft flying through this area would contact Clark to make sure that he was still free. Because of the threat in the area, Clark was passed a message directing him to move across a ridge if at all possible. This was similar to the techniques used with Bat 21Bravo. When he made the move, a Twenty-Third TASS Pave Nail OV-10 crew was able to proceed into

Clark's area and determine his loran location. On 26 April, A-1s and HH-53s launched from NKP but had to abort when they determined that the weather in the recovery area was just too poor for rescue operations. Capt. Dale Stovall and crew were flying the low Jolly and were able to get below the weather. However, the clouds were too low for the A-1s to escort them. Considering the enemy threat in the area, Stovall and crew did not proceed with the pickup attempt.[61]

The next day, support aircraft were available, and a Fast FAC reported that weather in the survivor's area was not restrictive. A task force consisting of Nail 40, Capt. Larry Cox in a Pave Nail OV-10, Sandys 01, 1st Lt. Bob Carlsen, 02, 1st Lt. Dave Blevins, 03, 1st Lt. Lamar Smith, and 04, 1st Lt. Lance Smith, and Jolly Greens 56 and 32, taxied as one flight and took off. En route, they maintained radio silence in an attempt to achieve surprise as they entered North Vietnam. As they crossed the Ho Chi Minh trail near the always dangerous Mu Gia Pass, there was no enemy response. They encountered layered clouds and had to maneuver in the open areas. At a predesignated holding point, the Jollys with Sandys 03 and 04 held as the Nail 40 crew led Carlsen and Blevins to the survivor's location. When Carlsen decided that the area was quiet enough for a pickup, he had Nail 40 go back and get Jolly 56, flown by Capt. Dennis Boroczk and crew, and Sandys 03 and 04 for the pickup. As they proceeded in, they crossed a road segment and the Sandys dropped cluster bombs on likely enemy positions. Carlsen and Blevins dodged SA-2s fired by SAM sites near Dong Hoi. In response, they fired full pods of rockets at the SAM site, and more SAMs were launched. As the helicopter approached, Carlsen called for Clark to pop his smoke. He did so, but the foliage kept it close to the ground and the Jolly crew did not see it. They had to expend a few minutes searching for him. Finally, the Jolly Green flight mechanic spotted Clark, talked the crew into a hover, and hoisted Clark in without incident. Sandy 01, Carlsen, then directed Jolly 56 to the departure heading as the Sandys swarmed around the helicopter, dropping ordnance and firing their guns at anything that looked threatening. It was a classic SEA SAR, which also showed the added value of the precise navigation capabilities of the Pave Nail OV-10s. Since all of the Sandy pilots were first lieutenants, they dubbed this mission the "Silver Bar SAR." Later, the parents of Woody Clark wrote a thank you letter to the men who flew in the SAR. Bob Carlsen later wrote, "That letter is my most cherished item from my tour in SEA."[62]

On 28 April, an F-4 from Da Nang, Gunsmoke 01, flown by Capt. Mike Francisco and Capt. Arch Arthur, was Fast FACing north of the DMZ when

Cosmic 16 Bravo, 1st Lt. Woody Clark returning to Udorn. (USAF photo)

it was seriously damaged by an SA-2 missile. They got out over the water before ejecting. An OV-10 FAC, Covey 255, and two A-1s from NKP were working strikes just south of there, supporting the ARVN in the battles around Quang Tri, and were diverted to SAR duties. Jolly Green 65, flown by Capt. Don Sutton and crew, and Jolly Green 71, flown by Capt. Rodney Griffith and crew, launched from Da Nang and were escorted by two more A-1s, led by Capt. Bob Burke, as they proceeded up the coast. Arriving over the survivors, the Jollys dodged several rounds of NVA artillery and then deployed their pararescue jumpers (PJs) into the water to recover both men.[63]

MR-3, Loc Ninh—An Loc

On 2 April, as the NVA forces in the north were battering the Third ARVN Division, fellow NVA units initiated the attack in MR-3 with two feints against ARVN forward units north of Tay Ninh. This area was defended by the Fifth ARVN Division, its US Army Advisory Team 70, and support elements. Two days later, the Fifth VC Division, supported by NVA armor, attacked an ARVN regiment at Loc Ninh. USAF FACs covered these operations, worked with Advisory Team 70, especially Capt. Mark "Zippo" Smith, and directed air strikes as they were called for and available, usually from the Eighth SOS, an A-37 equipped unit located at Bien Hoa Air Base, SVN. US Army aviation units were also available, usually the F Troop, Ninth

Cavalry (F/9), and F Battery, Seventy-Ninth Aerial Rocket Artillery (F/79). However, as it appeared that Loc Ninh was going to be overrun, F-4s and AC-130s from Thailand and US Army aviation units from MR-3 were diverted to the fight and devastated attacking enemy forces. In the melee, an AH-1 from F/79 was shot down and both men were killed. The battle raged until 7 April, when the South Vietnamese commander decided to surrender to the NVA. Advisory Team 70 was ordered to evacuate. Helicopters from F/79 tried to get in to pick up the remaining advisors, but the ground fire was just too heavy. The survivors left their firebase and began to evade. Other US Army helicopters tried to get in to them but suffered the same result. And the air strikes were endless, as the FACs worked seemingly unlimited fighters and gunships. One man was recovered by ARVN forces, four were captured, and two were killed.[64]

Another unit from the Fifth ARVN Division, Task Force 52, was cut off as it tried to reinforce Loc Ninh and suffered a savage blow from the invading forces. As their condition worsened, the three-man advisory team was directed to evacuate. Two US Army UH-1 medevac helicopters tried to get in to their location but were shot off by the NVA, with one of the pilots killed. They then called for USAF rescue to fly in an HH-53 but were told that the helicopter would take two hours to get there. It would be dark by then, and they could not operate in the darkness in such a high-threat area. That night, AC-130s orbited above and provided covering fire. The next morning, as FACs and A-37s dropping teargas cluster bomb units (CBUs) covered them, two OH-6s from the D Company, 229th Assault Helicopter Battalion (D/229 AHB), scooted in, picked up the three advisors and several ARVN, and flew the men to safety. It seemed as if the army aviators were fearless. The OH-6 helicopter was rated to carry four people. The lead OH-6 lifted off with five Americans and four Vietnamese. None of the passengers was belted in, and as the helicopter bucked along, barely clearing the trees, they had to struggle constantly to keep from falling out. The pilot and gunner of the aircraft, Capt. John Whitehead, and Sgt. Raymond Waite were both awarded the Distinguished Service Cross for this mission.[65]

However, the battle was really just getting started, and some senior commanders questioned the propriety of evacuating the advisors when the fighting got heavy. Major General James Hollingsworth, the commander of the Third Regional Assistance Command (TRAC), directed that nonessential personnel would be evacuated, but senior unit advisors would stay and fight with their units. They were much too critical to the application of US support in the form of logistics and firepower and had to remain in place as a matter of necessity and honor.[66]

As ARVN forces pulled back from Loc Ninh, they rallied at An Loc. Units from the Twenty-First ARVN Division were ordered to reinforce the ARVN units standing at An Loc. Additionally, a brigade from the Airborne Division was also ordered to move to the city. It was a foot race. On 13 April, the Ninth VC Division, with many AAA guns, attacked An Loc. The battle raged for three days as the defenders used every tool they had to beat back the combined arms attack. FACs were constantly overhead and the air strikes were continuous, utilizing attack helicopters, gunships, and fighters. The only resupply came from Vietnamese C-123s doing airdrops or helicopters that could quickly scoot in and out, mostly from the 229th AHB, and the CH-47s from the 362nd Aviation Company. Every helicopter that made that run came out with bullet holes. A VNAF CH-47 was shot down on one of these missions.[67]

Watching this battle closely, General Abrams diverted B-52 flights to decimate the attacking formations. Deconfliction became a real problem as support came in from everywhere: USAF gunships and fighters and US Navy air from the aircraft carriers. But the most effective were the A-37s of the Eighth SOS and the AH-1s from F/79 Artillery and F/9 Cavalry. These aircraft could work extremely close to friendly forces and precisely deliver their ordnance for maximum effect. They were the ones called for when the situation was most critical—when the tanks were in the wire. And when the weather was poor and the fighters could not work at all, the attack helicopters would still be there. But they were also the most vulnerable. On one particularly bad day, five AH-1s were downed, eight of the men were killed, and two were recovered by ground forces. Major General James Hollingsworth wrote to General Abrams, "Massive air support of all types tipped the scales in our favor."[68]

On 14 April, as the battle appeared to be shifting into a siege, the airborne brigade air assaulted into several locations around An Loc. The next day, the NVA unleashed another withering combined arms attack on the city. The VNAF had been striving to supply the forces in An Loc by air and had a C-123 shot down with no survivors. USAF C-130s began airdropping supplies into a soccer field at An Loc. They did so with FACs watching from above and fighters or attack helicopters on immediate call. Every aircraft was hit by ground fire, and one had to crash-land at Tan Son Nhut Air Base, Saigon. Three days later, one of the C-130s was badly damaged on its run in and crash-landed in a swamp near Lai Khe. All six American crewmembers and one Vietnamese crewmember were rescued by a UH-1 and two AH-1s from the 229th AHB and F/9, who followed them until they were on the ground. There were NVA units in the area, and the AH-1s held them at bay until the crew of the UH-1 pulled the C-130 crewmembers out of the wreckage and loaded them on the helicopters. Said Capt. Robert Frank, the air mission commander of the helicopters, "We did these sorts of things in the air cavalry all the time. . . . Heroic things were done every day. Sometimes somebody would see it, other times they wouldn't."[69]

On 19 April, the NVA unleashed another withering attack in an effort to take the city and shot down another VNAF C-123. Once again, the forces on the ground, with massive air support, beat the attackers back. The FACs also began looking for the NVA artillery and hit it with air strikes whenever they found a battery. They also routinely covered the supply runs of the helicopters of the 229th AHB as they brought in supplies and ammunition for the besieged troops and then tried to evacuate wounded.

Realizing that day drops were just far too dangerous, the VNAF and USAF C-130s began dropping at night. However, the accuracy of the drops was poor, with an estimated 30 percent actually being recovered by friendly forces and a significant amount falling into the hands of the enemy. On 25 April, a flight of eleven C-130s attempted another night drop. The enemy gunners were ready. All aircraft were damaged, and one was shot down with seven crewmembers, six US and one Vietnamese, killed. FACs searched the site the next morning, but there was nobody to rescue. However, regardless of the losses, An Loc held through April, but with the expectation that the climactic battle was not far in the future.[70]

MR-2, Kontum–Pleiku

US and Vietnamese intelligence were also concerned about the movement of strong NVA forces into the triborder area. There, the NVA Second and 320th Divisions with supporting armor and artillery regiments were well supplied and apparently ready for action. Additionally, the NVA Third Division was very active in the Binh Dinh province near the coast, and there was some concern about a possible linkup of those disparate units to split South Vietnam in half. This region of South Vietnam was defended by the ARVN Twenty-Second Division with two regiments in the Kontum area and two regiments in Binh Dinh province. It had also been reinforced with two cavalry squadrons and a brigade from the Airborne Division, one of the two strategic reserve forces usually kept in the Saigon area. Additionally, eleven ranger battalions covered the far western border of South Vietnam.

As the big battles were joined at Dong Ha and An Loc, the NVA forces northwest of Kontum began moving southeast as B-52 strikes rained on their columns. They were already assaulting ARVN positions on an escarpment west of Dak To called Rocket Ridge, and they shot down a US Army CH-47 from the 228th Assault Helicopter Company (AHC) on the perimeter of Fire Support Base (FSB) Delta, being held by an airborne unit on 31 March. For three days, other aviation units tried to rescue the five-man crew. On the morning of 3 April, a rescue team consisting of AH-1s and UH-1s from the 361st Aerial Weapons Company (AWC) and the 57th AHC flew to FSB Delta to provide resupply, evacuate wounded, and rescue the crew. As they arrived overhead, they were met with heavy AAA fire and the beginning of a two-battalion assault on the base. The AH-1s immediately attacked the AAA guns and enemy soldiers trying to get through the barbed wire around the base. For several hours, they engaged the enemy forces, refueling and rearming at Kontum and sustaining damage to all their aircraft. Their continuous fire, mixed in with air strikes from fighter aircraft, successfully stopped the attack and killed an estimated two hundred NVA soldiers before the crew of the CH-47 was finally rescued.[71]

The NVA continued to advance and surrounded the outlying ARVN forces at Dak To and Tan Canh as FACs constantly orbited overhead and called in incessant fighter and gunship strikes and US Army attack helicopters. These ARVN units also had US advisors assigned to them, and as the battle developed, many were increasingly at risk of being taken prisoner. The senior American advisor in MR-2, John Paul Vann, put out a directive that helicopters had to always be on call to recover advisors if they were in danger of being captured. On 15 April, US Army helicopters from Camp Holloway flew into one of the forward bases still held by the South Vietnamese on Rocket Ridge and rescued one of the US Army advisors.[72]

On 24 April, an OH-58, Gladiator 715, from the Fifty-Seventh AHC, flew into Dak To to rescue six advisors. They scrambled aboard, and the helicopter slowly rose and successfully cleared the local area. Unfortunately, while en route to Pleiku, they were shot down and crashed on a sand bar along a river. Four of the men survived, and after twelve days they were able to contact an FAC with their survival radio. The FAC brought in another recovery team to rescue them. However, these actions were problematic. Like the situation at An Loc, Vietnamese commanders realized that their American advisors were key to their units' receiving critical logistical and firepower support, which in many cases was critical to their very survival, and they threatened to forcefully prevent the evacuation of their advisors.[73]

The airpower was relentless. Four Pave Nail OV-10s from the Twenty-Third TASS were dispatched to support precision air strikes in the area. Additionally, the crews worked with local commanders to reestablish a direct air support center (DASC) to better coordinate the interaction of the ground units in the area and supporting aerial forces and overall priority of targeting. More than half of all B-52 strikes in South Vietnam in April went in against the NVA forces advancing toward Kontum. As they overran ARVN positions around Dak To and Tan Canh, the ARVN soldiers abandoned numerous artillery pieces and even tanks. Consequently, the fighters and AC-130 gunships trying to cover the retreating forces also had to destroy abandoned equipment—one estimate even stating that for several days, 80 percent of the air strikes were used for this purpose. As the month ended, ARVN forces had been pushed back to the environs of Kontum city, and the vital highway to Pleiku was threatened by an NVA flanking movement. Additionally, the Third NVA Division in Binh Dinh had pushed the two defending ARVN regiments out of the province and was consolidating their gains. If Kontum could be taken, then NVA forces could attain the long-term goal of bisecting South Vietnam.[74]

Edwards AFB, California—Pave Low

In late April, about seven thousand miles to the east, the 6512th Test Squadron at Edwards AFB started a new project. Major Paul Balfe was the project pilot assigned to consolidate what had been learned on Pave Imp and Pave Star and what still needed to be done to meet the requirements of MAC ROC19–70. He was assigned three other pilots, Maj. Jon Hannan, Maj. Don Jensen, and Maj. Frank Pehr, from MAC to conduct the equipment and flight tests over the next seven months. Jensen and Pehr had flown the HH-53s in SEA, and Pehr was now a lead instructor at the HH-53 qualification course at Hill AFB. They would conduct the test on HH-53B #14433. It was one of the first USAF HH-53s and was a combat veteran. Additionally, it had also been modified with the LNRS equipment. At Edwards, it would be further modified with the addition of an AN/APQ-141 forward-looking radar, recently tested on the US Army's new prototype attack helicopter, the AH-56. The test program was labeled Pave Low, and concurrent events in SEA would illustrate how much it was needed by the rescue forces in the theater.[75]

April was a dramatic month. The anticipated offensive began, and it caused a redirection of our efforts in the war. The reduction of ground forces continued. And since the beginning of the year, the US Army had reduced its aircraft inventory by one thousand fixed- and rotary-wing aircraft. USAF units continued to transfer to Thailand. However, in response to the enemy actions, American fighter, bomber, and tanker forces had been increased, with the reintroduction of USAF, US Navy, and USMC strike and support assets. Total sortie production dramatically increased as the reintroduced units became available. But sortie numbers for Laos and Cambodia dropped when these assets were shifted to South and North Vietnam.

The blitzkrieg-like NVA attacks initially found success against the generally tepid defense efforts of the South Vietnamese, and the aggressors advanced in all three attacks. Air power made a noted difference in each battle, but as the month ended, the results were in doubt. Air power was also unleashed against North Vietnam as the beginning of an air interdiction campaign attempted to staunch the flow of NVA troops and material from that nation.

For the month of April, according to Chris Hobson, in his seminal *Vietnam Air Losses*:

Fixed wing losses: USAF—17, US Navy—6, USMC—2
KIA—25/46%
POW—4/7%
Rescued—26/47%[76]

Rescues were made by USAF, US Navy, US Army, and Air America helicopters, US Navy ships, US Coast Guard personnel, and a special operations team. However, as the narrative shows, this picture, while representative, is incomplete. The stories of US Army, MACSOG, and Air America rescues are only partially represented. Their stories have to be told individually. And they tell us that it was not just downed aircrews that our forces were trying to rescue. In many cases, those needing rescue were South Vietnamese soldiers or airmen, American advisors fighting with the Vietnamese units, or just soldiers or marines caught up in the battles. During the month of April, rescue missions accomplished by the dedicated and designated rescue forces were a common occurrence across the breadth and depth of Southeast Asia.

CHAPTER FOUR

MAY AGAIN, GOING NORTH

The men flying combat in Southeast Asia could be assured that in the event they were downed, every conceivable effort would be made to get them back.

Lt. Col. LeRoy Lowe, Project CHECO Report, Search and Rescue Operations in SEA, January 1971–March 1972

MR-1

On 1 May, the movement of reinforcing units from the United States continued. Under Operation Constant Guard II, two more F-4E equipped squadrons, the 308th Tactical Fighter Squadron (TFS) and the Fifty-Eighth TFS, departed from their home bases in Florida for the long flights across the Pacific Ocean to Udorn Royal Thai Air Force Base (RTAFB), Thailand.[1]

Support also came from units already in the Pacific region. The Seventh Fleet deployed elements of the III Marine Amphibious Force into the combat area but not ashore. This included parts of the Ninth Marine Amphibious Brigade as a landing force component. Their initial assigned tasks were to provide Military Assistance Command Vietnam (MACV) security and emergency evacuation of US forces should the need arise. It also included detachment of both CH-46 and CH-53 helicopters, which could be used for air assault operations in support of the Army of the Republic of Vietnam (ARVN) or Vietnamese Marine Corps (VNMC), or for evacuation or rescue missions as the need arose. These helicopters would sit alert on the ships and monitor for emergency calls. They were another immediate asset available for rescue missions.[2]

Unfortunately, they would not arrive in time to affect the debacle that was unfolding at Quang Tri, South Vietnam. That morning, strong North Vietnamese Army (NVA) units continued to surround the city and prepare to force their way across the Thach Han River. Their heavy artillery steadily rained fire down on the unnerved ARVN troops, and they began to retreat, in spite of the efforts of their commanding officers to control their movements and even the ongoing battle. The commander of the Third ARVN Division, Brig. Gen. Vu Van Giai, and his attached US advisors from Team 155 worked feverishly to coordinate an effective defense as forward air controllers (FACs) orbited overhead and directed countless air strikes, using fighters from all services, gunships, army attack helicopters, artillery fire from batteries still in action, and gunfire from US Navy ships offshore. However, NVA units from the 304th Division were able to slip in south of the city and interdict QL-1, the main road to the south. That further panicked civilians and soldiers alike, and all control broke down. The FACs were from the Twentieth Tactical Air Support Squadron (TASS), based at Da Nang Air Base, about eighty miles to the southeast. They constantly had FACs in O-2s and OV-10s orbiting over the battle with a steady supply of air support. However, by noon the situation was hopeless, and the Third Division commander directed a general retreat of his units to the south. He and his command team and several US advisors were now trapped in the old French citadel in the center of the city. Anticipating such a possibility, his senior Air Force advisor, Maj. Dave Brookbank, had coordinated preplanning with the Thirty-Seventh Aerospace Rescue and Recovery Squadron (ARRSq) at Da Nang for an on-call emergency evacuation. There, Lt. Col. Bill Harris and USCG Lt. Cdr. Jay Crowe planned the operation and coordinated Sandy and FAC support. When Brigadier General Giai decided that it was time to go, Brookbank requested the evacuation plan be executed.[3]

At the time, the rescue forces were busy. On a Freedom Train mission, a US Navy A-7, Hoboken 401, flown by Lt. Michael Surdyk, from the USS *Coral Sea*, had been mortally damaged by an SA-2 near Dong Hoi. The pilot got out over the water, bailing out just one-half mile off the coast. A Fast FAC, Seafox 04, acted as the on-scene commander (OSC). He directed fighters against enemy personnel firing at the survivor and attempting to launch boats to capture him. Normally, an HH-53 from the Thirty-Seventh ARRSq would be dispatched for a pickup in this area. But they were scrambling for the Quang Tri evacuation, and instead an HH-3A from HC-7, flown by Lt. Jim Spillman and crew, responded. As the supporting fighters drove away the enemy boats, Spillman came to a hover over the downed pilot and dropped his rescue swimmer. The swimmer got on the hoist with Surdyk. Watching in the side mirror, as the two men approached the door, Spillman began to turn to the left for his exit. Unfortunately, at that exact moment, the lift cable broke. However, since the helicopter was banked

Sgt. Bob LaPointe. (Courtesy Bob LaPointe)

into a left turn, the two men fell into the cabin of the helicopter. Lucky is a good thing. The survivor was then flown to the USS *Denver*.[4]

Back at Quang Tri, one of the Twentieth TASS O-2 FACs, Bilk 34, 1st Lt. Bill Jankowski, was airborne and on station above the battle. Five HH-53s launched and headed north. They were escorted by two A-1s, Sandy 07, Capt. George Throckmorton, and 08, 1st Lt. Joe Seitz. Arriving in the Quang Tri area, Sandy 07 took over as the OSC and had Bilk 34 move off to the south and put in supporting air strikes and coordinate the movement of the Jollys into and out of the citadel.

As the helicopters approached the area, the Sandys had them hold east over the water. Jolly Green 71, flown by Maj. Jackson Scott and crew, was first to arrive in the Citadel. They received no ground fire. Their lead pararescue jumper (PJ), Sgt. Robert LaPointe, quickly guided the waiting troops onto the aircraft, and after two minutes on the ground, they departed with thirty-seven personnel. Second in was Jolly 65, flown by Capt. Rodney Griffith and crew. They quickly loaded forty-seven more troops and then uneventfully departed. Third in was Jolly Green 21, flown by Capt. John Weimer and crew. They picked up forty-five personnel. The fourth aircraft, Jolly 21, flown by Capt. Don Sutton and crew, then landed. However, it took his crew mere moments to realize that they were the only ones still there and that the next people that they would see would have a high probability of being NVA troops with the worst of intentions. So they rapidly departed. The fifth aircraft, Jolly Green 60, flown by Capt. Richard Wall and crew, did not need to land in the Citadel. A total of 129 soldiers, marines, and airmen, American and Vietnamese, were successfully rescued by the crews of the Thirty-Seventh ARRSq, under the watchful eyes of the Sandys of the First Special Operations Squadron (SOS).[5]

As the evacuation was proceeding, Bilk 34 was holding generally to the south of Quang Tri. As the A-1s were dropping smoke bombs to cover the movement of the helicopters into and out of the Citadel, Jankowski's O-2 was hit by a SA-7 missile, and he had to bail out. Fortunately, he landed among friendly troops and was safe. He immediately reported this to Sandy 7, and the evacuation continued. Covey 244 diverted from his mission to serve as the OSC for Bilk 34. He was immediately contacted by a flight of five AH-1s and an UH-1 from F Troop, Fourth Cavalry (F/4), who were working missions in the area and volunteered to make a rescue effort for Jankowski. As Covey 244 was trying to put together the recovery effort for Bilk 34, Sandys 07, Throckmorton, and 08, Seitz, were low on fuel but offered to provide their ordnance before returning to Da Nang. As they entered the fray over Bilk 34, Sandy 08 was hit by an SA-7 and critically damaged. With flames streaming out the right side of his engine, Seitz headed out over the water with Sandy 7 in escort and ejected. Throckmorton regretted that he did not have a camera, remembering "it looked like an old war movie of a smoking aircraft rolling off on one wing then plunging into the Gulf." A US Army UH-1, Centaur 06, flown by the commander of F/4, picked up Seitz.[6]

Two more A-1s, Hobo 42 and 43, had taken off from Da Nang to provide support for the fighting around Quang Tri, and they diverted to the ongoing SAR effort for Bilk 34. As they arrived over his location, Hobo 42 was hit by an SA-7 and seriously damaged but flyable. He headed back to Da Nang with Hobo 43 in escort as the sun was setting and made a gear-up landing. The Rescue Coordination Center, OL-A at Son Tra near Da Nang, was monitoring the ongoing events at Quang Tri. With this series of shootdowns by SA-7s, it was obvious that SAR procedures had to change. The senior controller there ordered all rescue forces out of the area. They knew that Jankowski was with friendly troops, and they would set up for an early morning recovery.[7]

Bilk 15 was airborne at dawn to act as the OSC. Arriving over Jankowski's position, he checked in with him and then began directing air strikes against NVA units in the area. Two A-1s, Hobo 20 and 21, Maj. Jim Harding and Capt. Don Screws, from the First SOS checked in to support the SAR and larger battle. Bilk 15 started working them to prepare for a rescue attempt. Harding and Screws had been briefed that the SA-2 sites up near the DMZ were very active, and they decided to stay relatively low as they delivered their ordnance. However, as Harding pulled up from a pass, he saw an SA-7 streak up toward his aircraft and strike the bottom of his engine. The engine cowling and propeller blew off and the aircraft began to descend. Harding quickly looked for a place to crash-land when the aircraft was hit with another SA-7. The aircraft pitched hard nose down, and Harding ejected. As he was floating down, he could hear enemy troops firing at him. Landing in the midst of foxholes and bunkers, he used his pistol and a recovered AK-47 to kill three NVA soldiers before he was finally able to take out his survival radio and contact the aircraft above.[8]

When he saw his flight lead go down, Captain Screws rolled in to support him with protective fire, and his aircraft was also struck by an SA-7. The result was the same and Screws also ejected, badly injuring his left shoulder in the process. Harding watched him descend and land about one-quarter mile away. On the ground, both pilots made immediate radio contact with Bilk 15. A team of army helicopters were supporting the battle and were immediately available to attempt to rescue the two A-1 pilots. Harding used his survival radio to vector them into his location. With AH-1s providing cover, another UH-1 from F/4, Centaur 22, slipped in, and before it had even landed Harding had jumped aboard. He then directed them over to Screws for another successful recovery. They were taken to Camp Evans, near Hue. There, Harding and Screws gave the army troops a thorough briefing on the SA-7s and the enemy positions that they had personally observed. The helicopters returned to pick up Bilk 34 and now five other ground personnel with him who also needed to be rescued. Centaur 22 landed under fire and picked up one American and two Vietnamese. As it was departing, it was hit with an

SA-7 and crashed with no apparent survivors. Centaur 21 landed and picked up Jankowski and two American advisors. As the helicopter was departing the area, it experienced a full engine failure for unknown reasons and made a hard landing in an open field. Nobody was seriously hurt. Almost immediately, two OH-6s, Centaur 13 and 17, dashed in and picked up all of the personnel from Centaur 21, made a safe escape, and delivered everybody safely to Camp Evans. However, the three A-1s lost and the one seriously damaged were a devastating blow to the USAF rescue forces. That left only twenty aircraft available for theaterwide Sandy duties, and there were no replacements. Additionally, as US forces departed the theater, rumors abounded that the remaining A-1s would be passed over to the Vietnamese Air Force (VNAF).[9]

The SA-7 was a threat to all allied aircraft. The fighters immediately modified their tactics to use steeper dive angles and steeper pullout so that they spent less time at lower altitudes. The O-2s, OV-10s, and AC-130s had no choice but to fly higher, approximately eight thousand feet above the ground to avoid the missiles until they could receive flare dispensers. The AC-130 and AC-119 gunships and cargo aircraft began designating onboard spotters to watch for the missiles. The spotters were equipped with Very pistols, which fired flares useful as decoys for the missiles.

The A-1s began carrying an SUU-25 flare pod loaded with decoy flares. It was, at best, a "Rube Goldberg" expedient and required the pilot to trigger the dispensing of flares. Additionally, the A-1 pilots modified their tactics. When in a suspected SA-7 area, the Sandy lead would stay high and provide overwatch as his wingman did any work that required low passes.[10]

The USAF rescue squadrons immediately put in requests for flare dispensers while engineers began looking for ways to run the engines cooler or somehow disperse the heat plumes from the helicopter engines. Exhaust diffusers were available for the US Army helicopters, but it would take a few weeks before they could be procured, shipped to Vietnam, and installed on the hundreds of machines still engaged in the war. In the interim, the helicopter crews heavily modified their tactics and began doing nap-of-the earth flying, slower and lower than they had been used to—effective against the SA-7s and the NVA antiaircraft artillery (AAA) guns but certainly easier to hit with small arms. It was a chance that they had to take to operate against the invading NVA units.[11]

Over Hanoi
At almost the same time that these dramatic events of 2 May were taking place at Quang Tri, two SR-71s flew over Hanoi at seventy thousand and

eighty thousand feet. This was not a rare occurrence because the reconnaissance aircraft based in Kadena Air Base, Japan, frequently flew over North Vietnam. However, these two aircraft passed over Hanoi exactly fifteen seconds apart. And before passing over the city, each crew slowed their aircraft to subsonic speed and then accelerated through the sound barrier to produce a dramatic "boom—boom," which swept across the city and environs. On 4 May, the SR-71s returned to Hanoi and repeated the maneuver.

This seemingly illogical maneuver over the most heavily defended area in North Vietnam actually served as a simple expedient. It was a signal to the American prisoners being held in North Vietnamese prisons that US national leadership authorized them to attempt to escape with the knowledge that military assets would be in place in the Gulf of Tonkin (GOT) to recover them. This was called Operation Diamond.

This plan was germinated out of necessity. By this late date in the war, more than six hundred Americans were being held by the North Vietnamese, and that number was increasing daily as US air power responded to the invasion. They wanted to get our prisoners home, especially as domestic pressure to do so steadily built up. After the disappointment of the Son Tay effort, President Nixon pushed his military leaders to develop other recovery options. Through their communications capabilities with the senior POW leaders in the prisons, US national intelligence agencies knew that some POWs wanted to make escape attempts. In fact, several had already tried, with no success. In early 1972, the POWs sent a message to President Nixon asking if they were cleared to attempt an escape, with a target window of early June. They asked that the answer be simple, delivered twice, and prove authorization from the national command authority. That affirmative was delivered on 2 and 4 May.[12]

In the prison, USAF Capt. John Dramesi and Maj. Jim Kasler were ready. They had developed a plan, had been hoarding provisions, had prepared disguises, and even had a fairly detailed map of Hanoi. However, when the senior POW leaders reviewed their proposal, they felt that the plan was far too risky and that if attempted, it could cause retribution to those who could not attempt the escape. They disapproved the escape attempt and made plans to communicate that to the national command authority—however long that took. Unfortunately, unaware of the decisions in Hanoi, senior military leaders in Washington and subordinate headquarters in the Pacific region initiated actions to ensure that during the agreed-upon rescue window, US military assets would be available in the Gulf of Tonkin to recover any escapees. The plan was labeled Operation Thunderhead.[13]

FACs and Fast FACs

Throughout the war in SEA, the USAF utilized forward air controllers to conduct visual reconnaissance and direct the fighter-bombers as they struck targets in support of friendly troops or interdiction operations. Initially, the FACs flew O-1s. As the conflict developed, the need for FACs increased, and as enemy forces began acquiring better AAA and surface-to-air missiles (SAMs), better, more capable aircraft were needed. This led to the procurement of the O-2 and the OV-10. However, the continued improvement of NVA air defenses forced USAF commanders to use faster—hence more survivable—F-100s and F-4s and a few USMC TA-4s in high-threat areas to perform strike control and reconnaissance (SCAR). Technically not FACs since they were not allowed to direct air strikes near allied ground troops, these aircraft took on the title of "Fast FACs" because of the easy alliteration of the term. In 1972, they were very busy over North Vietnam and those areas of Laos and even northern South Vietnam that were heavily defended by NVA air defense units.

Freedom Train

The number of missions being flown into North Vietnam, especially just north of the DMZ, was steadily increasing as flights of attack aircraft and B-52s hit the North Vietnamese storage areas, SAM sites, transshipment points, and convoys heading south. Enemy formations, too, were fair game for the hunters. On 3 May, another Fast FAC, an F-4 from Ubon, Musket 02, was mortally damaged by AAA near Bat Lake, and Capt. Tim Ayres and 1st Lt. Ted Sienicki ejected. Arriving on the ground, Sienicki was immediately captured. Ayres was able to hide in a small cave in dense underbrush and make voice contact with orbiting aircraft. The Joint Personnel Recovery Center (JPRC) began tracking this event. They requested that an RF-4 make a recce run from the two survivors' estimated locations to the coast so that an evasion plan could be developed for a possible sea-based recovery. However, voice contact with Ayres was lost. Fast FACs working through the area were unable to reestablish voice contact. JPRC put all plans on hold, pending any indication that either crewmember was still evading. Both men were transported to Hanoi and released in 1973.[14]

As directed by Operation Constant Guard III, starting on 4 May, the Forty-Ninth Tactical Fighter Wing (TFW) based at Holloman AFB, New Mexico, was alerted to deploy to SEA with its four F-4D equipped squadrons. The first aircraft departed two days later, and within a week, seventy-one of their aircraft had arrived at Takhli RTAFB, Thailand. Since most

aircrew members had already flown tours in SEA, requalification requirements were minimal and they were flying missions throughout the theater
within twenty-four hours of arrival.[15]

SAC also was directed to increase the number of B-52s in SEA. During
April and May, six iterations of aircraft were deployed from stateside units
to both Anderson AFB, Guam, and U-Tapao Royal Thai Navy Airfield, Thailand. By the end of May, the bases held eighty-five and fifty-three B-52s,
respectively, which were now flying missions throughout the theater.[16]

SAC also increased the number of KC-135s in the theater to 168, scattered at six different bases. They began providing 130 sorties per day to
service the swelling fleet of strike aircraft now operating across the breadth
and depth of SEA.[17]

Decisions in Washington

On 8 May, President Nixon met with his National Security Council and
cabinet. After reviewing the calamitous events in Vietnam and noting that
the North Vietnamese had canceled a secret meeting with Dr. Kissinger in
Paris, he opted for decisive action. He directed the resumption of bombing
in the Hanoi-Haiphong area, the mining of six North Vietnamese harbors,
and a countrywide interdiction effort. It would be called Linebacker. He
told them, "I have the will in spades," and added, "Those bastards are going to be bombed like they have never been bombed before." That evening,
the president addressed the nation on TV. He told his countrymen what
he intended to do and why. "There is only one way to stop the killing," he
said. "That is to keep the weapons of war out of the hands of the international outlaws of North Vietnam." The bombing, mining, and interdiction
of shipping and land transport would continue until Hanoi was prepared
to return all American prisoners of war and accept an internationally supervised cease-fire throughout all of Indochina. As he was giving his speech,
operational orders were streaming to the combat units in South Vietnam,
Thailand, and the GOT.[18]

But, in fact, the opening events of this campaign were already taking
place. Task Force 77 had been directed to prepare for the harbor mining
operations. This focused subcampaign was labeled "Pocket Money." The
USS *Coral Sea* was ordered to launch a force of three A-6s, six A-7s, and one
EKA-3B for electronic countermeasure support to deliver mines to block
the harbor at Haiphong and five smaller ports. This would prevent the
movement of ships in or out and effectively block and prevent the delivery
of 85 percent of war materiel shipped to North Vietnam. The strike went

in precisely as planned—literally as the president was giving his address to the nation. As the first mine hit the water, the flight lead sent a message to the *Coral Sea*. They immediately forwarded the message to the White House, where an aide to the president slipped a note to him as he was giving his address. Taking the note, he then said to the nation and world, "I have ordered the following measures, which are being implemented as I am speaking to you. All entrances to North Vietnamese ports will be mined to prevent access to these ports. United States forces have been directed to take appropriate measures within the international and claimed territorial waters of North Vietnam to interdict the delivery of supplies."[19]

This operation was supported by other actions. A diversion air strike was conducted by aircraft from the USS *Kitty Hawk* to draw NVA attention away from the mining aircraft. Two guided missile cruisers, the USS *Long Beach* and USS *Chicago*, moved within forty miles of Haiphong and maintained a watch over the low-flying A-6s and A-7s. When two NVA MiGs launched to attack the force, the *Chicago* fired two Talos missiles, which destroyed one MiG and drove the other away. Additionally, a force of three destroyers used their main batteries to bombard NVA air defense sites for thirty minutes as the mining force was delivering their ordnance. Consequently, no navy aircraft were lost in the raid. It was a good beginning to Linebacker. However, Pocket Money was not complete. More mines were dropped on 11 May, and by the end of 1972, more than eight thousand mines had been dropped to keep the ports closed.[20]

Linebacker

On 10 May, the sustained bombing of North Vietnam resumed with a vengeance. Guidance from Washington defined the overall objective: "Reduce to the maximum extent possible, North Vietnam's capability to support the war against South Vietnam." To accomplish this, US military forces were given three tasks:

1. Destroy war-related resources already in North Vietnam.
2. Reduce or restrict NVN assistance from external sources.
3. Interdict or impede the movement of men and materials into Laos and South Vietnam.[21]

The primary weapon for accomplishing these tasks would be US air power, with assistance from naval gunfire provided by US Navy ships of Task Force (TF-) 77. They would carry out fire missions as directed along the long coast of North Vietnam. Additionally, some of the ships had USMC attack helicopters aboard, and these hunter-killer teams could be used for attacks and supporting raids. When necessary, they could also do rescue duty.[22]

The strike forces were ready. Since the cessation of bombing over North Vietnam in 1968, the fighter units had been equipped with a new series of bombs called Paveway. Nicknamed "smart bombs," they were capable of being guided directly to a target by a laser designator and were vastly more accurate than the conventional unguided bombs that had to be dropped in quantity for any assurance of accuracy. The practical result of the Paveway weapons meant that fewer aircraft had to be sent to destroy a target, hence fewer men were put at risk of shootdown. Paveway-equipped fighters were led by a flight lead with a designator pod and three wingmen, each carrying two MK-84 two-thousand-pound bombs to roll in on the target. Additionally, most F-4s were now carrying jamming pods to protect against the SA-2 batteries, and some F-4s primarily assigned to MiG Combat Air Patrol (MiGCAP) duty were equipped with air-to-air radars specifically modified to detect and identify MiGs beyond visual range so that AIM-7 Sparrow missiles could be used to destroy them at longer ranges. New procedures had also been established to better coordinate with support electronic-jamming aircraft and to utilize the deployment of chaff corridors to protect the strike flights. Aerial warfare was becoming high tech. Disco, the US Air Force early warning EC-121s that orbited over northern Laos, and Red Crown, the early warning US Navy ships that operated in the GOT, were in place and equipped with radar to give the flights better warning of MiG and SAM activity.[23]

Large strike packages were launched by the fighter wings in Thailand and South Vietnam as well as aircraft carriers of TF-77 to hit petroleum, oil, and lubricants (POL) sites, storage areas, and transportation infrastructure. They clobbered the train lines coming into North Vietnam from China. The SA-2 and AAA sites were active, and NVA MiG-17s, -19s, and -21s took off to engage the US formations. In the initial melees, US forces shot down eleven MiGs.

But there were also American losses. A thirty-two-ship of F-4s was sent to drop the Paul Doumer Bridge in Hanoi. Near Yen Bai, the site of one of the main MiG bases, about sixty miles northwest of Hanoi, the package was attacked by MiGs, and one of the MiGCAP F-4s, Oyster 01, from the 432nd Tactical Reconnaissance Wing (TRW) based at Udorn, Thailand, was shot down by a MiG-19. Nobody reported seeing anybody eject from the aircraft, and no emergency calls were heard from the crewmembers, Maj. Bob Lodge and Capt. Roger Locher. A listening watch was maintained by assets in the area, but no contact was made with either man. A task force of A-1s and Jolly Greens was on orbit about one hundred miles south over Laos but did not move toward Yen Bai. In fact, because of all the MiG activity, the rescue task force was moved further south to an orbit over Paksane, Laos, about one hundred miles north of Nakhon Phanom RTAFB (NKP). Unknown to all, one man, Oyster 01Bravo, Roger Locher, had ejected and was evading. He wanted to move away from Yen Bai before he called for rescue forces.[24]

A large formation of US Navy aircraft was also engaged by a mixed force of MiGs. In the furball that ensued, an F-4 from the USS *Constellation*, Showtime 100, flown by Lt. Randy Cunningham and Lt. Willie Driscoll, shot down three MiGs, giving each of them five kills and making them the first "Aces" of this conflict. However, as they were egressing North Vietnam, an SA-2 site near Nam Dinh hit them with a missile, and they had to eject five miles out to sea over the Gulf of Tonkin. Fortunately, three HH-3As, Big Mothers 61, 62, and 65, had taken off from the USS *Okinawa* and immediately responded. As they arrived near the two survivors, the enemy AAA and SAM sites ashore were very active, and strike flights of A-7s were attacking them vigorously. Big Mother 62, flown by Lt. Frank Pinegar and crew, recovered Driscoll, and Big Mother 65, flown by Lt. Tom Kautsky and crew, recovered Cunningham. Both helicopters flew the two survivors back to the USS *Okinawa* and then returned to their SAR orbit points. There, Cunningham and Driscoll boarded a USMC helicopter and were flown back to the USS *Constitution*. A navy photographer duly captured Cunningham stepping off the USMC bird. [25]

Interestingly, after the war, Randy Cunningham told many an audience that he had been rescued by a USMC helicopter. It took the veterans of HC-7 twenty-three years to finally get him to acknowledge that it had been the Sea Devils who had fished them out of the Gulf of Tonkin on that fateful day and then delivered them for their ride in a marine helicopter.[26]

The next day, another large USAF formation attacked targets in the Hanoi area. In this action, Icebag 04, an F-105G Wild Weasel from the Seventeenth Wild Weasel Squadron (WWS), Korat, Thailand, flown by Maj. Bill Talley and Maj. Jim Padgett, was shot down by a MiG-21 as it was attacking a SAM site twenty-five miles southwest of Hanoi. Both men ejected, and when on the ground, they made radio contact with aircraft above. A Jolly and Sandy task force was on orbit in northern Laos and headed toward the survivors' locations. More A-1s launched from NKP and the alert Jolly Greens at Ubon were launched and directed to "head north." When the rescue task force began to encounter heavy ground fire and realized that there was no MiGCAP in the area, they withdrew. That night, the crew of Icebag 04 maintained contact with USAF aircraft in the area. The next morning, the pilot, Talley, could hear the well-organized local militia searching for them and coordinating their actions with shouted directions. He was captured as the SAR task force flew overhead. Throughout the day, Jolly Greens and several flights of A-1s tried to get in to Padgett. However, the Sandys were run out of the area several times as MiGs were able to make attack runs on them. Below, Padgett was evading in an attempt to get away from the enemy forces. Throughout, Fast FACs maintained radio contact with the survivor until the morning of 13 May, when all contact was lost. Padgett had also been captured. Both men were released in 1973.[27]

In the same general engagement, an F-4, Gopher 01, from the Thirteenth TFS at Udorn, Thailand, flown by Lt. Col. Joe Kittinger and 1st Lt. Bill Reich, was also shot down by a MiG-21. The crew of Gopher 02 saw two parachutes and made radio contact with Reich, who reported that he had a broken leg. That was the last contact with either man as both were quickly captured. On 16 May, the recovery effort for Gopher 01 was "suspended with the concurrence of 7th AF and the parent unit, due to the lack of leads or sighting of the crew." As losses mounted in the campaign, this was becoming an ever more common conclusion to rescue efforts for downed aircrews in SEA.[28]

On 17 May, another aircraft carrier, the USS *Ticonderoga*, rejoined Task Force 77. It had completed a tour with the unit in July 1971 but was sent back to reinforce the air armada.

Diplomacy

On the diplomatic front, Dr. Kissinger had tried to initiate talks with the North Vietnamese in Paris on 2 May. The North Vietnamese negotiator, Le Duc Tho, buoyed by North Vietnamese initial successes on the battlefields, was in no mood to negotiate. Ten days later, after the mines had been laid, he signaled that North Vietnam wanted to restart the talks. From 20 May to 30 May, President Nixon traveled to Moscow. He participated in summit meetings with Soviet leader Leonid Brezhnev and other Soviet officials, and they reached a number of agreements, including one that laid the groundwork for a joint space flight in 1975. Nixon and Brezhnev signed the Strategic Arms Limitation Treaty. The treaty limited the United States and the USSR to two hundred antiballistic missiles each. The Soviets did not make any demands that the air campaign against North Vietnam should be stopped. President Nixon used one of the joint sessions to state that the United States would accept a cease-fire in place in exchange for the removal of only those North Vietnamese forces that had entered South Vietnam since the start of the offensive. This was a major concession to North Vietnam, which it was hoped would lead to a cessation of hostilities. While the summit was ongoing, no air strikes were allowed in the Hanoi-Haiphong area.[29]

MR-1

As the fighter and bomber units were ravaging North Vietnam, the retreat south in MR-1 continued as the battered elements of the Third ARVN Division and its attached units continued to move south to the My Chanh River. Alarmed at the loss of Quang Tri, the NVA's first strategic objective, President Nguyen Van Thieu decided that he needed to make a change in MR-1, and he relieved the corps commander, Lt. Gen. Hoang Xuan Lam, and replaced him with South Vietnam's most competent officer, Maj. Gen. Ngo Quang Truong. Truong arrived at his headquarters in Hue a few hours after the Bilk 34 episode ended and quietly took charge. He straightened out all of the command and control issues bedeviling his command and supervised as his staff drew up a simple plan to stop the NVA and defend Hue. The Vietnamese Marine Division would defend along the My Chanh River, and the First ARVN Division would defend to the west of Hue. The units fell in on their assigned positions, and the lines held. Through the rest of May, the South Vietnamese forces in MR-1 licked their wounds and started rebuilding their forces, adding two airborne brigades and starting limited offensive maneuvers northward toward Quang Tri. The First ARVN Division also fended off enemy attacks from the west toward Hue. General Truong established a new Fire Support Coordination Center to better coordinate with his ever-present FACs above and almost endless air support from US and Vietnamese aerial forces, hopefully setting the conditions for offensive action in the summer to retake their lost ground. They also watched as the last American units in their area steadily packed up and went home. Hourly, they watched the formations of American and Vietnamese strike aircraft and bombers fly over en route to their targets as the invading forces and their logistical trail were constantly assailed from above.[30]

However, the North Vietnamese air defenses accompanying the invasion force were ready for the onslaught. On 5 May, they shot down another Fast FAC F-4, Musket 03, from the Eighth TFW at Ubon RTAFB, Thailand, ten miles southwest of Quang Tri. The crew, Capt. Peter Kulzer and Capt. Robert Comstock, ejected. Two FACs, Bilk 20 and Rustic 124, diverted to cap the survivors and put in air strikes around them for protection. Two A-1s, Sandy 07, Capt. George Throckmorton, and Sandy 08, 1st Lt. Dave Blevins, and Jolly Greens 65 and 21 launched from Da Nang and held over the water as the FACs moved the two survivors to a clear area for a pickup. The JPRC did a quick analysis of the area and determined that enemy units in the area were relatively benign. Sandy 07 took over as the OSC. A large thunderstorm was beginning to build over the area. After the A-1s laid down a smoke screen and Rustic 124 put in more supporting air strikes, Sandy 07 had Sandy 08 lead in Jolly 65, who picked up one man and departed for Da Nang. Sandy 08 then brought in Jolly 21, who picked up the second man and also returned him to Da Nang.[31]

Two days later, a USMC F-4 from VMFA 212, Bootleg 51, was hit while attacking SA-2 sites near the DMZ. The aircraft went down five miles west of Cam Lo, and Bootleg 52 reported that only one man, the backseater, Chief Warrant Officer 3 J. J. Castonguay, had ejected. Sandy 07, Maj. Zeke Encinas, and Sandy 08, 1st Lt. Lance L. Smith, departed Da Nang with Jollys 71 and 72. The Jollys held south of Khe Sanh over high terrain as the Sandys worked with a Fast FAC, Musket 02, to examine the area and make contact with Castonguay. North Vietnamese Army AAA was active in the area, but Sandy 07 decided to attempt a pickup as day was rapidly fading. However, heavy AAA fire caused the Jolly Green to abort his run in. Sandy 07 ordered all SAR forces to return to base (RTB). That night, Major Encinas worked with the Jollys and planners at the JPRC to arrange supporting strikes, area denial ordnance, and SAM suppression for a recovery attempt the next morning. At first light Sandys 07, 08, 09, and 10 and two Jolly Greens launched. A Fast FAC, Gunsmoke 05, was acting as the OSC and had the survivor moving to an open area. Sandy 07 took over as the OSC and determined that the area was quiet enough for a pickup. As the Fast FAC was putting in air strikes with area denial ordnance and smoke bombs, the Sandys protected the low Jolly Green as he made a low altitude run-in to successfully recover Castonguay. The pilot was not recovered. This rescue operation uncovered a glaring recovery difficulty with USMC aircrews: they had been issued survival radios that broadcast only on Guard frequency. This forced all of the recovery task force aircraft to work solely on that frequency too and prevented timely emergency calls warning of SAM activity in the area. Fortunately, none of the SAM sites tried to interfere with the SAR effort. As a result, USMC crews began to receive better four-channel survival radios.[32]

On 12 May, Lieutenant General Truong unleashed his VNMC forces in a dramatic assault to break out of the My Chanh line. He ordered one battalion of marines to attack north, across the river, while supported by two battalions of marines that would be airlifted to seize two landing zones a few miles north and set up a pincer maneuver to smash an NVA regiment. United States Marine Corps CH-46s and CH-53s from the Ninth Marine Amphibious Brigade (MAB), offshore, lifted the attacking units. They were escorted by F/4 Cavalry, who provided armed escort with its OH-6s, UH-1s, and AH-1s. All aircraft flew nap-of-the-earth to avoid the SA-7s and the AAA. All infantry forces were delivered in two lifts. One CH-53 was damaged in the landing zone. It could not be repaired on-site and was destroyed. The helicopters also medevaced 18 Vietnamese marines and shuttled supplies throughout the day. In the operations, 240 enemy soldiers were killed, 3 tanks were destroyed, 2 of the deadly 130mm artillery pieces were put out of action, and 150 civilians were freed from enemy detention. The operation was supported by copious amounts of naval gunfire from the US Navy ships on the gun line and top cover from the ever-present FACs. The success of the operation portended similar operations in the future.[33]

On 19 May, Covey 248, an OV-10 from the Twentieth TASS, directing naval gunfire from the US Navy ships off Quang Tri, was shot down near the destroyed city. Jolly Greens and Sandys were readily available because they were on orbit offshore in support of air strikes going on in southern North Vietnam. However, the crewmembers, Capt. Dave Mott, USAF, and Chief Warrant Officer 2 Bill Thomas, USMC, were quickly captured and immediately moved north. Subsequent intelligence reports indicated the movement of the two men, and the JPRC was tracking them. However, the intelligence data was not current enough for locally available forces to attempt a recovery. On 22 May, all further rescue efforts were suspended, "due to no trace of survivors." Both had been captured and were released in 1973.[34]

Two days later, another F-4, Speer 02, from Da Nang, was damaged by 23mm fire and headed out over the water for safety. When twenty-five miles north of Da Nang, Lt. Col. R. Ross and 1st Lt. W. Key ejected into the GOT. A FAC, Nail 68, served as the on-scene-commander. Jolly Greens 71 and 64 scrambled to take off from Da Nang. However, a US Navy minesweeper, USS *Impervious*, observed the ejection and recovered the two men before the helicopters could arrive.[35]

On 22 May, an F-4 from Korat RTAFB, Vien 02, flown by 1st Lt. Eugene Doyle and 1st Lt. Dennis Van Liere, was mortally damaged by an SA-7 as they supported South Vietnamese Marines five miles southeast of Quang

Tri. The crew ejected. A Twentieth TASS FAC, Covey 217, was in the area and took over as the on-scene commander. Two Jolly Greens launched from Da Nang. Sandys 07 and 08 were airborne and diverted to assist. Doyle landed in an open area among some of the marines. He did not recognize them as friendlies and feared that he was about to be captured or killed. To his surprise, they ran to him, helped him to his feet and said, "Friend Friend." Not far away, Van Liere landed in a stand of elephant grass in a slight ravine and hid as best as he could. He heard Vietnamese troops approaching, searching in the elephant grass. One of them spotted him, smiled and said, "Friend." The two men were then moved to an ARVN tank unit and secured until a UH-1, Centaur 28, flown by Warrant Officer Daniel Miller and crew, from F/4 Cavalry, arrived and flew them back to Da Nang. The USAF rescue forces were not needed.[36]

On 25 May, an OV-10, Rustic 124, from the Twenty-Third TASS, was shot down by an SA-7. The two pilots, 1st Lt. Jim Twaddell and 1st Lt. Jack Shaw, landed seven miles north of Hue and were immediately picked up by a VNAF UH-1 and flown to Camp Evans.[37]

The next day, in an almost exact repeat, a USMC TA-4, Wineleaf 04, from MAG-15 at Da Nang, flown by Capt. W. Ramsbottom and Chief Warrant Officer 2 Bruce Boltze, was hit and mortally damaged by NVA in almost the same area as Rustic 124. The crew proceeded out over the water to eject. When they did, an HH-43 from Da Nang, Pedro 61, plucked both men out of the water and returned them to Da Nang.[38]

The Jolly Greens were not launched for the Wineleaf recovery because they had their hands full on another mission. Concurrent with that event, another Fast FAC F-4, Gunsmoke 02, flown by Capt. A. Arnold and Capt. Tom Kincaid, had gone down in the ever-dangerous Khe Sanh area. Initially, Bilk 35 served as the OSC and initiated the SAR. Sandys 07, Capt. Don Morse, and 08, 1st Lt. Tex Brown, took off with the Jolly Greens from Da Nang. Arriving in the area, the helicopters held south as the Sandys went to work over the survivors and put in several air strikes to dampen the enemy threat. When Sandy 07 believed that the area was benign, he committed Jolly Green 21 for a pickup, and they recovered both crewmembers.[39]

In late May, the northern portion of South Vietnam was a dangerous place for aircraft and men as the fighting raged on.

MR-2 Kontum

After ARVN forces struggled to hold their positions along Rocket Ridge, their forces began to pull back from Tan Canh to consolidate in the Kontum area for what appeared would be the climactic battle in MR-2. On 6 May, a team of OH-6s and AH-1Gs from the H/17 Cavalry took off from Camp Holloway and flew to Polei Kleng to evacuate the two American advisors serving there with the Vietnamese unit. While the gunships provided covering fire and USAF F-4s bombed enemy positions near the camp, the OH-6s were able to slip in and extract the two advisors with no losses.[40]

At dawn on 9 May, several AH-1G Cobra helicopters from the 361st Aerial Weapons Company departed the airstrip at Camp Holloway, south of Pleiku, to provide support to ARVN units under attack at Polei Kleng. There, they expended all of their ordnance on advancing NVA troops and armored vehicles before diverting into the airfield at Kontum to refuel and rearm. Two of the aircraft, Panthers 36 and 37, led by Capt. Bill Reeder, relaunched and proceeded to the besieged camp at Ben Het, near the triborder area, to engage another attacking NVA force. They mixed in with USAF fighters and US Army helicopters firing the new XM-26 TOW missiles being fired by two UH-1B helicopters deployed forward to test these new weapons in an all-out effort to stop the enemy advance.

On their third sortie, they escorted a UH-1 that was carrying badly needed ammunition for the camp. As they approached Ben Het, the enemy gunners, firing an assortment of AAA guns, threw up a steady stream of fire at the helicopters. The UH-1 dropped to treetop level and headed for the camp as the two Cobras followed and tried to provide suppression fire. The UH-1 crew was able to drop their ammo to the defending troops. As they turned to leave, the Panthers passed overhead, returning fire on the enemy guns. However, Panther 36 was slammed by rounds from several directions. Remembered Reeder, "We took large-caliber hits all over the aircraft. Rounds came through the cockpit." His craft was decimated, and he spun down to a violent crash. Reeder called for Panther 37 to cover him. Its pilot, Warrant Officer Steve Allen, had been grievously wounded, and his gunner immediately headed toward Kontum to save him. Panther 36 crashed violently in heavy brush.

Reeder survived the crash. However, he was dazed—in and out of consciousness, partly paralyzed, and numb from head to toe. He took out his emergency radio, but it did not work. He looked for his partner, 1st Lt. Tim Conry, unaware that Conry had been killed in the crash. As helicopters passed overhead, he tried to use his signal mirror but could not draw any attention. He was able to crawl away from the wreckage and hide under a small tree. It began to rain and he was quickly cold soaked. Then he heard the sound of OH-6s buzzing overhead. He again tried to signal to them but was unable to get their attention. That night, he evaded away from the camp. He could see the AC-130s working with the camp to fend off the NVA forces and felt the rumble of the incessant B-52 strikes. The next day, he spotted a VNAF O-1. He tried his radio again, but it still would not work. He fired a pen-gun flare, but the pilot did not respond. Unfortunately, the flare did draw the attention of a team of NVA soldiers, and they began searching for him. He was able to evade them, but two days later, after several more fruitless attempts to signal orbiting allied aircraft, he was captured, and eventually moved up the Ho Chi Minh trail to Hanoi.[41]

An AC-130, Spectre 03, also supported the camp. It fired all of its ordnance, including sixty-nine rounds from its 105mm cannon, killing an estimated 350 NVA and breaking a major assault on the camp. The forces in the camp were able to hold for three more days until they were forced off, and the remaining South Vietnamese soldiers and their families were forced to evade as they could back to friendly territory. Several elements were able to contact orbiting FACs, who tried to bring in helicopters to recover as many as possible. This action bought some time for the defending ARVN units falling back into the Kontum area.[42]

Because of the added loss of Rocket Ridge and the Tan Canh positions, Kontum and possibly the key logistical center in the Pleiku area were vulnerable. President Thieu decided to appoint a new MR-2 corps commander, Maj. Gen. Nguyen Van Toan, and reinforced him with another infantry regiment, commanded by Col. Ly Tong Ba from the Twenty-Third ARVN division. Colonel Ba and his force were reinforced by two more regiments from the Twenty-Third Division, and he was also given operational control of several other units in the area. He had USAF FACs overhead around the clock and an almost unlimited stream of allied and Vietnamese fighters and gunships, to include AC-130s from Ubon, Thailand. Additionally, General Abrams directed several B-52 strikes into the area every day. The first major NVA attack occurred on 14 May. Allied air strikes and timely B-52 strikes devastated the attack.

As the MR-2 battle attack was developing, another iteration of US-based USAF aircraft was deploying from stateside bases to SEA. This time, it was two C-130 squadrons, from Langley AFB, Virginia, and Little Rock AFB, Arkansas, that flew to join the 374th Tactical Airlift Wing (TAW) located at Ching Chuan Kang Air Base, Taiwan. From there, they would deploy throughout SEA.[43]

For the next ten days, the NVA forces resupplied and repositioned for another attempt to overwhelm the ARVN at Kontum. They used their long-range 122mm and 130mm artillery to pummel the ARVN forces and airfield at Kontum. On 17 May, a C-130 was hit and crashed on takeoff. Seven crewmembers were killed, and two wounded were evacuated. The C-130s were then directed to land only at night, and on 22 May another, Spare 622, was destroyed by a rocket. As the fighting intensified, John Paul Vann, the senior US advisor in MR-2, directed that all advisors except those who were absolutely essential would be evacuated, and US Army helicopters from Camp Holloway came in and picked them up. This generated bitter resentment among the ARVN troops, who were fighting for their lives and saw this as abandonment by their supposed allies.[44]

FACs were constantly orbiting over Kontum and directing air strikes or working with the US Army aviation units from Camp Holloway. The UH-1Bs firing the TOW missiles were being particularly effective in destroying NVA vehicles. Consequently, four jeep-mounted firing units were sent to the Kontum area and quickly put to work by the US advisors with the Twenty-Third Division units.[45]

On 24 May, an O-2 FAC, Covey 533, from the Twentieth TASS, was reported missing near the ranger border camp at Plei Mrong, ten miles northwest of Pleiku. United States Air Force and US Army aircraft searched the area but could not find any indications of the pilot or aircraft. The FAC was never found.[46]

The main NVA attack into Kontum opened on 25 May and lasted for five days. The US advisors declared a tactical emergency, and aircraft of all sorts diverted into the battle. Two US Army helicopters were shot down in the middle of the melee, and several crewmembers were killed. But the C-130s and VNAF C-123s kept bringing in supplies at night, and CH-47s came in during the day, until the airfield was closed, and then the transports started airdrops outside the city. The TOW-equipped UH-1Bs were wickedly effective as the battle peaked. On 26 May, they fired twenty-one missiles, destroying five T-54 tanks, five PT-76 tanks, a truck, a bunker, and two enemy machine guns. They flew all day long. The air strikes were constant and deadly. But it was the South Vietnamese soldiers who held the ground. The NVA were broken and Kontum did not fall. Noted an intercepted NVA radio message, "We launched two assaults into Kontum City, but our forces were unsuccessful and suffered losses. Our units were ordered to pull back to regroup."[47] The NVA forces pulled back, but they did not leave South Vietnam. The fighting would continue throughout the year along the battle lines west and north of Kontum.

MR-3 An Loc

The ARVN position held at An Loc, but it was tenuous. The attempts to airdrop at night were just not working. In fact, they seemed to be supplying the NVA better than the ARVN fighting forces. Doing a quick analysis of the situation on 1 May, General Hollingsworth estimated that the ARVN were recovering only about 30 percent of the drops. Airdrop experts in Taiwan and back in the United States went to work on the problem as the siege continued.

As the experiences of the C-130 crews demonstrated, the NVA AAA crews were deadly. On 2 May, a USAF AC-119 gunship from the Eighteenth SOS at NKP, Thailand, Stinger 41, was dispatched out of Bien Hoa Air Base to work in the An Loc area during daytime. It rendezvoused with an O-2 FAC, Sun Dog 29, Capt. Tom Milligan, and he directed them to destroy ARVN supplies that had been erroneously airdropped outside of the city drop zone by the C-130s the previous evening. As the gunship began its attack, it was fired upon by the numerous enemy AAA guns arrayed around the city. The crew of Stinger 41 began to attack the guns, and Sun Dog 29 called for fighters to suppress the guns so that Stinger 41 could carry out its original assignment.

However, before the fighters arrived, Stinger was hit by several rounds of AAA and suffered severe damage to its right wing and engines. The aircraft commander, Capt. Terry Courtney, fought to control the aircraft as the crew scrambled to bail out. Milligan directed them to fly out southwest of the city. As the parachutes began to appear, he reported the loss to the direct air support center, who notified the Joint Rescue Coordination Center (JRCC) in Saigon. They launched the alert HH-3s at Bien Hoa, Jollys 23 and 33. They were joined by Sandys 05, 1st Lt. Lamar C. Smith, and 06, Capt. Denny Morgan, now sitting alert at Bien Hoa vice Ubon, and the rescue task force headed for An Loc. A US Army helicopter team from the 229th Assault Helicopter Battalion (AHB), working in the area, immediately responded. They placed protective fire around the survivors and picked up one crewmember. An AC-130 also diverted to the scene and began engaging the enemy guns. Arriving over An Loc, the Sandys received a quick brief from Sun Dog 29 and then led in the two HH-3s. Each recovered three crewmembers. However, Courtney and two other airmen could not be located and were not heard on their radios. The Jollys flew their survivors back to Tan Son Nhut, and a listening watch was maintained for several days for the remaining members of Stinger 41. An ARVN Ranger team also searched the area and wreckage of the AC-119, but no trace of the missing airmen was found. For the next several days, the FACs over An Loc destroyed every AAA gun that they could find.[48]

That night, another seven C-130s were scheduled to drop supplies into the besieged ARVN troops. However, when the first aircraft missed the drop zone by seven hundred meters, the remaining drops were canceled. The next night, another C-130 from the 374th TAW went down with no survivors on a resupply attempt. The cause of the loss was undetermined. But further C-130 drops were canceled until a better method could be determined.[49]

The air rigging experts worked tirelessly to develop a method to airdrop into besieged locations with the most accuracy and survivability for the aircraft and crews. They discovered that they could use high-velocity drogue parachutes instead of the regular airdrop type. This would decrease the drop time, allow for more accuracy, and allow the C-130s to drop from higher altitudes. The cargo would hit the ground harder, but that could be ameliorated with more packing and padding. The first tests were conducted on 8 May with increased effectiveness, and within a day, test drops were up to 90 percent effectiveness. Now, the ARVN units could be steadily supplied, and morale and overall fighting effectiveness improved quickly and dramatically—and not a minute too soon. Intelligence sources indicated that NVA forces were preparing for another all-out attack against the city. [50]

By 8 May, the intelligence sources were indicating that NVA forces around the city were reorganizing and consolidating for a new series of attacks with seven regimental-sized units and almost ten thousand fighters. They also indicated that the NVA commanders had the will to use them. This was confirmed when an NVA officer was captured and revealed their plans. The ARVN forces had about four thousand soldiers, of whom almost one thousand were wounded in some form. When the ARVN tried to heli-lift in some fresh soldiers, the NVA gunners shot the helicopter down. In the early morning hours of 9 May, enemy forces began probing all around the perimeter, and enemy artillery fire dramatically increased. At the headquarters, Major General Hollingsworth believed that these early attacks were a buildup to the main attack, which would occur on 11 May. Accordingly, he requested eighteen B-52 strikes and two hundred tactical air strikes, and then added seven more B-52 strikes, to be delivered in the next twenty-four hours. The FACs were busy, and the strikes went in. Additionally, the US Army aviation units in MR-3 also flew repeated missions to An Loc, as did the USAF AC-119 and AC-130 gunships. There was offensive air over An Loc continuously. Hollingsworth also allowed his advisory teams to plan missions to extract the advisors if their units appeared to be collapsing. He kept this quiet, however, lest the planning action itself cause flagging morale among the ARVN. But it had to be done.[51]

The NVA forces were ready for the onslaught. In addition to their massed AAA guns, they had just received the new SA-7s along with reports about how effective they had been up around Quang Tri. In fact, in the last two days a pilot of an AH-1 from F Troop, Ninth Cavalry (F/9) and an O-2 FAC had reported seeing them being used.[52]

In the early hours of 11 May, the NVA unleashed their main attack with heavy artillery attacks and waves of infantry buttressed with tank support. They also attacked outlying supporting ARVN positions in an attempt to decisively defeat the ARVN forces standing before Saigon. They also brought in more 23mm, 37mm, and even self-propelled ZSU-57/2 guns in an earnest desire to beat back the unremitting airpower raining down on their forces and, in particular, to shoot down the FACs, which they could clearly see were orchestrating much of the effectiveness of the air strikes. The FACs were directing A-37s right into the middle of the city to destroy tanks and using AC-130s to destroy enemy forces just yards away from friendly forces. At the height of the battle, up to five O-2 FACs orbited over the city at the same time, with one acting as the overall quarterback, organizing the strike flights—sometimes as many as ten flights of fighters with different ordnance and "playtime" available—and passing them off to the other FACs who were actually directing the air strikes. One observer called the airspace of An Loc a "mass of confusion." On 11 May, 297 strike aircraft delivered ordnance in the center area of the city and averaged 260 sorties per day for the four days afterward. And to that must be added the flow of US Army helicopters, USAF gunships, and the deconfliction, which had to be done for the B-52 strikes to go in. At one point in the fight, General Hollingsworth was able to divert five more B-52 strikes from the Pleiku area into the midst of the An Loc fight, catching and seriously damaging an enemy regiment beginning an attack on an ARVN Ranger battalion. Noted Hollingsworth in his after-action report, "That [B-52] crew diverted the strike in 20 minutes, put it in . . . and destroyed the whole damn regiment, right in the same holes where they had gone to reorganize."[53]

The A-37s from the Eighth SOS at Bien Hoa Air Base flew constantly in the An Loc fight. That morning Hawk 02, 1st Lt. Mike Blassie, was working with a FAC, Chico 11, when his A-37 was hit by 23mm AAA while dropping napalm on enemy positions. He did not eject. A US Army helicopter flew low over the burning wreckage but saw no sign of life. Friendly forces were not able to reach the wreckage until late October.[54]

A few minutes later, an AH-1 from F Battery, Seventy-Ninth Aerial Rocket Artillery Artillery (F/79) had just killed two tanks in the southwest corner of the city when it was hit by an SA-7. The two pilots, Capt. Robert Williams and Warrant Officer Rod Strobridge, were killed when the stricken machine violently crashed. A few minutes later, another F/79 AH-1 was similarly shot down while escorting a medevac UH-1. Again, both men were killed.[55]

At one point, a Vietnamese Ranger team north of the city spotted several NVA tanks getting ready to cross a small concrete bridge. They used an M-72 light antiarmor weapon (LAW) to immobilize the lead tank and then called in AC-130s, which destroyed the column. The NVA fought back against the lumbering gunships by firing several SA-7s. One struck one of the big aircraft, severely damaging it. However, the crew was able to contain the damage and fly it back to Ubon.[56]

After Hawk 02 went down, Chico 11, Capt. Barry Allmond, continued to put in air strikes. About two hours later, his O-2 was hit and destroyed by enemy fire. Nobody saw him bail out, and ground observers watched the aircraft violently crash and burst into flames. As the fire consumed the aircraft, its marking rockers exploded. AH-1s from F/79 Artillery responded to the crash, but there was nothing that they could do.[57]

Three hours after that terrible event, Sun Dog 34, another O-2, flown by 1st Lt. John Haselton, was also hit and destroyed by enemy fire. He did not bail out and suffered a similar fate as Chico 11. In both cases, SA-7s were suspected but not confirmed as the downing weapon. However, SA-7 launchings were now a common event in the An Loc area.[58]

The battle continued for several more days, but the combined strength of the ARVN ground forces and the US and South Vietnamese airpower held off the NVA forces. On 13 May, a VNAF A-1, Phoenix Black, was shot down on the southwest side of An Loc by an SA-7. The pilot ejected and landed in a grove of rubber trees. Garbled transmissions were heard on the Guard frequency. An HH-3 and two A-1s, Sandy 05, 1st Lt. Bob Carlsen, and Sandy 06, Capt. Ross Buchanan, launched and headed for An Loc. However, a helicopter team from F/79 Artillery searched the area. They found a parachute but could not find the pilot. The rescue forces continued to search for the airman, but there were no further indications that the pilot had survived. Both Sandys observed and avoided SA-7s and dropped ordnance on the launch sites.[59]

The next day, an SA-7 shot down another O-2, Sun Dog 07. Fortunately, this time the FAC, 1st Lt. Henry "Pep" McPhillips, was able to bail out. The missile hit and destroyed the rear engine, and he was able to escape through the left window. The top FAC at the time was Capt. Peter Collins, Rash 05. He immediately assumed OSC and watched McPhillips descend. Collins used the US Navy A-7s and F-8s that were working with Sun Dog 07 to now support his SAR. Sandy 05, 1st Lt. Bob Carlsen, and Sandy 06, Capt. Ross Buchanan, had just launched from Bien Hoa and immediately diverted to support the SAR. They checked in with Rash 05 along with a US Army helicopter team ready to attempt a pickup. However, the area was just too hot, and the ground battle was a confused mess. Rash 05 had the Sandys and fighters drop their bombs on the enemy SA-7 firing sites and other suspected positions. Several SA-7 missiles were observed, and Sandy 05 decided that the area was just too dangerous for A-1s. They returned to Bien Hoa.

Below, McPhillips landed hard and broke a foot. He took cover and made radio contact with Collins, who told him that ARVN forces—the Eighth Airborne Battalion—were near and looking for him. He came out of cover, and the ARVN troops were laughing at him and already cutting up his parachute for hammocks. He spent several days with them and acted as a ground FAC. While there, he met several of the ARVN commanders and their US advisors. They all expressed to him their great appreciation for the support that the FACs provided them. Several days later, he was flown out on a UH-1from the 229th AHB.[60]

On 15 May, the intensity of the battle noticeably slackened. General Hollingsworth concluded that the NVA were ceasing their attack and withdrawing their units to the north and west under the cover of the rubber plantations. He reported to General Abrams, "The enemy had lost his capability for further offensive operations in Binh Long Province." He later added that the enemy forces had "withdrawn from the immediate vicinity of An Loc as a result of the heavy losses inflicted by TACAIR and B-52 strikes." However, the NVA did not withdraw their artillery units, and they continued to rain several thousand rounds per day on the ARVN units north and west of Saigon.[61]

The next day, US Marine Air Group 12 (MAG-12) began to arrive at Bien Hoa with thirty-two A-4s of VMA 211 and VMA 311. Their pilots took orientation rides in the right seat of the A-37s of the Eighth SOS, and one pilot was killed by enemy fire on a mission over An Loc. Soon they were flying missions all over MR-2, -3, and -4 and added to the decimation of the invading NVA forces. The enemy high tide at An Loc had passed. Noted the official NVA history of the war, "Three waves of assaults against Binh Long city [An Loc] on [13 and 15 April and on 11 May] were all unsuccessful.

Sun Dog 07, 1st Lt. Pep McPhillips and Lt. Col. Art Taylor, ARVN advisor. (Courtesy Pep McPhillips)

Our units suffered heavy casualties and over half of our tanks we used in the battle were destroyed." Fighting did not stop in the area and would continue with some significant actions through the rest of the year. But the South Vietnamese forces, with staunch US airpower support, had held at the key place and time. Their actions had saved Saigon.[62]

Linebacker

The initiation of the broader campaign further increased the need for Fast FACs. Correspondingly, their losses mounted. On 12 May, Gunsmoke 07, an F-4 Fast FAC from the 366th TFW at Da Nang, crewed by Capt. Sam Adair and 1st Lt. Dennis Cressey, flew an afternoon mission into southern North Vietnam to work against interdiction targets. At the completion of their mission, the crew passed through the Quang Tri area and went down for unexplained reasons about five miles east of Quang Tri. Both men were killed, and no SAR effort other than visual confirmation was conducted.[63]

Similar to the Fast FAC program, the US Navy dispatched flights of strike aircraft on armed reconnaissance missions to find and destroy supply convoys. On 17 May, a flight of A-7s off the USS *Constellation* was searching for targets twenty miles north of Dong Hoi. North Vietnamese Army AAA hit and severely damaged one of the A-7s, Jason 404. The pilot, Cdr. Tom

Wilkinson, was the commander of VA-147. He flew out over the Gulf of Tonkin and ejected. Big Mother 64, an HH-3A from HC-7 flown by Lt. Jim Spillman and crew, picked him up as Rescue Combat Air Patrol (RESCAP) A-7s drove away enemy boats that tried to sprint out and grab the survivor.[64]

This scenario was repeated two days later when an A-7 from the USS *Midway*, Champion 411, flown by Lt. Aubrey Nichols, was shot down south of Vinh. The pilot successfully ejected, and an HH-3A from HC-7 was dispatched for a recovery as his wingmen capped him. However, before the helicopter could arrive, the pilot was captured. He was released in 1973.[65]

On 20 May, an F-4 from the 432nd TRW at Udorn, Bowleg 02, flown by 1st Lt. John Markle and Capt. Jim Williams, was downed twenty-five miles west of Hanoi on a MiGCAP mission. Wingmen reported two beepers and voice contact with both men. Two A-1s, Sandys 03, 1st Lt. Tex Brown, and 04, and two Jolly Greens, 53 and 30, diverted from their orbit point, with Disco providing critical navigational support. The Jollys rendezvoused with King 27 and refueled while the Sandys proceeded to the rescue area, where they generally located the two survivors. The area was very dangerous, with known AAA and SAM sites, and well within the range of MiG aircraft. Additionally, thunderstorms were building. After four hours, the recovery forces lost contact with Williams when he was captured. Sandys 09, Capt. Ron Smith, and 10, 1st Lt. Byron Hukee, and Sandys 01, Maj. Zeke Encinas, and 02, 1st Lt. Lance Smith, launched from NKP to support the recovery. At the holding point, Jolly 53 received a radar homing and warning (RHAW) indication of an SA-2 missile launch. The aircraft commander, Capt. Mark Schibler, saw the missile, called out a warning on the radio, and took vigorous evasive action, which caused the missile to pass harmlessly overhead. USAF and Navy fighters provided MiGCAP and engaged a MiG that tried to attack the force, as the Sandys escorted in Jolly 53 to recover Markle. After the recovery, Jolly 53 headed southwest, rejoined with Jolly 30, and received fuel from King 27. However, while heading south, they were again engaged by an SA-2 battery that fired several missiles and by several AAA sites that fired at the helicopters and escorting Sandys, fortunately without effect. King 27 provided key navigational support for the Sandys, who all recovered at NKP with minimum fuel. Jim Williams was released in 1973.

Schibler's copilot was a brand new pilot in the unit, 2nd Lt. Rufus Hutchinson. This was his first mission, and he was mightily impressed by the SA-2s that passed overhead. On the way back to NKP, Schibler signed him off as fully combat ready. Rufus had to wonder if split S's were routine for an HH-53. If so, it was going to be a long year.[66]

Left to right: *Capt. Mark Schibler, A1C Robert Mason, S.Sgt. Tom Bryant, 1st Lt. John Markle (Bowleg 02Alpha), 2nd Lt. Rufus Hutchinson, Sgt. Paul Perry. (Courtesy Mark Schibler)*

At the Third Aerospace Rescue and Recovery Group (ARRG), the commander, Col. Cy Muirhead, looked at this mission carefully. He noted that the RHAW gear on HH-53 provided the crew with timely warning of the SA-2 sites. However, without any onboard electronic countermeasures (ECM) capability, they needed SAM suppression to be able to accomplish rescues in SA-2 threat areas. He was also concerned about the MiG threat, which had endangered a recovery operation for the second time in ten days. He sent a message to Blue Chip requesting MiGCAP for any mission that took place whenever MiGs were within range of the recovery force. Air superiority was an absolute requirement for SAR operations because A-1s and HH-53s could not focus on recovering downed personnel if they had to maneuver to protect from aerial attack.[67]

Three days later, in the late evening, another Fast FAC, Owl 14 from the Eighth TFW, Ubon, was shot down by AAA eight miles above the DMZ while searching out targets for strike flights. Capt. Bill Byrns and Capt. Ray Bean ejected. Byrns made radio contact and reported that he was near AAA sites and had troops all around him. That was his last call before he was captured. However, Captain Bean was able to hide. Owl 14 had been working with Calcite, a flight of two F-4s. The flight lead was 1st Lt. Brian Nelson and 1st Lt. "Hoss" Hostenske. They immediately notified King that

Left to right: *1st Lt. Bob Carlson, Maj. Zeke Encinas, 1st Lt. Lance Smith, 1st Lt. John Markle, 1st Lt. Byron Hukee. (Courtesy Mark Schibler)*

Owl 14 was down and were directed to assume OSC over the downed crew. However, their aircraft was engaged by an SA-2 battery and was damaged by a missile, forcing them to divert to Da Nang.[68]

Other Fast FACs maintained voice contact with Bean. He was down in a very dangerous area overloaded with NVA ground and air defense units. The JRCC worked with the JPRC to develop a plan to have the survivor move to a more benign area to the southwest, but Bean replied that because of the enemy forces in the area, such a move was impossible. Instead, they considered deploying a special operations team to possibly attempt a recovery operation from the sea. As part of their preparation, they debriefed First Lieutenant Nelson and others who had been flying in that area and considered dropping in a Madden kit with food, water, and batteries. However, before a recovery effort could be carried out, Bean was captured. He was moved to Hanoi and released in March 1973. Captain Bean later said that the NVA knew where he was and built an AAA and SAM trap around him, hoping to use him as bait to destroy another Jolly Green.[69]

On 24 May, another navy A-7 off the USS *Coral Sea*, Hoboken 410, flown by Lt. Cdr. Harvey Eikel, was shot down just north of Haiphong while attacking SAM sites. He was able to get out over the water before ejecting, and his flight mates suppressed the enemy air defenses. Big Mother 67, flown by Cdr. John Woolam and crew, launched from the USS *Chicago*, and Big Mother 63 launched from the USS *Sterett*. Arriving in the area, another A-7 led Big Mother 67 in to pick up Eikel. This was the one-hundredth combat rescue for the squadron, and the second time that they had rescued Eikel.[70]

This was a stressful time for HC-7. Because of the now sustained air operations over North Vietnam, the unit was pressed to have as many aircraft as possible on flight status and airborne when the strike flights were going in. The pressure on the maintenance teams to keep the aircraft "up" stretched them to the limit. Many were working beyond their specialties and getting minimum rest as they were called to work fourteen-to-sixteen-hour shifts. And they were constantly cross-decking, on one occasion with only two hours' notice as the ships of TF-77 came and went. The young sailors performed absolute miracles to keep their life-saving helicopters ready to go.[71]

As the month of May waned, TF-77 had several aircraft go down on missions in the north. The USS *Hancock* lost an F-8 and two A-4s, with one pilot killed and two captured. They were released in 1973. The USS *Coral Sea* had an A-7 go down, but the pilot was recovered by an HH-3A from HC-7. It also lost a USMC A-6, Bengal 503, on a mission to a target near Haiphong on 29 May. The crew of Lt. Cdr. Philip Schuyler and Capt. Lou Ferracane were able to eject well out over the GOT and were also recovered by an HH-3A from HC-7, flown by Lt. Dennis Dilley and crew. Heading 130 degrees and going "feet wet" was an obvious tactic for the crews who were now daily striking targets in North Vietnam.[72]

By the end of the month, Linebacker was beginning to have its intended effects. Intelligence data indicated that NVA shelling on the southern battlefields had declined 55 percent and SA-2 firings in and around South Vietnam and Laos had markedly decreased.[73]

Nakhon Phanom RTAFB, Thailand

However, the First SOS had taken some serious losses. The enemy offensive in South Vietnam and the renewed bombing of North Vietnam put new pressures on the dwindling A-1 SAR force. Due to the heavy enemy offensive, fast mover strike flights were no longer readily available during SARs. The occasional lack of support, including the lack of MiGCAP and SAM suppression assets, was at times adding greatly to the challenge of

SARs in North Vietnam and probably contributed to the nonrecovery of Ice-bag 04Alpha and Bravo. Additionally, the SA-7s were showing up all over the theater and were a real danger to the A-1s and HH-53s, and everybody else. The First SOS received a new commander on 19 May, when Lt. Col. Martin Barbena completed his tour and returned to the United States. He was succeeded by Maj. Jim Harding, who moved up from operations officer. On his third tour in SEA and a below-the-zone selectee for lieutenant colonel, he brought a wealth of combat knowledge and experience to the job, and the Fifty-Sixth Special Operations Wing (SOW) commander, Col. Jack Robinson, picked him over several other available lieutenant colonels because he recognized that his drive and strength of character were what the squadron needed in the challenging times ahead.[74]

But Colonel Robinson had a larger concern. His wing was, de facto, the rescue wing for the theater. On reflecting upon this mission and its accomplishment over that last few months, he believed that overall tactical control of SAR should be consolidated into one tactical center versus two—OL-A at Son Tra and OL-B at Udorn. And he believed that such a center should be located at NKP. There, the Fifty-Sixth SOW had the First SOS with its A-1s and rescue expertise, the Twenty-Third TASS with its FACs and Pave Nails and rapidly expanding involvement in SAR, the Fortieth ARRSq with its HH-53s, and the tremendous intelligence capabilities of Task Force Alpha.

Unaware of the Air Force's plans for the A-1 or its replacement in SEA, he also addressed an expedient, at least on an interim basis. Noting that the Twenty-Third TASS had more than forty OV-10s assigned, he suggested using them as a replacement for the A-1s. He noted the strengths and weaknesses of the aircraft but cited the SAR experience of the crews, and especially the technological capabilities of the Pave Nail OV-10 with its Pave Spot laser system and loran navigational coupling, as real enhancers to mission accomplishment. As a combat wing commander, he had to address the mission requirements of his unit with the assets that he had available. His views and recommendations were duly forwarded to Seventh AF for consideration.[75]

Chris Hobson's *Vietnam Air Losses* presents us with the following statistics for May:

Fixed wing aircraft downed: USAF—28, USN—13, USMC—4
Results: KIA 32/38%
POW 18/21%
Recovered 35/41%

Recovery by: 10 USAF Heli
                 7 Army Heli
                 9 Navy Heli
                 1 Ground force
                 2 VNAF Heli
                 4 Unknown[76]

The data shows general trends. Again, though, the stories of US Army rescues are only partially represented, and the numbers do not reflect all of the troops evacuated at Quang Tri. Those are told individually. During the month of May, rescue missions were more challenging because of the increased enemy threat and the increased tempo of aerial operations across the breadth and depth of Southeast Asia.

CHAPTER FIVE

JUNE DESPERATE BATTLES, GROUND AND AIR

It was like a man returning from the dead. . . . This was the most gratifying mission I ever flew.

First Lieutenant Fred Hastings, 523rd Tactical Fighter Squadron, email to author, 20 August 2018

We are going in!

Captain Dale Stovall, quoted in Kevin O'Rourke and Joe Peters, *Taking Fire*

Oyster 01Bravo

Unbeknownst to US forces, an American airman was evading in North Vietnam. Captain Roger Locher, the weapons systems operator (WSO) shot down on 10 May, had evaded in an attempt to move away from the MiG base at Yen Bai, believing that no rescue helicopter could survive a pickup attempt anywhere near such a heavily defended facility. However, he had been able to use his survival radio to monitor the search and rescues (SARs) for Icebag 04Bravo and Bowleg 02Alpha and had come to believe that the SAR forces would be able to get in to him.[1]

On the morning of 1 June, Locher heard jets overhead his location and recognized the "whoosh" sound of an SA-2 missile roaring into the sky. Locher took out his survival radio and turned it on, monitoring the Guard frequency. When he did not hear any emergency calls, he realized that the SA-2 had not shot down another American aircraft. He waited a few minutes and then made a call himself: "Any US aircraft, if you read Oyster 01Bravo, come up on Guard." That call was heard by another flight using the Oyster call sign that day. They were part of the Linebacker Uniform strike package and were egressing North Vietnam. The pilot of Oyster 02, 1st Lt. Jim Dunn, from the Eighth Tactical Fighter Wing (TFW) at Ubon Air

Base, Thailand, quickly notified his flight lead, but the flight was swiftly egressing to the south and further calls to Locher were not received. Regardless, they reported the call to the Disco EC-121 that monitored strike flights in northern Laos. The controllers aboard Disco quickly notified "Bluechip," the Seventh Air Force (AF) command center in Saigon, and the notice was flashed to the Joint Rescue Coordination Center (JRCC), the two subordinate rescue coordination centers (RCCs), and the airborne King aircraft, one of which was orbiting over northern Laos with two Fortieth Aerospace Rescue and Recovery Squadron (ARRSq) HH-53s: Jolly Green 57, flown by Capt. Dale Stovall and crew, and Jolly Green 30, flown by Maj. Leo Thacker and crew. They were escorted by two First Special Operations Squadron (SOS) A-1s, Sandy 01, Capt. Ron Smith, and Sandy 02, Capt. Bob Herklotz, on orbit in northern Laos. Almost simultaneously, another flight of F-4s, Fletch Flight, passed over Locher, and the lead crew of Capt. Steve Ritchie and Capt. Chuck DeBellevue also heard Locher's calls and immediately recognized his voice. Locher asked, plaintively, "Guys, I've been here a long time. Any chance of picking me up?" Ritchie replied, "YOU BET!"[2]

Moments later, the two Jolly Greens and two A-1s turned north and started heading to Locher's reported position just four miles northeast of Yen Bai. En route, Smith made radio contact with Locher and authenticated him. Initial navigation into the Red River Valley was challenging because the terrain all looked the same. Fortunately, Jolly Green 30 was equipped with an electronic location finder (ELF), and as they got closer to the survivor's location, it began to provide accurate guidance to Locher's survival radio. The two Jolly Greens held behind a low ridge line four miles south of the Red River. Herklotz remained with them as Ron Smith proceeded north to determine Locher's position. In Saigon, the JRCC directed the launching of another King HC-130 and two more A-1s and HH-53s from Nakhon Phanom RTAFB (NKP).[3]

Flights of F-4s were vectored into the area to provide MiG Combat Air Patrol (MiGCAP). SA-2 batteries fired at them and damaged one F-4. That crew was able to fly back to Udorn Air Base before they had to eject. They were replaced by other F-4s. However, a MiG-21 attempted to attack the two Jolly Greens and Herklotz at the holding point. The aircraft scattered and the Jolly Greens dropped down to one hundred feet above ground level (AGL), forcing the MiG to pass by harmlessly. North of the Red River, Ron Smith was attempting to precisely locate Locher so that one of the Jolly Greens could be brought in for a recovery. However, he was having difficulties maintaining communications with the survivor and then discovered that the direction finder on his ultrahigh frequency (UHF) radio was inoperative. Additionally, antiaircraft artillery (AAA) batteries began to fire at the aircraft. With the realization that the Jolly Greens and A-1s were all now low on fuel and that the AAA guns would have to be dealt with, Ron Smith directed that all SAR forces leave the area and develop a plan to enter the survivor's location from the north or west. He also requested that the F-4s still in the area determine, as accurately as possible, the survivor's location.

The two Sandys had to immediately leave the Jollys because they had just enough fuel to get to a Laos Lima site. The Jollys did not have enough fuel to make it out of North Vietnam. They called King and said, "Have the other Jollys coming toward the Black River pick them up." King replied, "Jolly, I have been monitoring your fuel and I am in North Vietnam." (King's normal orbit was 125 miles south of the border.) The two Jollys had the five-minute low-level fuel lights on when they refueled fifty miles inside of North Vietnam at ten thousand feet. As the Jollys plugged into the tanker, two USMC F-4s arrived for MiGCAP. Other strike aircraft and Fast FACs (forward air controllers) operating in the area maintained radio contact with Locher. En route to NKP, Jolly Green 30 experienced a mechanical issue with one of its engines, and the crew had to land it in a flooded rice paddy in Thailand. Maintenance crews were flown to the aircraft and were able to repair it and return it to NKP.[4]

Arriving back at NKP, the Jolly Green and Sandy crews immediately debriefed with Intelligence and the controllers at Joker and then began intense preparations for an early SAR effort on 2 June. At the First SOS, the commander, Maj. Jim Harding, directed that Capt. Ron Smith would lead further efforts to recover Locher. Concerned about the MiG threat, he decided to join on as Sandy 03 with Lt. Col. Bill Latham as Sandy 04 because they were the only pilots in the squadron who had any experience as air-to-air pilots.

However, both Harding and Ron Smith realized that they were going to need a great deal of support to suppress the North Vietnamese MiGs at Yen Bai and the air defense forces in the survivor's area. This would require preplanned strike flights for AAA and surface-to-air missile (SAM) suppression and actual strikes on the Yen Bai airfield, and continuous MiGCAP, plus sufficient tankers to refuel all of the fighters—in all, adding up to a major effort, which would impact the overall Linebacker operations for the day. The planners at NKP talked to the planners of the 432nd Tactical Reconnaissance Wing (TRW) at Udorn Air Base and realized that they would have to ask Seventh AF for the support. When they made their request, they were told that only General Vogt could approve such a major modification to the Linebacker plan. Captain Ron Smith would fly as Sandy 01 for the recovery. Replicating his call to the JPRC for the Bat 21Bravo/Nail 38Bravo rescue effort, Smith (and Captain Stovall) spoke directly with General Vogt and specified the needs of the mission. The general recalled the conversation:

> The problem was that it was going to involve a substantial effort. Choppers would have to be sent up there; they would have to have enough support to deal with the possibility that when they got up around the Airbase at Yen Bai, the MiGs would come swarming in. There could be a major air battle, we might lose aircraft. I had to decide whether we should risk the loss of maybe half a dozen airplanes and crews just to get one man out. Finally, I said to myself . . . the one thing that keeps our boys motivated is the certain belief that if they go down, we will do absolutely everything we can to get them out. If that is ever in doubt, morale would tumble. . . . I didn't ask anybody for permission, I just said, "Go do it."[5]

In that pithy and concise statement, General Vogt encapsulated the "moral imperative" that defined the meaning and purpose of the rescue forces and their capabilities in that war in 1972.

At NKP, preparations were made for an early morning launch, and the maintenance crews scrambled to prepare the aircraft. The First SOS would launch four A-1s, Sandy 01, Capt. Ron Smith, Sandy 02, Capt. Buck Buchanan, Sandy 03, Maj. Jim Harding, and Sandy 04, Lt. Col. Bill Latham. The Fortieth ARRSq would initially launch four HH-53s, Jolly Green 30, flown by Capt. Dale Stovall and crew, Jolly Green 53, flown by Maj. Leo Thacker and crew, Jolly Green 60, flown by Capt. Jerry Shipman and crew, and Jolly Green 57. Because this was such a high-risk mission, both squadron commanders directed that all crewmembers would be volunteers only. They would be escorted by two HC-130 King aircraft. Additionally, the rescue task force would be supported by 119 F-4s, F-105Gs, EB-66s, and KC-135s. Backup A-1s and HH-53s would also be available for this all-out effort to rescue Captain Locher.[6]

The next morning, the first two Jolly Greens took off at 0530L. However, Jolly Green 53 had a mechanical problem and had to abort. Jolly Green 30 joined with Jollys 60 and 57 and refueled with one of the King HC-130s and proceeded to a holding point about twenty-five miles southwest of Yen Bai.

Captain Stovall activated their ELF system and was able to get good tracking guidance on Locher's survival radio whenever he transmitted. The four A-1s took off at 0745L and also proceeded to the holding point. As they arrived at about 0915L, the valleys were filled with morning fog. Jollys 30 and 60 joined them there, as the support fighters orbited above and strike flights bombed the Yen Bai Airfield. While Sandys 03 and 04 remained in orbit with the helicopters, Sandys 01 and 02 then proceeded north of the Red River to precisely determine Locher's position. Sandy 01 also authenticated him again with a question about a favorite pub at Locher's college. When he correctly answered, Smith declared, "It looks like you are the guy we are looking for!" Locher's response was classic: "You're damn right I am!"

Antiaircraft artillery sites began firing at the A-1s, and Ron Smith directed a supporting flight of F-4s to destroy them. They did so. Almost simultaneously, F-105Gs suppressed the SA-2 sites that had shot at the rescue aircraft the previous day. Smith was then able to generally determine Locher's position. He decided to bring the Jolly Greens in behind the protective cover of a ridgeline northwest of Locher.

Ron Smith briefed his plan to the Jollys and other Sandys. He would lead the helicopters to the north about fifteen miles west of Yen Bai, cross the Red River and ridgeline, and then turn right to take Jolly 30 in for the pickup. As the gaggle of aircraft proceeded, they began to receive fire from villages along the route. As they crossed the Red River, Ron Smith called MiGCAP and got no answer. The MiGCAP F-4s were provided by the squadrons at Udorn, to include the augmenting 523rd Tactical Fighter Squadron (TFS) from the Philippines. However, their time on station between Phuc Yen and Kep airfields was about twenty minutes, and to maintain that time on station, they had to cycle back to KC-135s holding over Laos. Consequently, there were gaps in the coverage, and Ron Smith had found one. Smith called Jolly 30 and said, "There is no MiGCAP, so what do you want to do?" Stovall replied, "Keep going. I don't want to come back here tomorrow." The A-1s provided suppressive fire as best they could, and the gunners on the HH-53s returned fire.

The Jollys and Sandys 03, Harding, and 04, Latham, then entered a holding pattern as Ron Smith and Buchanan proceeded toward the survivor. As they passed nearby, the survivor, Locher, flashed his mirror and Buchanan saw it. He began to give Jolly 30 vectors to the survivor. Stovall turned for his run-in to Locher. As he crossed over the hill on which Locher was located, his ELF pointed directly at the survivor. Ron Smith directed Locher to pop his survival smoke. He did so, and the copilot on Jolly 30,

Capt. Mel Gillespie, saw him and talked the crew into a hover over the survivor on what appeared to be a forty-degree slope. The hoist operator lowered the jungle penetrator as the gunners engaged enemy forces in the immediate area who were now firing at the helicopter. Jolly 60 held about one-third mile to the north and similarly engaged ground targets as the Sandys strafed several locations and laid down a smoke screen to block the AAA sites to the south and east. As Locher cleared the trees, Stovall added max power and began to ascend. When the machine reached the top of the ridge, the PJs were pulling Locher through the door, and Stovall began to accelerate to rejoin with Jolly 60 and head back to the northwest. The Sandys then joined them and they turned south to recross the Red River and head home.

But more challenges lay ahead. As the task force crossed over villages, enemy gunners fired at them, and the helicopter gunners and A-1s returned fire. At one point, Ron Smith spotted a train that they could not avoid. It had several guns on it. All four A-1s attacked it, with Harding and Latham making several passes. Harding hit the steam engine with his rockets and Mk-47 bombs. The attack severely damaged the rolling stock and cargo. Jolly 60 also spotted a MiG-17. Harding thought it was a MiG-19. Regardless, when it appeared to be setting up for an attack, Harding attacked it and drove it away.

Both HH-53s were now low on fuel. They rendezvoused with King 22 in North Vietnam and received enough fuel to fly to Udorn Air Base. They and the A-1s landed there and were welcomed by several hundred airmen, including General Vogt, who had flown up from Saigon just to greet Captain Locher and the men of the rescue task force. That night, there were joyous celebrations at Udorn and NKP.[7]

For their extraordinary actions in this SAR, both Capt. Ron Smith and Capt. Dale Stovall were awarded the Air Force Cross. The combat photographer aboard Stovall's helicopter was awarded a Silver Star, a very prestigious award for a non-crewmember.[8]

However, the SAR was not completely over. Oyster 01Alpha, Maj. Bob Lodge, was still missing. For the next three days, flights passing through the area were vigilant for any sign or signal from Lodge. However, nothing was forthcoming. Consequently, on 4 June, the recovery mission for the crew of Oyster 01 was suspended with the concurrence of Seventh AF and the 432nd TRW. Major Bob Lodge's remains were returned from North Vietnam on 30 September 1977.[9]

Three days later, two more aircraft carriers, the USS *America* and USS

Oyster 01Bravo, Capt. Roger Locher and Gen. John Vogt at Udorn. (USAF photo)

Oriskany, joined Task Force 77 and were quickly generating sorties to support Linebacker.

Operation Thunderhead

Support for this operation was ongoing. Unaware that the senior POW leaders in Hanoi had forbidden any rescue efforts unless there was a high chance for success, the chairman of the Joint Chiefs of Staff, Admiral

Jolly Green crews on the Oyster 01Bravo rescue. Jolly Green 60—High Bird, back row (left to right): Capt. Jerry Shipman, Capt. Stanley Zielinski, Sgt. William Lyles, S.Sgt. Donald Goodlett, Sgt. Dennis Williamson, S.Sgt. Hal Smith. Jolly Green 30—Low Bird, front row (left to right): Capt. Dale Stovall, Capt. John Gillespie II, A1C James Walsh, Sgt. Charles McQuoid II, A1C Kenneth Cakebread, T.Sgt. Bobby Welborn. (USAF photo)

Thomas Moorer, sent a staff officer to brief Admiral Holloway, commander of the US Seventh Fleet on the anticipated POW escape(s). The tasking, with straightforward and highly classified details, was passed to Task Force (TF-) 77 for execution. Only a few officers were told that the recoverees would be POWs. Instead, the cover story more broadly shared was that the effort was designed to pick up some defecting North Vietnamese Army (NVA) officers. From 1 June to 19 June, HC-7 helicopters were directed to fly two to four flights a day along specified routes offshore from the estuaries of the Red River and lesser waterways connected to it. They were to look for specified authentication signals.

Additionally, a small team of SEALs from Seal Team One and Underwater Demolition Team (UDT) 11, led by Lt. M. Spence Dry, would be deployed aboard a submarine, the USS *Grayback*, which had been modified for special operations missions. The submarine would carry them well forward into the shallower coastal waters of North Vietnam in the Gulf of Tonkin. The SEALs would then launch a two-man team aboard a swimmer delivery vehicle (SDV) to a small island off the mouth of the Red River,

A-1 Sandy pilots on the Oyster 01Bravo rescue. Left to right: Lt. Col. William Latham, Maj. Jim Harding, Capt. Ross Buchanan, Capt. Ron Smith. (Courtesy Jim Harding)

approximately sixty miles southeast of Hanoi. There they would set up an observation point to watch for any escaping POWs, swapping teams every forty-eight hours utilizing the SDV.

The HC-7 detachment's crews started flying their assigned routes. They also had to maintain their standard SAR alert, and the added tasking stretched their crews, support personnel, and aircraft to the limit. On 3 June, the USS *Grayback* arrived at its designated launch point. The SDV was launched with Lieutenant Dry, Chief Petty Officer Philip "Moki" Martin, and its two UDT operators for the observation point that night at 0200L. However, the SDV could not handle the strong currents. When the batteries for its motor were exhausted, the craft foundered. The SEALs onboard decided to abandon it and called for a pickup by HC-7. The next morning, one of the helicopters was dispatched to pick them up. They also used their machine gun to riddle the SDV so that it would sink and then delivered the four men to the guided missile cruiser USS *Long Beach*. *Grayback* was still submerged to maintain operational security and prevent detection.

The next night, an HC-7 helicopter, big Mother 61, flown by Lt. Craig Peterson and crew, picked up the SEALs and UDT operators to return them to the *Grayback* by night drop—called a "cast" in SEAL jargon—so that they

USS Grayback *and SEALs on Operation Thunderhead. (US Navy photo)*

could continue their mission. Lieutenant Dry briefed the helicopter crew that the maximum limits for the drop were "20/20," meaning no higher than twenty feet above the water and twenty knots of air speed. The helicopter crew was also told that they could find the submarine because it was showing an infrared beacon atop the ship's snorkel mast, which they could see with their night goggles. It was a very dark, overcast night with gusty winds estimated up to twenty knots and waves to four feet.

Under the best conditions at the time, a low-level night SEAL cast was a difficult task. On this night's mission, the helicopter crew faced many more challenges. Flying to the expected location, they had a very hard time finding the submarine—at one point inadvertently overflying the darkened shoreline of North Vietnam. Finally, after spotting what they thought was the submarine's beacon, the pilot was hard-pressed to make a suitable approach for the drop. After several attempts, he made a final approach, hovered, and told the four men to drop.

After hitting the water, Martin and the two operators found each other in spite of the surface visibility being only about ten feet. One man was seriously injured. The three men then discovered that the flashing beacon was not the *Grayback*. Instead, it belonged to one of the SEALs who had launched with his three teammates in the second SDV earlier that night. They also had to abandon it when it foundered owing to improper ballasting. Then they found the body of Lieutenant Dry. He was dead, having suffered "severe trauma to the neck" caused by impact with the water. The navy later concluded the helicopter was flying too high and too fast when the call to jump was made.[10]

Cdr. John Chamberlain (at right), commander of USS Grayback, swears in Chief Petty Officer "Moki" Martin as a chief warrant officer while Lt. "Spence" Dry, OIC SEAL Team One, Alpha Platoon, looks on. (Courtesy US Navy.)

At dawn, the men, towing the body of Lieutenant Dry, made radio contact with the *Long Beach*, and an HC-7 helicopter was diverted to pick them up and return to the cruiser. Later, on 12 June, they were flown back to the *Grayback*. In the interim, the submarine remained in shallower waters and maintained a periscope watch for escaped POWs.

The HC-7 aircrews continued to conduct their search routes. But they did not recover any escaping POWS. However, as air operations over the north continued to increase, and the mining of North Vietnam's harbors dramatically reduced sea traffic, Operation Thunderhead was terminated in late June. Lieutenant Spence Dry was the last SEAL killed in the war.[11]

In-Country Operations

MR-3
With the conclusion of the climactic and decisive battles of May, the fighting in MR-3 steadily reduced. The Army of the Republic of Vietnam (ARVN)

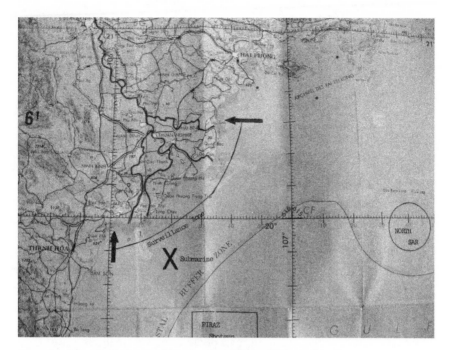

Operation Thunderhead map. (Courtesy Ron Milam, HC-7 Archives)

units in the area, still supported by the USAF and USMC units at Bien Hoa and Tan Son Nhut, and when necessary the fighters and gunships in Thailand, were able to hold their ground. Rescue forces were still provided by the USAF H-3s and TDY A-1s on alert at Bien Hoa, and the FACs still prowled for the enemy forces from above, always ready to initiate SAR missions if necessary. And the US Army units were still capable of immediate response when required, but under the ongoing US withdrawals, their numbers were steadily dwindling. Regardless, SARs still occurred.

On 5 June, Chico 64, an O-2, flown by 1st Lt. Craig Dunn, a FAC from the Twenty-First Tactical Air Support Squadron (TASS), was hit by AAA, and he crash-landed northwest of Bao Loc, South Vietnam. Sun Dog 01, another O-2 FAC, assumed OSC. Sandy 05, Capt. George Throckmorton, and Sandy 06, 1st Lt. Randy Scott, launched from Bien Hoa with two HH-3s, Jolly 35 and 36. The survivor's location was covered with low clouds and precluded jet air strikes, but the area was reportedly benign. Arriving in the area, Sandy 05 took over as on-scene commander (OSC) and was able to work down through the weather to the survivor's area. He brought in Jolly 35 for a pickup, but low clouds and high trees prevented it. Sandy 05 then had the survivor move down the hill into a clearer area. Sandy 05 was low on fuel and passed OSC to Sandy 06 so that he could return to Bien Hoa for fuel. However, the weather still precluded any pickup, and an hour later Sandy 06 also headed back to base for fuel.

When Sandys 05 and 06 were refueled, they returned to the survivor's site and joined Jollys 43 and 23 for another attempt. The clouds had broken up a bit, and they were then able to work down through the weather and vector the Jollys to Chico 64. Jolly 43 made the pickup, and its pararescue jumper (PJ) treated Dunn's broken jaw as they returned him to Tan Son Nhut.[12]

On 27 June, the Twenty-First TASS lost another O-2 when Sun Dog 42, Capt. Dave Baker, was shot down near Phum Prasol, in the "Parrott's Beak" region of Cambodia. He was captured before any rescue forces could respond, although a ground team did eventually make it to the wreckage. He was returned to US control in February 1973, the only US POW released from Cambodia.[13]

MR-2

As June began, the stout efforts of the ARVN Twenty-Second and Twenty-Third Divisions and the steady support of US airpower (including 699 B-52 strikes through 31 May) had broken the NVA attack against Kontum, and the NVA forces were pulling back to lick their wounds and reconstitute their units. Supporting FACs, including the Pave Nail OV-10s, and US Army aviation units continued to provide overwatch and attacked the enemy forces wherever they were found. But those forces were still very dangerous.[14]

During this period, fighting had also been going on further east in MR-2. In early June, the NVA Third Division attacked LZ Chrystal near the village of Phu My, approximately sixty miles east Kontum and about ten miles inland from the coast. The area was defended by elements of the ARVN Forty-First Regiment, which was supported by a US Army advisory team and aviation units in the area. On 5 June, an aviation team of OH-6s, UH-1s, and AH-1s from H Troop, H Troop, Tenth (H/10) Cavalry flew in direct support of the regiment. As they scouted for enemy elements in the area, 1st Lt. Frank Beall, flying one of the OH-6s, spotted several NVA soldiers and called for the supporting AH-1s to strafe them. An NVA soldier then launched an SA-7 missile at the helicopter. Beall spotted the missile and tried to take evasive action. However, the missile guided to the helicopter's engine exhaust, and the ensuing explosion blew off the tail rotor of the machine and it crashed.

The gunner, Sp5 Doug Hansen, was unhurt and was able to recover his M-60 and ammunition. However, Beall was unresponsive, and Hansen thought that he was dead. He moved to a tree line and began to fire on enemy soldiers swarming toward him. Then he noticed that Beall was alive and struggling to get out of the wreckage. Hansen helped him to get out and then took him back to the tree line, where Beall used his survival radio to contact the helicopters above for recovery.

As the AH-1s covered the survivors, they moved toward an open rice paddy to facilitate their recovery. A UH-1 from the H/10 Cavalry flown by Capt. Zane Brown and crew landed in the paddy, and the two survivors jumped on as the Cobras strafed overhead.

However, as Captain Brown lifted off with the two soldiers, his aircraft was hit by enemy fire from several quarters and crashed just one hundred meters from the still burning OH-6. The six stunned soldiers then formed a defensive position and fought off the enemy soldiers as Captain Brown used his survival radio to talk to the aircraft above and an USAF FAC, who then brought in a force of eleven army helicopters and two flights of fighters to protect the survivors.

Another UH-1, flown by Maj. Alan Jones from the 129th Assault Helicopter Company (AHC), diverted to join the recovery effort. As the strike aircraft swarmed above and smashed the enemy forces, he made three attempts to land before successfully touching down in the paddy. He carefully ensured that all six soldiers were onboard before successfully taking off and flying to the US Army Evacuation Hospital at Qui Nhon. A subsequent sweep of the area by ARVN forces discovered 150 NVA killed in action (KIA) and numerous weapons captured, including an expended SA-7 launcher.[15]

On 9 June, John Paul Vann, the civilian senior advisor to the ARVN in MR-2, mounted his personal OH-58 to fly up to Kontum, something that he had done every day since the intense fighting around the city had commenced on 14 May. Vann's personal call sign was Rogue's Gallery. He took off with a pilot, 1st Lt. Ronald Doughtie, and one passenger. It was a dark, cloudy night. Vann liked to fly the aircraft, but it is unclear who was flying that night. En route to Kontum, the helicopter collided with a tall stand of trees as they tried to clear the pass just south of the city, near Fire Base 41, an ARVN outpost. When the crash occurred, the word quickly spread that Rogue's Gallery was down, and aircraft swarmed into the area. Nail 76, Capt. Harrold Ownby, was working in the area and responded. He contacted King and tried to initiate a SAR. However, the chaotic scene with helicopters scampering about in the dark cloudy night precluded any good that he could contribute to the debacle. The next morning, ARVN soldiers reached the site and stole personal items from the three dead Americans. American forces arrived a little later and recovered the bodies.[16]

On 15 June, another dramatic event occurred that required the services of American recovery forces. Cathay Pacific Flight 700Z, a Convair 880, flying from Bangkok to Hong Kong, was destroyed when a bomb exploded in the passenger compartment as the aircraft was cruising at twenty-nine thousand feet above Pleiku. Many flight crews in the area observed the falling wreckage and initially assumed that it was a midair collision. Covey 53, an O-2 FAC, assumed OSC, but there were no signs of survivors. Regardless, US Army aviation units swarmed to the site. Wreckage and eighty-one bodies were strewn across a large area. Ground forces quickly established a security perimeter. Nobody survived the event.[17]

Ten days later, King 25 monitored a call that a US Army CH-47, Eagle 34, had gone down north of An Khe, South Vietnam. As King 25 was beginning to coordinate a recovery operation, another US Army helicopter, Bulldog 11, diverted to the area. When he determined that the area was relatively quiet, he landed, recovered all seven personnel, and transported them to Phu Cat Air Base. These types of operations occurred on an almost daily basis.[18]

MR-1

In the northern areas of South Vietnam, ARVN and Vietnamese Marine units, under the command of Lieutenant General Truong, continued to improve their positons, especially facing the A Shau Valley, and build up their strength for offensive operations toward Quang Tri, to reclaim some of the territory lost to the invading NVA forces. United States airpower of all forms was very active in the area. FACs continuously conducted visual reconnaissance to locate and attack NVA forces and directly provided close air support. United States Army units such as F Troop, Fourth and F Troop, Eighth (F/4 and F/8) Cavalry were also still providing direct support, although their units were also being withdrawn. North Vietnamese Army forces were especially active in the A Shau Valley. It was a major conduit for their forces from the Ho Chi Minh trail in Laos, and FACs and USAF AC-130 gunships from Thailand patrolled this area constantly and attacked enemy forces wherever and whenever they were detected. But those forces were well defended by massed AAA and the deadly SA-7 missile.

On 11 June early afternoon, Queen was notified that Blueghost White, an OH-6 from F/8 Cavalry, had gone down twenty miles west of Hue with three soldiers onboard while searching for enemy forces in that area. A Covey FAC was overhead and lending assistance. Teams of OH-6s and AH-1s from F/8 Cavalry and the F/4 Cavalry made several attempts to recover the soldiers as Covey and Nail FACs assisted with supporting air strikes.

However, by late afternoon, growing thunderstorms prevented any further attempts that day. Efforts by the troops of F/8 Cavalry and F/4 Cavalry continued the next morning. While making another recovery attempt, Blueghost 10, another OH-6, was shot down in the same area. Covey 116 was assisting, and he called King for Sandys and Jollys. Sandy 07, 1st Lt. Byron Hukee, and Sandy 08, Capt. Gene Bardal, launched with Jolly Greens 65 and 21. The Jollys held just east of the survivor, as the Sandys went directly to the recovery site and checked in with Covey 116. He showed them the location of the survivor(s)—he was not sure of how many he had because he did not have radio contact with them, but he was seeing mirror flashes near the crashed helicopter. He also pointed out several known enemy positions and then headed to Da Nang as Covey 15 replaced him.

Hukee spotted mirror flashes near the wreckage. They trolled the area to determine enemy activity and then used smoke bombs and CBU to lay down smoke screens to protect the Jolly. When all was ready, Hukee observed a mirror flash and assumed that it was the survivor. The Sandys then led Jolly 65 in for the pickup and orbited around the helicopter as its crew dashed in to recover one survivor, who reported that the other soldier had been killed.[19]

On 15 June, a Vietnamese Air Force (VNAF) UH-1, Eagle 02, was shot down west of Hue, on the edge of the A Shau Valley, with three Vietnamese soldiers aboard. King 25 heard their emergency call and took over as the OSC. The crash was in an area of high trees, and the VNAF requested USAF rescue support. Sandys 07, 1st Lt. Dave Blevins, and 08, 1st Lt. Joe Seitz, took off from Da Nang with Jollys 64 and 21. Jolly 64, flown by Maj. Jackson Scott and crew, was able to recover one survivor. Jolly 65 replaced Jolly 21 and deployed its PJs at the site. They reported that the other soldiers were all dead.[20]

While the Da Nang rescue forces were busy working with Eagle 02, the Fortieth ARRSq HH-53s at NKP were supporting US forces in Thailand. Knife 924, a CH-53 from the Twenty-First SOS at NKP, had made an emergency landing just west of the Mekong River in Thailand on a classified mission. All personnel were recovered and returned to their base. The aircraft was subsequently picked up and returned to NKP, where it was repaired and returned to duty. The aircraft, CH-53C #68–10924, continued to perform special forces duty with the USAF, and it flew its retirement mission in combat in Iraq on 27 September 2008.[21]

USAF Rescue Reorganization

On 17 June, as part of the continuing drawdown of American forces in South Vietnam, the Third Aerospace Rescue and Recovery Group (ARRG), acting upon the recommendations of Col. Jack Robinson at the Fifty-Sixth Special Operations Wing (SOW), inactivated OL-A (Queen, the RCC at Son Tra, South Vietnam) and OL-B (Jack, the RCC at Udorn). Jack would transfer to NKP and become a co-OL with the Fortieth ARRSq and retain the call sign Jack. Now, the JRCC at Tan Son Nhut would handle all SARs in South Vietnam and Cambodia, and Jack would handle all SARs in Laos and North Vietnam. Additionally, as Colonel Robinson had also envisioned, Jack would be colocated with several key rescue components, the intelligence capabilities at Task Force Alpha, the Jolly Green crews of the Fortieth ARRSq, the Sandy pilots of the First SOS, and the FACs of the Twenty-Third TASS, who were becoming ever more involved in SARs, especially with their Pave Nail OV-10s. Such colocation created its own form of synergy, as the young officers who were flying the missions got to know, understand, and appreciate each other.[22]

On the night of 18 June, an AC-130 from the Eighth TFW, Ubon Air Base, Spectre 11, was hit by an SA-7 over the A Shau Valley in South Vietnam. The missile hit the number-three engine, causing extensive damage. The aircraft commander, Capt. Paul Gilbert, turned the aircraft to the east as the crew fought to keep the aircraft functioning, However, with increasing system failures, Gilbert then gave the order to bail out—just before the aircraft exploded and fell to the ground in a fiery crash. Some of the crew were able to bail out, and later that night, radio contact was made with Spectre 11Delta, Golf, and Papa. Through the night, Nail and Covey FACs orbited overhead to maintain contact with the survivors as planners at the JRCC and Jack ordered up strike flights with bombs and CBU. They also planned for a first-light effort, with four Sandys each from NKP and Da Nang and four Jolly Greens from Da Nang.

Sandys 07, 1st Lt. Dave Blevins, and 08, 1st Lt. Joe Seitz, with Sandys 05, Maj. Don Milner, and 06, Capt. Lee Mazzarella, were airborne from Da Nang at first light with Jolly Greens 72 and 64. Nail 19, Capt. Gary Haile, was on scene and had located all three survivors. He continued to put in air strikes in the area as Sandy 07 assumed OSC. When he determined that a recovery was possible, he ordered Jolly 72, flown by Capt. Don Sutton and crew, to proceed. They then swept in as the Sandys protected them, recovered all three survivors, and returned to Da Nang. Aircraft maintained a visual and listening watch for the next several days for any more survivors of Spectre 11, but none appeared. After the war, the remains of the lost crewmembers were recovered, and on 17 November 1994, a group burial of the comingled remains of the AC-130A Spectre gunship crew was held at Arlington National Cemetery.[23]

On 20 June, a US Navy F-8J, Nickel 102, from the USS *Hancock*, was shot down on the north end of the A Shau Valley by 57mm AAA as part of a strike package destroying supplies and vehicles in that area. The pilot, Cdr. James Davis, ejected. Covey 111 responded, made contact with Davis, and reported his position. Nail 18, 1st Lt. Dale Holmund and 1st Lt. Vic Gedris, a Pave Nail OV-10 FAC, also responded and determined the survivor's location with loran coordinates. Sandy 07, Capt. Larry Highfill, and 08, 1st Lt. Tim Brady, launched from Da Nang with Jolly Green 71 and 72. However, Jolly 72 developed engine problems and was replaced by Jolly 64, who joined Jolly 71 in a holding pattern over Hue.

Sandy 01, Capt. Jim "Red" Clevenger, and Sandy 02, 1st Lt. Tex Brown, also launched from NKP. Arriving at the survivor's location, Sandy 07, as the OSC, directed them to join with the Jollys for a recovery attempt. They did so, but as they approached the survivor, the AAA was very heavy. Jolly 71 reported that their aircraft had been hit several times and the flight engineer had been wounded. They aborted the attempt and returned to Da Nang.

Jolly 21 launched from Da Nang and joined the group. Jollys 64 and 21 were then led in by the Sandys. However, again the AAA was heavy, and when Jolly 21 reported that they had been hit several times, this attempt was also aborted and the two Jollys returned to Da Nang. The Sandys continued to direct air strikes against the enemy forces. A few minutes later, Sandy 07 was hit and mortally damaged, and Captain Highfill ejected about five miles south of Nickel 102. The remaining Sandys made radio contact with him and plotted his location. Sandys 03, Captain Clevenger, and 04, First Lieutenant Brown, also launched from NKP and joined the effort. Jolly Greens 30 and 73 arrived from NKP. Jolly 30 was equipped with an ELF and was receiving very accurate guidance from Sandy 07's survival radio. However, again the AAA was heavy, and with darkness rapidly approaching, the helicopters aborted. Sandys 09 and 10 also launched from NKP and replaced Sandys 03 and 04. However, the Third ARRG commander, Col. Cy Muirhead, had been closely monitoring the SAR, and he ordered all recovery attempts to be terminated for that day. As darkness arrived, FACs maintained cover over both airmen and put in more air strikes on NVA forces as all SAR forces returned to Da Nang and began planning another attempt the next morning.

That night, the Sandys and Jollys developed their plans to recover both men and requested support from the fighter wings and aircraft carriers. HH-53s from the Fortieth ARRSq, Jolly Greens 62, flown by Capt. Bennie Orrell and crew, and 57, flown by Maj. Leo Thacker and crew, were ordered to deploy to Da Nang to support the effort, with two more helicopters to follow.

The next morning, as Nails 28 and 19 worked above the two survivors, the two Fortieth ARRSq helicopters and two Thirty-Seventh ARRSq helicopters, Jolly 72 flown by Maj. Chris Korper and crew, and Jolly 64, flown by Capt. Gary Dake and crew, lifted off from Da Nang to recover Nickel 102 and Sandy 07, respectively. Both flights of Jollys held along the coast east of Hue. Sandys 11, 1st Lt. Byron Hukee, and 12, 1st Lt. Tim Brady, also took off and proceeded to Sandy 07's location and assumed OSC. They were followed by Sandys 03, Captain Clevenger, and 04, First Lieutenant Brown, who rendezvoused with Jollys 72 and 64 and led them in for an attempt to pick up Sandy 07. Throughout the night and early morning, FACs had directed strikes against enemy formations and guns, including the use of BLU-52 and smoke screens. Jolly 72 was the low bird, and the crew proceeded in for the pickup as the Sandys orbited above, using smoke rockets and CBU to obscure suspected AAA positions. The Jolly crew was wearing gas masks because of the use of BLU-52, and that complicated communications.

Fortuitously, enemy AAA was negligible. The survivor was on a fairly steep slope but effectively used his smoke and flare to guide the Jolly crew right over him. They dropped the jungle penetrator, but Sandy 07 was slightly injured and affected by the BLU-52, and he had trouble moving through the jungle. One of the PJs went down to assist him. When they were on the penetrator, they were hoisted aboard as Korper turned the helicopter for an expeditious departure.

Clevenger and Brown then flew to Nickel 102's position, where they assumed OSC from the FACs who were putting in air strikes and directing fighters to lay down smoke screens. The A-1s flown by Hukee and Brady joined with Jollys 62 and 57. They were accompanied by Nail 59, a Pave Nail OV-10 that was providing precision navigation support. He led them all to Nickel 102. The survivor was not talking on the radio but was giving mirror flashes. As the helicopter approached, he fired a pen gun flare, revealing his exact position. He was in a steep ravine, and the helicopter had to "swing" the penetrator over to him. He grabbed it and strapped on as the Sandys orbited above, alert for any enemy action. The Jolly flight engineer then hoisted him in, and Orrell turned the helicopter for an uneventful departure.

Two more Jollys from the Fortieth ARRSq had joined the effort and were holding at 14,000 feet about three miles inland. Captain Dale Stovall was the aircraft commander on the fourth Jolly when he heard a call: "This is Teaball, on guard! SAM! SAM! Vicinity of . . ." The location was blocked by the aft PJ's simultaneous call: "Missile 6 o'clock!" "What the hell," Stovall thought. "An SA-2 in South Vietnam?!" He started to roll the lumbering helicopter into an evasive "split S" and was at 120 degrees of bank when his copilot, Mel Gillespie, yelled, "Strella [SA-7]! Fire your IR [infrared decoy flares]!" Stovall immediately rolled level. The Jolly crews fired the flare pistols mounted on the door and window frames, and the aft-ramp PJ threw out some thermite grenades. The helicopter was at 12,500 feet when the crew saw the SA-7 flame out and fall back to the earth. Regardless, the helicopters immediately flew out over the ocean. Stovall never could figure out if the flares had actually saved them. But he and the Fortieth ARRSq crews were now fully aware of the reality of the SA-7 threat in South Vietnam.

It was a tough and challenging two-day SAR. But because of the stalwart actions of the Jollys, Sandys, FACs, and strike flights, both men were rescued in a ninety-minute period.[24]

While working a night mission southwest of Hue on 26 June, Covey 27, Capt. C. Houston, an O-2 FAC from the Twentieth TASS, was shot down. A Pave Nail OV-10 from the Twenty-Third TASS, Nail 55, Capt. Mike Gaines and Maj. Quin Waterman, diverted to serve as the on-scene commander. Using their Pave Spot system, they were able to spot the survivor's strobe light and plot his location. The next morning, Sandys 07, Capt. Bob Herklotz, and 08, Capt. Bob Simica, took off from Da Nang. They orbited overhead as a US Army helicopter from F/4 Cavalry recovered the survivor and flew him to Camp Evans, where Jolly Green 65 picked him up and took him to Da Nang.[25]

On 28 June, Lieutenant General Truong initiated offensive actions to recapture Quang Tri, and the level of combat dramatically increased all along the line of contact with the NVA forces. The next day, Capt. Steve Bennett, Covey 87 from the Twentieth TASS, launched in his OV-10 to provide FAC support to ARVN forces north of Hue. In his back seat he had Capt. Mike Brown, USMC, who had authority to direct naval gunfire from the ships off shore. Bennett was contacted by one of the ARVN ground commanders, who was worried that an NVA force was massing on his front and about to launch an attack. Bennett requested any available air strikes, but the Direct Air Support Center (DASC) responded that none were immediately available. The OV-10s of the Twentieth and Twenty-Third TASSes were equipped with M-60 machine guns, and in emergency situations, the FACs were authorized to use them to strafe. Captain Darrel Whitcomb, Nail 70 from the Twenty-Third TASS, had just completed a mission in the Dong Ha area and was heading back to Da Nang when he heard Bennett's call for support. Whitcomb contacted him and offered to strafe if Bennett thought that it would help the ARVN forces. Bennett directed Whitcomb to rendezvous with him over the threatened ARVN unit. As they joined, Bennett pointed out the positions of the friendly and enemy units and directed that they would strafe with run-ins from the west to east, and Bennett would pull off to the south and Whitcomb off to the north to deconflict.

However, as Bennett pulled up from his strafe pass, he announced that he would pull off to the north and Whitcomb could pull off to the south. As Whitcomb strafed and then started his climbing right turn, he looked to the north and saw a large explosion. He remembered that in the morning intelligence briefing, the pilots had been told that the NVA gunners had brought in 100mm antiaircraft guns and that the large shells produced large and distinctive airbursts. He called Bennett and told him to watch out for the heavy guns. Bennett replied that his aircraft had been hit by an SA-7 and he was heading out over the water. Whitcomb then spotted his smoking aircraft and maneuvered to join with him on his left wing. Whitcomb also contacted King on Guard frequency and informed him that Covey 87 had been hit and was heading "feet wet." One of the SAR controllers on King acknowledged the call and notified the rescue forces at Da Nang. Jolly Greens 64 and 65 were launched.

Joining on Bennett's left wing, Whitcomb could see that his OV-10 was severely damaged. The left propeller was feathered, and the left engine was missing. The left landing gear was hanging down, and there were shrapnel holes along the left side of the aircraft. As the formation reached the shoreline, Bennett announced that he and Brown would be ejecting. Almost immediately, he stated that Brown's parachute, which was mounted in his ejection seat, had been damaged by the missile blast, and he was going to crash-land on the beach like Covey 299 in mid-April. Whitcomb could see the US Army airfield at Hue–Phu Bai about twenty miles away and instructed him to land there. Then, somebody said on the radio, "You had better ditch it, Covey!" The flying manual for the OV-10 clearly stated that the OV-10 could not be safely ditched, and Whitcomb started to call Bennett to remind him of that warning when King called and asked for an update on Covey 87's status. Distracted, Whitcomb failed to notice that Covey 87 then rapidly descended and ditched his OV-10 in the water about four hundred yards off the shore. When he saw the aircraft splash, Whitcomb notified King that Covey 87 was down and stated their location. Another OV-10, flown by Nail 64, 1st Lt. Bob Temko, had also joined them. He spotted Vietnamese along the shore who were launching a boat to proceed to the crash site. Whitcomb asked King for a determination of the local populace as friendly or enemy. By now, several flights of fighters had begun to orbit over the crash site and were immediately available if air strikes were necessary. King quickly responded that the local populace was friendly. Regardless, as the Vietnamese began to launch their boat, Temko and Whitcomb each laid down a line of strafe two hundred yards off shore. The Vietnamese desisted and acknowledged with a wave.

After hitting the water, Bennett's OV-10 quickly sank. Whitcomb could see one survivor. Then he heard a radio call from Wolfman 45, Captain Brown, stating that he was okay. A few minutes later, Greenbug, a USMC CH-46, launched off one of the US Navy ships offshore and recovered Brown. The alert A-1s from Da Nang arrived and took over. Whitcomb and Temko proceeded to Da Nang and were told that apparently Bennett had been killed when the OV-10 hit the water. The next morning, a US Navy dive team recovered his body. Two years later, Capt. Steven Bennett was awarded the Medal of Honor for his actions that led to the rescue of Capt. Mike Brown.[26]

On 30 June, another OV-10 FAC, Nail 37, 1st Lt. Ernie Steincamp, was working with South Vietnamese ground forces south of Quang Tri who had declared a tactical emergency because of a heavy NVA attack. He attempted to put in air strikes but was having difficulties doing so because of a low cloud deck. He made a pass down through the clouds to clearly determine the friendly and enemy force locations, and his aircraft was hit in the left engine by an SA-7, mortally damaging the machine. He made a quick emergency call and then ejected. Another FAC, Covey 110, diverted to his location to become the OSC and quickly made contact with Steincamp. Above, King 26 alerted the recovery forces at Da Nang. Friendly ground forces were only three hundred meters away. However, NVA forces were closer and closing in on the pilot as he evaded and found an area of heavy scrub brush in which he could hide. He could hear the enemy troops as they searched for him.

Sandys and Jollys launched from Da Nang. However, rescue forces were closer at hand. Captain James Elder, US Army, the executive officer of F/4 Cavalry, also monitored Steincamp's emergency calls at their airfield at Tan My, about six miles northeast of Hue. His unit routinely used its helicopter teams, consisting of an OH-6, UH-1s with three infantrymen aboard each aircraft, and AH-1s, for this contingency. Additionally, his crews had solid tactical knowledge of this area and the friendly and enemy forces involved. He grabbed Warrant Officer William "Pappy" Jones, one of the most experienced pilots in the squadron, and yelled, "Let's go." Quickly joined by two door gunners and a crew chief, they headed out to their aircraft, a brand new UH-1H with less than two hundred flight hours. This aircraft had been modified "just a bit" for its missions. Remembered Pappy Jones: "We changed the armaments a little, adding a 50 cal [machine gun] mounted on the left that would make your nose bleed . . . and trip[le] 60s [M-60 machine guns] on the right."[27]

But even they were not the quickest to respond. Captain Pete Barber, Centaur 25, the commander of the UH-1 platoon in F/4 Cavalry, had just returned from a flight down to the Marble Mountain airfield near Da Nang to have his helicopter modified with a new infrared kit as protection against the SA-7s. He monitored the calls about Nail 37, and instead of shutting down, he and his crew took off and headed up along the coast to find Steincamp.[28]

As Barber and his crew lifted off, Captain Elder and his crew were scrambling to follow. They were joined at the aircraft by the unit first sergeant and three infantrymen. Their call sign was Centaur 06.

They took off and joined Capt. Peter Barber and crew, who were already in contact with Steincamp and getting vectors from him as they flew nap-of-the-earth. As the two helicopters flew in, they could see NVA troops, some wearing new uniforms, and almost all of them shooting at the machines. They also counted at least eight *observed* SA-7 launches, none of which guided on the very low flying helicopters. The sky was overcast and the sun was setting over the mountains. Two AH-1s had also taken off to provide support but were driven off by the NVA guns and SA-7s in the area. The two UH-1s were on their own.

Arriving near Steincamp's location, both crews began a frantic search for him—about three feet off the ground. The survivor broke from the bushes and ran toward the nearest helicopter, which was Centaur 06, and Jones brought his aircraft to a hover. However, Steincamp's right leg was hurt and he could not move too quickly, especially when he got stuck on some old barbed wire. The first sergeant jumped out to assist, ripped him out of the barber wire, and literally threw Steincamp into the helicopter as the gunners engaged enemy soldiers on all sides. Above, Barber and his crew were laying down all of the suppressive fire that they could generate.

Capt. Pete Barber and an SA-2 booster. (Courtesy Pete Barber)

With the survivor and sergeant onboard, Jones then took off, and Barber followed. They initially headed north. Steincamp directed them to turn east just as Centaur 06 was hit by several rounds of 12.7mm fire, which ripped through the helicopter from nose to tail and severely wounded the first sergeant, who had been impaled in the belly by a piece of a door handle shattered by one of the 12.7mm bullets. However, the machine was still flying, and Jones headed out to the east as one of the Sandys rolled in over the two helicopters and bombed the NVA forces shooting at them.

As Centaurs 06 and 25 climbed to altitude, they intended to fly to Tan My and transfer the wounded to one of the Jolly Greens. However, they received a call on the Guard frequency from somebody with the call sign of Gallant Man, who offered immediate medical services if needed, with instructions to proceed to the east. It was the command center from the USS *Okinawa*, twelve miles off the coast. The ship's crew had been monitoring the rescue mission and onboard had a surgical team standing by. Jones was confused by the call and asked, "Are you a boat?" When they replied affirmatively, he was not sure that he could find it without any functioning navigational gear. Fortunately, Jolly Green 64 was following the UH-1 and directed him to the ship, where they received medical attention for the wounded soldier and Steincamp. And when firmly aboard the deck, they discovered that their "brand new" helicopter had collected eighty-four bullet holes for their heroic effort.[29]

Captain Pete Barber and his crew flew back to Tan My. They discovered that they had not received a single hit in the melee. Barber attributed that to his superior flying skills. He was also really impressed with the new infrared diffusers.

After they had recovered a downed crew, as the UH-1 platoon commander, Barber had gotten unit approval for his pilots to wear a shoulder patch that said "Hunter/Killer/Retriever." It was not long after arriving in MR-1 that all members of F/4 Cavalry were wearing the patch. Remembered Barber, "We were a busy group in '72."[30]

As the battle continued, the FACs were the fingers of the long arm of US airpower. That force, combined with the increasingly effective South Vietnamese armed forces, had by the end of June staunched the NVA offensive on all fronts. Estimates indicated that the NVA had suffered 50 percent attrition of their initial two-hundred-thousand-man invading force, with an estimated forty thousand killed. Additionally, most of their tanks and fully 50 percent of their artillery pieces were destroyed. And the wreckage of their failed offensive was there for all to see.[31]

Linebacker Operations

United States aerial forces were now routinely operating over North Vietnam on a daily basis, with a major strike package striking targets in the Hanoi region every day.

On 7 June, a US Navy RA-5, Commanche Trail 601, from the USS *Saratoga*, flown by Lt. Cdr. C. Smith and Lt. L. Kunz, was tasked to make a high-speed photo run among the islands off Haiphong. When it popped up to three thousand feet to get the pictures, it was engaged by an SA-2 missile battery. When Smith realized that his aircraft was targeted, he began evasive maneuvers. His efforts were in vain, and a missile slammed into the left side of the aircraft, destroying the port engine. Smith then headed southeast and made it five miles out into the Gulf of Tonkin, where he and Kunz ejected. As other navy aircraft orbited over their locations, Big Mother 66, flown by Lt. Craig Peterson and crew, launched from the USS *Long Beach*, and Big Mother 67, flown by Lt. James Kelly and crew, launched from the USS *Duluth*. Arriving in the rescue area, support aircraft suppressed the North Vietnamese guns and small boats as Big Mother 66 picked up Kunz and Big Mother 67 picked up Smith. This was one of the northernmost rescues in the conflict.[32]

On 8 June, a USAF QU-22, Vampire 21, suffered a mechanical failure on its orbit in west central Laos, and the pilot bailed out. The orbiting King HC-130 in that region heard his emergency call and contacted NKP to dispatch a recovery helicopter. A Laredo Fast FAC diverted to serve as the OSC. Jolly Green 56 took off and recovered the pilot an hour after he bailed out. The QU-22s were experiencing a very high rate of increasingly serious mechanical problems.[33]

An hour later, about 120 miles to the east, a USAF F-4, Seafox 06, based at Korat RTAFB, Thailand, was flying on a Fast FAC mission in the southern part of North Vietnam when it was hit and downed by AAA near Fingers Lake north of the DMZ. Both men, Capt. John Murphy, and 1st Lt. Lawrence Johnston, ejected. Murphy was the senior experienced pilot in the Seafox Fast FACs and was giving Johnston an orientation ride because he had just joined the program. While descending under canopy, Murphy heard lots of fire directed at him. He landed just inland from the beach and shed his parachute and harness. Initially, he headed for the water, but then realized that such a move would be suicidal. Instead, he ran to the west and found minimal coverage by a small tree. As he tried to take out his survival radio, he was captured by a group of NVA soldiers and taken into a bunker.

Johnston was a little luckier. He was in the back seat and ejected first at a higher altitude. Even though he had problems getting his parachute to deploy, once it was fully blossomed, he was able make a few radio calls and then drift/steer out over the water as the NVA gunners blazed away at him. He landed about six hundred yards offshore, and when enemy rounds started landing in the water around him, he did his best to move further out into the GOT.

Another Fast FAC, Musket 06, witnessed the ejections and maintained radio contact with Johnston. When Johnston spotted and reported an enemy boat leaving the shore to recover him, he called it out to the guys above and a second Fast FAC, Laredo 14, destroyed it with a lethal strafe pass. Remembered Johnston, "It was the most beautiful strafe pass that I had ever seen."[34]

Covey 299, an OV-10 FAC then took over as the OSC. He was assisted by Nail 73, a Pave Nail OV-10 flown by Capt. John McNabb and 1st Lt. Bob Jahns, which used their Pave Spot system to pinpoint the survivor locations and attack several gun sites with laser guided bombs (LGBs). When Sandys 07, 1st Lt. Lamar Smith, and 08, Capt. Lance Shotwell, arrived, they took over as the OSC and began to execute the SAR, requesting fighters to drop CBU-42 and BLU-52 around Murphy's estimated position.

Greenbug, a USMC CH-46, sitting alert aboard the USS *Joseph Strauss*, one of the offshore US Navy ships, launched and rendezvoused with the A-1s, successfully picked up Johnston, and delivered him to the USS *Tripoli*. Covey 299 and the Sandys continued to search for Murphy. His parachute and harness were about seventy yards inland, near some bunkers, and they requested that a team be inserted from the sea to find and recover the pilot. However, without any visual or electronic indications that Murphy was alive and loose, this request was denied, but the JPRC was monitoring the situation and began initial planning for an over-the-beach effort. Additionally, Queen made plans for a first-light recovery effort, and a Navy SEAL team was alerted to possibly support the effort. A visual and listening watch was maintained until 11 June and then suspended.[35]

There was a poignant substory to this event. Wrote John Murphy years later:

> I was in the front seat, my last scheduled Fast FAC mission. [Johnston] was in the back seat, his first Fast FAC mission. We were to make a couple of passes through RP-1, maybe a small amount of time in Laos and RTB. I was just pointing out a few landmarks. [We had] a big party planned for the evening. I was to return to the squadron and fly missions intent on killing MiGs. I had flown my first MiGCAP the day before, just east of Hanoi. And, prior to those flights, I was to go on R&R and meet my wife in Hawaii, on the 9th. In fact, I had an opportunity to fly out on the 8th, but we had made our plans, briefed and flew the scheduled mission.
>
> . . . My wife picked up the kids at school and drove to an American Airlines office in Lubbock to pick up the tickets. It was not long after getting home that the blue staff car pulled up and the blue suits were at the door. The next day she returned the tickets to American and they re-funded 100%.[36]

Such are the vagaries of war. Murphy had been shot down in Laos in early February, and he and his WSO had been recovered by a SAR task force. Twice was not a charm. After his capture, Murphy was held in southern North Vietnam for three months and then moved to Hanoi. He was released in 1973.[37]

Johnston also had a story to tell about his rescue. He remembered:

Unbelievably, despite the bad guys opening-up on us again, the Green Bug pulled to a hover above me . . . obviously the chopper pilots were packing Big Ones! The [rescue swimmer] was incredible, and snatched me from the water as bullets flew by the chopper.

Once on board, and after the Medic finished with me, I sat next to the [rescue swimmer] to thank him for saving my life. He was very stoically professional and said, "It's my job, Lieutenant." The Medic had told me the [swimmer] was also from Oklahoma . . . so I asked him where exactly he was raised. He responded that he was from a very small town that I'd probably never heard of . . . "Choctaw." "Dude," I said, "I went to Choctaw High School!" He then spun around, looked at my bandaged head and out-of-limits mustache and exclaimed, "Holy Shit, you're Lawrence Johnston, you're Keith's older brother!" When he pulled up the visor on his helmet I shouted, "Billy Thompson!!!" Billy, my brother and my wife were in the Class of '67, two years behind mine. We then compared other names and stories about Choctaw . . . a truly small town east of Oklahoma City. We both marveled at the improbability that two small-town-hicks in different Services would meet again like this![38]

There is more to Johnston's story. He later allowed that as the helicopter came to a hover over him, Thompson started to mount the hoist to ride down and get him but changed his mind when he saw tracers flying by the helicopter. Instead, he wisely and quickly determined that Johnston was well enough to ride up by himself. The helicopter egress was uneventful.

After arriving aboard the USS *Tripoli*, Johnston was examined by a flight surgeon. He later recalled that experience:

The Flight Surgeon, employing perfect bedside manner, asked me where I was from. I mumbled that I was from Oklahoma . . . and he responded, "I'll be damned, so am I." He asked where I'd gone to college, whereupon I said Oklahoma State, "Really, so did I!" I then looked at him and his no-nametag-smock and said, "Holy shit, you're Bill McDaniels . . . you wrestled 167-weight on the OSU Varsity!" When he said, "This is impossible that you just called my name here in the Gulf of Tonkin." I said, "Bill, that's nothing . . . you should have been on that helicopter with me about an hour ago!" . . . Who says there's no such thing as fate, or magic, or miracles in the Profession of Arms![39]

On 16 June, a US Navy RF-8, Baby Giant 601, from the USS *Midway*, was crippled by AAA as it attempted to take pictures of the Thanh Hoa

Bridge, which had recently been attacked by F-4s from the Eighth TFW, who dropped LGBs and destroyed a whole section of the structure. Fortunately, the aircraft was still flyable, and the pilot, Lt. Paul Ringwood, was able to get about ten miles out to sea before he ejected. Big Mother 61, flown by Lt. James Kelly and crew, was in the area performing one of the still ongoing sweep missions for Op Thunderhead and immediately volunteered to do the pickup. As support aircraft orbited above to dissuade MiGs and North Vietnamese boats, they entered the survivor's area, recovered him, and returned him to the USS *Midway*.[40]

The next day, TF-77 lost another aircraft when an A-7, Jury 304, off the USS *Kitty Hawk*, was hit and severely damaged by an SA-2 while bombing a rail yard near Thanh Hoa. The pilot, Cdr. Darrel Owens, was able to exit North Vietnam and make it back to the environs of the USS *Saratoga* before his hydraulic system failed and he had to eject. A Big Mother from HC-7 picked him up.[41]

That afternoon, the First SOS at NKP suffered a terrible loss when Maj. Zeke Encinas, flying as Hobo 42, was shot down and killed on a strike mission in southern Laos to support the recovery of a CH-53 from the Twenty-First SOS that had gone down for mechanical reasons and was being repaired in the field. He had been a stalwart member of the squadron and considered one of the best Sandy pilots. His wingman, 1st Lt. Byron Hukee, observed Hobo 42 being struck by 23mm rounds as he made a rocket pass. Encinas did not eject. Raven FACs searched the site. Another flight of Hobos, led by Maj. Jim Harding and Jolly Greens, launched from NKP and orbited over the area until nightfall, but there was nobody to rescue. After three days of unfruitful listening watch, the mission was terminated. An indigenous ground team subsequently searched the site and determined that Major Encinas had been killed in the cockpit. His remains were recovered and returned to friendly control.[42]

On 18 June, a US Navy F-4 from the USS *Kitty Hawk*, Black Lion 107, flown by Lt. Cdr. Roy Cash and Lt. Ron Laib, was conducting MiGCAP for a navy strike on North Vietnamese shipping near Vinh when it was hit and downed by 23mm AAA. The crew headed well out to sea before they had to eject. Big Mothers 60 and 67 scrambled and picked up Cash and Laib, respectively.[43]

In a reminder that the war was still going on in Laos, during the morning hours of 24 June, Jack received notification that a Laotian T-28, Chaophakhao Moon, had gone down east of Paksane. Raven FACs responded and tried to get Air America helicopters in for a pickup. However, they were driven off by NVA AAA. Sandys 01 and 02 and Jolly Greens 53 and 30 took off from NKP to render assistance. However, before they could arrive, voice contact with the survivor was lost, and Air America sources indicated that they could handle the recovery if one was warranted. Sometimes mysterious things happened in Laos.[44]

That afternoon, USAF flights engaged in a major air battle with North Vietnamese MiGs as a strike package bombed the iron and steel plant at Thai Nguyen, thirty-five miles north of Hanoi. In the melee, Loggy 03, an F-4 from the 366th TFW, Da Nang Air Base, flown by Capt. David Grant and Capt. William Beekman, was shot down by a MiG-21. Grant was quickly captured. However, Beekman made voice contact with other F-4s. But he was not far from a major concentration of AAA guns. A Fast FAC, Laredo 17, led Sandys 03 and 04, and Jollys 30 and 62 went in for a quick pickup. However, the NVA defenses were just too heavy, and they drove the helicopters away, wounding personnel on each aircraft. The two helicopters landed at a site in Laos, and Jolly Greens 56 and 73 recovered all personnel. Captain Dale Stovall at the Fortieth ARRSq suggested attempting a recovery with an LNRS helicopter, but Seventh AF would not approve the mission. SAR forces were not able to return to Beekman before he was captured.[45]

In the same battle, Salter 04, an F-4 from the Eighth TFW, Ubon Air Base, was shot down. The pilot, 1st Lt. James McCarty, was killed and the WSO, Capt. Chuck Jackson, ejected but suffered a badly broken arm and spinal injuries and was quickly captured. However, he escaped his captors and was free for a day, but his injuries and the rugged terrain precluded evasion. He was recaptured and taken to Hanoi. He and the two men from Loggy 03 were released in February 1973.[46]

On 27 June, another strike package struck the Bach Mai Airfield, on the south side of Hanoi. The package was being protected by a MiGCAP flight about forty miles to the west. During the strike, MiG-21s attacked the MiGCAP and downed Troy 04, another Udorn-based F-4, about fifty miles west of Hanoi. Other crews observed two parachutes, but the pilot, Capt. John Cerak, and WSO, Capt. Dave Dingee, were quickly captured. However, the USAF flights above did not know that, and a Fast FAC, Laredo 12, flown by Capt. Marty Cavato and Capt. Tony Marshall, was diverted into the area to find the survivors and initiate a SAR for them. Because of the consistent threat of MiGs, Valent, a flight of four F-4s, was diverted from a chaff escort flight and directed to provide MiGCAP for Laredo 12 as he served as the OSC for the two downed F-4 crews.

Valents 03 and 04

At the same time, Sandys 01 and 02 with Jolly 56, flown by Capt. Stan Zielinski and crew, and Jolly 60 were in the northern SAR orbit and headed for Troy 04. However, they turned back when Jolly 60 developed a severe problem with its flight controls. Regardless, Laredo 12 remained in the area to search for the two survivors with Valent flight providing MiGCAP. However, the crew of Laredo 12 were not able to make radio contact with either survivor and turned to return to Udorn. Then Red Crown contacted them and reported that two MiG-21s were twenty-five miles to the west and turning to attack. Valent flight immediately turned toward the MiGs with Laredo 12 in a loose wing position. Cavato described what transpired:

> You can imagine the scenario: GIBs are all heads down in their radars, front seaters looking for the Migs at 12 o'clock and also checking their formation position. As Red Crown called the distances down, 20 miles, 15 miles, etc, I was also checking 12 and then checking the formation, with #4 off my right wing at 3 o'clock high. After a couple of times checking Valent 4, I again looked up at them and [called], "4's on fire." I checked deep six and saw two MiG-21s in a trail formation and called "Valent flight, break right, break right, bandits 6 o'clock!" I saw #3 break right and immediately explode on fire.
>
> I began a climbing right turn toward the trailing MiG and told Tony to go boresight on the radar and punched off our wing tanks. I put the pipper on the MiG, locked on with the radar and reversed my turn to the left as he passed by—about 2000 feet away. Afterwards, I wished I had just ripple fired my 14 Willie Petes—probably would have had a good chance. As he passed me I rolled in trail—I'm sure he didn't see me since I came from so low. I was out of speed by then and he was supersonic. I squeezed the trigger, released and squeezed again to fire an AIM-7, but nothing happened. I watched the MiG make a slow wide left turn towards Hanoi. Then I rolled back right in time to see Valent 4 hit the ground like napalm. I looked around and found Valent 3 in a flat spin, falling like a leaf with a smoke trail going straight up like holding it with a thread. I then counted four parachutes so knew they all got out. . . . We had no missiles and no wing tanks so headed back to Udorn.[47]

Valent 03 was flown by Maj. Robert Miller and 1st Lt. Richard McDow, and Valent 04 was flown by Capt. Lynn Aikman and Capt. Tom Hanton. Both crews were from the 366th TFW, now located at Takhli RTAFB, Thailand.[48]

Sandys 03, 1st Lt. Byron Hukee, and 04, Capt. Lee Mazzarella, had taken off from NKP with Jolly Green 52, flown by Capt. Ben Orrell and crew, and Jolly Green 73, flown by Maj. Leo Thacker and crew. They proceeded north and joined with the guys already working the SARs. En route, Jolly 73 also developed a hydraulic problem. They subsequently joined with Jolly 60 and returned to NKP, while Jollys 52 and 56 headed north to attempt recoveries of the eight USAF airmen now down west of Hanoi.

Sandys 03, Hukee, and 04, Mazzarella, headed for Valents 03 and 04. Hukee could hear the survivors talking to Laredo 16, who had replaced Laredo 12, and proceeded to their general area and began searching for the downed airmen. He could see the burning wreckage of both aircraft and was able to make voice contact with all of the men from Valents 03 and 04. He also noticed that troops on the ground were firing at him. Valent 03Alpha, Major Miller, used his signal mirror, and Hukee had his precise location and called for Jolly 52 to make the pickup. Jolly 52 headed in for the survivor, and inbound, Jolly 56 reported that they were taking hits. The Jolly 52 crew spotted Miller on the side of a steep hill. As they went into a hover over him, enemy soldiers began to fire at the helicopter. Captain Orrell, in his later after-action report, described the crew's actions:

> Just prior to the penetrator reaching the ground, the copilot saw ground fire on a ridgeline at our 8 o'clock position. The #1 gunner put mini-gun fire in that area and suppressed the fire. . . . As the survivor reached [the penetrator], an enemy soldier stepped out with a rifle on the hill 50 feet above him and raised his gun. The Combat Photographer, [T.Sgt. Bobbie Welborn] who was in the door with the engineer . . . grabbed his AR-15 and dropped the man. . . . Another soldier stepped out and the photog shot him also. At that point, the engineer called for me to pull out and we did so with the survivor 10 feet below the aircraft.[49]

Sandy 03 then vectored Jolly 52 to the position of Valent 03Bravo, First Lieutenant McDow. As they moved through the valley, they were shot at by more enemy troops, and the gunners engaged in all quarters. They spotted the survivor's parachute but could not find him. They hovered for five minutes as they and the Sandys frantically searched. But McDow had already been captured. Finally, Captain Orrell departed and had to evade small arms fire and an active 23mm AAA site to escape. As they climbed out with Jolly 56, King 27 picked them up on its onboard radar and rendezvoused with them near the Laotian border. He refueled both aircraft, and they then proceeded directly to NKP.

Sandys 03 and 04 were also low on fuel and had to return to NKP. Before leaving, they were replaced by Sandy 09, 1st Lt. Randy Scott, and Sandy 10, Capt. Lance Shotwell, and showed them the general locations of Valent 04Alpha, Captain Aikman, and Valent 04Bravo, Captain Hanton. Aikman was badly injured including a broken jaw, making it difficult for him to talk on the radio. He landed in a tree and struggled to get himself to the ground. Hanton had landed near a village. He made several calls on his survival radio but got no response. He tried to hide in a bamboo thicket but was quickly captured and beaten by three peasants. The rescue forces did not know his status.[50]

One Brave Pararescue Jumper

More helicopters were dispatched for the rescue. At Udorn, Jolly Green 73 was repaired and relaunched. At NKP, Jolly Green 57, flown by Capt. Dale Stovall and crew, took off for another attempt. They were escorted by Sandy 01, Maj. Jim Harding, and Sandy 02. Both helicopters rendezvoused over Laos and headed for the rescue scene. There, Sandys 09, Scott, and 10, Shotwell, had been able to work with Aikman to get a fairly accurate fix on his location. As the replacement aircraft arrived, Scott decided to attempt to recover Aikman with Jolly 73. While he and Shotwell orbited above the survivor, Sandys 01, Harding, and 02 would escort him in and Jolly 57 would hold about two miles away. In preparation, the Sandys dropped ordnance and smoke bombs on several likely enemy locations in the valley where Aikman was located. When all was set and briefed, Jolly Green 73, still being flown by Major Thacker and crew, made its run-in for the pickup as the Sandys orbited above.

Arriving over Aikman, Major Thacker needed to offset his hover because of the large tree near him. When settled, the lead PJ on his aircraft, Sgt. Chuck McGrath, rode down on the penetrator to render immediately needed first aid to the wounded survivor and get him on the hoist. Just as he touched ground, enemy fire erupted from several directions. The Jolly gunners immediately answered with all of the firepower that they had, while Thacker held the hover. Free of the penetrator, McGrath began to furiously search for Aikman as he could hear enemy fire being directed at him. He found Aikman in dense brush and began dragging him to a clearing for extraction.

Above, the helicopter was taking fire from every quarter. The combat photographer manned one of the guns and was injured by the enemy fire. Rounds were slamming into the machine and beginning to damage vital components: one minigun was knocked out, and critical flight instruments were being fifty-eight-page draft of the agreement and completely reviewed it with the president. The details were daunting. Kissinger planned to fly to Saigon to brief President Thieu on 19 October and then directly to Hanoi for two days to wrap up all loose ends. The agreement would be announced on 26 October and signed on 31 October. As a sign of goodwill, Seventh AF was directed to reduce Linebacker sorties to 150 a day, but in a sign of strength, B-52s would bomb as far north as twenty degrees latitude. At the same time, the NVA was directed by their leaders in Hanoi to seize as much territory in South Vietnam as possible, and they increased the flow of supplies, especially to their forces in MR-1. In response to these brazen actions, some of the sorties not sent into North Vietnam were still generated but used in South Vietnam.[47]

Kissinger met with President Thieu 19–23 October. The discussions did not go well. Thieu completely rejected allowing the NVA to remain in South Vietnam or letting the communists to have any role in the South Vietnamese government. When he finally got a copy of the proposed agreement *in Vietnamese*, he and his staff analyzed it and quickly presented Kissinger with a list of required changes. Kissinger went back to Paris, but the North Vietnamese were in no mood to accept any changes.

In an effort to mollify President Thieu, President Nixon directed that a huge aid package called Enhance Plus, including 619 aircraft, would be shipped to South Vietnam by 1 November. It included the last USAF A-1s. Regardless, President Thieu would not back away from his requirements for changes, and it was obvious to President Nixon and Henry Kissinger that the agreement could not be signed by 31 October.

However, to reassure the North Vietnamese that the United States still desired to sign the agreement, President Nixon on 23 October directed the cessation of all bombing north of twenty degrees latitude. Two days later, the North Vietnamese released to the world press the entire text of the draft agreement. With expectations of peace dramatically heightened, Kissinger held a press conference to explain the need to revise the agreement, but he inexplicably declared that "peace is at hand."[48]

Regardless of what the politicians were doing, the aircrews had missions to fly. Another F-111, Coach 33, flown by Capt. James Hockridge and 1st Lt. Allen Graham, was lost on 16 October. It was scheduled to hit the Dai Loi railroad bridge twenty miles northwest of Hanoi. This was an area heavily defended by multiple SAM and AAA sites, and the aircraft disappeared with no friendly witnesses or contact. Nail FACs from NKP were directed to search along its planned route in Laos, and an RF-4 was sent to search along its route in North Vietnam. Nothing was found, and rescue forces were not dispatched. However, press and photo releases by international agencies did indicate that an F-111 had gone down in the area west of Hanoi at about the time that the aircraft was flight-planned to be there.[49]

On 27 October, another F-4 Fast FAC, Wolf 01, from Ubon, was putting in air strikes on AAA sites north of the DMZ when it was seriously damaged by 57mm fire. The crew of Capt. Robert Jones and Capt. Eldon Bleak flew out over the GOT and headed south, steering east of Tiger Island. Abeam the DMZ, both men ejected. A US Army U-21, Vanguard 917, orbited above them. Jolly 71, flown by USCG Lt. Jack Stice and crew, launched out of Da Nang and were joined by Jolly Green 65, flown by Capt. Dennis Boroczk and crew. Arriving at the SAR site, Jolly 65 picked up the pilot, while Jolly 71 picked up the WSO. Both aircraft deployed a PJ for the recovery. While they were accomplishing the pickups, a US Army CH-47 from the Sixty-Second Aviation Company also responded to the SAR. However, he passed close to Tiger Island and was fired upon and hit by AAA sites on the island. He headed south with wounded crewmembers and an engine on fire. An HH-3A from HC-7 also responded to Wolf 01 and escorted the CH-47 back to his base at Tan My. Like the effort to rescue Bat 21Bravo back in April, this rescue involved personnel from the US Army, Navy, Air Force, and Coast Guard.[50]

Two days later, an A-7 off the USS *America*, Sidewinder 404, flown by Lt. Cdr. James Sullivan, was hit by automatic weapons fire from a boat while performing visual reconnaissance along the coast about twenty-five miles north of Vinh. The aircraft burst into flames. Sullivan was able to turn out over the GOT before ejecting about two miles offshore, but in an area of numerous Vietnamese boats. His wingman reported that he had ejected and took over as the OSC. Big Mother 65, an HH-3A flown by Lt. Karl Rolls and crew, launched off the USS *Reeves* and was vectored into the SAR area. Additionally, Big Mother 62, another HH-3A flown by Lt. Franklin Lockett and crew, diverted from a logistics mission to the USS *Cochrane* and headed to the SAR area to join the effort. As Big Mother 65 approached the coast, they discovered that the aircraft serving as OSC had left the area to find a tanker. Rolls and his crew searched in vain for the survivor among the Vietnamese boats. When the OSC returned, he pointed out which boat had picked up Sullivan. As Rolls and crew flew over the boat, one of the crewmembers thought that he saw Sullivan. However, they began to take fire from the men on the boat. Rolls directed his crew to fire on the boat in an attempt to recover Sullivan. In the melee, the helicopter was hit several times and seriously damaged. They had to leave the area. En route to the

USS *Kitty Hawk*, they had to secure the #2 engine but landed aboard the aircraft carrier uneventfully.

As Big Mother 65 was departing the SAR area, Big Mother 62 arrived to help. The OSC pointed out to them the boat carrying Sullivan. The crew hovered near the boat and received heavy fire. When they returned fire, several of the Vietnamese jumped out of the boat. However, the individual who they thought was Sullivan did not move. Now low on fuel, Lockett decided to head to the USS *Long Beach* for fuel. While they were refueling, the crew was notified that the rescue operation was terminated.

This rescue attempt was noted in the war history of the Nghe An Province of North Vietnam, which stated for this date:

> On 29 October [1972] the soldiers and civilians along the coast of Quynh Luu District scored a glorious success. At 1215 hours Quynh Thuan Village militia forces fired twelve 12.7mm rounds at an F-8 [A-7]. The aircraft crashed, but the pilot ejected and parachuted into the sea . . . ten kilometers from the coastline. Ordered nine boats to quickly transport . . . village guerrillas out to sea to capture the pilot. Twenty enemy jets swarmed in and circled over the pilot. . . . Bombs and bullets could not alter the zeal of the soldiers . . . in a determined effort to pluck the pilot out of the ocean. The American pilot, with all of his personal equipment, was pulled into the boat by the Quynh Long militia fighters, who then took the pilot back to the shoreline as the modern enemy aircraft watched, impotent.[51]

Later that evening Radio Hanoi reported that an American pilot had been captured just off the coast but killed by the fire of American aircraft. Sullivan's remains were returned in 1985. The mission was a bitter failure to the men of HC-7.

On 30 October, an HH-43, Pedro 60 from the Thirty-Seventh ARRSq, was conducting a training flight when it was notified by the Da Nang Air Base control tower that a US Army helicopter, Sabre 26, from Delta Troop, Seventeenth Cavalry (D/17 Cav), had crashed on a small island in the middle of the river south of the city. First Lieutenant William Latham and crew diverted to the site and worked with a US Army UH-1 medevac helicopter to recover all six survivors. They also flew in the sling-loaded fire suppression kit to extinguish a lingering fire.[52]

Special Operations

Early in the afternoon of 30 October, two South Vietnamese Navy junks departed the small South Vietnamese Navy base at Thuan An located just a few miles east of Hue. They were carrying a team consisting of two US Navy SEALs, Lt. Tom Norris (who did the Bat 21Bravo and Nail 38Bravo recoveries), and Petty Officer Mike Thornton, and three South Vietnamese sea commandos. The junks proceeded out into open sea. After sunset they turned north, intent on inserting the team over the beach. The team would then reconnoiter the abandoned naval facility and environs on the south side of the mouth of the Cua Viet River in preparation for potential South Vietnamese amphibious operations in that area. It was a small part of a larger plan to return the area to South Vietnamese control. Offshore, two US Navy ships, the destroyer USS *Morton* and the cruiser USS *Newport News*, provided nominal radar guidance for the junks and on-call naval gunfire support if necessary for the team.

Unfortunately, the team was inserted several miles further north and just south of the Ben Hai River, which separated South and North Vietnam. Fortunately, the team was equipped with an AN/PVC-1 first generation night-vision device, which helped them determine that they were in an area occupied by significant enemy forces with vehicles and a tank. They found an abandoned bunker and decided to use it as a hide site if they were not able to depart the area before sunrise. While trying to determine their location, they spotted two enemy soldiers patrolling along the beach. They took one prisoner, but the other escaped and alerted the local forces, who began to organize and attack the team. As the enemy force swarmed around the team, Norris called the *Morton* for gun support and directed them to fire a round onto a predesignated target. They did so, but Norris did not hear the round impact.

Still unsure of their position, they showed the prisoner their map and he showed them their real location, several miles north of their intended target. Norris then directed the junks to move north to pick up the team and directed the *Morton* to begin moving its gunfire north. Norris also began to move his team to a better defensive position about five hundred yards further north as the sun began to rise.

The *Morton* responded as requested, adjusting its fire further north until Norris could hear and then see the rounds impact. When the fire was in their vicinity, Norris directed them to "shoot, just shoot." *Morton* responded with a ten-round salvo that landed on an advancing group of enemy soldiers and decimated them.

Norris had lagged behind his group to cover their movement to the north. In the melee, he was hit in the head by an AK-47 round and grievously wounded. When Thornton discovered that Norris had been hit, he bolted back, picked him up in a fireman's carry, and rejoined the rest of the team as continued fire from the *Morton* held back the enemy forces. Thornton was also wounded but led the team as they entered the water and swam out so that the junks could return and pick them up. They then proceeded out to the USS *Newport News*, which had a doctor and crack medical team onboard that could provide initial care for Lieutenant Norris and the other wounded team members. Almost one year later, Petty Officer Mike Thornton was presented the Medal of Honor by President Richard Nixon for his rescue of Lieutenant Norris north of the Cua Viet River on Halloween morning 1972.[53] Later, Thornton spoke of this event: "It was a mission—the job for which I was trained. . . . We did our job, and when we fought, we fought for each other." Among the American soldiers, sailors, airmen, and marines still engaged in the war, this was a common refrain.[54]

New Sandys

In late September, the 354th TFW at Myrtle Beach Air Force Base, South Carolina, was notified that it would be deploying 1,574 personnel and its seventy-two A-7D aircraft to Korat RTAFB, Thailand, as part of Constant Guard VI. This allowed two squadrons of F-4s to return to their bases in the Pacific region and two others to return to Eglin and Homestead AFB in Florida. The 354th TFW began its mobilization process on 5 October. Five days later, the aircraft began to depart in six-ship cells for the long flight. Upon arrival, the support personnel immediately began to settle in as the aircrews went through theater indoctrination. The first combat sorties were flown on 16 October, and the immediate reports from the FACs who directed them on strikes in South Vietnam, Laos, and Cambodia were very complimentary. Their improved weapons delivery systems provided for very accurate ordnance delivery. On 26 October, a forward operating location (FOL) was established for the A-7s at Bien Hoa Air Base, and this doubled the number of sorties that could be flown in MR-3. They were an excellent replacement for the Eighth SOS, which had just inactivated and given its A-37s to the VNAF. The USAF A-7s quickly developed a reputation for delivering very accurate ordnance, especially in troops-in-contact situations. On 19 October, a flight of A-7s helped a team of US Navy A-7s off the USS *Saratoga* and a US Army Cobra team prevent the overrunning of an ARVN firebase near Pleiku in MR-2.[55]

Their aircraft were optimized for missions like this with improved bombing avionics, in-flight refueling capability, forward-looking radar (FLR) with radar altimeter interface, projected map display systems, and a navigation/

weapons delivery computer integrated with INS, all reflecting how aviation was modernizing. The USAF commanders in SEA were very pleased with the A-7s.

The commanders also had another mission in mind for the A-7s: they wanted to use them as a replacement for the A-1s in the Sandy role. For over a year, Seventh AF knew that it had to find a replacement for the venerable A-1s. The problem was twofold: First, the A-1 fleet was slowly being reduced by losses. Second, they were slated to be given to the VNAF as the USAF departed South Vietnam. Studies had been conducted to consider a replacement, and the A-37, the OV-10, the A-7, and even the F-4 were considered. However, all of the analysis pointed to the A-7 as the best available aircraft for the mission. Now that they were in SEA, the transition could begin.

In late October, Seventh AF held a joint A-1/A-7 SAR conference to examine the problems inherent in the replacement. Additionally, SAR training for twelve A-7 pilots began immediately. A-1 pilots serving as "instructors" rode along on HH-53s as practice SARs were staged, critiquing exercises as they were conducted. Several A-1 pilots then stayed at Korat to help the 354th TFW develop an ongoing SAR training course for those pilots who would assume the Sandy role, primarily from the 353rd Tactical Fighter Squadron (TFS). Since the First SOS was now projected to inactivate soon and turn its aircraft over to the VNAF, the 354th TFW A-7s were also directed to assume the Hobo missions that directly supported indigenous forces in Laos.[56]

First Special Operations Squadron

October was rather anticlimactic for the squadron. It was obviously drawing down. With only nineteen aircraft and twenty-five pilots, it still had aircraft on alert at Ubon, Da Nang, and NKP. They also flew daily sorties as Hobos, supporting indigenous forces in both northern and southern Laos, as they had been doing since the early days of the war. On 19 October, the Hobos provided escort for the CH-53 Knives of the Twenty-First SOS in a major infiltration mission in the Saravane area. For five days, they flew cover for the operation. Five of the CH-53s were hit by AAA, and an Air America helicopter also supporting the operations was shot down. The crew was recovered by another Air America aircraft. The Hobos took out several enemy gun positions, and their accurate air strikes helped the indigenous forces to recapture Saravane.

The unit also experienced a big turnover in maintenance personnel as several experienced A-1 maintainers went home and were replaced by airmen from the now defunct QU-22 maintenance team.

On 22 October, the First SOS gathered for a going-away, or "Sawadee," party for now Lt. Col. Jim Harding, 1st Lt. Byron Hukee, 1st Lt. Tex Brown, 1st Lt. Lance L. Smith, and Capt. Ross Buchanan. They had several distinguished participants: the US ambassador to Laos, McMurtrie Godley; Laotian Maj. Gen. Vang Pao; deputy commander for the Seventh/Thirteenth AF, Maj. Gen. James Hughes; and deputy chief, Military Assistance Command, Thailand (MACTHAI), Brig. Gen. Jack Vesey. All made remarks, but Ambassador Godley and Gen. Vang Pao both spoke passionately and eloquently about the role that the First SOS and the A-1s had played in supporting the Laotian forces in the long war in Laos. Ambassador Godley then announced that in early November the A-1s of the First SOS would be transferred to the VNAF and the Hobo and Sandy missions would transfer to the A-7s.

The next day, Lieutenant Colonel Harding passed command of the First SOS to Lt. Col. Bill Latham. Latham accepted the assignment stoically, noting in the squadron history: "If the A-1s are to be lost to the VNAF, based upon the impending ceasefire, the return of the POWs and subsequent peaceful solutions to the problem of SE Asia, then the loss of our A-1s will be more acceptable." To say the least, he and his squadron faced a most uncertain future.[57]

NOVEMBER

With the restriction on Linebacker operations, sortie rates were reduced in the north, and the focus of the air strikes was now on the southern portion of North Vietnam, greatly reducing the risk to US aircraft and aircrews. But rescues still occurred.

On 2 November, changes were made to the Sandy A-1 alert posture. Four aircraft were still on alert at NKP. However, the 2 A-1s at Ubon were moved to Da Nang so that six aircraft would be on alert there. Linebacker sorties had been reduced but were still flying into southern North Vietnam and the Quang Tri area. The next day, the JRCC also put out guidance that within a few days, the 354th TFW at Korat would be able to prepare 4 A-7s to be on Sandy alert. They would use the call signs of Sandys 05, 06, 09, and 10, to deconflict with the A-1s while they were still available.[58]

That same day, an A-7 off the USS *Kitty Hawk*, Jury 300, suffered a mechanical failure while attacking trucks south of Vinh with a Walleye missile. The pilot, Lt. R. Deremer, turned well out to sea and ejected. An HH-3A from HC-7 recovered him.[59]

A little before noon on 5 November, King 25 monitored an emergency call that Sabre 73, an AH-1 from D/17 Cavalry, was down fifteen miles south of Da Nang. Covey 26 was the OSC. Sabre 16, an OH-6, tried to make a quick recovery of the crew but was driven off by heavy AAA and had one man wounded. Sabre 16 landed on a road a few miles further south. At that point, Jolly Greens 64 and 71 were scrambled out of Da Nang, with Sandys 07 and 08. Additionally, Sandys 05, 06, 09, and 10, all A-7s, were scrambled out of Korat. United States Navy A-7s also arrived to assist as a US Army medevac helicopter, Dustoff 15, arrived and recovered one survivor and three bodies from Sabre 73. Dustoff 15 then recovered the four survivors from Sabre 16, and all SAR forces returned to base.[60]

On 6 November, Coachman 159, a US Army UH-1 Huey helicopter from the Sixty-Second Aviation Company went down in jungle mountains approximately fifteen miles west of Quang Ngai. It was carrying a crew of four and three passengers, an army, a navy, and a marine officer, serving as advisors to the First ARVN Division. They were on a mission to direct gunfire from US Navy ships offshore. The terrain consisted of low mountains and jungle. This area was a known enemy stronghold and was potentially extremely hostile. During the night, the downed crew made weak radio contact with an army U-21, Vanguard 19, who determined a general location. The crew and passengers were together in a defensive laager. An HC-130, King 27, assumed AMC duties. A VNAF AC-119 and army helicopters tried to enter the area but were constrained by terrible weather, heavy rain, turbulence, low clouds, poor visibility caused by a developing typhoon, and enemy ground fire. King 27 began coordinating a first-light SAR.[61]

At first light, army helicopters tried to mount a recovery operation, but had to abort because of the persistent weather. When conditions appeared to be improving, the alert A-1s from Da Nang, Sandy 07, Capt. Don Screws, and Sandy 08, launched ahead of them to locate the survivors. They were forced to fly at dangerously low altitudes (two hundred feet or less) in order to find them. When their position was determined, Jolly Greens 71 and 72, HH-53s from the Thirty-Seventh ARRSq, took off and proceeded to the survivors' area. Two A-7s, Sandys 09 and 10, also launched from Korat RTAFB to support the operation.

Once the survivors' exact location had been determined, Sandy 07 became the OSC and remained overhead the crash site. Sandy 08 went out to escort the Jollys in for the pickup. The two HH-53s flew in formation at treetop level during the ingress. Both helicopters landed close to the survivors, and the seven men climbed into Jolly Green 71, flown by Capt. James

Bruner and crew. They flew to the airfield at Quang Ngai and returned the soldiers to their unit. These survivors were saves number 878 through 884 for the Thirty-Seventh ARRSq and the last combat saves by the Jollys based at Da Nang.

This was also the last SAR for the USAF A-1s. Just prior to this event, all A-1s remaining in Southeast Asia began transferring to the South Vietnamese Air Force. However, on 9 November 1972, Seventh AF decided that six A-1s were still needed for Sandy Alert at Da Nang. Four A-1 pilots were flown to Bien Hoa Air Base, South Vietnam, where they signed hand receipts for the Skyraiders and flew them to Da Nang. First Lieutenant Bob Carlsen was sent with another pilot to Pleiku, where they signed hand receipts for two more VNAF A-1s and also flew them to Da Nang. They were not used on a SAR mission. On the fifteenth, they were returned to the VNAF and the First SOS pilots took the occasion to fly one last grand six-ship formation as a salute to their great aircraft. With that poignant gesture, the Sandy mission was fully and finally passed to the newly arrived A-7s. The remaining A-1 pilots were either sent home early or assigned to staff jobs in various headquarters. On 15 December, the squadron was transferred to Kadena Air Base, Okinawa, without personnel or equipment, for a new identity and new life.[62]

Reelection

On 7 November, President Nixon was reelected with a massive majority over his opponent, Senator George McGovern. Public polling also showed that the American people supported his actions in the war. However, the Senate and House of Representatives also elected that day held strong majorities against continuing support for the war and would probably take legislative action in the new year to restrict or even end funding for military action there. Nixon realized that he had to convince the South Vietnamese to accept the agreement and force the North Vietnamese to sign it. He began to consider the use of B-52s in a concentrated attack in the Hanoi area, and he directed his military to begin planning for such a contingency.[63] Meanwhile, air operations continued over North and South Vietnam and almost forgotten Cambodia and Laos, and the residual American forces in South Vietnam continued to leave.

The Thirty-Seventh Air Rescue and Recovery Squadron

In early November, Lieutenant Colonel Sutton at the Thirty-Seventh ARRSq used the alert klaxon to call all of his squadron members together for a squadron meeting. When his airmen were gathered, he told them that the unit had just received orders to inactivate at the end of the month. Some helicopters and about one-third of the personnel would be transferred to the Fortieth at NKP, but most members would be home for Christmas. The squadron was a beehive of activity as the troops began accounting for and shipping out all unit equipment. All individual weapons had to be collected and turned in. This was a problem because the PJs had, over the years, collected quite an unofficial collection of weapons, including grenades, foreign-made rifles, and even crew-served machine guns. Lieutenant Colonel Sutton had to declare a collection amnesty to protect his men from legal action.

When the unit finally went off alert status, the parties started. However, the "official" last party was at the Jolly Green Inn. There, the alcohol flowed and mixed with the memories. The men realized that many would never see each other again as they departed to other rescue units far-flung around the globe. Many had forged deep and enduring friendships from their common experience of war. The next day, the squadron formed up to salute the HH-53s as they departed for NKP. Lieutenant Colonel Sutton told a reporter for the Da Nang base newspaper, "I cannot begin to describe the dedication these guys have for the job. It is 24 hours a day, seven days a week, always alert and ready to pick up someone. . . . When we bring a downed pilot back, the guys act like he is a long-lost brother. They really have empathy for the jet jocks and all men in trouble. They are the greatest bunch of guys I have ever known." The Fortieth would occasionally post HH-53s to sit alert at Da Nang and would still have its detachment with HH-43s there for local base rescue (LBR). But the proud Thirty-Seventh ARRS was gone.[64] Now, USAF responsibility for combat SAR in SEA would rest singly and solely upon the Fortieth ARRSq.

In the early morning hours of 7 November, another F-111, Whaler 57, flown by Maj. Robert Brown and Maj. Robert Morrissey, disappeared while on a mission to bomb a fording site nine miles north of the DMZ. As with previous F-111 losses, FACs and RF-4s searched along the projected flight plan for several days, but no indications that the crew had ejected were ever found. Consequently, no rescue effort was extended. This was the fourth F-111 and crew lost on this deployment.[65]

Later that day, Raven 20, USAF Maj. John Carroll, took off from Long Tieng, Laos, in an O-1 to seek out enemy targets over the PDJ. His aircraft was hit by enemy ground fire, severely damaging his aircraft engine. He made emergency calls on Guard frequency, and Air America helicopters began to track him. When his engine seized, he crash-landed on a ridge. Enemy troops were immediately upon him. He reported that he was under his aircraft and fighting. That was his last radio call. Another Raven, USAF 1st Lt. Terry Pfaff, diverted to initiate a SAR for Carroll, then had to leave for fuel and passed the mission to USAF Capt. Steve Neal, who continued the effort. The orbiting HC130 King aircraft monitored the emergency calls and launched HH-53s from NKP. However, the A-1s were no longer available. They had been inactivated and the "Sandy" mission was now being performed by A-7s based at Korat Air Base, Thailand, who were at least an hour away. Jack alerted the Fortieth ARRSq. They realized that they could not be there before dark and began planning for an LNRS recovery.

Neal called for any nearby Air America helicopters. Two crews responded. The first aircraft, a UH-1, call sign N8535F and flown by M. Jarina and G. Taylor, was driven off by intense enemy ground fire that seriously damaged the aircraft. Its crewmembers reported that enemy troops were within one hundred feet of Major Carroll's position. The second aircraft, call sign N8512F and flown by T. R. Cash and R. A. Heibel, was able to hover next to Carroll's aircraft. The flight mechanic, G. R. Neufeld, reported he could see the body under the aircraft with multiple grievous fatal wounds. Concentrated fire from enemy forces precluded a successful recovery, and the crew aborted their pickup attempt. Hearing of this, Jack terminated recovery operations for Raven 20. That night, an enemy radio message indicated that the pilot killed that day was John Carroll. The next morning, the first Raven airborne over the PDJ was USAF Capt. Darrel Whitcomb. He observed enemy forces swarming around the aircraft and directed F-4s who delivered a two-thousand-pound laser-guided bomb (LGB) on the wreckage.[66]

On 10 November, US Navy attack aircraft were very busy over southern North Vietnam, searching for and attacking whatever NVA targets that they could find. In the morning, an A-7 from the USS *Midway*, Raven Jet 314, flown by Lt. Michael Cobb, was working with his flight just south of the ever-dangerous Thanh Hoa area when the aircraft was seriously damaged by 57mm AAA. Following now standard procedure, he turned east over the water and when away from the coast, ejected. As his wingmen capped him, a Big Mother flown by Lt. Franklin Lockett and crew launched off the USS *Long Beach* and recovered the pilot without any significant enemy interference.[67]

Three hours later, another A-7, Red Falcon 300, from the USS *Saratoga*, flown by Lt. Cdr. Frederick Wright, was downed by an unknown weapon just a few miles above the DMZ. Nobody observed an ejection or heard any beeper or voice calls. His wingmen and F-4 Fast FACs maintained a watch over the area for several hours with no contact. Photography of the wreckage by an RF-4 showed catastrophic damage to the aircraft and no sign of ejection. The pilot's remains were returned in September 1990.[68]

That night, this almost same scenario played out again when another A-7 from the USS *Midway*, Champion 401, flown by Lt. Wayne Lotsberg, was shot down by 23mm AAA while hunting trucks south of Vinh. Again, the pilot turned east and ejected over the water. His wingman remained over him to serve as the OSC. Once again, Big Mother 60, flown by Lt. James Spillman and crew, launched off the USS *England* for the recovery. They contacted the OSC, and he vectored them to the survivor using flares. Overhead, they hoisted down their rescue swimmer, who ignited a flare to mark the survivor's position. Unfortunately, the flare dropped by the A-7 burned out and he did not have another. The Big Mother pilots both experienced vertigo and almost descended into the water. They repositioned the helicopter to establish a more stable approach and were then able to recover the survivor and swimmer without further difficulties.[69]

On 15 November, just before noon, a JRCC controller dryly noted in the JRCC log: "Sandy A-1—the 6 Sandy aircraft are making their Fini-flight to Bien Hoa to become VNAF aircraft." So ended the spectacular service of the USAF A-1s as strike aircraft and rescue escort aircraft in the long war in SEA. They had flown literally from one end of the theater to the other. And their efforts had protected allied forces, destroyed countless NVA troops, trucks, and supplies, and helped bring home allied soldiers and airmen in uncounted desperate rescues. During the conflict, the USAF had lost 150 A-1s in combat and another 41 in other operational losses. They would be sorely missed.[70]

Bobbin 05

On 16 November, another aircraft carrier, the USS *Ranger*, arrived to join in combat operations with TF-77. That evening, a USAF F-105G, Bobbin 05, from the 388th TFW at Korat, was escorting a cell of B-52s on a night strike near Thanh Hoa when it was shot down by an SA-2. The two crewmembers, Maj. Norman Maier and Capt. Kenneth Theate, ejected and landed on a ridge. The next morning, an F-4 Fast FAC contacted them and determined their location. USAF A-7s had assumed the Sandy role and tried to initiate a rescue. However, low ceilings and massed AAA guns along the coast precluded an attempt.

At first light on the eighteenth, a package of forty-seven aircraft launched. Jolly Green 32 was flown by Capt. Mel Gillespie and crew, and Jolly Green 56 was flown by Capt. Dale Stovall and crew. They would be led in by Sandy 01, Maj. Arnie Clarke. The rescue area was covered with a blanket of low clouds. Using his INS navigational system, Clarke led the Jollys down below the clouds to make the run-in to the survivors. They were supported by twelve other A-7s carrying a variety of ordnance. Stovall later recalled: "Mel auto-rotated from 8,000 feet through the clouds following Clarke, who had popped up through the clouds and said, 'There is a 400-foot ceiling.' He dove back down and said, 'Follow me.'"[71]

The A-7s utilized their inertial navigation system and projected map displays to guide the Jolly Greens into the area. However, the enemy gunners were waiting, and multiple AAA sites engaged the two helicopters. The Sandys suppressed the enemy gunners with ordnance and a smoke screen while both men were recovered and the Jolly Greens egressed back to Thailand.

Major Arnie Clarke logged nine hours of flight time that day, and his aircraft was damaged by AAA. However, he was able to climb back above the clouds and return to Korat with his fellow Sandys. Noted Dale Stovall later, "Clarke was a GREAT Sandy lead!"[72]

Actually, Maj. Arnie Clarke was well familiar with SAR. On his first combat tour as an F-100 pilot, his aircraft was badly damaged while flying SAR support for a downed Laotian T-28 near the Plain of Jars in northern Laos on 18 August 1964. He tried to fly back to Takhli, but his engine failed and he bailed out over northern Thailand and was recovered by an Air America helicopter. On a subsequent tour, also flying F-100s, he was shot down on a Misty FAC mission on 22 January 1969 near Kham Duc, South Vietnam. This time, he was rescued by a USAF HH-3. For his efforts on the Bobbin 05 mission, he received the Air Force Cross. Clarke's actions that day replicated the actions of Capt. John Lackey, Maj. Jim Harding, and Capt. Ron Smith for their missions earlier in 1972, for which they had also received this prestigious award. Being a Sandy 01 was a very challenging and dangerous occupation.[73] **

** Captain Dale Stovall and Capt. Mel Gillespie were slated to return home from their Jolly Green tour on 10 November—a forty-three-day rollback, as the Thirty-Seventh ARRSq was inactivated and personnel were being sent home early. However, he and Gillespie stayed on for a few more weeks because the Fortieth ARRSq was short of instructor pilots and the two wanted to be primary commanders for any missions. Gillespie did a superb job as Stovall's copilot on the Oyster 01Bravo rescue. As payback, Stovall agreed to be his high bird on any SAR that they flew after 10 November.

A-7 of Maj. Arnie Clarke on the Bobbin 05 rescue. (Courtesy Lou Drendel)

This was the first serious SAR for the new USAF A-7s. With their modern navigational systems, they brought some much-needed technological improvement to combat rescue. However, their higher speed as compared to the old A-1 dictated that they could not maintain visual contact with the Jolly Greens and overall situational awareness of rapidly changing SAR situations. Overall, their performance revealed several weaknesses in the use of this aircraft in the rescue effort (RESCORT) role:

1. They did not have the loiter time of the A-1s and had to utilize KC-135s as they cycled back and forth for gas. This increased the utilization rate for the tankers.
2. The standard communications plan that had been developed over years of use had to be modified for the communications capabilities of the A-7.
3. The A-7s needed to be equipped with ELF to better and more quickly locate survivors.[74]

The rescue community could not help but compare the A-7 to the sorely missed A-1. Beyond the equipment differences, other concerns were voiced, especially by the HH-53 crews. They had operated for years with the A-1s providing close support for them when they were ingressing, hovering over the survivors, and exiting the battle area. De facto, the A-1s were the Jolly Greens' navigational systems.

The Jolly crews purely liked the feel of the A-1s in close and were hesitant, initially at least, with the A-7s with their higher speeds and larger turn radius, which prevented them from maintaining that close contact. It made the Jolly crews feel "naked" in the face of the enemy gunners. They also noticed that the pilots were different. The A-1 guys were "low and slow" pilots, trained as close-in attack specialists and flying aircraft straight out of World War II. When not on SAR duty, they flew missions providing tight close air support for primarily indigenous coalition forces in Laos and had a real feel for ground battle. They did interdiction too, but as a secondary mission. They had a fundamental feel for air-to-ground battle, and many SARs ended up as air-to-ground battles.

Additionally, the Jollys also really appreciated having the A-1 squadron right there at NKP with them and the Nail OV-10 FACs of the Twenty-Third TASS. These disparate groups of young airmen developed a close bond through their combined efforts in the rescues. And there at NKP they also had colocated with them Jack and the intelligence capabilities provided by Task Force Alpha. It was a cohesive and fortuitous grouping of all the key SAR elements, and it provided for a robust synergy among the various groups. Nakhon Phanom RTAFB was the home of the "complete" rescue wing.[75]

In contrast, the A-7s were located at Korat. They kept liaison officers at NKP, but that was not the same as having the actual Sandy pilots themselves right there with the other SAR experts and having opportunities to mix with them on a daily basis and swap the inevitable "bar talk," which in many cases created the unique tactics and techniques that enabled the SAR forces to perform so many incredible rescues. That was a loss to the rescue community.

In comparison to the A-1 pilots, the A-7 drivers were a different breed. They were jet guys, flying higher and faster. They were focused on flying quickly to a target, bombing it, and returning home. Yes, they did close air support, but they were not down low and in the fight like the A-1 guys were. They were really more designed and optimized for interdiction or preplanned targets designated in a campaign plan. Their aircraft were optimized for it, with improved bombing avionics, in-flight refueling capability, FLR with radar altimeter interface, projected map display systems, and navigation/weapons delivery computers integrated with the INS, all reflecting how aviation was modernizing. SAR procedures had to be modified to take advantage of the new equipment. As a plus, with their higher speeds, the A-7s could get to the rescue location quicker, and history had shown that reduced reaction time was a key determinant in recovery success.

After the Bobbin 05 mission was complete, one A-1 pilot speculated that the uniqueness of the A-7, with its advanced capabilities, enabled this rescue when it is probable that the A-1 pilots would have had a much more difficult time completing the mission so far from home base and in such a dangerous area. Starkly stated, the A-1 was the proud past—the A-7 was the exciting future. Regardless, the A-1s were gone, and for operational reasons, the A-7s were the new Sandys in town. And they were flexible, as Bobbin 05 showed. The A-7 pilots would adapt their aircraft and themselves for the mission and reshape the mission to exploit the new technologies and ideas. In that, they would replicate the earlier efforts of the helicopter crews who incorporated in-flight refueling and the limited night recovery system into their tactics and techniques, and the OV-10 FACs of the Twenty-Third TASS who adapted the new Pave Spot laser/loran system, which provided highly accurate position designation and navigation. The A-7 airmen would also evolve as necessary to do the mission.

Recognizing that, perhaps the best commendation for the Bobbin 05 effort came from the commander of the Third Aerospace Rescue and Recovery Group (ARRG), Col. Cy Muirhead. He had been at the helm of the theater rescue forces for all of 1972 and knew better than most the reality of rescue in Southeast Asia. He wrote to the airmen of the new Sandy force: "Your extraordinary display of calmness and heroism under pressure are in the highest traditions of the [Aerospace Rescue and Recovery Service] and the USAF. For the Sandys of the 354th: Welcome to the rescue family.

You couldn't have upheld the highly respected tradition of the Sandys in a finer manner. It's great having you with us." It was a timely but almost bittersweet thought because some of the greatest challenges for rescue were looming just beyond the horizon.[76]

Continued Diplomacy

On 20 November, Henry Kissinger was back in Paris, where he presented President Thieu's proposed changes. Le Duc Tho flatly rejected them and began proposing changes to items already agreed upon. Kissinger reminded him that bombing had been halted above the twentieth parallel with the expectations that negotiations would proceed "seriously" and suggested that the bombing could be resumed. Tho pointed out that the North Vietnamese were negotiating "seriously" and that it was the Americans who had backed away from the proposed agreement by introducing a new series of demands. "The October 31 deadline is past," Tho declared. "The election is over and, from our point of view the war can continue." Tho was aware that it was very possible that when it reconvened in January, the US Congress could very possibly vote to end all funding for the war. Time, he felt, was on their side. On 25 November, both delegations returned home for further instructions.[77]

On the afternoon of 20 November, Motion 05, a USMC F-4 from MAG-15 at Nam Phong, Thailand, was working with a Nail FAC from the Twenty-Third TASS and striking trucks along the Ho Chi Minh trail about twenty miles southeast of Tchepone. The very heavy AAA severely damaged the jet as he released his bombs. When it began to lose controllability, the pilot, Capt. Bill Anderson, ejected. The status of the radar intercept officer (RIO), Capt. Donald Breuer, is unknown. Nail 75, Capt. Jeff Colbath, diverted to their location and assumed OSC. King 21 also diverted into the area and notified Jack and the JRCC.

When on the ground, Anderson made radio contact with the aircraft above and pointed out active AAA positions in his area. "The guns were all around me," he recalled. Colbath began attacking the guns with flights of fighters that diverted to support the SAR. Jack scrambled Jolly Greens 57 and 56 from Ubon and also Sandys 01, 02, 03, 04, and 05 from Korat. Arriving over the area, Sandy 01 took over as the OSC and assessed that a pickup attempt was warranted. He directed Sandys 02 and 03 to lead the Jolly 57, flown by Capt. Roger Bradley and crew, in for a pickup attempt. Colbath continued to put in air strikes on the enemy gun positions. To take advantage of terrain and weather, the Jolly Green made his approach to the survivor from the east as Anderson gave them vectors, called out gun sites, and ignited his day flare. As the helicopter came in to a hover and the flight engineer began to drop the jungle penetrator, a 12.7mm gun started firing at them. The PJ on that side engaged with his minigun. When it jammed, he used his AR-15 to shoot the gunners. When Anderson was safely on board, Bradley turned and egressed the area. No contact of any sort was made with Captain Breuer.[78]

Later that evening, an F-4 from the USS *Saratoga*, Clubleaf 210, flown by Lt. Cdr. Vincent Lesh and Lt. Donald Cordes, was escorting a cell of B-52s as they bombed a target near Vinh when it was seriously damaged by an SA-2. They turned east and proceeded six miles out over the GOT before ejecting. Once again, Big Mother 60, flown by LTJG Timothy Dewhirst and crew, launched off the USS *Jouett* and followed their vectors to the projected location of the two survivors. Arriving in the area, they spotted a flare and made an approach to what they thought was a survivor. The rescue swimmer was lowered on the hoist and found one very wet sailor. Both men were hoisted up as the pilots struggled to control the helicopter in the pitch-black conditions. Then the crew spotted a pen gun flare from the other survivor, and they hovered over to his location and recovered him. Big Mother proceeded to the USS *Truxtun* and dropped off the two flyers.[79]

Following a now sadly familiar pattern, in the early morning hours of 21 November, another F-111, Burger 54, flown by Capt. Ron Stafford and Capt. Charles Caffarelli, disappeared on a fragged mission to attack a transshipment point eight miles southwest of Quang Khe in Route Pack 1. There were no witnesses to the loss and no enemy reports that they had downed an aircraft in that area. Fast FACs searched Route Pack 1 but found nothing. Several days later wreckage identified as honeycomb sections from an F-111 washed up on the shores north of Da Nang.[80]

On 22 November, one of the B-52s that aircraft like Bobbin 05 and Clubleaf 210 had been escorting, Olive 02, was itself badly damaged by an SA-2 missile after dropping its bombs on a target near Vinh. The crew fought to control the aircraft as its systems failed and fire began to burn through the wings. They were able to coax the aircraft back across the Mekong River before all engines failed. The crew then bailed out about fifteen miles southwest of NKP. There, the local base rescue HH-43, Pedro 21, began searching for the crew. It was joined by Knife 30, a CH-53 assigned to the Twenty-First SOS at NKP, which was conducting local training. Pedro 21 recovered two crewmembers, and Knife 30 recovered the other four. This was the third B-52 hit by enemy fire over North Vietnam in the last month.

Capt. Bill Anderson, Motion 05, arriving at NKP. (Courtesy Bill Anderson)

However, it was the first B-52 actually downed by enemy action in the entire war and a harbinger for worse to come.[81]

It was interesting, too, that the crew would head toward NKP. That base in far northeast Thailand stood as a beacon for the combat crews flying into northern or eastern Laos and certainly into North Vietnam. It was the center for SEA rescue—figuratively and literally—and every combat aviator knew that when you needed help, NKP, TACAN Channel 89, was the place to go.

On 23 November, 1st Lt. John Sundgren, Nail 36, an OV-10 FAC from the Twenty-Third TASS, was taking off from Da Nang when one of his engines failed and his heavily laden aircraft would not maintain altitude. Sundgren ejected about three miles south of the airfield. Pedro 61, flown by 1st Lt. William Latham and crew, was airborne on a local training sortie and quickly diverted to pick up Sundgren. The elapsed time from ejection to recovery was about one minute and thirty-two seconds—probably the fastest rescue in a combat theater ever.[82]

About thirty minutes later and three hundred miles to the south, Rash 31, 1st Lt. Robert Martensen, an O-2 FAC from the Twenty-First TASS, had to bail out when his aircraft was hit by an SA-7 near An Loc. He was supporting the ARVN forces still defending that area from the NVA. Fortunately, a "red" team consisting of an OH-6, two AH-1s, and a UH-1 from F/8 Cavalry, which had relocated to Bien Hoa Air Base, was in the area and responded to the mayday call. Martensen's parachute partly tangled in a tree, but he was able to lower himself to the ground. Orienting himself quickly, he said a prayer and later remembered, "I felt a physical experience . . . like a bolt of lightning going through me. It was different than adrenaline, and an overwhelming sense of calm and optimism came over me." Above, he was heartened to see the team AH-1s orbiting as the OH-6 flown by Chief Warrant Officer 2 Fred Page and gunner Sgt. Randy Yetton zipped over just above the trees as they searched for and then spotted Martensen below. Page carefully descended through the trees and hovered just fifty feet from Martensen as Yetton engaged enemy forces rushing into the area. Martensen quickly ran to the OH-6 and scrambled aboard. Under continuous enemy fire, Page quickly lifted them out of the trees. Once clear, they accelerated to maximum speed and proceeded to the airfield at Tay Ninh. There, a US Army general officer had been reviewing army operations in the area and was able to monitor the recovery effort. On the spot, he presented Chief Warrant Officer 2 Page an "impact award" Silver Star for his quick and selfless actions. Martensen then boarded a medevac UH-1, which flew him back to Bien Hoa. It was another save for the dwindling army forces still operating in South Vietnam.[83]

On 26 November, another Raven went down for unknown reasons in Laos. Raven 41, Capt. Mike Stearns, was forced to land near a village about thirty miles northeast of Pakse when his engine failed. Four Sandy A-7s were airborne, and they diverted to his location as Raven 43 took over as the OSC and organized a rescue operation. An Air America H-34, call sign H-63, responded and picked up Stearns and his Laotian interpreter and returned them to Pakse.[84]

1st Lt. Bob Martensen returns on a white MEDEVAC helicopter. (Courtesy Bob Martensen)

On 28 November, the USS *Kitty Hawk* completed its tour and departed Task Force 77. It had been on the line for eight and a half months of sustained combat operations. Two days later, Jolly Greens 64, 66, and 71 departed Da Nang and the Thirty-Seventh ARRSq for NKP and duty with the Fortieth ARRSq. Jolly Green 65 had a maintenance abort. However, four hours later, it and Jolly Green 71 followed, as required by the inactivation of the Thirty-Seventh ARRSq as part of the nation's withdrawal from South Vietnam. Subsequently, there would occasionally be rescue helicopters at Da Nang, but only on a temporary duty travel (TDY) status.[85]

Another Campaign

On 30 November, acting on President Nixon's direction, Admiral John S. McCain, commander in chief, Pacific (CINCPAC), sent a message to General John C. Meyer, commander in chief, Strategic Air Command (CINCSAC); General Lucius Clay, commander in chief, Pacific Air Forces (CINCPACAF); and Admiral Bernard Clarey, commander in chief, Pacific Fleet (CINCPACFLT), stating, "We must be prepared for contingency breakdown in cease-fire negotiations," and the subsequent cancellation of restrictions above the twentieth parallel. He asked them for a plan for "an integrated and sustained air campaign against North Vietnam," to interdict the southward flow of supplies and to isolate the North Vietnamese "heartland"—where targets should be such that their destruction would achieve the maximum psychological impact while causing minimum risk to the population. It was beginning to look like the aircrews of Seventh AF and TF-77 would once again be busy over the skies of Hanoi.[86]

Linebacker was an interdiction campaign directed at the North Vietnamese supply system and designed to attrite their forces so that the military of South Vietnam could defend its nation. Conducted across the breadth and depth of the theater, it challenged the rescue forces in innumerable and unforeseen ways. Again, macro data provided by Chris Hobson in *Vietnam Air Losses* presents a comparative picture for this campaign from 10 May through the end of November:

Fixed-wing aircraft lost: USAF—99, USMC—14, USN—59.
Results:

182 KIA	46%	
68 POW	17%	
149 recovered	37%	
Recovery by:		
Army helicopters	8	
USAF helicopters	49	
USMC helicopters	2	
USN helicopters	39	
USN ships	11	
Ground forces	18	
VNAF helicopters	2	
Crash home base	10	
AirAm helicopters	3	
Unknown	6	[87]

The reduced rate of recovery and higher rate of capture from earlier periods were the result of the increased intensity of the fighting and threats arrayed against our aerial forces. Again, the numbers do not include the anecdotal rescues noted in ground unit histories, the special operations taking place in Laos, and all Air America recoveries.

CHAPTER EIGHT

DECEMBER GÖTTERDÄMMERUNG

It was bombing that settled the question, bombing that got our prisoners out.

Gen. Alexander Haig and Charles McCarry, *Inner Circles: How America Changed the World*

Theater Air Operations

As December started, USAF, USMC, and US Navy strike flights were still bombing in the southern half of North Vietnam as well as all regions of South Vietnam. Additionally, some sorties were still going to Cambodia and Laos, as USAF forward air controllers (FACs) still patrolled over all of those areas, and the Ravens were still on-station in their sectors in northern and southern Laos. On 2 December, the 354th Tactical Fighter Wing (TFW) suffered its first loss when one of its A-7s, Hobo 01, flown by Capt. Anthony Shine, was reported missing in the Fish's Mouth area on the Laos–North Vietnam border. He and his wingman had provided support for an Air America helicopter infiltration, and he was last seen descending through a cloud deck to look at a possible target. When his wingman reported that he was missing, a flight of six Sandy A-7s were launched from Korat but were not able to establish contact with him. For the next thirty hours, RF-4s with escorting fighters and Pave Nail OV-10s were dispatched to the area to search, and MiG Combat Air Patrol (MiGCAP) flights were on orbit to patrol between them and Hanoi. However, nobody saw or heard any signs of a survivor. Shine's remains were returned to the United States in 1995.[1]*

---

*Hobo 02 was diverted to a Raven FAC in an O-1 over the PDJ to expend his ordnance. Hobo 02 was low on fuel, and in that hurried airstrike, the A-7 almost had a collision with the O-1 as the A-7 pilot pulled off the target. The A-7 pilots had a bad habit of looking back at their ordnance and not forward as they recovered from

Air America Operations

As the air campaign was ongoing, Air America crews conducted a little noticed but consequential mini-operation in North Vietnam. It involved a one of a kind highly modified OH-6 helicopter designated the Hughes 500P, a limited-edition stealthy machine built by the Aircraft Division of the Hughes Tool Company. Its moniker was "The Quiet One." It was developed by the CIA's Special Operations Division Air Branch and optimized to provide a long-range, quiet, and precision capability to drop off and pick up agents deep in enemy territory. Two aircraft were so modified with forward-looking infrared (FLIR), engine noise baffling devices, and a loran navigational package. Additionally, the pilots were trained to use first-generation SU-50 night-vision goggles. After testing in Nevada, the aircraft were shipped to SEA for use by Air America. There, aircrews trained to adapt to the new technology, determine its limitations, and optimize it for operational missions.[2]

On the night of 5/6 December, weather and moonlight conditions were favorable for a penetration mission. Pilots George Lamothe and Daniel Smith took off with two indigenous commandos onboard. The commandos were equipped to attach a transmission device to a key North Vietnamese command cable detected by CIA intelligence sources near Vinh. They were escorted by another helicopter with a SAR recovery team, which entered an orbit as Lamothe and crew entered North Vietnam. Utilizing the precise loran system, they inserted their commandos and proceeded to another location to insert a radio repeater/relay device. On the ground, the two commandos found the communications cable and inserted the monitoring device and small solar power panels. A surveillance aircraft orbiting over Laos was immediately able to pick up the signal and notified Lamothe. He then returned to the site, recovered the two commandos, and returned to their base in Laos.

Those involved were never told what type of information was being collected. Allegedly, it included inside information from North Vietnamese commanders useful in the negotiations ongoing between the United States and North Vietnam to achieve a ceasefire in the war. Regardless, that Air America crew displayed a developing capability that could have had direct application to SAR in SEA. However, for reasons unknown, it was not so applied. It would take another six years before that capability would be adapted to the rescue mission.[3]

---

their bomb passes. This information was passed along to the other Ravens and was a major concern when working with the A-7s.

About eight hours after the mission into North Vietnam was completed, a fellow Air America crew found themselves in need of rescue. A C-123K, Air America #648, departed from Pakse in southern Laos to air-drop supplies to several Laotian units fighting in the Bolaven Plateau region against North Vietnamese Army (NVA) forces west of the Ho Chi Minh trail. When it was hit by antiaircraft artillery (AAA), the aircraft commander, Capt. Neil Hansen, ordered the crew to bail out. The two pilots and two "kickers" successfully made it out of the aircraft. Just taking off from Pakse, Raven 44, 1st Lt. Lew Hatch, heard the emergency calls and immediately flew to the location of the downed crew to serve as the on-scene commander (OSC) for recovery operations. En route, he checked in with King 21, who began diverting USAF strike flights to Hatch. King 21 notified Jack. When the controllers there checked with the Air America operations center at Udorn, they were told that Air America would handle this mission.[4]

Fortunately, several Air America helicopters were operating in the area and diverted to pick up the crew. Before Hatch could arrive at the scene, one of the helicopters, Hotel 52, with eighteen wounded soldiers onboard, swooped in and recovered the copilot and one of the kickers. However, as it maneuvered to pick up the captain, its tail rotor hit a tree. The pilot completed the pickup, but his aircraft was at maximum load and he could barely clear the trees. The pilot intended to fly to Pakse but instead decided to land the damaged and maxed-out helicopter at an old Japanese airfield.

Another Air America helicopter, Hotel 81, arrived, picked up the second kicker, and then took him to Pakse. Overhead, Hatch had USAF F-4s and A-7s on station, and he directed them against enemy forces in the area as a third Air America helicopter, Hotel 53, landed next to Hotel 52 and cross-loaded his entire load. The pilot also had his hands full with the now overloaded machine and had to carefully fly it just above the trees. As Hotel 53 was heading for Pakse, Hatch was joined by another Raven, Capt. Hal Mischler. Unfortunately, Hotel 53 did not have enough fuel to make it to Pakse and had to land on a road. Mischler orbited above with a flight of Laotian T-28s until another Air America helicopter, XW-PHE, could arrive. The crew of XW-PHE then took all of the passengers from Hotel 53 and flew them to Pakse, with Mischler and the T-28s in escort.

Hatch stayed in orbit above Hotel 53 until another helicopter could arrive with a barrel of fuel. As the crew began to pump fuel into their machine, Hatch spotted enemy forces in the area and attacked them with the F-4s and A-7s holding above. When the fuel was transferred, the crew of Hotel 53 took off and proceeded to Pakse.

As the helicopter departed, Hatch received a call informing him that a Laotian force further east was being attacked and needed air support. He started heading east and then realized that he was seriously short on fuel. He quickly passed the target off to another Raven and turned for Pakse himself. Unfortunately, he had been running his engine at maximum power as he orbited to support the downed helicopters and did not realize how precarious his fuel state was; his engine quit several times en route and he twice considered putting the aircraft down in a field. Instead, he nursed it back to the Pakse area, and as he approached the airfield, told the control tower that he had to land immediately. One of the Air America helicopters heard his call and scrambled to assist him. Unfortunately, the pilot lifted off directly into Hatch's flight path and Hatch had to overshoot the runway. As he did, his engine quit and would not restart. Hatch was able to unceremoniously put the aircraft down on the Air America ramp. It was a long and eventful day for the young lieutenant.[5]

Diplomacy

As the Air America rescue operation was taking place near Pakse, Henry Kissinger was back in Paris dealing with a very stubborn North Vietnamese contingent. Time was now on their side, and they clearly knew it. They intended for the war to go on. While they were meeting, Viet Cong forces in Saigon bombarded the Tan Son Nhut airport on the night of 6/7 December with its heaviest rocket attack since 1968. In response, "red" teams from US Army air cavalry troops in the Saigon area launched to find the enemy launch sites and destroy whatever enemy forces they could find. One team from the F Troop, Eighth (F/8) Cavalry searched to the east of the city. While checking out one likely launch site, one of the OH-6 aircraft, Blueghost 13, flown by 1st Lt. Chris Cole and gunner Sp4 Don Russell, was hit and downed by enemy fire. Cole was wounded with bullets through both legs. This was his second shootdown. Fortunately, Russell was not hurt, and he helped Cole out of the aircraft. As they moved away from the wreckage, Russell fired his and Cole's weapons at pursuing enemy troops. Above, the escort AH-1s joined the fight with their cannons and rockets as the accompanying UH-1 command and control bird landed and picked up both men.[6]

The rocket attacks were a clarion signal from North Vietnam. Kissinger could not get the North Vietnamese to accept any of the proposed changes, and President Thieu refused to accept any political interference with his government in Saigon. By 12 December, they were at an impasse. North

Vietnamese leaders ordered the evacuation of large sections of the Hanoi/ Haiphong region in anticipation of air attacks. The next day, Kissinger and Tho both returned home, leaving their deputies in Paris.[7]

Linebacker Operations

As the bombing continued over the panhandle area of North Vietnam, USAF RF-4s were constantly running through that area to photograph targets. In preparation for "sustained" and increased air operations in the northern sections of North Vietnam, RF-4s were also photographing known prominent locations to verify loran navigational systems to provide accurate bombing in heavy weather conditions as had been attempted a year earlier in the Operation Proud Deep missions. In the afternoon of 9 December, an RF-4 from Udorn, Kansas 01, flown by Maj. Billie Williams and 1st Lt. Hector Acosta, was conducting one of these missions with an escort of four F-4Es. Kansas 01 was hit and severely damaged by an SA-2 about thirty-five miles north of Vinh. When the aircraft burst into flames, the two men ejected. A Fast FAC, Wolf 13, established contact with Acosta. Sandys 01–05 were launched but were unable to establish voice contact or pinpoint his location. With darkness rapidly approaching, plans were made to resume recovery efforts the next day. Fast FACs patrolled that area and maintained a listening watch throughout the night.

The next morning at about 0700L, Wolf 03 reestablished radio contact with Acosta and authenticated him. Supported by fifteen aircraft providing MiGCAP, surface-to-air missile (SAM) suppression, and other duties, Sandys 01–08 swarmed into the area and were able to make weak radio contact with Acosta and locate him. Four HH-53s had taken off from Nakhon Phanom Royal Thai Air Force Base (NKP) and were in the area with King 21. Sandys joined with strike flights to drop area denial ordnance and to attack gun and troop positions around the survivor. Sandy 01 then led in Jolly Green 32 for a pickup attempt as other Sandys screened their approach with smoke. The crew of Jolly Green 32 searched for twenty minutes but could not spot the survivor. The helicopter was being hit by enemy fire. When a pararescue jumper (PJ) and the copilot were wounded, Jolly 32 flew out of the area and returned to NKP.

That afternoon, after more air strikes were put in on the enemy forces now moving into the area, Sandys 06, 07, 10, and 11 escorted in Jolly Green 60 for another attempt. The crew spotted a survivor and was able to hover over him. However, the survivor made no effort to climb aboard the jungle penetrator. After taking several hits causing serious damage to the aircraft including the loss of one engine and the wounding of a crew-member, Jolly Green 60 had to abort and depart. The PJs aboard said that the survivor appeared to be sitting but was motionless—almost as if he was being propped up and used as bait to draw them into a trap. A listening watch was maintained over the site, and four more Sandys again tried to establish voice contact with either man. But they were unsuccessful, and further efforts by follow-on Fast FACs were unrewarded.

This event was recorded in the war history of the Nghe An Province, which noted:

> At 1400 hours on 9 December one of the 267th Missile Regiment's missile battalions, located at a launch site in Nghia Dan, scored a hit on one RF-4C. The aircraft began to burn and crashed into a mountain jungle region along the border between Nghia Dan and Quynh Luu districts. Quynh Chau militia forces (Quynh Luu District) saw the parachute come down in the area of Chop Dinh Mountain and immediately headed toward the target. A[n] . . . enemy aircraft also arrived over the area and began bombing and strafing to block our efforts to reach the downed airman. . . . A Quynh Chau militia squad reached the downed aircraft and found the body of one US airman lying near the wrecked aircraft, dead. Based on their examination of the aircraft, the militia fighters thought that another airman might still be alive and that the enemy were searching for this airman so that they could rescue him. After one night and almost the entire next day, 10 December, the squad searched this jungle area. Enemy aircraft attacked, dropping napalm and chemical weapons, but the entire squad successfully evaded these attacks and continued to carry out its search.
>
> At 1400 hours on 10 December a helicopter arrived and lowered a rope ladder for the down airman to climb up to be rescued. At that moment the Quynh Chau militia forces were close by. They focused heavy fire on the helicopter as it was hovering in the air. The helicopter was hit. The damage forced the helicopter to fly away after dropping the ladder and the downed airman. The Quynh Chau fighters arrived and captured the surviving airman after twelve straight hours of searching for him.[8]

Consequently, rescue efforts for the crew of Kansas 01 were suspended on the thirteenth. In fact, 1st Lt. Acosta had been taken prisoner and was released in April 1973. The remains of Maj. Williams were returned in December 1990.[9]

More Diplomacy

Returning to Washington on 14 December, Kissinger met with President Nixon for eight hours over two days. Nixon sent a strongly worded cable to Hanoi warning that "serious negotiations" would have to be resumed within seventy-two hours—or else bombing of the North would be resumed. Then he had Kissinger brief the results of the Paris negotiations to top government officials, military leaders, and his White House staff.

Meanwhile, the US military was preparing for what seemed inevitable, a wholesale attack on the North Vietnam heartland. In response to Admiral Gayler's request on 30 November, the Strategic Air Command (SAC) staff had developed a list of sixty targets in North Vietnam suitable for attack by B-52s. On 14 December, the Joint Chiefs of Staff (JCS) authorized the resumption of manned photo reconnaissance flights above the twentieth parallel starting 16 December. The next day, the chairman of the JCS, Admiral Thomas Moorer, directed that air and naval gunfire operations be resumed north of the twentieth parallel at 1200Z (1900L Hanoi time) on 17 December for a maximum three-day effort, and he forwarded a list of fourteen targets for B-52 strikes. The start time was subsequently slipped twenty-four hours to 1200Z on 18 December.[10]

Decision

Hanoi did not respond to President Nixon's cable. Accordingly, on 17 December, Nixon ordered the resumption of concentrated US air attacks against North Vietnam, including the use of tactical air and B-52s against targets in the Hanoi and Haiphong area, beginning later that evening in Washington-area time. The JCS then alerted both the commander in chief, Pacific (CINCPAC) and the commander in chief, Strategic Air Command (CINCSAC) that the operations could be extended beyond the three-day limit. In explaining to the nation what was about to happen, White House press secretary Ron Ziegler indicated that Linebacker II, as the attacks were now called, was a campaign, not just one attack. He said that it would continue "until such time as a settlement is arrived at," adding, "We stand ready to end the conflict rapidly." They wanted a quick end to this. As Ziegler further explained, "It is the President's view that neither side can gain from prolonging the war or from prolonging the peace talks."[11]

Linebacker II

The airmen and sailors of the Seventh Air Force (AF) and Task Force (TF-) 77 were ready. For the new campaign, strike packages of F-4s and

Linebacker II—the high road to Hanoi. (Courtesy Jack Fellows)

A-7s (US Navy and USAF), would be striking targets during the day, and A-6s, F-111s, and B-52s with support packages would be striking at night. The need for rescue could arise anywhere at any time. The B-52 crews now going into the heart of North Vietnam were briefed on what to expect from the rescue forces. They were shown the selected area for evasion (SAFE) areas around Hanoi and briefed on the preplanned contact times for evaders. All were equipped with full survival vests and had at least one survival radio and a secondary beeper. They had all been through survival school and knew what to expect. They understood the function of the rescue task forces and knew how to interact with the Jolly Greens, Sandys, and FACs who would try to rescue them, although some were not as trusting of the A-7s as they had been with the old A-1s. They knew that the US Navy would recover them over the Gulf of Tonkin (GOT) but were not as sanguine about the Jolly Greens coming into the Hanoi area.[12]

18–19 December
As evening settled over North Vietnam, their intelligence sources in Thailand reported that a large force number of fighters and bombers were taking off from the US bases, and especially U-Tapao. Their long-range radars also spotted HH-53s from the Fortieth Aerospace Rescue and Recovery Squadron (ARRSq) as they orbited over northern Laos—just as the

radars had during the Valent 04 rescue mission in June. A few hours later, 121 B-52s began striking targets in the Hanoi area. They were divided into three waves, about four hours apart. Each wave was escorted by a gaggle of about forty-five fighters of various types for MiGCAP, SAM suppression, chaff dispensing, and standoff jamming. The B-52s were also preceded and followed by F-111s from Takhli and A-6s from the aircraft carriers. Over two hundred SAMs were fired at the aircraft, damaging two and bringing down three of the big bombers.[13]

At about 2200L, Charcoal 01, a B-52G, from the Ninety-Seventh Bomb Wing (BW), Blytheville Air Force Base, Arkansas, was in the first wave as it attacked the Yen Vien railway yard on the northern edge of Hanoi. The aircraft was mortally hit by two SA-2s just before bomb release and went down near its target. Several other B-52 crews watched the bomber go down. Three men ejected and were quickly captured. They were released in March 1973. The other three crewmembers went down with the aircraft. Their remains were returned in 1978.[14]

An hour later, an F-111 from Takhli, Snug 40, flown by Lt. Col. Ronald Ward and Maj. James McElvain, struck the Hanoi International Radio Communication Transmitter located in the Hanoi environs, the most heavily defended area in North Vietnam. After expending their bombs, the crew reported to a monitoring agency that they were outbound. That was their last communication. The wreckage was never found, and postmission analysis suggested that the terrain-following radar failed as they flew across the Gulf of Tonkin and caused them to hit the water. There was nothing to rescue.[15]

As the second wave attacked its targets in the Hanoi region, another B-52G, Peach 02, from the Second BW at Barksdale Air Force Base, Louisiana, was hit and severely damaged by an SA-2 just after releasing its bombs and turning away from the target. The crew was able to fly their aircraft out of North Vietnam, intending to land at U-Tapao RTAFB, Thailand. However, while they were passing Udorn, a fire in the left wing worsened and the aircraft began to come apart. All seven crewmembers, including the squadron commander, who was in the jump seat, bailed out and were rescued by two USMC CH-46s from MAG 15 at Nam Phong Air Base, Thailand. They flew the survivors to Udorn.[16]

Just at sunrise, a B-52D, Rose 01, from the Ninety-Ninth BW, Westover Air Reserve Base, Massachusetts, dropped its bombs on Hanoi's main radio station. As it was turning away after release, it was hit by an SA-2 and caught fire. Four crewmembers bailed out and were quickly captured. There was no SAR effort. The wreckage of the B-52 landed in a lake in central Hanoi and became a popular photo opportunity for the international press. The POWs were released in March 1973.[17]

The POWs

The American POWs certainly heard the noise of the heavy bombers and escort aircraft. They immediately understood what was happening and saw the fearful reaction of their North Vietnamese guards. Recalled Capt. Jerry Singleton, USAF, who was being held at a camp north of Hanoi not far from the Chinese border: "The guards started shouting, 'Nixon has gone crazy. He is going to kill us all.'"[18]

Aboard the ships of TF-77, the HH-3s of HC-7 were ready. They were also flying aircraft along the shoreline when strikes were going in. At dawn, Jolly Greens 32 and 66 took off and flew north to orbit in northern Laos. They were joined by Sandys 01–05. But they were not used and were returned to their bases when their coverage window was ended. This would be a common pattern throughout the campaign.[19]

19–20 December

Air operations were also continuing in South Vietnam, Laos, and Cambodia. In the early afternoon, a Twentieth Tactical Air Support Squadron (TASS) OV-10, Covey 64, was seriously damaged by an SA-7 near Quang Tri. It was flown by Capt. Francis Egan and USMC 1st Lt. Jonathan Patterson from the First Air and Naval Gunfire Liaison Company (ANGLICO). The missile strike was witnessed by Vanguard 969, a US Army U-21, which orbited in the Quang Tri area to snoop on NVA communications. Its crew contacted King 26 to alert them to Covey 64's emergency. When Egan realized that the aircraft would not maintain altitude on one engine, he glided down over friendly lines before both men ejected. A Vietnamese Marine Corps (VNMC) element was nearby and secured Patterson when he landed. However, Egan's parachute did not deploy, and he was found still strapped in his ejection seat. A UH-1, Centaur 03 from F/4 Cavalry, flown by Chief Warrant Officer 2 Joe Bowen and crew, picked up both men, but Captain Egan had died of injuries. They were taken to Camp Eagle, near Hue. Interestingly, Bowen had a Vietnamese soldier on his aircraft as an interpreter. As they were inbound to pick up Egan and Patterson, the soldier told Bowen that the troops holding the two men were, in fact, NVA soldiers who wanted to surrender and thought that turning over the two Americans would help that process.[20]

On the second night of Linebacker II, ninety-three B-52 sorties were sent in, again in three equal waves, against targets in the Hanoi area. Tactical modifications were applied based on the results from the night before. All waves were also escorted with the same support packages. Over 180 SAM firings were reported by the crews. Two aircraft were damaged, but none were shot down.[21]

In the early morning hours of 20 December, an A-7, Streetcar 303, off the USS *America*, was part of a flight that was attacking an SA-2 site twelve miles south of Haiphong in support of the B-52s. The aircraft, flown by Lt. Carl Wieland, was struck and destroyed by a missile. The pilot ejected, but in the chaos ongoing around him, his loss was not immediately noticed. Before any rescue actions could be taken, he was captured. He was released in March 1973.[22]

20–21 December

On the third night, ninety-three B-52s were scheduled to go in. Their main target was the big rail yard at Gia Lam and also the Yen Vien railroad complex near Hanoi. Over 220 SAMs were fired, and six B-52s were shot down.

At about 2200L, Orange 03, a B-52D from the Ninety-Ninth BW was on its bomb run at Yen Vien when it was attacked and slightly damaged by a MiG-21. Oranges 01 and 02 both released their bombs on the target. Just prior to bomb release, Orange 03 was hit and mortally damaged by an SA-2, a few miles north of Hanoi. The aircraft went into a flat spin, and the electrical system failed. The aircraft commander ordered the crew to bail out, and two men ejected and were quickly captured. They were released in February and March 1973. The other four men went down with the aircraft.[23]

Almost simultaneously, another B-52G, Quilt 03, from the 456th BW, Beale Air Force Base, California, was on its bomb run against the Yen Vien rail yards when it was hit by at least one SA-2. Two men were wounded and subsequently died when the aircraft depressurized. The other four men all ejected and were quickly captured. They were released in 1973, and the remains of the other two men were returned in 1977.[24]

Just a few minutes behind Quilt 03 was Brass 02, in another flight of three aircraft to attack the same target. It was another B-52G from the Forty-Second BW at Loring Air Force Base, Maine. On its bomb run, it was hit by two missiles, which knocked out four engines. But the aircraft was still flyable, and the crew turned to the southwest in an attempt to get out of North Vietnam. Fortunately, the crew was able to hold the aircraft together, and they were attempting to make it to U-Tapao when the aircraft went out of control about ten miles southwest of NKP. All six of the crewmembers were able to bail out. Knife 30, a CH-53 from the Twenty-First Special Operations Squadron (SOS) was on a night sortie and picked up two men; Jolly Green 71 picked up one; Pedro 42, an HH-43, picked up two; and the sixth man caught a bus that brought him to the front gate.[25]

Just past midnight, an A-6 from the USS *Enterprise*, Milestone 511, was shot down by AAA or possibly an SA-7, as the aircraft was making a low-level run on the Haiphong shipyards. The crew, Cdr. Gordon Nakagawa and Lt. Kenneth Higdon, both ejected but were quickly captured before any SAR effort could be mounted. Both were released in 1973.[26]

Three losses in the first wave certainly got the attention of commanders in Saigon and at SAC headquarters at Offutt Air Force Base, Nebraska. Since the B-52Gs seemed to be more vulnerable than the other B-52 types, two cells scheduled in the second wave were recalled, and that wave suffered no losses. In fact, analysis showed that when the B-52Gs turned at more than forty-five degrees of bank angle, the antennas pointed to the horizon and the G model had zero electronic defense.[27]

At about 0600L, a US Navy flight working east of Hanoi reported a huge fireball over Hanoi just as the third wave was approaching its targets. Straw 02, a B-52D from the 306th BW at McCoy Air Force Base, Florida, had just completed its bomb run and release and was making a poststrike turn when it was hit by an SA-2 missile and badly damaged. Two engines were on fire, and the electrical system failed. However, the crew was able to turn toward the southwest and attempt to get out of North Vietnam. Thirty minutes later, the aircraft became uncontrollable, and five members of the crew bailed out east of Ban Ban Valley in Laos, an area under the control of Pathet Lao forces. The status of the radar navigator was never established. Jolly Greens 71 and 73 had already launched and were heading to the holding point in Northern Laos, and Sandys 01, 02, and 03 were scrambled from Korat, followed an hour later by Sandys 11, 12, 13, and 14. Everybody headed for the area of the survivors, and two MiGCAP flights were diverted to cap the area from MiGs. Once there, everyone began searching for the survivors. Once they were located, the Sandys had to eliminate some AAA as the two helicopters worked to recover the survivors. Jolly 73 picked up two survivors and Jolly 71 picked up three. Jolly 71 lowered a PJ to the ground to search for the sixth man. No trace of him was found. Jollys 71 and 73 then returned to NKP, leaving the continuing search for the missing crewmember to Jollys 30 and 66 and the Sandys. They never found him.[28]

While the rescue forces were working hard to recover the Straw 02 survivors, several additional cells were arriving to attack more targets in the

Hanoi area. Olive 01 was a B-52G from the Ninety-Second BW at Fairchild Air Force Base, Washington. It was leading a cell of three aircraft directed at a target near Kinh No in the Hanoi area. While making its turn after bomb release, it was hit by several SA-2s and destroyed. The aircraft erupted in flames and went straight down. There were seven men onboard. Three of the crew were known to have ejected. All three were quickly captured, and one died in captivity. Two were released in March 1973. The remains of one man were released in 1974 and the other four in 1988. There was no SAR effort. The Joint Rescue Coordination Center (JRCC) log-in mentions Olive 01 only once: "20/2250Z Olive 01 No Contact—NX (Notified) Jack."[29]

But even as the first glimmer of dawn began to arrive, the drama was not over. Two more cells of B-52s were headed for Kinh No. In the second cell, Tan 03, a B-52G from the Ninety-Seventh BW had a problem. Their radar-navigation system had failed, and they needed to rely on release guidance from their cell lead. Unfortunately, they were lagging behind the two other B-52s, and the aircraft was rocked by an SA-2 detonation just below it. The aircraft went into a dive, but the pilots were able to recover it. Another SA-2 hit the aircraft, and the pilots lost complete control. The aircraft commander directed the crew to bail out. Then the aircraft exploded. Only the gunner escaped, and as he arrived on the ground, he was quickly captured. He was released in March 1973. The remains of one man were returned in 1975 and the other four in 1988. The JRCC log holds just one cryptic comment on this event: "Tan 03 lost contact after Bullseye from King 22 NX B/C (Blue Chip)."[30]

The Whistle

It had been a horrible night. At one point, as the SAMs were streaking through the sky, an electronics warfare officer on one of the B-52s decided to take matters into his own hands. He carried a whistle as a good-luck charm and would occasionally whistle on the radio at opportune times for a bit of comic stress relief. While watching several SAMs streak up at him and his compatriots, he let go with a blast from his whistle on the North Vietnamese air defense control frequency and then followed it up with a shrill "Time out!" call. For ninety seconds, not a single missile was fired. In that time, his crew was able to drop their bombs, make their poststrike turn, and escape. He was either smart or lucky but didn't care which because they got out alive. Countermeasures come in all forms.[31]

Maybe the SAC commanders should have issued whistles to all crew-members, because they had to do something. The night was a disaster. Four B-52Gs and two B-52Ds had been shot down, and another B-52D had been seriously damaged but was able to make it back to U-Tapao. Over two hundred SAMs had been fired at the attackers. But after three nights of bombing, some key points were now evident:

1. The B-52Gs had fundamental deficiencies in their electronic counter-measures equipment that could not be quickly fixed. They were at high risk over Hanoi.
2. Six of the B-52s had been hit as they turned after bomb release.
3. Changes had to be made to the basic plan of attack.

All of this was discussed in detail as CINCPAC and SAC commanders and staffs conferred. They also determined that much more SAM suppression was needed, especially just before the B-52s arrived.[32]

From a rescue perspective, the numbers from night three of the campaign were bad. Of the thirty-seven men who crewed these aircraft, only eleven were rescued, and none from the Hanoi area. The Linebacker II campaign was clearly showing the limits of the theater rescue capability. The men of rescue were more than ready to fly the missions. However, their aircraft were just not capable of operating in a high-threat area like Hanoi.

21–22 December

In the evening hours of 21 December, an AC–130, Spectre 17, from the Sixteenth SOS at Ubon, was attacking trucks along the Ho Chi Min trail, twenty-five miles west of Saravan, in clear skies with a bright moon. The NVA gunners were very active and hit the lumbering gunship with several rounds of 37mm fire. The Spectre crew turned to head for Ubon only seventy miles to the west. Spectre 07 was also in the area and turned to trail their stricken squadron mate. However, Spectre 17 was mortally damaged and filling with fuel when the crew started to bail out. The crew of Spectre 07 made radio contact with two survivors. They assumed OSC and used their guns to suppress the enemy gunners. King 21 was on orbit in northern Laos, and King 22 was directed to launch from Korat to serve as the airborne mission commander (AMC). However, King 22 had an engine problem and had to abort. Jack directed Spectre 07 to assume AMC duties until King 22 could get airborne. Jolly Greens 32—equipped with limited night recovery system (LNRS)—and 63 launched from NKP. Three Sandy A-7s, 11, 12, and 13, also launched from Korat.[33]

At Pakse, the Raven FAC detachment was notified of the downing of Spectre 17. Raven 10, Capt. Ed Chun with Capt. Harrold Ownby in his back seat, and Raven 44, 1st Lt. Lew Hatch with 1st Lt. Terry Pfaff in his back seat, took off in their O-1s. After only a few miles, they could see the burning wreckage and the shells streaking down from Spectre 07. Approaching the area, Chun called back to Pakse and asked for Air America to launch helicopters for the pickup. The Ravens were very familiar with the enemy forces in that area and knew that they were not far away. They spotted two parachutes on the ground and heard the survivors on the radio. Time was of the essence, and they knew that the Air America helicopters would arrive before the Jolly Greens. However, Jack overruled the use of the Air America helicopters. The recovery would be made by Jolly Green 32 with its LNRS.

Another AC-130, Spectre 12, also diverted to support the operation. The Jollys arrived an hour and ten minutes after the crash, and Jolly 32, flown by Capt. Jerry Shipman and crew, successfully utilized the LNRS and low light television (LLTV) systems to recover the two crewmembers in five minutes. They then hovered over the area for another twenty minutes in a fruitless search for any other survivors. Shipman and crew flew the two airmen to NKP. King 22 finally arrived on the scene and assumed AMC. They orbited over the area for the rest of the night but did not detect any sign of any other survivors.

This was the first actual/full night recovery utilizing the LNRS system. Stated Captain Shipman in his mission report, "The darkness protected us from ground fire in the SAR area."[34]

Lew Hatch was airborne again before sunrise to cap an insertion of a Laotian infantry force to scour the crash site. He found two main areas of wreckage and oversaw the infil. Enemy forces were waiting for them, and the Laotians suffered one killed and several wounded. Hatch called in flights of T-28s on the enemy troops. The Laotian force made it to the two crash sites but did not find any more survivors. Raven FACs stayed over the force until they moved overland to the southwest and were met by trucks, which took them back to Pakse.[35]

One of the men lost on Spectre 17 was actually a fighter pilot from the 497th Tactical Fighter Squadron (TFS). Major Francis Walsh had been grounded by a medical problem for several days and just recently cleared to fly. He visited the Sixteenth SOS and asked to fly with them so that he would get his combat pay for the month. Normally, he would have been able to get the necessary sortie with his squadron. However, he asked to be allowed some time off the flying schedule so that he could spend Christmas with his wife, who was coming to Ubon for a visit. She arrived at Ubon on the morning of the twenty-second, expecting to be greeted by her husband. Instead, she was met by the squadron commander, flight surgeon, and chaplain.[36]

Hanoi

While the Jollys, Sandys, Spectres, and Ravens were working to recover the two men from Spectre 17, another B-52 strike force was heading for North Vietnam on night four of the campaign. This one included thirty bombers and was focused on targets in the Hanoi area. Tactical changes had already been made. Now the bombers would no longer make the poststrike turn. Instead, they would proceed straight ahead and depart North Vietnam over the GOT. All of the aircraft on this raid were from U-Tapao; the aircraft from Guam were sent to targets in South Vietnam.

At about 0430L, Scarlet cell of three B-52Ds was approaching its bomb run on the Bach Mai storage complex on the southwest side of Hanoi. The flight lead was Scarlet 01, from the Twenty-Second BW, March Air Reserve Base, California, but that aircraft had a problem with its radar system, and its aircraft commander directed Scarlet 02 to take the lead and direct their bombing. Scarlet 01 then became Scarlet 03. The electronic warfare officer on board, Capt. Pete Camerota, described what happened:

> Just as we approached the Initial Position (IP), our radar nav[igator] lost his computers. . . . We were lead for the cell . . . [the aircraft commander] said that we would fly through the target turn, 2 and 3 would pass us in the turn, and then we would fall in as the new number 3. The purpose of that maneuver was to try and save the mission, save time, [and] make sure the change gets done before the IP.
>
> Falling back in to the number 3 position, we got hit with an SA-2, went off probably a couple of hundred feet below us and to the left. We were making a right turn and were belly up to the SAM site. . . . We got our bombs off and then we made a right turn to egress over the Gulf.
>
> We lose our interphone. Don't know what is going on. I could hear the guns firing. My equipment is faulting, and I am trying to reset it. I expended chaff and flares. I have all the jammers going. My TV screen with all the frequencies on it starts flickering and finally quits. I kept trying to reset my gear, some would reset, and some would not. . . . Since the intercom was not working, I was waiting for the bailout light. . . . When the light came on, I ejected.
>
> Next, I am hanging in my chute . . . mask is gone, helmet is gone. I look up, the chute is good; I guess we were really low. . . . I was looking

around, undercast as far as I could see. I see three parachutes, 2–300 meters, damn, flashing their Habu lights at each other. I got mine out and shined it at them, and then started slipping my parachute over toward them, to get closer to them.

[It was] a very clear and beautiful night. So, as I get a bit closer to them . . . I sink into the clouds and then I land in a rice paddy. Shocking, the water is cold. I hear shouting, shooting and screaming over there. I found a spider hole and put my parachute into it and run along on the top of a [*sic*]–like you are not supposed to, as fast as I could for a minute or two to get away from that shooting and shouting. Then, I started to evade . . . staying down on the side of the dike, sneaking and crawling along. . . . Two things saved my life: those three guys ejected after I did. They were only 300–400 meters away from me, a couple of seconds away from their ejection and my ejection. . . . I had waited a few more seconds, I would have been with those three guys, the two navigators and the co-pilot.[37]

The pilot and gunner were quickly captured. They were released in March 1973. The remains of the two navigators were returned in 1988. The copilot is still missing. However, Capt. Peter Camerota was free and evading in North Vietnam, but nobody knew that yet.[38]

The Evader
Captain Camerota heard voices all around him. He had left his survival pack with his parachute but had his vest and survival radios. He ran along the edges of the fields, stopping only long enough to make a quick call on his radio. He did not get a response. After about an hour, he evaded around a village and saw what appeared to be a deep stand of trees and headed that way. However, he soon discovered that it was actually a small hill, about eight hundred feet high. He found a small cave and crawled in as the air war above continued.[39]

Literally fifteen minutes behind the Scarlet cell was the Blue cell of three B-52Ds, striking the same target. The crew of Blue 01, from the Seventh BW at Carswell Air Force Base, Texas, watched ten SA-2s come up as they made their bomb run. One of them hit Scarlet 03. As Blue 01 was releasing its bombs, the aircraft was bracketed by two exploding SA-2s. The pilots fought to control the plane as windows cracked, the aircraft rapidly depressurized, the electrical system failed, and the left wing erupted in fire. The aircraft commander directed the crew to bail out. All six men successfully escaped the dying aircraft before it exploded and made it to the ground, where they were all quickly captured and thrown into prison. They were

Crew of Scarlet 03. Back row: *Capt. Pete Giroux, Capt. Robbie Howe (replaced by 1st Lt. Joe Copack, not shown), Capt. Waring Bennett.* Front row: *M.Sgt. Louie LeBlanc, Capt. Pete Camerota, Maj. Gerry Alley. (Courtesy Pete Camerota)*

released in March 1973. Unfortunately, some of their errant bombs struck a hospital in Bach Mai and caused an international outcry that the attacks were indiscriminate carpet bombing of Hanoi.[40]

At sunrise, the Jolly Greens from NKP and the A-7s from Korat arrived on orbit in northern Laos. However, there was nothing that they could do for the downed B-52 crewmen. And they had not a clue that Pete Camerota was still loose somewhere near Hanoi.

Pave Low

As these events were occurring, the commander of Military Airlift Command (MAC), Gen. Paul Carlton, was visiting NKP, and Captain Shipman and his crew were able to brief him on the successful use of the LNRS and take him for a demonstration ride. The general was pleased with the professionalism of the crew but clearly saw the limits of the LNRS. He took the opportunity

Spectre 17 LNRS recovery. Gen. Paul Carlton with Capt. Jerry Shipman (door), Brig. Gen. Glen Sullivan, and helicopter crew. (Courtesy Jerry Shipman)

to give them a highly classified briefing on the results of the test of the Pave Low modified HH-53B, which had just concluded at Edwards Air Firce Base, California. Major Balfe and his team had flown the aircraft on seventy-three flights, logging 100.2 flight hours. They flew in flat and mountainous terrain and in varying weather conditions. The general explained that the test showed that the combination of the forward-looking radar with the current LNRS configuration was an advancement toward a full capability to perform night/all-weather rescues. However, the system still needed major improvements in overall area navigation capability, night vision capability, avionics integration, aircrew cuing, terrain following radar, and numerous collateral issues. He also told them that his design engineers and test pilots could not tell him how long that was going to take, and he could not promise them that the system would ever be ready in time for service in SEA. Overall, he felt that all of the challenges could be worked out. He would later commit MAC to fully developing the aircraft and providing the combat forces with a full night/all-weather rescue capability in accordance with MAC ROC

19–70. A few weeks later, at the "request" of General Carlton, Jerry Shipman traveled to an air force conference in Puerto Rico and briefed the combined leaders of the USAF on the successful LNRS recovery.[41]

22–23 December

That afternoon rescue forces were also needed in central Laos, near the North Vietnam border. The US embassy in Vientiane contacted Jack and requested assistance at Lima Site 241, where an Air America H-34 was reported to have gone down with a load of passengers at about 1600L. King 21 diverted into the area. Jolly Greens 66 and 64 were returning from the northern Linebacker orbit with Sandys 01–05; they also headed to the location. Arriving over the area, Sandy 01 discovered that in fact, two H-34s were down at the end of the airfield runway and a pitched battle was in progress. He directed the Jollys to hold to the west until the ground situation was fully determined. None of the survivors could speak enough English to explain to Sandy 01 what was going on. Fortunately, a Laotian O-1 FAC, Nokateng 201, also diverted to the area and began working with Sandy 01 to organize a recovery for the twelve survivors of the two aircraft. Once the situation was clear, Nokateng 201 had the survivors move away from the airfield. Sandy 01 then directed air strikes against the enemy forces, who were equipped with mortars and 12.7mm AAA. Once the threat was reduced, Sandys 04 and 05 led in Jolly Green 64 to recover the twelve persons, all indigenous personnel. They then flew them all to Udorn, where they were returned to Air America control.

In Laos, sometimes strange and unexplained things happened. However, such events were well within the capabilities of an overall theater rescue capability. The Laotian FACs were trained by the Ravens. They were fully capable of directing Laotian and US air assets and were designed to carry on the FAC duties and mission if and when the Ravens were removed from Laos. That would happen soon, and the Nokateng FACs would be on their own.[42]

The Bob Hope Mission

As this recovery operation was being carried out, the airmen at the huge U-Tapao RTAFB were playing host to Bob Hope and his traveling Christmas Show. They were on their ninth and final visit to the forces in Southeast Asia. As they arrived, Hope was met by the senior leaders on the base and apprised of the losses that the force had suffered over the last four nights. He and his troop put on another of their boffo performances designed to entertain the troops and provide them a respite from the war. Hope and several of his performers also visited several units and talked privately with the airmen. Afterward, Hope noted:

We also played to the worst kind of audience that last year—the airmen of the B-52 base at U-Tapao, Thailand. When we got there, we were told confidentially, that they had lost 15 airplanes. . . . If they ever needed a morale boost, it was then, because I believe that those flyers were the guys who got the job done. . . . They asked me to brief the B-52 crews before they went out that night, so I went and talked separately to the pilots, navigators, the gunners and the radar men. . . . Before they left, they did me the honor of naming their mission the Bob Hope mission. They were bound for Haiphong, a very dangerous target, and I found out about three weeks later that they did not lose a single plane.[43]

That evening, thirty B-52s launched from U-Tapao to hit the targets in the Haiphong area. They were preceded by a strong force of US Navy A-6s and USAF F-105Gs against the SA-2 sites in the area. As the bomber force clobbered its targets, forty-three missiles were sighted, but no B-52s were downed or even damaged.[44]

However, Bob Hope's luck had its limits. About five hours later, Jackel 33, another F-111 from the 474th TFW at Takhli, struck the Hanoi Port Facility with a load of twelve Mk-82 bombs. The crew reported their successful strike and egress, adding that the right engine had been shut down. However, when the aircraft lost both hydraulic systems and the flight controls would no longer respond, the pilots, Capt. Robert Sponeybarger and 1st Lt. Bill Wilson, ejected in their capsule, about seventeen miles southwest of Hanoi. They landed on the side of a hill and had a bit of trouble climbing out of the capsule. When clear, both were unhurt, and they decided to separate, figuring that their chances of evasion were better if they did it alone. Both had full survival vests with two radios and extra batteries. The area was mixed jungle and cleared land, with small villages interspersed. Evasion would be a challenge for both, and they could hear people in the area. Neither made an initial radio call. However, the emergency beacon in their ejection capsule was broadcasting, and Moonbeam, the orbiting EC-130 airborne battlefield command and control craft (ABCCC) in northern Laos, heard their beacon and reported it to the JRCC at 1512Z, 2212 local time in Hanoi. Throughout the night, several other aircraft and agencies reported the strong beeper emitting from about twenty miles southwest of Hanoi. At 1648Z, the calculated fuel exhaustion time for Jackel 33, the aircraft had not landed at any friendly airfield, indicating that the aircraft and crews were missing. United States aircraft traversing the Hanoi skies would now call, listen, and watch for any indication that the crew of Jackel 33 was alive and free, as they were already doing for the other men shot down in the last few days.[45]

23–24 December
Jackel 33

During the early morning hours, several aircraft reported seeing what appeared to be burning wreckage in the area of the reported beacon, which was still transmitting. On the ground, North Vietnamese forces were reacting to the downing of the F-111. Over the years of bombing, all villages and local militia had been organized and taught to track down and capture downed aircrews. Villages and local leaders heard the crash of the aircraft and saw the burning wreckages. Some reported seeing a parachute, and the search teams were called out. They also knew that American flyers were equipped with radios and that their leaders would send helicopters to rescue them. Consequently, the locals were reinforced with military units equipped with electronic search devices and heavier machine guns to deal with the rescue forces. The crew of Jackel 33 was in grave danger.[46]

At about 1700L, members from Walnut and Bronco flights reported contact with two different individuals whispering, "Jackel 33," three times. They seemed to correlate to the locations of the beacon and burning wreckage. Briefed on the data, the Third Aerospace Rescue and Recovery Group (ARRG) commander, Col. Cy Muirhead, authorized a recovery attempt based on a "valid objective" and under the cover of the assets in the area as part of Linebacker II.[47]

As the personnel at the JRCC were putting together a rescue plan, Captain Sponeybarger and First Lieutenant Wilson established radio contact and quickly talked. But the weather in the Hanoi area was dismal, with low ceilings and limited visibility. A rescue operation could not be mounted that day. Instead, a listening watch was maintained that night for the crew of Jackel 33, as the two men tried to stay warm, deal with the ever-increasing thirst and hunger pains, save their precious batteries, and move away from the crash site.[48]

Laos

At the direction of President Nixon, Linebacker II operations were suspended for thirty-six hours over the Christmas holiday. However, air operations were still being conducted in Laos. At Pakse, USAF Capt. Hal Mischler, Raven 40, took off in an O-1 to support Laotian Army units operating near Saravane, on the western periphery of the Ho Chi Minh trail. He had a Laotian soldier in his back seat who was bilingual and could coordinate with the ground units. While on station, their aircraft was severely damaged by enemy guns. Mischler was mortally wounded and the aircraft began to smoke. The Laotian backseater had been given some rudimentary flight instruction and took control of the aircraft. He turned the aircraft toward the airstrip at Saravane. But as he crossed a river, the smoke turned into fire, and he jumped out of the aircraft at an estimated two hundred feet above the water. Tragically he overshot the river, impacted a wall, and was killed. The Laotian ground commander in the area notified Hillsboro, the Southern Laos ABCCC, and then dispatched a platoon of commandos to the crash site, hoping to rescue the pilot.[49]

First Lieutenant Jack Shaw, USAF, Raven 43, had taken off just a few minutes behind Mischler to perform visual reconnaissance along the Ho Chi Minh trail when he got a call from Hillsboro notifying him that Raven 40 was down. Shaw and Mischler had earlier flown together as Nail FACs with the Twenty-Third TASS. Shaw had just joined the Ravens, and Mischler was his roommate. This was Shaw's first Raven sortie. He had in his back seat 1st Lt. Lew Hatch, an experienced Raven FAC, who would provide him with an area orientation. They headed for the crash site. As they approached the burning wreckage, the enemy guns began to fire at them. Above, flights of fighter aircraft arrived over their location to support the SAR, and Air America helicopters began to divert to the area to attempt a pickup. Below, the ground team arrived at the crash site and found that Raven 40 had been killed. They removed the body and brought it back to a friendly position.

Unaware of Mischler's fate, Shaw and Hatch tried to organize a rescue effort. However, their aircraft was also hit by numerous rounds of enemy fire. The engine quit. Shaw spotted an unused small runway nearby and began a glide toward it while also calling on the radio that they were now going down. However, he was only minimally qualified to fly the O-1, so he asked the more experienced Hatch to land the aircraft while Shaw guided him around the bomb craters and wreckage all over the old runway.

Another FAC, Raven 41, USAF Capt. Ed Chun, diverted to their location to begin the effort to rescue them. As he orbited above, Hatch told him where they were landing on the runway and then brought their aircraft to a ground-looping stop, well short of their intended stopping point. The two FACs quickly climbed out of the aircraft with their weapons, maps,

Raven FAC 1st Lt. Lew Hatch and Laotian interpreter. (Courtesy Lew Hatch)

and survival radios, and reported their status to Chun. They could not hear any enemy forces in the immediate area and began walking toward where they thought a helicopter would land. However, Chun was not so sanguine. He could see enemy forces quickly moving toward them as an Air America H-34, flown by Mel Cooper, landed his helicopter where Hatch had reported that they were going to stop. When he saw the two FACs walking, he filled the radio waves with furious invective. They sprinted and clambered aboard, and Hatch and the crew chief began firing at the advancing enemy troops, who returned fire as the helicopter lifted off.

Clear of the fire, Hatch put on a headset to talk on the intercom with Cooper. He told Hatch that they were going to land at a nearby firebase to pick up some wounded indigenous troops. Shaw sat in the back of the helicopter, trying to sort out the overwhelming events that had just occurred on his first Raven sortie. When they landed at the firebase, four wounded soldiers climbed aboard. As they were about to lift off, several more soldiers ran toward the helicopter and loaded a body wrapped in a parachute shroud. Shaw did not realize that the body was Mischler. Perhaps in a state of shock, he thought, "This poor sucker's dead—I wonder what happened to him? I made it—this poor sucker didn't." Shaw noticed a stream of blood out of the parachute shroud, across the helicopter floor, and slipping out into the windstream. "I wonder who this guy is, spilling his blood over Laos."[50] As the helicopter landed back at Pakse, Shaw saw several Americans whom he did not yet know approach the helicopter. One took out an American flag and draped it over the shrouded body. Shaw had still not realized what had just happened. He turned to Lew, "What the hell is this? Some CIA guy get blown away on the firebase out there?" Hatch replied, "Jack, that's Hal." Shaw was stunned. He watched as they loaded Hal's body on a stretcher and walked it across the ramp to an Air America CH-47, which then flew it to Udorn Air Base in Thailand for return to the United States. Such was the dirty "secret" war in Laos.[51]

Jackel 33

NVA military units continued to move into the area where the F-111 had crashed. They set up 12.7mm machine guns on high points and organized teams that swept through the area, finding items that seemed to be equipment used by American flyers.

Based on a favorable weather forecast, that morning of 24 December rescue forces were launched to try to recover Jackel 33Bravo. Shortly after sunrise, Jolly Greens 30, 63, 66, and 73 departed NKP heading north, but Jolly 63 had to abort with a mechanical problem. The Jollys were escorted by a Pave Nail OV-10 from the Twenty-Third TASS, which used its loran to take them to the designated holding point in northern Laos. Sandys 01, 02, 03, 04, 05, 06, 07, 08, and 09 took off from Korat. They were also accompanied by Smokes 01–04, which were loaded with a cluster bomb unit (CBU) to produce a smoke screen, and Slams 01–04, a strike flight with bombs, rockets, and antipersonnel CBU. King 21 also joined the force to serve as AMC and tanker for the Jollys. As the task force approached North Vietnam, Sandys 01, 02, and 03 proceeded ahead to locate and authenticate the survivors to ascertain that each was a "valid objective" and not an NVA trap. However, it took more than an hour before Jackel 33Bravo responded. And he was not with 33Alpha. Jackel 33Alpha would only answer with a beeper.

The Sandys tried to get down over the survivors, but the weather was just too poor for visual operations. Consequently, Slams 01–04 were released for strike duties, and they diverted to work with a Raven FAC near the Plain of Jars (PDJ) in Laos. The Sandys did finally make voice contact with both men, and Sponeybarger relayed some messages for Wilson. At one point, Sandy 06 was able to make a low pass over both men and get better positions on each. He determined that the area was just far too difficult and dangerous for a rescue operation and recommended that the survivors be moved. The JRCC planners quickly developed movement plans for both men, and Sandy 06 delivered the messages to them. All of the Sandys except Sandy 06 then returned to Korat, and the Jollys returned to NKP. Sandys 11, 12, 13, 14, 15, and 16 joined Sandy 06, but they were not able to do anything more for the survivors because of the poor weather and the constant threat of the NVA air defenses in the Hanoi area. Later that afternoon, Wilson talked a bit with Sponeybarger. A few minutes later, Wilson heard gunfire, and Sponeybarger no longer responded. In fact, he had been captured. An NVA team was searching for him and had gear to track his radio. They followed him over a ridge and found him in the grass. He was marched off to prison. The after-action report of the NVA forces stated: "At 1645 hours that afternoon, a cell led by Comrade Nguyen Van Binh spotted a pilot hiding behind a rock pile and very carefully camouflaged. [The soldiers] charged forward together, captured the pilot, and confiscated all the equipment he was carrying with him."[52]

Bill Wilson was all alone, except for the North Vietnamese he could hear looking for him and the voices he had on the radio. He found some tall grass and hunkered down in the miserable cold wetness of North Vietnam.[53]

Not too far away, a USMC F-4 from the USS *America*, Shamrock 210, was escorting a reconnaissance aircraft taking photographs of North Vietnamese torpedo boats when it was hit and severely damaged by 85mm AAA. The crew of Lt. Col. John Cochran and Maj. Henry Carr turned southeast and were able to get out beyond the coastal islands before ejecting. They turned on their beepers and made voice contact with their wingmen, who reported their downing. That alert was passed to the USS *Horne*. It had Big Mother 63 sitting on its helicopter pad at fifteen-minute alert. As Lt. Craig Peterson and his crew lifted off, they contacted an RA-5 crew who were orbiting the survivors as the OSC. He described the enemy situation in the area of small islands and warned them to expect AAA and shore artillery fire. As Big Mother arrived and began searching for the F-4 crew, other naval strike aircraft began attacking the North Vietnamese guns. The crew spotted the two survivors and came to a hover over the first. The rescue swimmer dropped into the water and joined one of the men while Peterson moved away from his position and then returned when they were ready to be hoisted up. Big Mother 67 had also launched off for the recovery and was approaching to do the second pickup. However, Big Mother 63 was very close to the second man and hovered over so that the rescue swimmer could link up with him too. When both men were on the hoist and out of the water, Peterson began to accelerate and hastily leave the area as enemy fire had increased and the helicopter had taken some hits. Once clear of the SAR area, the flight back to the USS *Horne* was uneventful. This was the last HC-7 rescue for 1972. For his actions on this mission, the rescue swimmer, AT2 Thomas McCann, received a Silver Star.[54]

Laos

On the afternoon of 24 December, USAF Capt. Paul "Skip" Jackson, Raven 21, took off from Long Tieng Airfield, Laos, in his O-1 to attack NVA trucks and supplies northeast of the PDJ. When he spotted a large supply area, Hillsboro dispatched a Slam flight of four A-7s to him. This flight had earlier been dispatched to assist in the rescue operation for Jackel 33Alpha and Bravo but was released when the weather precluded any effort to recover them. Instead, they were redirected to work with Raven 21.

As they arrived overhead the Raven FAC, the enemy gunners were active in the area with 14.5mm and 23mm guns. Jackson quickly briefed the flight on the target and then began to direct the A-7s to deliver their ordnance. Unfortunately, as Slam 04 made his bomb pass, Jackson's O-1 was in the A-7's twelve o'clock position. As Slam 04 pulled up, it collided with Jackson's O-1, ripping off one of the O-1's wings. The fatally damaged aircraft then fell to the ground, killing Jackson. The pilot of the A-7, USAF Capt. Chuck Riess, was able to eject. Unfortunately, after one swing in his parachute, he landed next to an NVA unit headquarters and was immediately captured by several soldiers who rifled through his pockets, took his boots, and then threw him into a bunker. Raven 20, USAF Maj. Chuck Hines, diverted to the area and quickly started a search for the downed aviators. He contacted King and requested that the alert Sandys and Jollys be dispatched. Hines made a low pass over the wreckage and determined that Jackson was dead. The Sandys arrived and relieved Hines, but they never made contact with Riess. He was taken to Hanoi and returned home in March 1973. Skip Jackson was the last Raven FAC killed in combat in Southeast Asia.[55]

Later that afternoon, a US Navy A-7, Battle Cry 314, from the USS *Ranger*, was shot down while dropping mines in the Chateau Renaud Channel near Hon Gay. The pilot, Lt. P. Clark, was able to eject. He made several radio calls, and his beeper was received by the other aircraft in the formation. However, search operations were hampered by low visibility in the area and approaching darkness. A listening watch was maintained for the pilot, but he was not recovered or reported as a POW. His remains were returned in 1988.[56]

25 December

On 25 December in the late afternoon, Pigeon 09, a Vietnamese Air Force (VNAF) O-1, was shot down while searching for enemy units in the rolling foothills about eight miles northwest of Quang Tri. The pilot was VNAF 1st Lt. Nguyen Tin, and in the back seat was USMC 1st Lt. Dwight Rickman from the First ANGLICO. They were looking for indications that NVA units in the area were violating the ceasefire agreement. Neither man made an emergency call. USAF FACs searched the area, and aviation units were available and willing to attempt recovery. However, without indications that anybody was alive to be rescued, no attempts were made. Dwight Rickman is still missing.[57]

Southwest of Hanoi, the NVA forces searching for Jackel 33Bravo noted the lack of American jets as they steadily searched for the young airmen. They had found what appeared to be his trail and were optimistic that they would have him soon. Anticipating that he would take advantage of the higher terrain, they moved their teams up into the foothills and brought in more AAA to emplace on the ridgelines.[58]

The Evader

Captain Pete Camerota was getting tired of his small cave. Using his survival map, he determined his approximate position and realized that he would not be able to walk to the nearest SAFE area. For obvious reasons, he would venture out only at night, and he was frustrated that his furtive radio calls were not being acknowledged. Physically, he was okay, in good shape and unhurt. His spirits flagged a bit as he could only wonder if anybody knew that he was alive. And he had another problem on his mind. His wife, Joy, had traveled to Thailand and was staying with him in the U-Tapao area. She was expecting their first child, and he knew that she would worry about him. He wanted to make sure that his USAF compatriots knew that he was down on the ground and evading, trusting that they would so notify her. Perhaps, he thought, his signal was being blocked by the terrain. But he had to be careful. Throughout the day, the nearby fields were full of locals who were tending to their crops. And he noticed that there were individuals with them wearing quasi-uniforms and carrying rifles. Moving only at night, he decided to go up his small hill and see if that helped. Ascending, he found another small cave, just perfect to hide in. While it was adequate for hiding, it did not assuage the thirst—he had lost his water bottles in his travels—or hunger pains now roiling in his gut. And every night he would keep making his calls and waiting for a response. He tried to call on

Jackel 33: 1st Lt. Bill Wilson and Capt. Bob Sponeybarger. (USAF photo)

the designated contact times, but that also was a problem, because he was wearing two watches and they were not showing the same time.[59]

26–27 December
Jackel 33

Bill Wilson was also still evading. On the twenty-fifth, Christmas Day, the weather was just impossible for rescue operations. Wilson followed his evasion instructions. However, he continued to dodge the enemy search teams and maintain intermittent radio contact with passing flights. On the twenty-sixth, the weather looked like it might allow a rescue effort, and another task force consisting of Jolly Greens 63, 73, 66, and 30 headed north, to be joined by Sandys 01, 02, 03, 04, 05, 06, 07, 08, and 09. Two of the Sandys, Capt. Cliff Montgomery and 1st Lt. John Penney, reentered the area, determined Wilson's location, and reauthenticated him as a "valid objective." They also got actively engaged with some AAA sites that they had to destroy. Penney learned an important lesson that day. As Montgomery was searching for Wilson by homing in on his radio, Penney was also trying to use his ADF to get directional cuts on the survivor. While doing so, he was flying behind Montgomery, and he was shocked at all of the tracers that passed between their two aircraft—that Montgomery never saw.[60]

Wilson told the Sandys that he was in good shape but running out of water and batteries. However, the Jolly Greens had mechanical troubles with their helicopters and were not committed for a pickup attempt. In fact, two of the HH-53s had to divert into and spend the night at Lima 16 (Van Vieng), in northern Laos.[61]

The NVA forces now surrounding Wilson watched the A-7s swarming around the area. Familiar with American rescue tactics, they anticipated that this indicated that a recovery attempt with helicopters would soon occur. They ordered their forces not to fire unless directly attacked so as not to reveal their positions. Their commanders also ordered more AAA to be brought into the area by the next morning.[62]

That day, overall Linebacker II operations were resumed, with the second-heaviest efforts of the campaign. In the late afternoon, a flight of F-4s operating north of Hanoi monitored a call on Guard from someone claiming to be a crewmember of Scarlett 03, downed on 22 December. He was not authenticated and his positions could not be determined. Four hours later, ten streams of B-52s, consisting of 116 aircraft, attacked ten targets in the Hanoi/Haiphong area in a compressed fifteen-minute period. Seventy SA-2s were fired at the aircraft, damaging two and downing two more.[63]

Ash 01, a B-52D from the Twenty-Second BW, Robins Air Force Base, Georgia, was part of a wave that attacked the Kinh No railway yard. After dropping its bombs, it was struck and seriously damaged by an SA-2 about fifty miles southwest of Hanoi. Two engines were knocked out, and the aircraft was leaking fuel. The crew diverted out over the GOT for possible ejection. However, the aircraft was still flying reasonably well and, with the assistance of some KC-135s, they decided to proceed to U-Tapao. There, the crew lost control of the aircraft on final approach to the runway and crashed. The copilot and gunner were rescued by ground teams.[64]

Ebony 02, another B-52D, but assigned to the 449th BW at Kincheloe Air Force Base, Michigan, was in the fourth wave that made the attacks in the Hanoi area. As the aircraft was in its poststrike turn, it was hit by an SA-2, mortally wounding the aircraft commander. The copilot took the controls, but when the aircraft was hit and critically damaged by another SA-2, he ordered the crew to bail out. Two men were killed, and their remains were returned in 1977. The other four men were captured and released in 1973.[65]

But even with the losses, this night was a success. Tactical changes like the elimination of the postbomb immediate turn, better positioning of chaff clouds, and one concentrated time-over-target versus three different ones appeared to pay off. The B-52s dropped more than two thousand tons of bombs and appeared to completely overwhelm the North Vietnamese air defenses. The next day, their Politburo sent President Nixon a message that they were willing to restart discussions in Paris on 8 January. Nixon replied that he wanted the Paris meeting to resume on 2 January, and he would direct Kissinger to join them on 8 January. But the air campaign would continue.[66]

27–28 December
Jackel 33

Bill Wilson was due to catch a break, and on the twenty-seventh it seemed to arrive as the weather appeared to be breaking up. Perhaps a rescue team could get in. He needed to come out because he was out of potable water, one of his radios had failed, and he was down to his last battery. In late morning, Jolly Green 73, flown by Capt. Richard Shapiro and crew, and Jolly Green 66 were launched out of NKP for another attempt to rescue him. They were followed shortly by Jolly Greens 32 and 52. En route, they joined with King 27 and were then met by Sandys 01–09, led by Capt. Cliff Montgomery, Smoke 01, Maj. John Morrissey, and Smokes 03 and 04. However, the Sandys had been delayed a bit because as they were waiting for takeoff clearance at Korat, they had to hold for a while because an F-105G preceding them had an engine problem on takeoff. The pilot had jettisoned his external stores at the end of the runway. That debris had to safely be cleared away before the A-7s could line up and take off. Regardless, with the rescue task force joined, they would also be supported by a mass of thirty-two F-4s and F-105s conducting another Linebacker II raid and also providing MiGCAP and SAM suppression for the rescue effort.

BARCAP and MIGCAP was being flown by the fighter squadrons out of Thailand. Captain Bill Anderson, USMC, was fully recovered from his SAR in Laos in November and was leading one of the Nam Phong flights. As a satisfied customer of the SAR forces, he really wanted to be a part of the rescue effort for a fellow countryman, and he would log five hours of flight time over North Vietnam that day. He listened to Wilson's whispers on his survival radio and watched as the SAR forces below positioned themselves for another rescue attempt while remaining vigilant for the MiG warning calls from Disco or Red Crown.[67]

Entering North Vietnam, Jolly Greens 32 and 52 went into a holding pattern with Sandys 08 and 09 as escort. Then Sandy 01, Captain Montgomery, had to make a decision. Major Morrissey remembered the quick discussion they had:

A rescue this close to the CITY [Hanoi], had never been attempted, or considered. . . . That decision to go for Bill was not made by 7th [Air

Force] or King. I told King that the weather and defenses looked reasonable for a try and that we were going in—I did not ask, and no one said no. . . . We joined with the two Jollys and started our joint ingress.[68]

The decision was not quite that simple. Morrissey was monitoring King on one of his secondary radios and they informed him that a MiG-21 had taken off but did not appear to be heading toward the SAR package. However, it would cause other problems in a few minutes. King also notified him that an SA-2 site a few miles to the east was tracking the rescue armada and going into launch mode. Serious gut-check time.

Regardless, Montgomery ordered his force to execute. He and Sandy 02 escorted Jollys 73 and 66 for the run in to Jackel 33Bravo. Crossing the Black River, they and Morrissey's flight laid down a smoke screen to shield the vulnerable helicopters as they flew in toward the survivor. The other Sandys flew ahead to Wilson's location to contact and authenticate him and strike whatever needed to be destroyed.

The Sandy pilots and Jolly crews had no idea what was waiting for them. The NVA had fairly well located Wilson and were intent on using him as bait. Their after-action report states: "Eleven members of the 115th Company deployed two 12.7 mm [AAA] on top of [the hill]. [Another unit] deployed two machineguns along the sides of [the hill]. . . . Militia units deployed platoons and squads equipped with light machineguns in the area. . . . Province militia personnel were ordered to deploy three 12.7 mm . . . on [another highpoint]."[69]

Past the river, Jolly 66 went into a holding pattern with Sandy 08 as Jolly 73 then went for the survivor, drawing heavy fire from a 12.7mm gun, which hit the aircraft with several rounds. The NVA forces were waiting for them. Their after-action report indicates:

Between 1400 and 1500 hours on 27 December, one flight of two F-4s and one flight of two F-8s [A-7s] were active in the skies over [the hill]. At 1530 hours, enemy aircraft fired twelve bursts of 12mm machinegun fire [sic] along the slopes of [the hill] and dropped four cluster bombs and six high-explosive bombs on Ram and Xam hamlets of Cu Yen village. The bombs wounded one civilian, set dozens of houses, the local general store, and a warehouse containing 200 tons of paddy [un-husked rice] on fire, and killed eight pigs. The enemy aircraft also dropped poisonous chemical gas on Trung Son, Tan Phong, Lien Son, and Cao Duong villages to block our forces on the outer perimeter from moving in to search for and capture the missing pilot. . . . The enemy spotted our

Capt. Rick Shapiro. *(Courtesy Chuck Rouhier)*

positions and attacked the positions of our anti-aircraft machineguns. A number of cadre and militia members were wounded and two light machineguns . . . and two 12.7mm machine guns manned by Ha Tay province militia forces became jammed. However, all cadre and militia personnel held their positions, and the rest of our weapons continued to fire at the enemy aircraft. Medics quickly treated the wounded. . . . At 1630 hours on 27 December, an observer stationed at the forward command post spotted an HH-53 helicopter flying in at low altitude through the valley, and our forces all opened fire at the same time. . . . The enemy aircraft circled back and then hovered over Van Hill for about ten minutes. One five-man cell, made up of two personnel from 115th Company and three militia members equipped with two AK-47s and three rifles, fired simultaneous volleys at the enemy aircraft.[70]

Under the swarm of A-7s, Jolly 73 crossed a ridge and spotted Wilson about one-third of the way down the slope on a small ledge with tall grass. They were fired at by another 12.7mm gun, and one of the Jolly Green gunners destroyed it with his minigun. Wilson popped his smoke. Shapiro saw it and hovered toward it. The flight mechanic, Sgt. Chuck Rouhier, spotted Wilson and began to lower the penetrator and give Shapiro directions.

Enemy troops were firing at the helicopter from all sides, and the gunners and photographer were firing back. Rounds were flying through the helicopter.

Wilson ran for the penetrator and was almost on when he either was blown over by the rotor wash, fell down, or was zapped by a static electric charge from the helicopter. At any rate, at that critical moment he could not quickly get on the jungle penetrator. Shapiro did not have any more time to wait. As he noted in his after-action report:

> I looked over at the copilot. . . . He said, "Hey man, I'm hit, let's get out of here!" He nodded towards his right arm and I could see a large open wound the size of my fist right above the elbow. There was blood all over the cockpit. I decided that the situation was becoming increasingly hopeless; the enemy had the cockpit zeroed in and all 3 guns were returning fire. So I executed an immediate egress. . . . I thought I was going to lose control of the aircraft as it went into an almost uncontrollable oscillation and required full right rudder.[71]

Struggling with the now badly damaged aircraft, Shapiro rendezvoused with an HC-130 tanker over northeastern Laos because he did not have enough fuel to get back to any base in Thailand. Unfortunately, the enemy fire had also damaged the aircraft's refueling probe, and it could not extend to safely reach the tanker refueling drogue or even pressurize to transfer fuel. Facing fuel starvation, Shapiro put the helicopter down in an open area, and his wingman, Jolly Green 66, picked up Shapiro and his crew. Jolly 32 then landed, and its crew salvaged weapons, classified equipment, and documents from Jolly 73. However, enemy troops were not far away and began shooting at the airmen as they scoured the wreckage. The accompanying Jolly Greens above provided covering fire for the airmen below as they reboarded Jolly 32 and departed. Then all of the Jollys rejoined with King 27, refueled, and headed back to NKP. As the enemy troops swarmed toward the wreckage of Jolly 73, the escorting A-7Ds destroyed HH-53C #69-5788 and as many of the enemy as they could. When that was done, all of the A-7s returned to Korat.[72]

Noted the North Vietnamese, "The enemy helicopter was hit and struggled to fly away toward the Vietnamese-Lao border."[73]

But the NVA troops still had not captured Wilson. Bitterly frustrated and demoralized, he had no choice but to continue evading. He was able to find small amounts of water and did eat some vegetation—sparingly. He was given more evasion instructions and continued to evade. That night,

Jolly 73 down. (Courtesy Tom Green)

he watched F-111 strikes come through his area. At least that boosted his morale a bit.[74]

As the final flight of Jolly Green 73 was ongoing, another large package of aircraft was attacking targets in the north as part of the overall campaign, and two more USAF aircraft were lost.

Vega 02, an F-4 from the 432nd Tactical Reconnaissance Wing (TRW) at Udorn, was part of a flight providing MiGCAP for the strike package and SAR operation when it was shot down by a MiG-21, fifty miles west of Hanoi. The crew of Capt. John Anderson and 1st Lt. Brian Ward both ejected. In the confusion caused in the command centers by the ongoing Jackel 33, and now Jolly Green 73 SARs and continuous larger air operations, their loss was barely even noted, and they were quickly captured. Anderson broke both arms in the ejection. Anderson and Ward were released in 1973.[75]

A few minutes later, Desoto 03, another F-4 also from the 432nd TRW at Udorn, was on a strike escort mission covering the attack forces when it was engaged and shot down by a MiG-21 that Major Morrissey had been warned about. The crew of Maj. Carl Jeffcoat and 1st Lt. Jack Trimble ejected. Bill Wilson heard the emergency calls and welcomed them to the club! However, before any SAR effort could be mounted for them, they were quickly captured.[76]

Major Morrissey and the A-7s were aware of the loss of the two aircraft.

Morrissey was also told by King that the MiG that had attacked Desoto 03 had landed at the small Hoa Loc airfield twenty miles west of Hanoi. He and his wingman still had ordnance on board, and he seriously considered attacking the MiG on the ground. However, he was dissuaded by two thoughts: (1) His job was to escort and protect the Jolly Greens, and they were not yet out of "harm's way." (2) As a young F-105 pilot, he had flown on a mass strike mission into this very area on 27 July 1965 and watched six F-105s get shot down in a decoy/ambush by NVA guns and the new SA-2s.

At that time and moment, he passed on the fleeting opportunity. He still occasionally thinks about that decision.[77]

As the rescue task force was leaving, an RF-4 from Udorn, piloted by Capt. Sherwood "Woody" Cox, was directed to inform Jackel 33Bravo that the SAR effort was over. Cox and Jack Trimble were good buddies from Udorn. Cox remembered:

We went to the tanker and asked where the Jollys were and were told that they were not only not ready then but were not coming back at all and that we should advise 33B[ravo] to do a Hogan's heroes and surrender with hands in the air. This is what has had me pissed for all these years and continues to bug the hell out of me. We had to go back in and advise a fellow crewmember whose hopes we had just skyrocketed that the SAR was not just being delayed but was being cancelled. I have never had to do anything so wrong in my life. I guess they knew the peace talks were going well and that a release would be imminent . . . but still . . . ![78]

As Sandy 01 was shepherding the Jolly Greens and his wingmen home, 1st Lt. Jack Trimble, Desoto 03Bravo, was experiencing his own misfortune. He remembered his actions:

After I was captured in the early evening/late afternoon all I could do was listen for the sound of jets and gaze skyward in hopes of seeing one of "us." As each echo faded it was strangely comforting to know they would be back in Thailand soon. I was surrounded by quite a collection of militia, farmers and their families and being led down a country road very near where Bill Wilson's SAR effort had gone on.

As we came around a bend in the road, one gomer with a radio marshaled us all under this large oak tree. There we waited. I couldn't hear anything but I did have a clear look at the sky above me. Suddenly, out of the west came the roar of a single F-4, pretty low. It flew right through the patch of sky I could see. It was in a left turn or knife edge and it was an RF-4. I could see the pilot silhouetted against the sky. "It's Woody" and it was, my friend. I'd flown so many weather recce's [*sic*] and post-strike escorts with [him] that I could tell it was [him] by the way [he] leaned forward in the seat. I teared up and hoped [he] would stay safe. I knew I was OK.[79]

Morale was a bit down at Korat that night. Remembered 1st Lt. John Penney:

That was a somber night at the Korat Club. We had the Jolly Green in the hover and Bill Wilson had actually gotten to the penetrator. It may have been a blessing in disguise that he was not hoisted above the elephant grass as, from what I heard the PJs said in debrief, he may have been shot off the penetrator and never made it home alive. We'll never know.[80]

Morale was no better at Udorn. They had another four members of their wing missing with status unknown as Linebacker II continued.

But, while the rescue news was bad, the air campaign was gaining in effectiveness. That evening, another wave of sixty B-52s was dispatched to attack several main storage areas and SAM sites. On its bomb run, Ash 02, a B-52D from the Twenty-Eighth BW, Ellsworth Air Force Base, South Dakota, was the target of an estimated fifteen missiles just after it released its bombs. The detonating missiles severely damaged the aircraft, but the crew was able to fly it back toward Thailand as F-4s escorted it. In the vicinity of NKP, the crew lost control of the aircraft, and the aircraft commander directed the crew to bail out. All six men successfully escaped from the crippled aircraft. They were picked up by Pedro 42, Knife 30, Jolly 32, and Jolly 52, all from NKP.[81]

As Ash 02 was experiencing its travail, another B-52D, Cobalt 01, from the Seventh BW, Carswell AFB, was running its own gauntlet. It was one of twelve aircraft slated to attack the railway yards near Hanoi. On its bomb run it was targeted by several SAMs, and its crew took evasive actions. Unfortunately, one missile slammed into the aircraft and extensively damaged it. Forty seconds later, the aircraft commander ordered the crew to bail out. Four men successfully got out and were quickly captured as they landed. Two men were killed. The POWs were released in 1973; the remains of the two men killed were returned in 1977 and 1985. Ash 02 and Cobalt 01 were the last two B-52s lost in Linebacker II.[82]

Overall, Crews reported ninety missiles launched at the bombers. The results showed how much more effective the tactics were and how the North Vietnamese air defenses were losing effectiveness. After reviewing the results, the commander in chief, Pacific Air Forces (CINCPACAF), General Lucius Clay Jr., sent a message to Washington questioning whether any target in North Vietnam was worth the loss of any more B-52s and crewmembers. Questions were also being raised in North Vietnam, where their military leaders were beginning to question whether or not their forces could any longer defend their nation against the onslaught. They ordered their MiG-21 units to attack the Americans at night and fervently hoped that their dwindling stock of SA-2 missiles would survive.[83]

28–29 December

At midday, the new assistant director of operations for Seventh AF, Maj. Gen. Jack Bellamy, was briefed about the ongoing saga of Jackel 33. Traversing flights were still talking to Wilson, but battery exhaustion was now a concern, and he reported that he was moving as directed but water was short and there were "bad guys all around." The general told the JRCC that they had the authority to direct another rescue attempt if they felt it was warranted. Accordingly, they put the Sandys and Jollys on alert for the day but never directed the package to launch.[84]

That afternoon, an RA-5 from the USS *Enterprise*, Flint River 603, was making a photo reconnaissance run over a petrol, oil, and lubricants (POL) storage area near Haiphong when it was attacked and seriously damaged by a MiG-21. The crew of Lt. Cdr. Alfred Agnew and Lt. Michael Haifley headed southeast. They reached the water, but their aircraft went out of control and they ejected. The status of the two crewmembers was unknown. In fact, Agnew had ejected but was quickly captured. He was released in March 1973. Haifley was killed in the incident, and his remains were returned in 1985. This was the last American aircraft lost to a North Vietnamese MiG.[85]

That evening, sixty B-52s and supporting aircraft attacked railroad yards and storage areas in and around Hanoi. The SAM sites fired only forty-eight missiles. MiG-21s did launch, but one was shot down by an escorting USAF F-4. No B-52s or supporting aircraft were lost or even damaged.[86]

Jackel 33 and the Evader

The next morning, Dakota, a flight of US Navy F-4s, did a radio check with Jackel 33Bravo. He was okay but weak. They also got a call from somebody calling himself Scarlet 03 and a rough fix on his location. Intelligence determined that this was a survivor of the B-52 crew that was shot down the night of 21/22 December. Captain Pete Camerota was elated. In this and a subsequent contact, he indicated that he was not injured but was on a hilltop with villages below and would like to be picked up. Now, the evidence was clear that there were two Americans loose in North Vietnam who needed to be picked up. But by now Camerota was very weak and could sense that he was occasionally passing into mental confusion. He had not eaten anything and had only been able to scrape off a small amount of dew from some large leaves. He had also moved to the top of his hill, which probably facilitated his radio contact. But he also discovered that one of his radios had a dead battery, and he did not have a spare.[87]

Meanwhile, two Sandy A-7s, flown by Capt. Cliff Montgomery and 1st Lt. John Penney, took off from Korat. They flew to Wilson's location and after making contact with him determined that he had moved in the wrong direction. They then dropped him a Madden kit, full of supplies, food, water, radios, compass, signal mirror, and batteries. Wilson saw the pod drop. He proceeded to retrieve it and was captured by NVA soldiers.[88]

Bill Wilson's capture was not just bad luck. Frustrated at not grabbing him during the defeated rescue attempt, the NVA forces had redoubled their efforts and resolve. They observed the flight paths of the A-7s and adjusted their forces accordingly. When they observed that one of the aircraft had dropped something that had not exploded, they carefully surrounded the impact point and waited for Wilson. When he arrived, they were waiting. Later that evening, the local commander gathered his forces and congratulated them for their achievement. He also read to them a message from the General Staff in Hanoi confirming that they had badly damaged the rescue helicopter when it tried to recover Wilson and it had later crashed on the Vietnamese-Lao border. The meeting erupted in cheers and applause to celebrate their great victory.[89]

While working with Jackel 33Bravo, the A-7s also got a call from Capt. Pete Camerota, who heard them above. They were able to get a general idea of his location but were not able to do much more before they had to leave. Camerota realized then that he was in a very dangerous area and his chances of rescue were slim, but others now knew of his situation and perhaps they might try a rescue. It was the best that he had felt since he had been shot down.[90]

At some point, Pete Camerota made contact with Cadillac Flight. They tried to generally determine his location and promised that they would pass along his information for follow-on actions. As before, the realization that his compatriots knew that he was alive and still waiting for rescue heartened him and raised his spirits. However, his thoughts again went to his wife, Joy, alone in Thailand at Christmas. He could only hope that she was being cared for by his unit mates at U-Tapao.[91]

The airmen in the JRCC and Jack did not know that Wilson had been captured and had only the briefest indications that Camerota was alive and evading. However, they now had indications that perhaps a third man, one of the crewmembers of Flint River 603, was also evading. These developments were briefed to General Bellamy. He was presented with a plan to use all of the Sandys fragged for Linebacker II support flights the next day to attempt to find and, if warranted, call in the on-orbit Jollys to recover the three men. The general approved the plan for execution, and the frag orders went out to the units.[92]

29–30 December

The next night, 29 December, a similar force again raided the Hanoi area, with only twenty-five SAM firings in response. The NVA were clearly beaten down. One B-52 crewmember, obviously elated, stated: "There was no threat. It was easy pickings."[93]

Apparently, the North Vietnamese leadership had come to the same conclusion. They notified Washington that they were ready to resume "technical discussions" in Paris on 2 January. President Nixon agreed and directed that all bombing be terminated north of the twentieth parallel.[94]

The next morning, the White House announced that negotiations would resume in Paris on 8 January 1973, between the president's national security advisor, Henry Kissinger, and Le Duc Tho.

Accordingly, as directed, Admiral Moorer ordered US military forces to cease operations in North Vietnam and adjacent waters north of the twentieth parallel at 0659L, 30 December. President Nixon sent a congratulatory message: "I would like to commend those who have so skillfully executed the air campaign against North Vietnam. . . . The courage, dedication, and professionalism demonstrated by our men is a source of enormous satisfaction to me as their Commander-in-Chief."[95]

During the operation, 714 B-52 sorties and 1,773 tactical strike and support sorties had dropped more than fifteen thousand tons of ordnance on thirty-four targets of vital importance to North Vietnam's war-making capability, primarily in the Hanoi/Haiphong area. Rail transport and POL storage were crippled, and electrical power capacity was reduced by 90 percent. More than 1,250 SAMs had been fired, almost the total national inventory. When faced with such utter destruction, the North Vietnamese leadership agreed to resume the peace process.[96]

Additionally, there had been minimal damage to homes and infrastructure, the North Vietnamese themselves admitting that in the entire eleven-day campaign there had been 1,318 civilian casualties. However, after the bombing was ended, the North Vietnamese tried to intimate that the United States, through its "indiscriminate" bombing, had hit the Hoa Lo prison and killed some POWs. Using a covert radio, the POWs were able to send a brief message in Morse code that stated, "V LIE WE OK," which conclusively refuted these spurious allegations.[97]

The American POWs certainly understood the meaning and importance of what had been accomplished in Linebacker II. They shouted and cheered as the bombs fell and later reported that some of the NVA guards apologized for their incarceration and asked for their protection. Said USAF Col. John Flynn, the senior POW officer, "When I heard the B-52 bombs go off, I sent a message to our people. It said, 'Pack your bags—I don't know when we are going home, but we are going home.'" Rudy Zuberbuhler said exactly the same thing.[98]

Jackel 33 and the Evader

On 30 December, radio contact could not be established with Jackel 33Bravo and the weather was bad all over the area, so the SAR plan was canceled. Additionally, with the cessation of Linebacker II, any further SAR operations above twenty degrees north had to be specifically approved by General Vogt. The JRCC log noted cryptically: "Neg[ative] attempt or com[munications] search for Jackel 33, F/R [Flint River] 603, or Scarlet 03 due to bad wx [weather] forecast in A. M. [3,000 feet overcast, 3 miles visibility, rain] and new rules for above 20 [degrees] north."[99]

Pete Camerota did not know any of that. He kept making radio calls and listening, as the villagers below tilled their fields and the skies above no longer resonated with the roar of American airplanes.[100]

As the events of the last few days showed, as optimistic as Colonel Flynn was about going home, he would soon have a few more cellmates.

Rescue Forces

The Linebacker II operation was over. However, little changed for the rescue forces because combat operations were still ongoing in South Vietnam, Cambodia, Laos, and North Vietnam up to the twentieth parallel. And American personnel were still at risk. At General Vogt's directions, rescue operations could still be ordered in the Hanoi area, but by exception. Intelligence sources did not know that Jackel 33Bravo had been captured. They suspected that he and Capt. Pete Camerota were still evading, and another man, possibly somebody from Flint River 603, was still roaming in North Vietnam. But with so many uncertainties, no more rescue efforts would be mounted into North Vietnam.[101]

As 1972 ended, HH-53s from the Fortieth ARRSq were on alert at NKP and Da Nang. Helicopters from HC-7 were cocked and ready aboard ships of TF-77. Six A-7s were on alert at Korat RTAFB. A King HC-130 from the Fifty-Sixth ARRSq was on orbit over north central Laos, and another was on alert at Korat. Jack, the Rescue Coordination Center (RCC) at NKP, was fully manned, and the controllers were alert and standing by. The JRCC at Tan Son Nhut was also fully up and alert. Captain Marck and Master Sergeant White at the JRCC were on duty and at their stations, waiting for that next mayday call. That was their job. That was what the men of rescue did in Southeast Asia in 1972 as they covered the withdrawal of our now residual forces from South Vietnam and our continued operations throughout the theater.[102]

The Linebacker II campaign, conducted 18–30 December, was designed to force the North Vietnamese to the negotiating table to conclude a ceasefire agreement. It involved heavy air strikes "aimed at sustaining maximum pressure through destruction of major target complexes in the vicinity of Hanoi and Haiphong." To defend against the strikes, the North Vietnamese air defense forces were at full strength and at full alert. Chris Hobson noted the following American losses during the campaign:

Fixed-wing aircraft lost: USAF—22, USMC—3, USN—5
Results:

54 KIA	42%
43 POW	34%
30 recovered	24%

Recovered by:

USAF helicopters	18
USMC helicopters	6
USN helicopters	2
Crash home base	2
Unknown	2 [103]

Reflecting the much higher threat to the aircraft and crews, the "recovered" percentage was lower and the "POW" rate was dramatically higher than the earlier campaigns in 1972. It was an inauspicious ending to the year. Additionally, as the record shows, nobody was rescued from the Hanoi area during Linebacker II; all of the B-52 crewmen rescued were in either Laos or Thailand. Adding to the Hobson narratives, other sources reveal the rescues that occurred in Laos and South Vietnam and the continuous efforts of Air America wherever they were operating.[104]

Regardless, on 31 December, there were about twenty-six thousand American troops in South Vietnam. The force still included two air cavalry units—H Troop, Tenth Cavalry, and H Troop, Seventeenth Cavalry—and four medevac detachments: the 57th, 237th, 247th, and 571st, which could and would support rescue operations. However, they departed in February 1973, and by 29 March and the signing of the cease-fire agreements, all American combat forces had departed South Vietnam. However, the Fortieth ARRSq was still at NKP, and the men of HC-7 were still aboard the ships of TF-77. The "American Experience" in Southeast Asia still had two and a half years to go before it would end on a small island called Koh Tang, off the southern end of Cambodia. And the men of rescue would be right in the middle of that episode too.[105]

CHAPTER NINE

THE EVADER UNREQUITED HOPE

I didn't know anything about helicopters. I never got to fly on one.

Pete Camerota*

Captain Pete Camerota did not know about the agreement with the North Vietnamese and was not aware of President Nixon's congratulatory message. All that he knew was that he was still on top of his small hill, somewhere south or southwest of Hanoi, and nobody was answering his radio calls.[1]

But he had not been forgotten. Airmen in Seventh Air Force were doing all that they could to determine the status of him and Bill Wilson. One controller suggested using a Strategic Air Command (SAC)–controlled "Buffalo Hunter" drone, which could be equipped with an ultrahigh frequency (UHF) radio and flown over the projected locations of both men. The drone engineers stated that it could be done and would take twenty-four hours to modify the craft. Air operations were still ongoing over North Vietnam up to twenty degrees north latitude, and on 3 January, General Vogt was briefed on the status of the two men. He approved sending aircraft into the vicinity to attempt radio contact, but no full SAR package of A-7s, HC-130s, and HH-53s. A flight of two RF-4s and then a single F-4 Fast Forward Air Controller (FAC) did make passes in the vicinity of both men, with negative radio contact. On 5 January, Radio Hanoi broadcast that they had captured Bill Wilson. Camerota's file was kept open, and ten A-7s were ready for a SAR effort, pending any firm information that he was alive and free and General Vogt's approval.[2]

Pete Camerota did not know about any of that either. He had lost any sense of what day it was and took stock of his situation. He was uninjured and still had most of his survival gear, although he did not know how much longer his radio battery would last. Obviously, the North Vietnamese did not know of his presence, and were not even searching for him. It was almost as if only he knew that he still existed—or at least that was the thought that was growing in his mind.

His physical condition was clearly deteriorating. He had not had any food and just a few sips of water since his shootdown. Now, he was beginning to suffer urinary problems and could tell that he was quickly losing weight. Any attempt to move from his hill or even to sneak into the villages to steal food and water was now beyond his physical capabilities.

And he could also sense that he was slipping mentally. Even when he was awake, it seemed as if he was in at least a half-trance. It was a challenge to even determine what was real and what was a dream. He remembered:

> Well, it comes down to nut cutting time. Am I going to live or am I going to die. I am a young guy. I don't want to die. I am now in a situation where I am looking at dying, or I am looking at living. It is my choice to make. Because in another day or two, or hours, I do not know, I knew that I was sick, hurting physically, no chance that I was going to live much longer unless I had food and drink. The only way that I was going to get food and drink was to surrender myself.[3]

The young airman realized that he was no longer an evader. He was not going to get rescued. His goal, now, was to survive, to live to see his wife again and meet his child.

But even that was not that simple for an emaciated man. He physically did not have the strength to walk down the mountain. He would have to get the local populace to come up for him. So he destroyed his survival radio by smashing it with his pistol. He threw his pistol and bullets as far as he could so that his captors could not shoot him with his own weapon. Then, seeing workers in the field, he stood up and tried to yell.

Nothing came out. He did not have enough energy to create any sound. Now fully exasperated, he began to believe that he was going to die up on this small hill. But the residual engineer in him began the problem-solving process. He remembered that in his survival vest he had a signaling device, his gyro-jet flares. He took out the package and tried to load a flare into the firing barrel. Unfortunately, this required him to push back on a spring to lock the flare into the mechanism so that it could be shot up into the air, where the flare would burst and draw attention to his position. But even using two hands, he could not generate enough force to lock the flare in. Instead, he had to wedge the trigger against a rock and use his legs to force the flare to lock in the firing position. Then, he had to use both thumbs to click the trigger, firing the flare into the sky.

The flare worked perfectly. Pete saw the farmers look up at him. Then the guys with the weapons started shooting at him. He dropped down on the rocks and went to sleep—only to wake up when they had surrounded him. All were speaking in Vietnamese. They searched him, but he had thrown away anything of value, and they tightly tied his arms behind his back. They also gave him some water. They did not strike or abuse him but ordered him to walk down the mountain. He indicated that he could not do that. The soldiers built a truss with a pole and tarp and carried him down to the nearest road, where they were met by military personnel who immediately began interrogating him. He would remain a prisoner until release with all of the other POWs in the spring of 1973.[4]

CHAPTER TEN

IN REDUCTION NUMBERS AND

MEANING OF RESCUE

The story of Air Rescue may well become one of the outstanding human dramas in the entire history of the Air Force.

Secretary of the Air Force Dr. Harrold Brown*

Numbers

Using an analysis of numbers from Chris Hobson's book, we can derive macro numbers for the entire year.

Fixed-wing aircraft lost: USAF—169, USMC—22, USN—79
Results:

305 KIA	44%	
126 POW	18%	
261 recovered	38%	

Recovered by:

Army helicopters	18
USAF helicopters	101
USMC helicopters	8
USN helicopters	59
USN ships	12
Spec Ops	2
Ground forces	18
VNAF helicopters	2
Crash home base	12
AirAm helicopters	8
Unknown	21.[1]

Rescue helicopter losses:

USAF

HH-3   1

| | HH-53 | 4.[2] |
| | USN | 0.[3] |

Macro SAR numbers for the theater provided by Military Assistance Command Vietnam (MACV) are organized differently. They show the following USAF rescues by HH-43s, HH-53s, and HC-130s (medical evacuations) for the year for individuals by service and by combat/noncombat:

		USAF	USN	US Army	Allies	Civilian
HH-43	9/16	0/2	3/0	9/1	0/0	
HH-53	83/21	19/9	87/4	31/3	35/9	
HC-130		0/33	0/0	0/2	0/0	0/5

Total:

combat 276

noncombat 105.[4]

The USAF also kept statistics of recoveries but with less specificity. For the period of 1 January through 31 December 1972, they recorded a total of 301 saves, delineated by service of the recovery asset:

USAF	102
USN/USMC	22
US Army	94
Foreign Mil	74
Civilian	9

They also broke the data out by country location of save:

N. Vietnam	15
S. Vietnam	224
Laos	51
Cambodia	1
Thailand	10.[5]

As noted throughout, Chris Hobson's numbers do not reflect a comprehensive accounting of Air America rescues, operations in Laos, or US Army and USMC rescues, which are all covered with any specificity only through anecdotal research. The MACV numbers do not indicate rescues by any assets other than the USAF rescue aircraft. The USAF totals are sparse on details but do break out rescues by service and country. In fact, each set of numbers presented is generated from a different perspective, and no one set seems to give us an entire picture. In total, though, they display the theaterwide results for a full year of heavy combat and reveal the importance and success of our rescue efforts that year.

In a more focused vein, the accomplishments of HC-7 are quite remarkable. Whenever US assets were operating over North Vietnam, they kept a minimum of two aircraft airborne and prepositioned along the coast for the quickest possible response. Their maintenance personnel worked miracles and provided 85 percent availability during the year. Their crews accomplished forty-eight rescues, thirty-five of which were in combat. Many were at night or in poor weather conditions, and under direct and occasionally intense enemy fire, which frequently caused battle damage to their aircraft. During the year, they logged almost five thousand hours of flight time and operated off seven different classes of aviation and nonaviation ships.[6]

Medals and Other Awards

The valor of the crews who flew the recovery missions is reflected in individual awards for 1972 rescue- or recovery-related actions:

Medals of Honor:
> Three—all were for actions that led to the recovery of personnel in distress. Interestingly, all three missions occurred in a roughly twenty-mile zone in the Dong Ha–Quang Tri area.[7]

Service Crosses:
> Air Force, seven of twenty total awards for the year were presented for rescue efforts: HH-53 pilots—2, pararescue jumpers—1, A-1/A-7 pilots—4.[8] These awards were for actions on the Nail 31, Bengal 505 (two awards), Oyster 01 (two awards), Valent 04, and Bobbin 05 recoveries. One recipient, Capt. Dale Stovall, was a participant in all five of the missions.
>
> Army, twelve of twenty-seven total awards were presented for rescue efforts.[9]
>
> Navy, five of thirteen total awards were presented for rescue efforts.[10]

Other awards:
> The number of Air Medals, Commendations Medals, Distinguished Flying Crosses, and Silver Stars is unknown. However, from 1966 through 1973, USAF rescue personnel were awarded almost seventeen thousand individual awards.[11]

Capt. Ben Orrell receives the AF Cross from Lt. Gen. Jay Robbin, vice commander, MAC. (USAF photo)

The American soldiers, sailors, marines, and airmen still fighting in 1972 understood that America was pulling out of the war. However, they all understood the moral imperative so clearly stated by General Vogt during the Oyster 01Bravo recovery. Their bravery is reflected in the award numbers above.

Postmortems

During 1972, the commander of the Third Aerospace Rescue and Recovery Group (ARRG) was Col. Cecil Muirhead. He gave up command on 9 January 1973 to Col. Herbert Zehnder. In their end-of-tour reports, both commanders discussed rescue operations in 1972, citing successes and failures and suggestions for the future:

1. The A-7s with their new technology brought new capabilities to the Sandy role. However, their higher speeds impacted their compatibility with rescue helicopters and necessitated modifications to classic escort tactics. The A-7s also needed to be equipped with the electronic location finder for quicker survivor location.

Lt. Tom Norris receives the Medal of Honor from President Gerald Ford. (US Navy photo)

2. Overall, the rescue forces needed an ability to more quickly locate survivors.
3. Night vision goggles enhanced the performance of the aircrews at night and should be exploited.
4. AC-130s, with their sensors and firepower, could very effectively serve as on-scene commander in a low-threat environment, especially at night.
5. Rescue needed a better, smaller, and faster helicopter that could survive in a high threat environment. Zehnder added: "Recovery by air of survivors downed in extremely heavily defended areas, such as Hanoi itself, is generally impossible."[12]

Additionally, SEAOR #114—consolidated in MAC ROC 19-70—the requirement for a night/all-weather rescue capability, was still on the books, and the current effort to address that deficiency, the Pave Low project, was far from any successful result.

The research for this book has revealed data that supports and amplifies the following considerations.

First, the totality of rescue assets available, either dedicated—like the USAF and US Navy units—or designated like the US Army, USMC, Air

America, or MACVSOG teams, created a ubiquitous presence of recovery assets across the theater. The King HC-130s were the constant presence above. Constantly monitoring tactical frequencies, they covered the theater from end to end and had the ability to work anywhere with communications links to command centers, tactical units, and even individual flights or ground units. With their navigation and their refueling capability, they could take the HH-53s with them. They facilitated many rescues like the US Army recovery of Volunteer 538 near Dalat in September, just by responding to emergency calls and alerting units, command centers, and recovery forces.

Then the young combat airmen, soldiers, marines, and sailors applied great creativity to technological exploitation and tactical innovation in a constant quest to derive newer and more successful methods to recover downed or isolated personnel. They utilized new equipment such as the OV-10 Pave Nail system and the A-7D to provide more precise navigation and quicker survivor location. They accepted the fact that there was a fundamental difference between SAR—someone who was rescued at sea or after becoming lost in the wilderness—and combat recovery—someone who was isolated in enemy-controlled territory with hostile forces actively opposing the rescue. The latter could require significant combat actions and had to be dealt with as a war-fighting event.

Air America helicopters in Laos had a company support net and excellent area knowledge of both friendly and enemy locations that gave them the ability to quickly respond to calls for help from isolated personnel, thus shortening response time.

Likewise, HC-7 dispersed aboard the ships of TF-77 in the GOT held similar advantages out over the water. All US strike flights working over North or South Vietnam were prepared to head "feet wet" if they had an emergency. The Sea Devils of HC-7 were afloat with TF-77 from late 1967 to September 1973. They cross-decked from ship to ship 142 times and were truly the "orphans of the Seventh Fleet." It is interesting to note that during the conflict, they referred to their missions as combat SAR versus the SAR used by the other services throughout the theater. In later years "combat search and rescue" (CSAR) would become the more common term for the rescue of isolated personnel in neutral or enemy-controlled territory. It was a prescient act by the sailors of rescue.[13]

US Army aviation units had the same advantages in South Vietnam and even into some areas in eastern Laos and Cambodia. The US Army air cavalry units, with their mix of aircraft and capabilities, were very adept at forming ad hoc task forces capable of very quick rescue responses. They also had a full suite of tactical radios that allowed them to communicate with anybody to coordinate with King or FACs, A-1s, or strike flights who could assist in a rescue. And their air assault doctrine, well-honed after ten years of war, was well vetted to define their modus.

Further, the addition of auxiliary receivers on military UHF radios tuned to frequency 243.00mhz provided an immediately available conduit for those in distress to call for and receive timely assistance. Aircraft, ships, and headquarters across the theater were equipped with these radios, and that web of instant communications capability facilitated countless rescues across all service components.

Clearly, the most ubiquitous recovery vehicle was the helicopter. But those machines, as marvelous as they were, were limited in what they could do, as were the forces that supported them. These limitations had several dimensions:

- Air superiority is a requirement for SAR. HH-53s, HC-130s, and A-1s/A-7s could not perform their SAR duties if they had to react to enemy MiGs. This was clearly demonstrated by events in the Oyster 01Bravo, Crow 01, and the Valent 03/04 SARs. At least local air superiority must be attained and maintained to facilitate SAR operations.
- Likewise, the rescue forces could not operate in areas where SA-2s were active, such as the recovery of Bowleg 02. They were not equipped with the necessary electronic equipment to defeat or neutralize the surface-to-air missiles (SAMs) and had to have SAM suppression support for their missions. SA-7s were also a growing concern and a great threat to the SAR task forces. The HH-53s were being equipped with decoy flares, and the US Army and USMC helicopters were being modified with decoy modifications. However, the A-1s were not modified and had limited capability to operate in SA-7–infested areas.
- North Vietnamese Army (NVA) antiaircraft artillery challenged our rescue forces throughout the theater. As navy rescue operations showed, one of the best ways to negate the guns was to operate at night. However, our rescue forces were not equipped and were only minimally trained to do this. Consequently, night recoveries occurred only by exception. The air force did develop the limited night recovery system (LNRS) and placed it on several HH-53s. However, the only truly successful use was for the recovery of the two airmen from the Spectre 17 shootdown. This was an unfulfilled requirement from this

war, exacerbated by the realization that the CIA had actually developed the highly modified Hughes 500D helicopter, which had both forward-looking infrared radar (FLIR) and loran navigational capability and successfully used it to insert and extract personnel at night deep in North Vietnam. It could just as easily be used for rescue missions.[14]

- To support the Jolly Greens, the escort Sandy A-1s and A-7s actively and aggressively sought out and attacked any enemy guns that challenged the SAR task force. However, they could deliver their ordnance only in a manner that did not itself threaten the vulnerable helicopters. The requirement for close-in defense—literally around and below the helicopter—could be accomplished only by the helicopter crews themselves. Accordingly, the USAF HH-3s and -53s and USN SH-2s and -3s were equipped with machine guns, miniguns, and, later, even fifty-caliber machine guns. However, the rescue squadrons were not manned with gunners. Instead, the guns were operated by the crewmembers, rescue swimmers, and pararescue jumpers (PJs). However, when the crewmembers were engaged with their crew duties such as running the hoist during a pickup, or the PJs were engaged with PJ duties to facilitate the recovery, their guns were not manned. This is an astounding revelation! After-action reports such as Jackel 33Bravo, Bat 21Bravo, Valents 03/04, Kansas 01, and others show the cost of this deficiency. During 1972, the Fortieth Aerospace Rescue and Recovery Squadron (ARRSq) did develop an expedient for this problem. Throughout the year, they had four combat photographers assigned to them. All were trained to fire the guns and all could and did fill in for the PJs and flight engineer. Of course, while acting as gunners, the photographers could not do their primary job. Additionally, all four were wounded on combat missions. One photographer, T.Sgt. Bobbie Welborn, was awarded two Silver Stars for his actions in 1972.[15]

- Concerning the efficacy of NVA air defense operations overall, air force historian Brian Laslie wrote, "Enemy surface-to-air missiles, enemy aircraft, and enemy antiaircraft artillery posed a serious and ongoing threat to American air operations over Vietnam."[16]

Finally, the rescue forces themselves needed a theaterwide navigation capability. The HC-130s had navigators and could operate anywhere. However, the HH-53s were equipped with tactical air navigation systems (TACAN), and a few had Doppler systems, which reportedly nobody trusted, understood, or even used. They were led by either the HC-130s, the OV-10 Pave Nails, or the A-1 pilots, who were utilizing maps. When required to operate by themselves, like on the Date 03 recovery attempt, the HH-53 crews could not do it, especially at night. By 1972, loran was in general use in SEA and the theater had been templated for missions. However, the HH-53s were not so equipped with loran. When the A-7s took over the Sandy mission, they were able to utilize their inertial navigation and moving map navigation systems. But their higher airspeeds made it very difficult for them to work with the much slower HH-53s.[17]

In summary, the bravery and enthusiasm of the airmen, soldiers, marines, and sailors to honor the moral imperative to rescue their fellow warriors in those last days in Vietnam was not matched by the machines available to them. There were just places in the theater where the helicopters could not go.

Many years later, Pete Camerota squared this point cleanly when he said: "Everybody has heard stories about rescue guys coming in and killing themselves trying to save people. That was a real boost to the combat crewmembers. These guys were going to come in and try to save your butt at their expense. . . . It just turned out that in my particular case, as in many particular cases, there was no way to get these folks out, including me."[18]

Camerota's honest comment reflects the truism of Dr. Earl Tilford, who in his seminal work on the war, *Search and Rescue in Southeast Asia*, captured this dichotomy when he wrote: "The rescue crews gave each mission all they had. Nevertheless . . . there was only so much the helicopters could take."[19] It all pointed to one inescapable fact: no amount of moral imperative, as well intended as it was, could override the immutable laws of physics by which these men and machines had to operate.

Finally, as noted, our rescue results during Linebacker II were disappointing and highlighted clear deficiencies. However, as disappointing as the results were, there is another way to look at this climactic campaign. The all-out effort of Linebacker II convinced the North Vietnamese to reengage in discussions leading to a peace agreement being negotiated over the last two years. The "Agreement on Ending the War and Restoring Peace in Vietnam" was signed by representatives of the United States, North Vietnam, South Vietnam, and the Viet Cong in Paris on 27 January 1973. Within it, Article 8 stipulated "the return of captured military personnel and foreign civilians." In February and March, 591 prisoners, including those captured during Linebacker II, were returned to US control. Perhaps

The rescue alert shack on the flightline at NKP. Every combat flyer knew what it meant. (Courtesy Dale Stovall)

it can be argued that Linebacker II itself was our greatest SAR effort of the war, because it precipitated the return of those Americans held by the North Vietnamese. Said General Alexander Haig in his memoirs: "It was the bombing that settled the issue, the bombing that got our prisoners out." That is a pungent and provocative thought.[20]

And so it was in 1972, the Year of Rescue in the Vietnam War.

THE SAGA OF RESCUE CONTINUES

The usefulness of search and rescue task forces in future conflicts will be determined by such factors as the geographic and demographic nature of the battlefield and, of course, enemy defenses. . . . Flexibility will require a continuation of the same spirit of innovation and ingenuity that made rescue successful in the wars in Southeast Asia.

Earl Tilford, *Search and Rescue in Southeast Asia*

The next Chuck Horner to fight an air war had better pay close attention to the way he (or she) organizes and controls the employment of his or her combat search and rescue efforts.

General Chuck Horner, quoted in Darrel Whitcomb, *Combat Search and Rescue in Desert Storm*

After our return from Southeast Asia, the USAF's Military Airlift Command, which commanded the air force rescue units, directed the full development of a night–all weather rescue capability under a program called Pave Low. In the late 1970s, nine HH-53Cs were modified with inertial navigation systems and terrain-following radars, which provided this capability for rescue forces. The aircraft were slated for service with the Forty-First Aerospace Rescue and Recovery Squadron (ARRSq) at McClellan Air Force Base, California. However, when the Iranian hostage rescue failed, these aircraft were transferred to the Twentieth Special Operations Squadron (SOS), at Hurlburt Field, Florida, to serve as lead aircraft for a second rescue effort. That effort was never executed. However, the aircraft stayed with the Twentieth SOS and became a bedrock element of the buildup of special operations forces that culminated with the activation of the Special Operations Command in 1987 and its subordinate Air

Force Special Operations Command in 1989. Subsequently, the aircraft were also assigned to the Twenty-First SOS in Europe and the Thirty-First SOS in Korea. They were also assigned gunners and modified with global positioning navigation systems, integrated navigation packages, electronic countermeasures, and jamming systems and were redesignated as MH-53J aircraft.

After Vietnam, the A-7 force continued to train for the Sandy mission. However, with the introduction of the A-10, that aircraft and its pilots were assigned the Sandy role. They performed what was now called combat search and rescue (CSAR) duties in Desert Storm, Allied Force, and Operation Iraqi Freedom and continue to train as the primary Sandy force for worldwide duty.

In addition to their special operations duties, the MH-53s served as primary CSAR aircraft in Operations Desert Storm, Deny Flight, and Allied Force. In Desert Storm, Pave Low crews conducted a rescue mission for a downed F-16 pilot in daytime low-visibility conditions. The crew flew to the location of the downed pilot in Iraq, but he had already been captured. They also conducted a successful rescue of a USN F-14 pilot in daytime and clear skies.

In Serbia, MH-53Js and further modified MH-53Ms, with A-10 Sandy support, led recovery task forces for the successful night recoveries of an F-117 pilot, Lt. Col. Dale Zelko, and an F-16 pilot, Lt. Col. David Goldfein, by accompanying MH-60Gs. The recovery of the F-117 pilot was under low-visibility conditions and gave the ultimate validation for a night all-weather recovery capability requirement (SEAOR #114) first drafted in Southeast Asia in 1967. The MH-53s also saw service in Afghanistan and Iraq, primarily in their special operations role, and were inactivated in 2008. Of the block of fifty-two HH-53s and twenty CH-53s that served in SEA, and that were later designated for conversion to Pave Low aircraft, only thirty actually made it to retirement.[1]

On 1 July 2016, General David Goldfein became the twenty-first chief of staff of the US Air Force. Under his direction, the air force began procuring new HH-60W helicopters, specifically optimized for recovery operations and reflecting hard-learned lessons of Vietnam and later conflicts. The rescue saga continues.[2]

GLOSSARY

AAA	antiaircraft artillery
AB	air base
ABCCC	airborne battlefield command and control craft
ACS	air commando squadron
ADF	automatic direction finder
AF	Air Force
AFB	Air Force Base
AFHRA	Air Force Historical Research Agency
AGL	above ground level
AHB	assault helicopter battalion
AHC	assault helicopter company
AMC	airborne mission commander
ANGLICO	air and naval gunfire liaison company
ARRG	aerospace rescue and recovery group
ARRS	Aerospace Rescue and Recovery Service
ARRSq	aerospace rescue and recovery squadron
ARVN	Army of the Republic of Vietnam
BARCAP	barrier combat air patrol
bingo fuel	just enough fuel to return to an airfield
BLU-52	chemical incapacitant munition
BN	bombardier navigator in an A-6 (USMC)
BW	bomb wing
CARA	combat aircrew recovery aircraft
CBU	cluster bomb unit, a teargas munition
CINC	commander in chief (theater commander)
CINCPAC	commander in chief, Pacific
CINCPACAF	commander in chief, Pacific Air Forces
CINCPACFLT	commander in chief, Pacific Fleet
CINCSAC	commander in chief, Strategic Air Command
CONUS	continental United States
CROC	combat required operational capability
CSAR	combat search and rescue
CWO	chief warrant officer
D/17	Delta Troop, Seventeenth Cavalry (Sabre)
D/229	D Company, 229th Assault Helicopter Battalion
DASC	Direct Air Support Center
DMZ	Demilitarized Zone
ECM	electric countermeasures
ELF	electronic location finder
EWO	electronic warfare officer
F/4	F Troop, Fourth Cavalry (Centaur)

F/8	F Troop, Eighth Cavalry (Blueghost)
F/9	F Troop, Ninth Cavalry
F/79	F Battery, Seventy-Ninth Aerial Rocket Artillery (Blue Max)
FAC	forward air controller
FLIR	forward-looking infrared radar
FLR	forward-looking radar
FOL	forward operating location
FRAC	First Regional Assistance Command
GOT	Gulf of Tonkin
Guard	emergency radio frequency on UHF radios (243.00 megahertz)
H/10	H Troop, Tenth Cavalry
H/17	H Troop, Seventeenth Cavalry (Undertaker)
HIFR	helicopter in-flight refueling
INS	inertial navigation system
IOT&E	initial operational test and evaluation
JPRC	Joint Personnel Recovery Center
JRCC	Joint Rescue Coordination Center
JSARCC	Joint Search and Rescue Coordination Center
JTF	joint task force
L (time)	local time
LAW	light antiarmor weapon
LBR	local base rescue
LGB	laser guided bomb
LLTV	low light television
LNRS	limited night recovery system
LS	Lima Site, Laos
MAAG	military assistance and advisory group
MAB	marine amphibious brigade
MABS	Marine Air Base Squadron
MAC	Military Airlift Command
MACSOG	Military Assistance Command, Studies and Observations Group
MACV	Military Assistance Command Vietnam
MAU	marine amphibious unit
MiG	Russian fighter aircraft
MiGCAP	MiG Combat Air Patrol
MR	military region
NKP	Nakhon Phanom RTAFB
NV	North Vietnam
NVA	North Vietnamese Army
OL-A	Operating Location Alpha, Son Tra, SVN
OL-B	Operating Location Bravo, Udorn RTAFB, Thailand
OSC	on-scene commander
PACAF	Pacific Air Forces
PARC	Pacific Air Rescue Center
PDJ	Plain of Jars

PJ	pararescue jumper
POL	petroleum, oil, and lubricants
QRF	quick reaction forces
RCC	rescue coordination center
RESCAP	rescue combat air patrol
RESCORT	rescue escort
RHAW	radar homing and warning
RIO	radar intercept officer (US Navy, USMC)
RS	reconnaissance squadron
RT	reconnaissance team
RTAFB	Royal Thai Air Force Base
RTB	return to base
SAC	Strategic Air Command
SAFE	selected area for evasion
SAM	surface-to-air missile
SAR	search and rescue
SARCC	Search and Rescue Coordination Center
SCAR	strike control and reconnaissance
SDV	swimmer delivery vehicle
SEA	Southeast Asia
SEAOR	SEA operational requirement
SEATO	Southeast Asia Treaty Organization
SERE	survival, evasion, resistance, and escape
SOG	studies and observation group
SOS	special operations squadron
SOW	special operations wing
SRAC	Second Regional Assistance Command
SVN	South Vietnam
TAC	Tactical Air Command
TACAN	tactical air navigation system
TAS	tactical airlift squadron
TASS	tactical air support squadron
TAW	tactical airlift wing
TDY	temporary duty travel
TF	task force
TFR	terrain following radar
TFS	tactical fighter squadron
TFW	tactical fighter wing
TRAC	Third Regional Assistance Command
TRS	tactical reconnaissance squadron
TRW	tactical reconnaissance wing
UDT	underwater demolition team
UHF	ultrahigh frequency
VC	Vietcong
VHF	very high frequency
VMA(AW)	marine all-weather attack squadron

VNAF	South Vietnamese Air Force
VNMC	South Vietnamese Marine Corps
WWS	wild weasel squadron
WO	warrant officer
WSO	weapons systems operator (USAF)
Z (time)	Greenwich Mean Time

NOTES

PREFACE

1. Maj. James Overton, Project CHECO Southeast Asia Report, USAF Search and Rescue November 1967–June 1969, 3, Air Force Historical Research Agency, Maxwell AFB, AL.

2. Earl Tilford, *Search and Rescue in Southeast Asia, 1961–1975* (Washington, DC: Office of Air Force History, 1980), 33, 146–148.

3. Tilford, *Search and Rescue in Southeast Asia, 1961–1975*; George Galdorisi and Tom Phillips, *Leave No Man Behind: The Saga of Combat Search and Rescue* (Minneapolis, MN: Zenith, 2008).

CHAPTER ONE. A LONG WAR

1. Chris Hobson, *Vietnam Air Losses: United States Air Force, Navy, and Marine Corps Fixed Wing Aircraft Losses in Southeast Asia, 1961–1973* (Hinkley, UK: Midland, 2001), 4.

2. Hobson, *Vietnam Air Losses*, 4.

3. John Correll, "The Opening Bell in Laos," *Air Force Magazine*, November 29, 2012, https://www.airforcemag.com/article/1212laos/.

4. Earl Tilford, *Search and Rescue in Southeast Asia, 1961–1975* (Washington, DC: Office of Air Force History, 1980), 34.

5. Tilford, *Search and Rescue in Southeast Asia, 1961–1975*, 33.

6. Victor Anthony and Richard Sexton, *The United States Air Force in Southeast Asia: The War in Northern Laos, 1954–1973* (Washington, DC: Center for Air Force History, 1993), 39–42.

7. Tilford, *Search and Rescue in Southeast Asia, 1961–1975*, 35; Col. George R. Hofmann Jr., *Operation Millpond: US Marines in Thailand, 1961* (Quantico, VA: History Division, United States Marine Corps, 2009).

8. Tilford, *Search and Rescue in Southeast Asia, 1961–1975*, 35; Correll, "The Opening Bell in Laos," np.

9. Darrel Whitcomb, "Farm Gate," *Air Force Magazine*, May 17, 2008, https://www.airforcemag.com/article/1205farmgate/; Col. (ret) John Schlight, "A War Too Long: Part 1," *Air Power History* 62, no. 2 (Summer 2015): 30.

10. Whitcomb, "Farm Gate," np.

11. Hobson, *Vietnam Air Losses*; Tilford, *Search and Rescue in Southeast Asia, 1961–1975*, 39.

12. Tilford, *Search and Rescue in Southeast Asia, 1961–1975*, 40–45; Hobson, *Vietnam Air Losses*.

13. Tilford, *Search and Rescue in Southeast Asia, 1961–1975*, 45–46.

14. Tilford, 47; Hobson, *Vietnam Air Losses*; Victor Anthony and Richard Sexton, *The United States Air Force in Southeast Asia: The War in Northern Laos, 1954–1973* (Washington, DC: Center for Air Force History, 1993), 39–42; John Wiren, "It Takes

Five to Tango," January 3, 2002, https://www.air-america.org/files/documents/It TakesFivetoTango.pdf.

15. Hobson, *Vietnam Air Losses*; Anthony and Sexton, *The United States Air Force in Southeast Asia*, 109–110.

16. Hobson, *Vietnam Air Losses*; Anthony and Sexton, *The United States Air Force in Southeast Asia*.

17. Tilford, *Search and Rescue in Southeast Asia, 1961–1975*, 52–53.

18. Hobson, *Vietnam Air Losses*.

19. Wayne Thompson, *To Hanoi and Back: The U.S. Air Force and North Vietnam, 1966–1973* (Washington, DC: Smithsonian Institution Press, 2000), 32–33; *History of the Air Defense Service*, vol. 2 (Hanoi, Vietnam: People's Army, Hanoi, 1993), 15–16.

20. *History of the Air Defense Service*, 2:15–16.

21. *History of the Air Defense Service*, 2:15–16, 44–45.

22. Tilford, *Search and Rescue in Southeast Asia, 1961–1975*, 52–53; Capt. Conn Anderson, Project CHECO (Contemporary Historical Examination of Current Operations) Report, United States Air Force Search and Rescue in Southeast Asia (hereafter referred to as USAF SAR in SEA for all editions), 1961–66, 135, Air Force Historical Research Agency, Maxwell AFB, AL (hereafter AFHRA); Scott Harrington, *They Called It Naked Fanny* (Ashland, OR: Hellgate, 2016), 17, 40, 43.

23. Tilford, *Search and Rescue in Southeast Asia, 1961–1975*, 54–55.

24. Jan Churchill, *Classified Secret: Controlling Airstrikes in the Clandestine War in Laos* (Manhattan, KS: Sunflower University Press, 1999), 1–2.

25. Hobson, *Vietnam Air Losses*.

26. Hobson, *Vietnam Air Losses*.

27. Hobson, *Vietnam Air Losses*; Harrington, *They Called It Naked Fanny*, 325.

28. George Galdorisi and Tom Phillips, *Leave No Man Behind: The Saga of Combat Search and Rescue* (Minneapolis, MN: Zenith, 2008), 227.

29. Hobson, *Vietnam Air Losses*.

30. Hobson, *Vietnam Air Losses*.

31. Hobson, *Vietnam Air Losses*; *History of the Air Defense Service*, 2:44; "Fobair, Roscoe Henry," updated February 6, 2001, http://www.pownetwork.org/bios/f/fo22.htm; "Keirn, Richard Paul," http://pownetwork.org/bios/k/ko46.htm, accessed 16 July 2018.

32. Hobson, *Vietnam Air Losses*; Galdorisi and Phillips, *Leave No Man Behind*, 235–237.

33. Tilford, *Search and Rescue in Southeast Asia, 1961–1975*, 66.

34. "38th Aerospace Rescue and Recovery Squadron," accessed June 12, 2020, http://airwarvietnam.com/38arrs.htm.

35. Tilford, *Search and Rescue in Southeast Asia, 1961–1975*, 66.

36. Hobson, *Vietnam Air Losses*; Harrington, *They Called It Naked Fanny*, 241, 328–329.

37. Tilford, *Search and Rescue in Southeast Asia, 1961–1975*, 71; Hobson, *Vietnam Air Losses*, 32; Briefing by Lt. Col. (ret) Jerry Singleton, at the Jolly Green Reunion, 4 May 2018.

38. Tilford, *Search and Rescue in Southeast Asia, 1961–1975*, 73–77; Galdorisi and Phillips, *Leave No Man Behind*, 240–241.

39. Tilford, *Search and Rescue in Southeast Asia, 1961–1975*, 88.

40. Hobson, *Vietnam Air Losses*.

41. Hobson, *Vietnam Air Losses*.

42. Robert Gillespie, *Black Ops Vietnam: The Operational History of MACSOG* (Annapolis, MD: Naval Institute Press, 2017), 11–12.

43. Gillespie, *Black Ops Vietnam*, 81–82.

44. Hobson, *Vietnam Air Losses*.

45. Hobson, *Vietnam Air Losses*; John Plaster, *The Secret Wars of America's Commandos in Vietnam* (New York: Simon and Schuster, 1998), 372.

46. Tilford, *Search and Rescue in Southeast Asia, 1961–1975*, 76, 84.

47. Lt. Col. (ret) Pat Finnigan, recorded interview by author, February 26, 2018. He was an HC-130 aircraft commander in 1972.

48. Galdorisi and Phillips, *Leave No Man Behind*, 413.

49. Galdorisi and Phillips, *Leave No Man Behind*, 413; Anderson, Project CHECO Report, USAF SAR in SEA, 1961–1966, 76.

50. Maj. John McLeaish and Maj, John Silvis, "Southeast Asia Operational Analysis," 3d. ARRG study, 6, 10, AFHRA.

51. McLeaish and Silvis, "Southeast Asia Operational Analysis," 12–18.

52. History of the Aerospace Rescue and Recovery Service (hereafter referred to as History of ARRS), 1 July 1970–30 June 1971, vol. 1, 191, AFHRA.

53. History of ARRS, 1 July 1970–30 June 1971, vol. 1, 190.

54. History of ARRS, 1 July 1970–30 June 1971, vol. 1, 191.

55. McLeaish and Silvis, "Southeast Asia Operational Analysis," 12.

56. Tilford, *Search and Rescue in Southeast Asia, 1961–1975*, 90, app. A.

57. Maj. Richard Durkee, Project CHECO report, USAF Search and Rescue, July 1966–November 1967, 1–3.

58. Galdorisi and Phillips, *Leave No Man Behind*, 327–329.

59. Ron Milam, "HC-7 Command Histories & Rescue Reports–1972," Historical documents pertaining to HC-7, collected by and in possession of Ron Milam.

60. Ron Milam, HC-7 historian, email to author, August 2, 2018.

61. Hobson, *Vietnam Air Losses*; Galdorisi and Phillips, *Leave No Man Behind*, 337–342.

62. Hobson, *Vietnam Air Losses*; Galdorisi and Phillips, *Leave No Man Behind*, 326.

63. Hobson, *Vietnam Air Losses*; Gillespie, *Black Ops Vietnam*, 157.

64. Gillespie, *Black Ops Vietnam*, 160; Hobson, *Vietnam Air Losses*.

65. History of the 40th Aerospace Rescue and Recovery Squadron (hereafter referred to as History of 40th ARRSq), Detachment 1, 1 January–31 March 1968, 1, AFHRA.

66. Maj. James Overton, Project CHECO Report, USAF SAR in SEA, November 1967–June 1969, 39. Kenny Fields, the A-7 pilot, eloquently tells this story in his book, *The Rescue of Streetcar 304: A Navy Pilot's Forty Hours on the Run in Laos* (Annapolis, MD: Naval Institute, 2007).

67. "Armed Helicopter Employment," Department of the Army Field Manual 1–110, July 1966, 25, 36, https://bits.de/NRANEU/others/amd-us-archive/FM1 -110%2866%29.pdf,

68. Hobson, *Vietnam Air Losses*; Ron Fogleman File, Robert F. Door collection, Glen L. Martin Archive, Middle River, MD.

69. "Millions Have Been Rescued by Igor Sikorsky's 'Angels of Mercy.' His Spirit Lives On—Saving Lives," *Sikorsky Archives News*, April 2011, https://www .sikorskyarchives.com/pdf/news%202011/News%20april%202011.pdf.

70. Overton, Project CHECO Report, USAF SAR in SEA, November 1967–June 1969, 54.

71. History of ARRS, 1 July 1970–30 June 1971, vol. 1, 194.

72. "H-53 Night Operation," *Sikorsky News*, May 1972, 4–9.

73. Overton, Project CHECO Report, USAF SAR in SEA, November 1967–June 1969, 54–57; History of ARRS, 1 July 1970–30 June 1971, vol. 1, 194; Darrel Whitcomb, *On a Steel Horse I Ride: A History of the MH-53 Pave Low Helicopters in War and Peace* (Maxwell AFB, AL: Air University Press, 2012), 24.

74. Galdorisi and Phillips, *Leave No Man Behind*, 360.

75. Thompson, *To Hanoi and Back*, 164–165.

76. "Ending the Vietnam War, 1969–1973," US Department of State, Office of the Historian, accessed April 6, 2017, https://history.state.gov/milestones/1969–1976 /ending-vietnam.

77. Thompson, *To Hanoi and Back*, 139–152; Hobson, *Vietnam Air Losses*, 166; Tilford, *Setup: What the Air Force Did in Vietnam and Why* (Maxwell AFB, AL: Air University Press, 1991), 165.

78. Tilford, *Search and Rescue in Southeast Asia, 1961–1975*, 96; Galdorisi and Phillips, *Leave No Man Behind*, 328–329.

79. Capt. Gordon Peterson and Capt. David Taylor, "Intelligence Support to Communications with US POWs in Vietnam," *Studies in Intelligence* 60, no. 1 (Extracts, March 2016), 1–16.

80. Tilford, *Search and Rescue in Southeast Asia, 1961–1975*, 92.

81. Overton, Project CHECO Report, USAF SAR in SEA, November 1967–June 1969, 42–6, app. A.

82. Hobson, *Vietnam Air Losses*.

83. History of the 3d Aerospace Rescue and Recovery Group (hereafter referred to as History of 3d ARRG), 1 January–31 March 1970, 17, AFHRA.

84. Lt. Col. LeRoy Lowe, Project CHECO Report, USAF SAR in SEA, 1 January 1971–31 March 1972, 27.

85. Hobson, *Vietnam Air Losses*; Thompson, *To Hanoi and Back*, 164, 173.

86. John Plaster, *SOG: A Photo History of the Secret Wars* (Boulder, CO: Paladin, 2000), 382.

87. Plaster, *The Secret Wars of America's Commandos in Vietnam*, 283; "Helicopter UH-1E 152427," May 26, 2019, http://www.vhpa.org/KIA/incident/70032110KIA .HTM.

88. Glines, C. V., "The Son Tay Raid." *Air Force Magazine*, November 1995, https://www.airforcemag.com/article/1195raid/.

89. Glines, "The Son Tay Raid."

90. Peterson and Taylor, "Intelligence Support to Communications with US POWs in Vietnam."

91. Walter Lynch, Project CHECO Report, USAF SAR in SEA, 1 July 1969–31 December 1970, table 3.

92. History of 3rd ARRG, 1 April–30 June 1971, 13.

93. Hobson, *Vietnam Air Losses.*

94. Robert Sander, *Invasion of Laos, 1971: Lam Son 719* (Norman: University of Oklahoma Press, 2014); 150–151; J. F. Loye, Project CHECO Report, Lam Son 719, 30 January 1971–31 March 1972.

95. Sander, *Invasion of Laos, 1971,* 170–171; "Mayday, Mayday, Mayday," personal story of Ralph Elliot, given to the author; "William Rogers Carter," updated October 29, 2006, http://www.arlingtoncemetery.net/wrcarter.htm.

96. Hobson, *Vietnam Air Losses*; Plaster, *the Secret Wars of America's Commandos in Vietnam,* 282–284.

97. Sander, *Invasion of Laos, 1971,* 192–193; Tilford, *Setup,* 203–205.

98. Stephen Randolph, *Powerful and Brutal Weapons: Nixon, Kissinger, and the Easter Offensive* (Cambridge, MA: Harvard University Press, 2007), 4, 32–39.

99. Thomas McKenna, *Kontum: The Battle to Save South Vietnam* (Lexington: University Press of Kentucky, 2011), 40.

100. Randolph, *Powerful and Brutal Weapons,* 4, 32–39; Tilford, *Setup,* 205–207.

101. History of 3d ARRG, 1 July–30 September 1971, 13, 24.

102. Walter Lynch, Project CHECO Report, USAF SAR in SEA, 1 July 1969–31 December 1970, 16–18; and History of the 3d ARRG, 1 April–30 June 1971, 16.

103. Lt. Col. John H. Morse, "Final Evaluation Pave Imp Operational Test Order 6-6-71, HH-53," 9 July 1971, AFHRA; message, 120900Z AUG 71, HQ 7AF TSN AFLD RVN to PACAF and various, subject: Pave Imp; message, 251620Z AUG 71, MAC to PACAF et al., subject: Pave Imp Combat Eval; and message, 130800Z SEP 71, HQ 7AF TSN AFLD RVN to CINCPACAF/DO, subject: Pave Imp. See also History of 3d ARRG, 1 October–31 December 1971, vol. 1, 14.

104. Message, 120900Z AUG 71, HQ 7AF TSN AFLD RVN to PACAF and various, subject: Pave Imp.

105. History of ARRS, 1 July 1971–30 June 1972, vol. 1, 139.

106. Capt. David Francis and Maj. David Nelson, Project CHECO Report, USAF SAR in SEA, 1 April 1972–30 June 1973, 17.

107. Tilford, *Search and Rescue in Southeast Asia, 1961–1975,* 113–114.

108. Darrel Whitcomb, "'Bar Napkin Tactics,' Combat Tactical Leadership in Southeast Asia," *Air Power History* 61, no. 4 (Winter 2014): 26–31.

109. Hobson, *Vietnam Air Losses*; JRCC Log, AFHRA.

110. Whitcomb, "'Bar Napkin Tactics,'" 26–31.

111. Letter, Col. Jack Robinson, 56th SOW Commander, to 7AF/CC, subject: Improvements to Search and Rescue (SAR) Capabilities, 30 December 1971, in History of the 56th SOW, 1 October–31 December 1971, vol. 2, AFHRA.

112. Graham Cosmas, *MACV: The JOINT Command in the Years of Withdrawal, 1968–1973* (Washington, DC: Center for Military History, 2007), 348.

113. Hobson, *Vietnam Air Losses*; Galdorisi and Phillips, *Leave No Man Behind*, 399; Commando Hunt VII, June 1972. K740.04–14, 144–146, AFHRA.

114. Cosmas, *MACV*, 351–352; John Correll, "Lavelle," *Air Force Magazine*, November 1, 2006, https://www.airforcemag.com/article/1106lavelle/; Col. (ret) Rick Atchison, document comments, January 22, 2019.

115. Stephen Randolph, *Powerful and Brutal Weapons: Nixon, Kissinger, and the Easter Offensive* (Cambridge, MA: Harvard University Press, 2007), 47–48.

116. Galdorisi and Phillips, *Leave No Man Behind*, 406.

117. Capt. David Francis and Maj. David Nelson, Project CHECO Report, Search and Rescue Operations in SEA, 1 April 1972–30 June 1973, HQ PACAF, 27 November 1974, 13, 15, 17, AFHRA.

CHAPTER TWO. JANUARY–MARCH

1. Chris Hobson, *Vietnam Air Losses: United States Air Force, Navy, and Marine Corps Fixed-Wing Aircraft Losses in Southeast Asia, 1961–1973* (Hinkley, UK: Midland, 2001), 217; JRCC Log, by date, Air Force Historical Research Agency, Maxwell AFB, AL (hereafter AFHRA).

2. Darrel Whitcomb, *The Rescue of Bat 21* (Annapolis, MD: Naval Institute Press, 1998), 142–145.

3. Squadron History, accessed 13 July 2016, http://blackpony.org/history.htm; Kevin Dockery, *Operation Thunderhead* (New York: Berkley Caliber, 2008), 207.

4. Ron Milam, "Historical Documents Pertaining to Helicopter Combat Support Squadron Seven (HC-7)" (Unpublished, undated), used with permission.

5. History of the 56th SOW, January, February, March 1972, vol. 3, 1st SOS History, 1–31 March 1972.

6. Ron Smith, interview by author, 29 April 2015, Scottsdale, AZ.

7. Drew Middleton, *Air War—Vietnam* (New York: Bobbs-Merrill, 1978), 110–112.

8. Maj. Charles Melson and Lt. Col. Curtis Arnold, *U.S. Marines in Vietnam: The War That Would Not End* (Washington, DC: Headquarters, U.S. Marine Corps, 1991), 7–11.

9. Melson and Arnold, *U.S. Marines in Vietnam*, 11–18.

10. Melson and Arnold, 2–6.

11. MACV Command History, vol. 1, B-44 thru B-50, 15 July 1973, http://www .vietnam.ttu.edu/virtualarchive/; James Willbanks, *The Battle of An Loc* (Bloomington: Indiana University, 2005), 11; 196th Light Infantry Brigade Association, "Order of Battle," accessed 14 July 2016, http://www.196th.org/Orderofbat.htm; William Reeder, *Through the Valley: My Captivity in Vietnam* (Annapolis, MD: Naval Institute, 2016), 1; Darrel Whitcomb, *Call Sign—Dustoff: A History of U.S. Army Aeromedical Evacuation from Conception to Hurricane Katrina* (Frederick, MD: Borden Institute, 2011), 54.

12. US Army Field Manual 1–110, July 1966 (Washington, DC: Department of the Army, 1965), 45–46.

13. Willbanks, *The Battle of An Loc*, 10; Jeffrey Clarke, *Advice and Support: The Final Years, 1965–1973* (Washington, DC: Center for Military History, 1988), 449–450.

14. Willbanks, *The Battle of An Loc*, 2–3;

15. Commando Hunt VII, June 1972, File K740.04–14, 227–229, AFHRA.

16. Joshua Kurlantzick, *A Great Place to Have a War* (New York, NY: Simon & Schuster Paperbacks, 2016), 211–213.

17. Commando Hunt VII, June 1972, K740.04–14, 8–13.

18. Stephen Randolph, *Powerful and Brutal Weapons: Nixon, Kissinger, and the Easter Offensive* (Cambridge, MA: Harvard University Press, 2007), 51–52.

19. Whitcomb, *The Rescue of Bat 21*, 58–59.

20. Whitcomb, *The Rescue of Bat 21*, 58–59.

21. Commando Hunt VII, June 1972, K740.04-14, 14–15.

22. Mission report, File K318.3912-5, pt. 1, by date, AFHRA.

23. Mission reports, File K318.312, 19 December 1971–4 January 1972, by date, AFHRA; John Plaster, *SOG: The Secret Wars of America's Commandos in Vietnam* (New York, NY: Simon & Schuster, 1998), 32.

24. Mission report, Mission Files, K318.3912-5, pt. 2, AFHRA.

25. Hobson, *Vietnam Air Losses*, 218; History of the 23rd TASS, January–March 1972, 23, AFHRA; Document, accessed 24 June 2016, www.cia.gov/library/readingroom/docs/c05266397.pdf; Mission report, Mission Files, K318.3912-5, pt. 2, AFHRA; Brian DeLuca, email to author, 29 October 2017.

26. Hobson, *Vietnam Air Losses*, 218; Mission reports, File K318.3912-5, pt. 1, by date, AFHRA.

27. JRCC Log; Bob Kain, email to author, 1 August 2017.

28. April Davila, "The Rescue of Raven 11," 2007, accessed 7 December 2015, https://www.youtube.com/watch?v=7HG45ptKsgw; Mike Kelly, email to author, 8 December 2015.

29. John Murphy, email to author, 17 September 2018.

30. Mission reports, File K318.3912-5, pt. 1, by date, AFHRA; History of the 23rd TASS, January–March 1972, 24, AFHRA; History of the 1st SOS, February 1972, 7, AFHRA; History of the 40th ARRS, January–March 1972, mission statements, AFHRA.

31. Letter to Commander, 41st ARRW, from Col. Cy Muirhead, in Mission reports, File K318.3912-5, pt. 1, by date, AFHRA.

32. Wayne Thompson, *To Hanoi and Back: The U.S. Air Force and North Vietnam, 1966–1973* (Washington, DC: Smithsonian Institution Press, 2000), 246–247; Col. Cy Muirhead, End-of-Tour Report, 9, AFHRA; Brig. Gen. (ret) Dale Stovall, document review comments, 28 July 2018; USAF Search and Rescue, July 1966–November 1967, 19 January 1968, 17, AFHRA.

33. Graham Cosmas, *MACV: The Joint Command in the Years of Withdrawal, 1968–1973* (Washington, DC: Center for Military History, 2007), 350; Dale Andrade, *America's Last Vietnam Battle: Halting Hanoi's 1972 Easter Offensive* (Lawrence: University Press of Kansas, 2001), 9, 23.

34. Marshall Michel III, *Clashes: Air Combat over North Vietnam, 1965–1972* (Annapolis, MD: Naval Institute Press, 1997), 193–194.

35. Hobson, *Vietnam Air Losses*; JRCC Log.

36. Hobson, *Vietnam Air Losses*; JRCC Log; History of the 1st SOS, February 1972; Commando Hunt VII, June 1972, K740.04–14, AFHRA, 148, 170.

37. Mission reports, File K318.3912–5. pt. 1, by date, AFHRA; Doug Aitken, "Sun Dog 12: Search and Rescue"; *The Rustics, a Top Secret War in Cambodia* (Destin, FL:

LuLu, 2011), 126–128; History of the 1st SOS, February 1972; Doug Aitken, email to author, 15 July 2017.

38. Doug Aitken, "Sun Dog 12: Search and Rescue," in *Cleared Hot: Forward Air Controller Stories from the Vietnam War: A Collection of Histories by US Air Force and Allied Forward Air Controllers from the Southeast Asia War, 1961–1975*, comp. Charlie Pocock, Bob Gorman, and Peter Condon, vol. 2 (Fort Walton Beach, FL: Forward Air Controller Association, 2009), 465–467; Claude G. Newland, James W. Reese, and Fellow Rustics, eds., *The Rustics: A Top Secret War in Cambodia, History of the Rustic Forward Air Controllers, 1970–1973* (Destin, FL: LuLu, 2001), 329.

39. Hobson, *Vietnam Air Losses*.

40. JRCC Log; "Award—Ronald Radcliffe," Centaurs in Vietnam, 1966–1973, accessed 4 June 2020, http://www.centaursinvietnam.org/Roster/infoNotesRoster /InfoSilverStarRadcliffeRon.html.

41. In 2006, the former commander of F/4 Cavalry, Lt. Col. (ret) John Spencer, submitted an affidavit requesting that the Silver Star that Capt. Radcliffe had received for this mission be upgraded to the Medal of Honor. "Medal of Honor Recommenda-tion—Ron Radcliffe," Centaurs in Vietnam, 1966–1973, accessed 22 July 2017, http:// www.centaursinvietnam.org/WarStories/WarEssays/E_MOHRadcliffe.html.

42. Brig. Gen. (ret) Dale Stovall, manuscript review comments to author, 23 May 2018.

43. Hobson, Vietnam Air Losses; JRCC Log; Mission File, K318.3912–5, pt. 2, January–December 1972, AFHRA; Kevin O'Rourke and Joe Peters, *Taking Fire— Saving Captain Aikman: A Story of the Vietnam Air War* (Havertown, PA: Casemate, 2013), 84; Ron Smith, interview by author.

44. *Remembering Our Debt to the Martyrs of the People's Air Force of Vietnam* (Ha-noi, Vietnam: People's Army Publishing House, 2010), 176–197.

45. Milam, "Historical documents."

46. Hobson, *Vietnam Air Losses*; JRCC Log; History of the 37th ARRSq, 1 Janu-ary–30 March 1972, 10–11, AFHRA.

47. Mission reports, File K318.3912–5, pt. 1, by date, AFHRA; Ben Van Etten, "Rescue," Terry Turner File, Air America Files, Eugene McDermott Library, Uni-versity of Texas, Dallas; Bob Humphrey, email to author, 20 March 2017; Col. (ret) Rick Atchison, email to author, 21 March 2017.

48. Mission reports, File K318.3912–5, pt. 1, by date, AFHRA; personal narrative provided by Maj. Gen. (ret) Randy Jayne; History of the 23rd TASS, January–March 1972, AFHRA; History of the 1st SOS, March 1972, AFHRA; History of the 40th ARRS, January–March 1972, AFHRA; Ron Smith, interview by author.

49. "John E. Lackey," Veteran Tributes: Honoring Those Who Served, accessed 13 June 2020, http://www.veterantributes.org/TributeDetail.php?recordID=422; Maj. Gen. (ret) Randy Jayne, personal narrative provided to author.

50. John Correll, "Lavelle," *Air Force Magazine*, 1 November 2006, https://www. airforcemag.com/article/1106lavelle/.

51. Correll, "Lavelle." But the story of General Lavelle did not end there. He faced hearings before the House of Representatives and the Senate. However, his retirement as a major general was not changed, and President Nixon never publi-cally supported him. Lavelle died in 1979. In 2007, retired General Aloysius Casey

discovered audio recordings of President Nixon discussing the relief of General Lavelle and declassified message traffic from the JCS that changed the ROE in effect in early 1972. They concluded that the new material showed that Lavelle had "unequivocal authorization" to conduct the strikes. Casey shared his findings with Lavelle's widow, Mary Jo, and family. They applied to the Air Force Board of Correction of Military Records, which endorsed the general's exoneration in 2009. This action was supported by Air Force Secretary Michael Donley and Defense Secretary Robert Gates. In 2010, President Barack Obama nominated Lavelle for posthumous restoration to the grade of general. In December 2010, the Senate Armed Services Committee, chaired by Senator Carl Levin, reviewed Lavelle's nomination. However, citing "apparent inconsistencies" in recently released State Department records from the war, Levin refused to call for a vote on the nomination until the inconsistencies could be resolved. See: Craig Whitlock, "Effort to Restore Honor of Vietnam-Era General Hits Resistance," *Washington Post*, 16 December 2010, http://www.washingtonpost.com/wp-dyn/content/article/2010/12/16/AR 2010121601373_pf.html; David Zucchino, "Fight to Vindicate General Dies in Senate," *Los Angeles Times*, 23 December 2010, http://articles.latimes.com/2010 /dec/23/nation/la-na-1223-lavelle-20101223. Secretary of the Air Force Heather Wilson, after her appointment in 2017, called for a review of the case of General Lavelle. See: Oriana Pawlyk, "Air Force Reviewing Petition to Restore Rank of Vietnam-Era General," Military.com, 19 July 2017, http://www.military.com/daily -news/2017/07/19/air-force-reviewing-petition-restore-rank-vietnam-era-general .html.

52. Whitcomb, *The Rescue of Bat 21*, 132–133.

53. Letter to author from Marty Cavato, 25 January 1995.

54. Lt. Col. LeRoy Lowe, Project CHECO Report, USAF SAR in SEA, 1 January 1971–31 March 1972, 71, AFHRA; History of 40th ARRSq, 1 January–31 March 1972, mission narrative; History of the 1st SOS, March 1972.

55. Randolph, *Powerful and Brutal Weapons*, 52–53.

56. "Home of the AC-130 Spectre Gunships," Spectre Association, accessed 30 June 2016, http://spectre-association.org/; Hobson, *Vietnam Air Losses*, 219; "SAM Downs Gunship, Fear Crew of 14 Lost," newspaper clipping, accessed 30 June 2016, http://spectre-association.org/aircraft/displayPrometheus4.htm.

57. Mission reports, File K318.3912–5, pt. 1, by date, AFHRA; History of 40th ARRSq, 1 January–31 March 1972, mission narrative, AFHRA; History of the 1st SOS, March 1972; History of the 23rd TASS, January–March 1972, 25, AFHRA; Sgt. Robert D. Jacobs, "A Night to Remember: 'Spectre 22' Rescue," accessed 30 June 2016, http://www.spectre-association.org/pdfs/Spectre_Rescue.pdf; Hobson, *Vietnam Air Losses*, 219; Allen Cates, "The Easter Egg Hunt from the America Perspective," Terry Turner File, Eugene McDermott Library, University of Texas at Dallas; Allen Cates, *Honor Denied: The Truth about Air America and the CIA* (Bloomington, IN: IUniverse LLC, 2011), 82–89.

58. Randolph, *Powerful and Brutal Weapons*, 54.

59. Ron Smith, interview with author.

60. Hobson, Chris, *Vietnam Air Losses*, 218–220.

61. Randolph, *Powerful and Brutal Weapons*, 55–56.

CHAPTER THREE. APRIL

1. Dale Andrade, *America's Last Vietnam Battle: Halting Hanoi's 1972 Easter Offensive* (Lawrence: University Press of Kansas, 2001), 25, 29.

2. Andrade, *America's Last Vietnam Battle*, 51–58.

3. Andrade, 39–50.

4. Chris Hobson, *Vietnam Air Losses: United States Air Force, Navy, and Marine Corps Fixed-Wing Aircraft Losses in Southeast Asia, 1961–1973* (Hinkley, UK: Midland, 2001); Darrel Whitcomb, *The Rescue of Bat 21* (Annapolis, MD: Naval Institute Press, 1998), 21–22; History of the 37th ARRSq, 1 April–30 June 1972, 14, AFHRA.

5. Whitcomb, *The Rescue of Bat 21*, 22–23; Andrade, *America's Last Vietnam Battle*, 85–88.

6. Ken Mick, "Easter Offensive—Mick 1972," Centaurs in Vietnam: 1966–1973 (F/4 Cavalry narrative), accessed 22 July 2017, http://www.centaursinvietnam.org /WarStories/WarEssays/E_EasterOffensiveMick.html.

7. Whitcomb, *The Rescue of Bat 21*, 23–24; Andrade, *America's Last Vietnam Battle*, 65–69. Some reports suggest that the VNAF A-1 was shot down by an SA-7 heat-seeking missile. That has never been verified.

8. Whitcomb, *The Rescue of Bat 21*, 26–28.

9. *History of the 236th SAM Regiment (1965–2005)* (Hanoi, Vietnam: People's Army Publishing House, 2004), 305–306.

10. *History of the 236th SAM Regiment (1965–2005)*, 305–306. Added note by transcriber: "In 2000 an MIA team looking for Americans missing in action (59th Iteration) informed us that the aircraft that was shot down . . . on 2 April 1972 was an EB-66."

11. Whitcomb, *The Rescue of Bat 21*, 28–31.

12. Whitcomb, *The Rescue of Bat 21*, 146–147.

13. Commander (USCG) Joseph (Jay) Crowe, After Action Report, Coast Guard–Air Force Exchange, May 1971–May 1972. Provided by family.

14. Whitcomb, *The Rescue of Bat 21*, 55.

15. *History of the 236th SAM Regiment (1965–2005)*, 306.

16. Whitcomb, *The Rescue of Bat 21*, 66–69; Hugh Mills, email to author, 4 February 2016.

17. Ted Sienicki, email to author, 20 September 2019.

18. Gen. (ret) Bill Begert, email to author, 15 September 2019.

19. *Air War—Vietnam*, introd. Drew Middleton (New York: Merrill, 1978), 114–122; History of the 3rd ARRG, April–June 1972, 2–2, AFHRA; Edward Marolda, *By Sea, Air, and Land: An Illustrated History of the U.S. Navy and the War in Southeast Asia* (Washington, DC: Naval Historical Center, 1994), 388; Maj. A. J. C. Lavalle, *Airpower and the 1972 Spring Invasion* (Washington, DC: Office of Air Force History, 1985), 19; Charles Melson and Curtis Arnold, *U.S. Marines in Vietnam: The War That Would Not End* (Washington, DC: Headquarters, U.S. Marine Corps, 1991), 155; Ron Milam, "Historical Documents Pertaining to Helicopter Combat Support Squadron Seven (HC-7)" (Unpublished, undated, used with permission).

20. Whitcomb, *The Rescue of Bat 21*, 71–75; Lt. Col. (ret) Bob Carlsen, email to author, 9 August 2016; History of the 56th SOW, April, May, June, 1972, vol. 2, doc. 23-8, AFHRA.

21. Gen. Alexander Haig and Charles McCarry, *Inner Circles: How America Changed the World—A Memoir* (New York, NY: Warner, 1992), 282.

22. Whitcomb, *The Rescue of Bat 21*, 82.

23. Ron Smith, interview by author, 29 April 2015, Phoenix, AZ.

24. Whitcomb, *The Rescue of Bat 21*, 77–82.

25. *History of the Air Defense Service* (Hanoi, Vietnam: People's Army Publishing House, Hanoi, 1994), 3:36.

26. Hobson, *Vietnam Air Losses*; Center for Naval Analysis SEA Data Base, E12; Mark Morgan, "The Story of HC-7/CSAR: Orphans of the 7th Fleet," *The Hook, Journal of Carrier Aviation*, Fall 1998, 41.

27. Whitcomb, *The Rescue of Bat 21*, 81.

28. Ron Smith, interview by author.

29. Hobson, *Vietnam Air Losses*; JRCC Log, AFHRA; History of the 23rd TASS, April–June 1972, 12–13, AFHRA; History of the 56th SOW, April–June 1972, 111–112, AFHRA.

30. Hobson, *Vietnam Air Losses*; History of the 40th ARRSq, 1 April–30 June 1972, Mission Narrative, AFHRA; History of the 1st SOS, 1–30 April 1972, 4, AFHRA; History of the 23rd TASS, April–June 1972, 12, AFHRA.

31. Hobson, *Vietnam Air Losses*; History of the 40th ARRSq, 1 April–30 June 1972, Mission Narrative; History of the 1st SOS, 1–30 April 1972, 4; History of the 23rd TASS, April–June 1972, 12; Hall of Valor: The Military Medals Data Base, accessed 5 August 2016, http://valor.militarytimes.com; "Ketchie, Scott Douglas," accessed 5 August 2016, http://www.taskforceomegainc.org/k075.html.

32. Ron Smith, email to author, 8 June 2015.

33. Whitcomb, *The Rescue of Bat 21*, 83–89; Tom Norris, Mike Thornton, and Dick Couch, *By Honor Bound* (New York: St. Martin's, 2016), 13–15.

34. Whitcomb, *The Rescue of Bat 21*, 97–108.

35. Ron Smith, interview by author.

36. Whitcomb, *The Rescue of Bat 21*, 100–101; Ron Smith, interview by author.

37. Ron Smith, email to author, 8 June 2015.

38. Ron Smith, email to author, 8 June 2015.

39. Whitcomb, *The Rescue of Bat 21*, 97–108; Robert Gillespie, *Black Ops Vietnam: The Operational History of MACSOG* (Annapolis, MD: Naval Institute Press, 2011), 237, 239–241.

40. "Medal of Honor Recipients," Home of Heroes: Medal of Honor and Military History, http://www.cmohs.org/recipient-detail/3374/norris-thomas-r.php; http://www.sealtwo.org/kietvannguyen.htm. Initially, the navy submitted Lieutenant Norris for the Silver Star. In late 1973, Capt. Dale Stovall, now serving at Scott AFB, Illinois, got a call from an officer at the Third ARRG who told him they were starting a letter-writing campaign with AF rescue officers to upgrade Norris's Silver Star to the Medal of Honor. Stovall wrote a personal letter to the secretary of the navy explaining that after Jolly Green 67 was shot down, the commander of MACV made the determination that no more helicopter rescue attempts would be made. Stovall further explained that he had been awarded the AF Cross and two Silver Stars for missions that paled in comparison to what Tommy Norris did. His letter was accompanied by many more from other highly decorated men of rescue.

41. Hobson, *Vietnam Air Losses.*

42. History of the 37th ARRSq, 1 April–30 June 1972, 15, AFHRA.

43. Capt. David Francis and Maj. David Nelson, Project CHECO, *The 1972 Invasion of Military Region I: Fall of Quang Tri and Defense of Hue,* 15 March 1973, 40, AFHRA.

44. Mick, "Easter Offensive."

45. JRCC Log, AFHRA; History of the 56th SOW, April–June 1972, 116.

46. Capt. David Mann, Project CHECO, *The 1972 Invasion of Military Region I: Fall of Quang Tri and Defense of Hue,* 15 March 1973, 31–42, AFHRA.

47. Graham Cosmas, *MACV: The Joint Command in the Years of Withdrawal, 1968–1973* (Washington, DC: Center for Military History, 2007), 356–358.

48. Ken Curry, "My Miracle Day," *Friends Journal,* Spring 2017, 5–7.

49. Hobson, *Vietnam Air Losses*; E. H. Hartsook, *Airpower Helps Stop the Invasion and End the War, 1972* (Washington, DC: Office of Air Force History, 1978), 68.

50. Hobson, *Vietnam Air Losses*; Stephen Randolph, "Turning on Both Sides: The Linebacker II Air Campaign, December 1972," presentation, Fighting While Negotiating: Force and Diplomacy in the Vietnam War, George C. Marshall Conference Center, Washington, DC, 30 September 2010, accessed 6 April 2017, https://history.state.gov/conferences/2010-southeast-asia/fighting-while-negotiating.

51. *History of the Air Defense Service,* 3:97–98.

52. Marshall Michel III, *Clashes: Air Combat over North Vietnam, 1965–1972* (Annapolis, MD: Naval Institute Press, 1997), 202.

53. USS *Worden* Chronology/Narrative 1 January–31 December 1972, Naval History and Heritage Command, Washington, DC.

54. Morgan, "Orphans of the 7th Fleet," 42–43; "Robert Allen Sterling," Virtual Wall Vietnam Veterans Memorial, accessed 16 January 2019, http://www.virtualwall.org/ds/SterlingRA01a.htm.

55. Morgan, "Orphans of the 7th Fleet," 44.

56. W04 (ret) John Dill, email to author, 9 December 2018.

57. Hobson, *Vietnam Air Losses*; Brian DeLuca, email to author, 29 October 2017.

58. Milam, "Historical Documents Pertaining to Helicopter Combat Support Squadron Seven (HC-7)."

59. Hobson, *Vietnam Air Losses*; JRCC Log.

60. Hobson, *Vietnam Air Losses*; JRCC Log; Mission Narrative, K318 2411–6, 10 March–21 May 1972, AFHRA.

61. Brig. Gen. (ret) Dale Stovall, email to author, 11 May 2018.

62. History of the 40th ARRSq, 1 April–30 June 1972, Mission Narrative, AFHRA; History of the 1st SOS, 1–30 April 1972, SARCO Report, AFHRA; History of the 23rd TASS, April–June 1972, 13, AFHRA; Lt. Col. (ret) Bob Carlsen, emails to author, 9 August 2016 and 28 August 2018.

63. Hobson, *Vietnam Air Losses*; JRCC Logs; History of the 56th SOW, April–June 1972, 115; Mission Report, K318 3912–5, pt. 2, AFHRA.

64. James Willbanks, *The Battle of An Loc* (Bloomington: Indiana University Press, 2005), 42–54.

65. Willbanks, *The Battle of An Loc,* 60.

66. Willbanks, 59–61, 65.

67. Willbanks, 72.

68. Willbanks, 78; Hartsook, *Airpower Helps Stop the Invasion and End the War, 1972*, 56.

69. Maj. Paul Ringenbach. Project CHECO Southeast Asia Report Airlift to Besieged Areas, 7 April–31 August 1972, 8, AFHRA; Willbanks, *The Battle of An Loc*, 106. The four members of the UH-1 were awarded the Silver Star for this mission on 18 April 2017: "Four Vietnam Veterans to Receive Silver Stars for 1972 Rescue," Military.com, accessed 18 April 2017, http://www.military.com/daily-news/2017/04/18/four-vietnam-veterans-to-receive-silver-stars-for-1972-rescue.html.

70. Willbanks, *The Battle of An Loc*, 107; JRCC Log.

71. The Battle of Kontum, accessed 12 April 2017, http://www.thebattleofkontum.com/; Reeder, *Through the Valley*, 20–21.

72. William Reeder, *Through the Valley: My Captivity in Vietnam* (Annapolis, MD: Naval Institute Press, 2016), 24–25.

73. Thomas McKenna, *Kontum: The Battle to Save South Vietnam* (Lexington: University Press of Kentucky, 2011), 122, 150, 147.

74. Hartsook, *Airpower Helps Stop the Invasion and End the War, 1972*, 58–61.

75. Whitcomb, *On a Steel Horse I Ride: A History of the MH-53 Pave Low Helicopters in War and Peace* (Maxwell AFB, AL: Air University Press, 2012), 94–96; Richard Boivin, John Schmidt, and Paul Balfe, *PAVE LOW—Evaluation of a Terrain Following Radar System for the HH-53 Helicopter*, Technical report No. 73–11 (Edwards AFB, CA: Air Force Systems Command, US Air Force, March 1973), 1–2.

76. Hobson, *Vietnam Air Losses*.

CHAPTER FOUR. MAY

1. A. J. C. Lavalle, *Airpower and the 1972 Spring Offensive* (Washington, DC: Office of Air Force History, 1985), 24.

2. Charles Melson and Curtis Arnold, *U.S. Marines in Vietnam: The War That Would Not End* (Washington, DC: Headquarters, U.S. Marine Corps, 1991), 90, 95.

3. Col. (ret) Gerald Turley, *The Easter Offensive: The Last American Advisors, Vietnam, 1972* (Annapolis, MD: Naval Institute Press, 1985), 283.

4. Chris Hobson, *Vietnam Air Losses: United States Air Force, Navy, and Marine Corps Fixed-Wing Aircraft Losses in Southeast Asia, 1961–1973* (Hinkley, UK: Midland, 2001); JRCC Log, Air Force Historical Research Agency, Maxwell AFB, AL (hereafter AFHRA); Mark Morgan, "The Story of HC-7/CSAR: Orphans of the 7th Fleet," *Hook, Journal of Carrier Aviation*, Fall 1998, 44.

5. History of the 37th ARRSq, 1 April–30 June 1972, 17–18, AFHRA; History of the 56th SOW, April–June 1972, 117, AFHRA; Mission narratives, File K318.2411-5, pt. 2, AFHRA.

6. Incident report, History of the 56th SOW, April, May, June 1972, vol. 2, doc. 14, AFHRA; SpadNET thread provided by Byron Hukee to author, 14 May 2017.

7. JRCC Log, AFHRA; History of the 56th SOW, April–June 1972, 117–118, AFHRA.

8. Personal mission narrative provided by Col. (ret) Jim Harding to author, 28 April 2017.

9. Mission reports, File K318.2411–6 OLA, 1 January–31 May 1972, AFHRA;

JRCC Log; History 56th SOW, April–June 1972, vol. 1, 40, 131; vol. 2, docs. 15, 16, AFHRA; Personal mission narrative provided by Col. (ret) Jim Harding to author, 28 April 2017.

10. Lt. Col. (ret) Byron Huckee, review of manuscript comments.

11. Centaurs in Vietnam, 1966–1973, updated June 2020, http://www.centaurs invietnam.org/.

12. Kevin Dockery, *Operation Thunderhead* (New York: Berkley Caliber, 2008), 218–222, 232.

13. Dockery, *Operation Thunderhead*, 276–277.

14. Hobson, *Vietnam Air Losses*; JRCC Log.

15. Lavalle, *Airpower and the 1972 Spring Offensive*, 24.

16. Lavalle, 27.

17. Lavalle, 29.

18. Alexander Haig with Charles McCarry, *Inner Circles: How America Changed the World—A Memoir* (New York: Warner, 1992), 287; Wayne Thompson, *To Hanoi and Back: The U.S. Air Force and North Vietnam, 1966–1973* (Washington, DC: Smithsonian Institution Press, 2000), 229; Thomas McKenna, *Kontum: The Battle to Save South Vietnam* (Lexington: University Press of Kentucky, 2011), 151.

19. John Sherwood, *Fast Movers: Jet Pilots and the Vietnam Experience* (New York: Free Press, 1999), 86–88.

20. Sherwood, *Fast Movers*, 86–88.

21. M. Porter, Project CHECO Report, Linebacker: Overview of the First 120 Days, 12 September 1973, HQ PACAF, 1, AFHRA.

22. Porter, Project CHECO Report, Linebacker, 1.

23. Marshall Michel III, *Clashes: Air Combat over North Vietnam, 1965–1972* (Annapolis, MD: Naval Institute Press, 1997), 217–227.

24. Hobson, *Vietnam Air Losses*; JRCC Log.

25. Hobson, *Vietnam Air Losses*; Bill Driscoll, *Peak Performance under Pressure* (Bloomington, IN: Triple Nickel, 2013), 2–4; Morgan, "Orphans of the 7th Fleet," 47; Ron Milam, "Historical Documents Pertaining to Helicopter Combat Support Squadron Seven (HC-7)" (Unpublished, undated), used with permission.

26. Morgan, "Orphans of the 7th Fleet," 47.

27. Hobson, *Vietnam Air Losses*; JRCC Log; Mission narratives, File K318.2411–6, AFHRA; "Icebag 01B SAR," 12 May 1972, http://www.skyraider.org/skyassn/sar tapes/icebag1/icebag1.htm; Howard Plunkett, "F-105 SEA Losses–1972" (Unpublished, n.d.), used with permission.

28. Hobson, *Vietnam Air Losses*; JRCC Log; Mission narratives, File K318.2411–6, suspended Msn, AFHRA.

29. Earl Tilford, *Setup: What the Air Force Did in Vietnam and Why* (Maxwell AFB, AL: Air University Press, 1991), 237–238; Stephen Randolph, *Powerful and Brutal Weapons: Nixon, Kissinger, and the Easter Offensive* (Cambridge, MA: Harvard University Press, 2007), 233–234.

30. Phillip B. Davidson, *Vietnam at War: The History, 1946–1975* (New York: Oxford University Press, 1991), 684–687.

31. Hobson, *Vietnam Air Losses*; JRCC Log.

32. Hobson, *Vietnam Air Losses*; JRCC Log, "Sandy 07 Statement," doc. 30-1, History of the 56th SOW, April, May, June 1972, vol. 2.

33. Melson and Arnold, *U.S. Marines in Vietnam*, 95–97.

34. Hobson, *Vietnam Air Losses*; JRCC Log; Mission narratives, File K318.2411-6, OL-A, AFHRA.

35. Hobson, *Vietnam Air Losses*; JRCC Log; Mission narratives, File K318.2411-6, AFHRA.

36. Hobson, *Vietnam Air Losses*; JRCC Log; Mission narratives, File K318.2411-6, AFHRA; Charles Banks, who served as an F-4 pilot with the Thirty-Fifth TFS in 1972, personal narrative, email to author, 14 January 2019.

37. Hobson, *Vietnam Air Losses*; History of the 23rd TASS, April–June 1972, 11, AFHRA.

38. Hobson, *Vietnam Air Losses*; History of the 37th ARRSq, 1 April–30 June 1972, 28, AFHRA.

39. Hobson, *Vietnam Air Losses*; JRCC Log.

40. William Reeder, *Through the Valley: My Captivity in Vietnam* (Annapolis, MD: Naval Institute Press, 2016), 28.

41. William Reeder, "A POW Story," Untold Stories, accessed 11 May 2017, http://vnafmamn.com/vietnam_POWstory.html; "John Timothy Conry," HonorStates.org, accessed 11 May 2017, http://www.honorstates.org/index.php?id=267454; Reeder, *Through the Valley*, 38–48.

42. McKenna, *Kontum*, 156.

43. Lavalle, *Airpower and the 1972 Spring Offensive*, 25.

44. McKenna, *Kontum*, 193.

45. McKenna, 164–165.

46. Hobson, *Vietnam Air Losses*; JRCC Log.

47. McKenna, *Kontum*, 247.

48. Hobson, *Vietnam Air Losses*; Tom Milligan, email to author, 12 May 2015; Mission narrative, Mission File K318.3912–5, pt. 2, AFHRA.

49. Maj. Paul Ringenbach, Project CHECO Report, Airlift to Besieged Areas, 7 April–31 August 1972, 21–22, AFHRA.

50. James Willbanks, *The Battle of An Loc* (Bloomington: Indiana University Press, 2005), 108–109.

51. Willbanks, *The Battle of An Loc*, 116–117.

52. Willbanks, 118.

53. Willbanks, 120–123.

54. Hobson, *Vietnam Air Losses*; JRCC Log; Maj. Paul Ringenbach, Project CHECO Report, *The Battle for An Loc*, 5 April–26 June 1972, 67, AFHRA.

55. Willbanks, *The Battle of An Loc*, 123.

56. Willbanks, 124.

57. Hobson, *Vietnam Air Losses*; JRCC Log.

58. Hobson, *Vietnam Air Losses*; JRCC Log.

59. JRCC Log; Tom Milligan, Sun Dog 29, email to author, 5 May 2015; "Statement," doc. 31-1, History of the 56th SOW, April, May, June 1972, vol. 2.

60. Hobson, *Vietnam Air Losses*; JRCC Log; Pep McPhillips, email to author, 12

April 2015; "Statement," doc. 31-1, History of the 56th SOW, April, May, June 1972, vol. 2.

61. Willbanks, *The Battle of An Loc*, 126.

62. Willbanks, 126–127; Melson and Arnold, *U.S. Marines in Vietnam*, 160.

63. Hobson, *Vietnam Air Losses*; JRCC Log.

64. Hobson, *Vietnam Air Losses*; JRCC Log; Morgan, "Orphans of the 7th Fleet," 48; Milam, "Historical Documents."

65. Hobson, *Vietnam Air Losses*; JRCC Log.

66. Hobson, *Vietnam Air Losses*; JRCC Log; Mission narrative, File K318.3912–5, pt. 2, AFHRA; "Statement," docs. 33-1, 33-2, 33-3, 33-4, History of the 56th SOW, April, May, June 1972, vol. 2.

67. Col. Cy Muirhead, End-of-Tour Report, 14 January 1972–9 January 1973, 9, AFHRA.

68. Brian Nelson, email to author, 24 October 2017.

69. Hobson, *Vietnam Air Losses*; JRCC Log; Mission narrative, File K318.3912–5, pt. 2, AFHRA; Darrel Whitcomb, *The Rescue of Bat 21* (Annapolis, MD: Naval Institute Press, 1998), 151–152; Brian Nelson, email to author, 24 October 2017.

70. Morgan, "Orphans of the 7th Fleet," 48; Milam, "Historical Documents."

71. Morgan, "Orphans of the 7th Fleet," 48.

72. Hobson, *Vietnam Air Losses*; JRCC Log; Milam, "Historical Documents."

73. Dale Andrade, *America's Last Vietnam Battle: Halting Hanoi's 1972 Easter Offensive* (Lawrence: University Press of Kansas, 2001), 476.

74. History of the 56th SOW, April, May, June 1972, vol. 3, doc. A, 15; Col. (ret) Jim Harding, email to author, 1 July 2017.

75. Col. Jack Robinson, End-of-Tour Report, 18–24, AFHRA.

76. Hobson, *Vietnam Air Losses*.

CHAPTER FIVE. JUNE

1. Lt. Col. (ret) Byron Hukee, manuscript review comments, email to author, 14 August 2017.

2. Jeffrey Ethell, *One Day in a Long War: May 10, 1972, Air War, North Vietnam* (New York: Random House, 1989), 150–157; Ross Buchanan, "The SAR Rescue of Roger Locher," accessed 23 May 2017, http://www.talkingproud.us/Military/Military/Locher.html; Mission File, K318.3912–5, pt. 3, January–December 1972, Air Force Historical Research Agency, Maxwell AFB, Alabama (hereafter AFHRA).

3. Mission File, K318.3912–5, pt. 3, January–December 1972; Statement, Sandy 1 and 2 (Oyster 01B), doc. 34-4, History of the 56th SOW, April, May, June 1972, vol. 2, AFHRA.

4. Mission File, K318.3912–5, pt. 3, January–December 1972; Statement, Sandy 1 and 2 (Oyster 01B), doc. 34-4; Chris Hobson, *Vietnam Air Losses: United States Air Force, Navy, and Marine Corps Fixed-Wing Aircraft Losses in Southeast Asia, 1961–1973* (Hinkley, UK: Midland, 2001).

5. Mission File, K318.3912–5 pt. 3, January–December 1972; Statement, Sandy 1 and 2 (Oyster 01B), doc. 34-4, AFHRA; Ethell, *One Day in a Long War*, 150.

6. Mission Number: B-03-047, Narrative, Mission File, K318.3912–5, pt. 3, January–December 1972, AFHRA.

7. Mission Number: B-03–047, Narrative, Mission File, K318.3912–5 pt. 3, January–December 1972, AFHRA; Sandy Statements, docs. 34-1, 34-2, 34-3, 34-4, 34-5, 34-6, 34-7, History of the 56th SOW, April, May, June 1972, vol. 2, AFHRA; Ethell, *One Day in a Long War,* 162–163; Brig. Gen. (ret) Dale Stovall, manuscript review comments, email to author, 30 June 2018; Fred Hastings, email to author, 20 August 2018. In 1972, he was a WSO in the 523rd TFS and flew as part of the MiGCAP for the recovery mission.

8. Brig. Gen. (ret) Dale Stovall, manuscript review comments, email to author, 30 June 2018.

9. Rescue Suspending Report, Mission File, K318.3912–5, pt. 3, AFHRA; "Lodge, Robert Alfred," accessed 23 May 2017, http://www.pownetwork.org/bios/1/1068 .htm.

10. Capt. Michael G. Slattery, USN (ret) and Capt. Gordon I. Peterson, USN (ret), "Spence Dry: A SEAL's Story," *Proceedings* 131, no. 7 (July 2005); Gordon Peterson, email to author, 9 April 2017; Ron Milam, "Historical Documents Pertaining to Helicopter Combat Support Squadron Seven (HC-7)" (Unpublished, undated), used with permission.

11. Slattery and Peterson, "Spence Dry." The author thanks Captain Peterson for his support in the telling of this humbling story. See also "Melvin Spence Dry," Arlington National Cemetery Website, accessed 4 April 2017, http://www.arling toncemetery.net/msdry.htm.

12. Hobson, *Vietnam Air Losses*; JRCC Log, AFHRA; Sandy Statements, docs. 35-1, 35-2, 35-3, History of the 56th SOW, April, May, June 1972, vol. 2, AFHRA.

13. Hobson, *Vietnam Air Losses*; JRCC Log.

14. Phillip B. Davidson, *Vietnam at War: The History, 1946–1975* (New York: Oxford University Press, 1991), 693.

15. Phil Marshall, *Helicopter Rescues Vietnam* (San Bernardino, CA: Self-published, 2016), 3:197–202.

16. Thomas McKenna, *Kontum: The Battle to Save South Vietnam* (Lexington: University Press of Kentucky, 2011), 258; JRCC Log; Harrold Ownby, interview by author, 6 June 2017, Plano, TX.

17. JRCC Log; "Cathay Pacific Flight 700Z bombing," Wikipedia, accessed 8 June 2017, https://en.wikipedia.org/wiki/Cathay_Pacific_Flight_700Z_bombing.

18. JRCC Log; Mission Report, File K318.2411–6 2 June–18 December 1972, AFHRA.

19. JRCC Log; Mission File, K318.3912–5, pt. 3 January–December 1972, AFHRA; Personal narrative from Byron Hukee, http://a-1combatjournal.com/bg10.htm.

20. JRCC Log; History of the 37th ARRSq, 1 April–30 June 1972, 19, AFHRA; Mission File, K318.3912–5, pt. 3, January–December 1972, AFHRA.

21. JRCC Log; Darrel Whitcomb, *On a Steel Horse I Ride: A History of the MH-53 Pave Low Helicopters in War and Peace* (Maxwell AFB, AL: Air University Press, 2012), 656.

22. JRCC Log; Darrel Whitcomb, "'Bar Napkin Tactics': Tactical Leadership in Southeast Asia," *Air Power History* 61, no. 4 (Winter 2014): 26–33.

23. Hobson, *Vietnam Air Losses*; JRCC Log; History of the 37th ARRSq, 1 April–30 June 1972, AFHRA; History of the 23rd TASS, April–June 1972, 14, AFHRA;

"Patterson, William B., Sgt," TogetherWeServed.com, accessed 9 June 2017, http://airforce.togetherweserved.com/usaf/servlet/tws.webapp.WebApp?cmd =ShadowBoxProfile&type=AssignmentExt&ID=180607.

24. Hobson, *Vietnam Air Losses*, JRCC Log; History of the 37th ARRSq, 1 April–30 June 1972, 20–21, AFHRA; History of the 40th ARRSq, 1 April–30 June 1972, Mission Statements, AFHRA; Sandy Statements, docs. 38-1, 38-2, 38-3, 38-4, 38-5, 38-6, AFHRA; History of the 56th SOW, April, May, June 1972, vol. 2, AFHRA; Mission File, K318.3912–5, pt. 3, January–December 1972, AFHRA; Lt Col. (ret) Byron Hukee, document review comments, email to author, 17 August 2017; Brig. Gen. (ret) Dale Stovall, manuscript review comments, email to author, 30 June 2018.

25. Hobson, *Vietnam Air Losses*; History of the 23rd TASS, April–June 1972, 15, AFHRA.

26. Hobson, *Vietnam Air Losses*; JRCC Log; History of the 23rd TASS, April–June 1972, 15; author's personal recollections.

27. "Rescue of LT Steincamp" and "CW4 'Pappy' Jones First Person Account," documents provided to author by email from Dale Dow, 19 July 2017.

28. Peter Barber, email to author, 22 July 2017.

29. Hobson, *Vietnam Air Losses*; JRCC Log; History of the 56th SOW, April–June 1972, 134, AFHRA; Letter of Recommendation and Air Mission Commander Report, Record Group 472, Records of US Forces in SEA, F Troop 4th Cavalry, Box 90, National Archives, College Park, Maryland; "Rescue of LT Steincamp" and "CW4 'Pappy' Jones first person account."

30. Peter Barber, emails to author, 22 and 24 July 2017.

31. E. H. Hartsook, *Air Power Helps Stop the Invasion and End the War, 1972* (Washington, DC: Office of Air Force History, 1978), 119; Stephen Randolph, *Powerful and Brutal Weapons: Nixon, Kissinger, and the Easter Offensive* (Cambridge, MA: Harvard University Press, 2007), 280.

32. Hobson, *Vietnam Air Losses*; JRCC Log; Milam, "Rescue 103," and "Rescue 104," 7 June 1972, "Historical Documents Pertaining to Helicopter Combat Support Squadron Seven (HC-7)."

33. Hobson, *Vietnam Air Losses*; JRCC Log.

34. Maj. Gen. (ret) Lawrence Johnston, email to author, 9 September 2018.

35. Hobson, *Vietnam Air Losses*; JRCC Log; Mission narrative, File K318.2411-6 OLA, 1 January–31 May 1972, AFHRA; John Murphy, email to author, 4 September 2018.

36. John Murphy, emails to author, 6 and 8 September 2018.

37. Hobson, *Vietnam Air Losses*; JRCC Log.

38. Maj. Gen. (ret) Lawrence Johnston, email to author, 9 September 2018.

39. Maj. Gen. (ret) Lawrence Johnston, email to author, 9 September 2018.

40. Hobson, *Vietnam Air Losses*; Milam, "Rescue 105, 16 June 1972," Historical Documents pertaining to HC-7.

41. Hobson, *Vietnam Air Losses*; JRCC Log.

42. Hobson, *Vietnam Air Losses*; JRCC Log; History of the 56th SOW, April–June 1972, vol. 1, 66, AFHRA; Byron Hukee, *Spad Guy Blog*, 20 January 2003, http://a-1combatjournal.com/ToC.htm.

43. Hobson, Vietnam Air Losses; Milam, "Rescue 106" and "Rescue 107," 18 June 1972, "Historical Documents Pertaining to Helicopter Combat Support Squadron Seven (HC-7)."

44. JRCC Log.

45. Hobson, *Vietnam Air Losses*; JRCC Log; Capt. Dale Stovall, Oral History Interview #835, AFHRA.

46. Hobson, *Vietnam Air Losses*; JRCC Log.

47. Marty Cavato, email to author, 24 September 2019.

48. Hobson, *Vietnam Air Losses*; JRCC Log.

49. Mission Narrative, File K318.3912–5, pt. 3, January–June 1972.

50. Jon Couch, *Caged Heroes: American POW Experiences from the Revolutionary War to the Present* (Bloomington, IN: AuthorHouse, 2011), 196–197.

51. Hobson, *Vietnam Air Losses*; JRCC Log; Mission Narrative, File K318.3912–5, pt. 3, January–June 1972; Kevin O'Rourke and Joe Peters, *Taking Fire: Saving Captain Aikman: A Story of the Vietnam War* (Havertown, PA: Casemate, 2013), 118–190; Hukee, *Spad Guy Blog*; History of the 56th SOW, April, May, June, 1972, vol. 2, doc. 39, AFHRA.

52. *Home of Heroes: Medal of Honor and Military History*, accessed 12 June 2017, http://www.homeofheroes.com/airforcecross/index.html.

53. Marshall III Michel, *Clashes: Air Combat over North Vietnam, 1965–1972* (Annapolis, MD: Naval Institute Press, 1997), 239.

54. M. Porter, Project CHECO Report, Linebacker: Overview of the First 120 Days, 27 September 1973, HQ PACAF, 10, AFHRA.

55. Michel, *Clashes*, 243.

56. History of the 3rd ARRG, 1 April–30 June 1972, 1–1 thru 3–3, AFHRA.

57. History of the 56th SOW, April–June 1972, 58, 40.

CHAPTER SIX. JULY–AUGUST

1. Marshall Michel III, *Clashes: Air Combat over North Vietnam, 1965–1972* (Annapolis, MD: Naval Institute Press, 1997), 250.

2. Chris Hobson, *Vietnam Air Losses: United States Air Force, Navy, and Marine Corps Fixed-Wing Aircraft Losses in Southeast Asia, 1961–1973* (Hinkley, UK: Midland, 2001); JRCC Log, Air Force Historical Research Agency, Maxwell AFB, AL (hereafter AFHRA); Mission File, K318.2411-6, 2 February–12 November 1972, AFHRA.

3. Phillip B. Davidson, *Vietnam at War: The History, 1946–1975* (New York: Oxford University Press, 1991), 687.

4. Hobson, *Vietnam Air Losses*; JRCC Log.

5. Hobson, *Vietnam Air Losses*; JRCC Log.

6. JRCC Log; Rescue Report, doc. 6A1, History of the 56th SOW, July–December 1972, vol. 2, AFHRA; Charles Melson and Curtis Arnold, *U.S. Marines in Vietnam: The War that Would Not End* (Washington, DC: Headquarters, U.S. Marine Corps, 1991), 114; Record Group 472, Records of US Forces in SEA, F Troop 4th Cavalry, Box 92, National Archives, College Park, Maryland; "Award—Frederick D. Ledfors," Centaurs in Vietnam: 1966–1973, accessed 8 August 2017, http://www.centaursinvietnam.org/Memoriam/InfoMemoriam/InfoDFCLedforsFredrick.html;

"Award–Westley Franklin Walker," Centaurs in Vietnam: 1966–1973, accessed 8 August 2017, http://centaursinvietnam.org/Roster/infoNotesRoster/InfoDFCWalker Westley.html.

7. Lt. Gen. (ret) Tex Brown, email to author, 4 October 2017.

8. Lt. Gen. (ret) Tex Brown, email to author, 4 October 2017.

9. Darrel Whitcomb, *The Rescue of Bat 21* (Annapolis, MD: Naval Institute Press, 1998), 32.

10. Pete Barber, email to author, 27 July 2017.

11. JRCC Log; Rescue Report, doc. 6B3, History of the 56th SOW, July–December 1972, vol. 2, AFHRA.

12. Hobson, *Vietnam Air Losses*; JRCC Log; Mission statements, File 318.3912-5, pt. 3, January–December 1972, AFHRA.

13. Hobson, *Vietnam Air Losses*; JRCC Log; George Galdorisi and Tom Phillips, *Leave No Man Behind: The Saga of Combat Search and Rescue* (Minneapolis, MN: Zenith, 2008), 433.

14. History of the 56th SOW, July–December 1972, vol. 3A, doc. A, 1–6, AFHRA.

15. Hobson, *Vietnam Air Losses*; JRCC Log.

16. JRCC Log; Mission Report, File, K318.2411–6, 2 February–12 November 1972, AFHRA.

17. Hobson, *Vietnam Air Losses*; JRCC Log; History of the 56th SOW, July–December 1972, vol. 2, doc. 7, AFHRA.

18. JRCC Log.

19. Hobson, *Vietnam Air Losses*; JRCC Log.

20. Hobson, *Vietnam Air Losses*; JRCC Log.

21. Hobson, *Vietnam Air Losses*; JRCC Log.

22. Hobson, *Vietnam Air Losses*; JRCC Log; Mission Report, File K318.3912–5, pt. 3, January–December 1972, AFHRA.

23. Capt. David Francis and Maj David Nelson. Project CHECO Report, Search and Rescue Operations in SEA, 1 April 1972–30 June 1973, 10, AFHRA.

24. Hobson, *Vietnam Air Losses*; JRCC Log.

25. Michel, *Clashes*, 253; Maj. Calvin Johnson, Project CHECO Report, Linebacker Operations, September–December 1972, 29, AFHRA.

26. Hobson, *Vietnam Air Losses*; JRCC Log; Ron Milam, "Rescue 109, 20 July 1972," "Historical Documents Pertaining to Helicopter Combat Support Squadron Seven (HC-7)" (Unpublished, undated), used with permission.; Joe Lee Burns, "A Ridge Too Far: Shot Down by AAA & Rescued Off of Haiphong," F-4 Phantom, accessed 15 January 2019, https://www.keytlaw.com/f-4/a-ridge-too-far/#more-91. (This site identifies the downed aircraft as Caddy 03. Official records identify it as Scuba 03.)

27. Hobson, *Vietnam Air Losses*; JRCC Log.

28. Hobson, *Vietnam Air Losses*; JRCC Log; Milam, "Rescue 110, 7 July 1972," "Historical Documents Pertaining to Helicopter Combat Support Squadron Seven (HC-7)."

29. Michel, *Clashes,* 250–252.

30. Hobson, *Vietnam Air Losses*; JRCC Log; Milam, "Rescue 112, 24 July 1972,"

"Historical Documents Pertaining to Helicopter Combat Support Squadron Seven (HC-7)."

31. Hobson, *Vietnam Air Losses*; JRCC Log.

32. Hobson, *Vietnam Air Losses*; JRCC Log; Mission Statement, File K318.3912–5, January–December 1972, AFHRA; Stan Goldstein, email to author, 8 August 2018.

33. Hobson, *Vietnam Air Losses*; JRCC Log; Milam, "Rescue 113, 30 July 1972," "Historical Documents Pertaining to Helicopter Combat Support Squadron Seven (HC-7)."

34. Hobson, *Vietnam Air Losses*; JRCC Log; Milam, "Rescue 114 and 115, 30 July 1972," "Historical Documents Pertaining to Helicopter Combat Support Squadron Seven (HC-7)."

35. Hobson, *Vietnam Air Losses*; JRCC Log.

36. Hobson, *Vietnam Air Losses*; JRCC Log; Galdorisi and Phillips, *Leave No Man Behind*, 416–418; Milam, "HC-7 Rescue 116, 7 August 1972," "Historical Documents Pertaining to Helicopter Combat Support Squadron Seven (HC-7)."

37. Hobson, *Vietnam Air Losses*; JRCC Log; Harrold Ownby, interview by author, 6 June 2017, Plano, TX; "Townsend, Francis Wayne," POW Network, accessed 8 June 2017, http://www.pownetwork.org/bios/t/t047.htm; Mark Alexander, "Miraculously, We Found Bill's Crash Site," *Patriot Post*, 14 February 2018, https://patriot post.us/alexander/54143.

38. Hobson, *Vietnam Air Losses*; JRCC Log.

39. Michel, *Clashes*, 252–253.

40. Hobson, *Vietnam Air Losses*; JRCC Log; Mission Statement, File K318.3912–5, pt. 3, January–December 1972, AFHRA.

41. Hobson, *Vietnam Air Losses*; JRCC Log.

42. Hobson, *Vietnam Air Losses*; JRCC Log; History of the 56th SOW, July–December 1972, vol. 2, doc. 12.

43. Hobson, *Vietnam Air Losses*; JRCC Log.

44. "Chuyện bắt sống giặc lái Mỹ," accessed 29 April 2019, http://hoitruongson .vn/tin-tuc/2121_11089/chuyen-bat-song-giac-lai-my-.htm; in Vietnamese and translated by Merle Pribbenow.

45. Hobson, *Vietnam Air Losses*.

46. Dale Andrade, *America's Last Vietnam Battle: Halting Hanoi's 1972 Easter Offensive* (Lawrence: University Press of Kansas, 2001), 499–500.

47. Graham Cosmas, *MACV: The Joint Command in the Years of Withdrawal, 1968–1973* (Washington, DC: Center for Military History, 2007), 373.

48. Hobson, *Vietnam Air Losses*; JRCC Log.

49. JRCC Log; History of the 56th SOW, July–December 1972, vol. 2, doc. 9.

50. Capt. David Francis and Maj. David Nelson, Project CHECO Report, Search and Rescue Operations in SEA 1 April 1972–30 June 1973, 5, AFHRA.

51. Hobson, *Vietnam Air Losses*; JRCC Log; "All for One," video, Periscope Film, 15 August 2015, https://www.youtube.com/watch?v=y-CF_rgTtlg.

52. Brig. Gen. (ret) Dale Stovall, manuscript review comments, email to author, 19 July 2018.

53. History of the 56th SOW, July–December 1972, vol. 2, doc. 10; Mission Statement, File K318.2411–6, 2 June–18 December 1972, AFHRA.

54. Hobson, *Vietnam Air Losses*; JRCC Log.

55. "Obituaries for Muscatine, Iowa: Lanny A. York, First Lt.," 27 March 2001, http://iagenweb.org/muscatine/obituaries/yobit.htm; History of the 56th SOW, July–December 1972, vol. 1, 81–85, AFHRA.

CHAPTER SEVEN. SEPTEMBER–NOVEMBER

* History of the 56th SOW, July–December 1972, doc. A, 3A:21–24, Air Force Historical Research Agency, Maxwell AFB, Alabama.

1. Chris Hobson, *Vietnam Air Losses: United States Air Force, Navy, and Marine Corps Fixed-Wing Aircraft Losses in Southeast Asia, 1961–1973* (Hinkley, UK: Midland, 2001); JRCC Log, Air Force Historical Research Agency (AFHRA), Maxwell AFB, AL (hereafter AFHRA); Mission File, K318.2411–6, 2 June–18 December 1972, AFHRA.

2. Hobson, *Vietnam Air Losses;* JRCC Log; Ron Milam, "Historical Documents Pertaining to Helicopter Combat Support Squadron Seven (HC-7)" (Unpublished, undated), used with permission.

3. Hobson, *Vietnam Air Losses;* JRCC Log; Marty Cavato, email to author, 19 September 2019.

4. Lou Drendel, *And Kill Migs* (Warren, MI: n.p., 1974), 24.

5. Hobson, *Vietnam Air Losses;* JRCC Log; Mission Statement, File K318.3912–5, pt. 3, January–December 1972, AFHRA; Marty Cavato, email to author, 19 September 2019.

6. Hobson, *Vietnam Air Losses*; Data sheet, D13, Center for Naval Analysis, Washington, DC, n.d.

7. Hobson, *Vietnam Air Losses;* JRCC Log.

8. Hobson, *Vietnam Air Losses;* JRCC Log; Milam, "HC-7 Rescue 121, and 122, 19 September 1972," "Historical Documents Pertaining to Helicopter Combat Support Squadron Seven (HC-7)."

9. JRCC Log; Fred McMurray, phone interview by author, 21 August 2018; Fred McMurray, personal narrative shared with author.

10. Hobson, *Vietnam Air Losses*; JRCC Log; Rudy Zuberbuhler, phone interview by author, 20 August 2018.

11. Hobson, *Vietnam Air Losses;* JRCC Log.

12. McMurray, personal narrative.

13. Zuberbuhler, interview, 20 August 2018; McMurray, interview, 21 August 2018.

14. Brig. Gen. (ret) Jim Latham, email to author, 28 August 2018.

15. Brig. Gen. (ret) Dale Stovall, manuscript review comments, 19 July and 28 July 2018.

16. Msg FROM 40th ARRS to various rescue units and HQs, DTG 132230Z, Rescue Opening Report 13 September 1972; Msg FROM 40th ARRS to various rescue units and HQs, DTG 171100Z, Rescue Suspending Report 17 September 1972, Mission statement by Capt Dale Stovall; File K318.3912.5 Part 3, 1 January–31 December 1972, JRCC Log, AFHRA.

17. FBIS Intercept, acquired through FOIA, from the US Air Force Personnel Center, Joint Base San Antonio–Randolph, TX.

18. Roger Reynolds, *Operation Linebacker: Two USAF Project CHECO Reports:*

Linebacker: Overview of the First 120 Days (West Chester, OH: Nafziger Collection, 2017) 27; Linebacker, September–December 1972, 33–36.

19. Hobson, *Vietnam Air Losses;* JRCC Log; History of the 56th SOW, July–December, vol. 2, doc. 16, AFHRA.

20. Hobson, *Vietnam Air Losses;* JRCC Log; Howard Plunkett, "F-105 SEA Losses–1972" (Unpublished, n.d.), used with permission.

21. Hobson, *Vietnam Air Losses;* JRCC Log; Milam, "HC-7 Rescue 122, 19 September 1972," "Historical Documents Pertaining to Helicopter Combat Support Squadron Seven (HC-7)."

22. Hobson, *Vietnam Air Losses;* JRCC Log; Mission statement, File K318.3912–5, pt. 3, January–December 1972, AFHRA.

23. Col. A. Picinich, Project CHECO Report, The F-111 in Southeast Asia, September 1972–January 1973, HQ PACAF 21 February 1974, 23, AFHRA.

24. Steven Hyre and Lou Benoit, *One-Eleven Down: F-111 Crashes and Combat Losses* (Atglen, PA: Schiffer Military History, 2012), 92.

25. Hobson, *Vietnam Air Losses;* JRCC Log.

26. Hobson, *Vietnam Air Losses;* JRCC Log; Charles Melson and Curtis Arnold, *U. S. Marines in Vietnam: The War That Would Not End* (Washington, DC: Headquarters, U.S. Marine Corps, 1991), 160–162.

27. JRCC Log.

28. JRCC Log; History of the 56th SOW, July–December 1972, vol. 2, doc. 14, AFHRA; Mark Schibler, email to author, 29 July 2017.

29. JRCC Log.

30. Hobson, *Vietnam Air Losses;* JRCC Log.

31. M. Porter, Project CHECO Report, Linebacker: Overview of the First 120 Days, 27 September 1973, 54, AFHRA.

32. Stephen Randolph, *Powerful and Brutal Weapons: Nixon, Kissinger, and the Easter Offensive* (Cambridge, MA: Harvard University Press, 2007), 324.

33. Hobson, *Vietnam Air Losses;* JRCC Log; History of the 56th SOW, July–December, vol. 2, doc. 17.

34. Hobson, *Vietnam Air Losses;* JRCC Log; Melson and Arnold, *U.S. Marines in Vietnam,* 163.

35. Hobson, *Vietnam Air Losses;* JRCC Log.

36. Lt. Col. (ret) Chris Cole, email to author, 2 October 2018.

37. Randolph, *Powerful and Brutal Weapons,* 325.

38. Hobson, *Vietnam Air Losses;* JRCC Log; Mission Report, File K318.2411–6, September–December 1972, AFHRA.

39. Hobson, *Vietnam Air Losses;* JRCC Log; James Latham, "Prairie Fire FAC, Fighter Pilot, POW," *Drop* (Summer 2018): 34–42.

40. Hobson, *Vietnam Air Losses;* JRCC Log; Mission Report, File K318.2411–6, 2 June–18 December 1972, AFHRA.

41. Hobson, *Vietnam Air Losses;* JRCC Log.

42. Maj. Calvin Johnson, Project CHECO Report, Linebacker Operations, September–December 1972, 29, AFHRA.

43. JRCC Log.

44. JRCC Log.

45. Hobson, *Vietnam Air Losses*; JRCC Log.

46. Phil Marshall, *Helicopter Rescues Vietnam* (San Bernardino, CA: Self-published, 2016), 2:343–405.

47. Randolph, *Powerful and Brutal Weapons*, 325–326.

48. Wayne Thompson, *To Hanoi and Back: The U.S. Air Force and North Vietnam, 1966–1973* (Washington, DC: Smithsonian Institution Press, 2000), 253–259; Hartsook, *Airpower Helps Stop the Invasion and End the War, 1972* (Washington, DC: Office of Air Force History, 1978), 136.

49. Hobson, *Vietnam Air Losses*; Col. A. Picinich, Project CHECO Report, The F-III in Southeast Asia, September 1972–January 1973, HQ PACAF 21 February 1974, 47, AFHRA.

50. Hobson, *Vietnam Air Losses*; JRCC Log; Mission Report, File K318.3912–5, pt. 3, January–December 1972, AFHRA.

51. Hobson, *Vietnam Air Losses*; JRCC Log; Milam, Binder 21A-L, "Historical Documents Pertaining to Helicopter Combat Support Squadron Seven (HC-7)"; *Nghe An: History of the Resistance War against the Americans to Save the Nation (1954–1975)* (Hanoi, Vietnam: People's Army Publishing House, 1995), 262, trans. Merle Pribbenow.

52. Hobson, *Vietnam Air Losses*; JRCC Log; Mission Report, File K318.3712–5, pt. 3, January–December 1972, AFHRA.

53. Tom Norris, Mike Thornton, and Dick Couch, *By Honor Bound* (New York: St. Martin's, 2016), 117–161.

54. Norris, Thornton, and Crouch, *By Honor Bound*, 235.

55. History of the 354th TFW, 1 October–31 December 1972, 1:3–10, AFHRA.

56. History of the 354th TFW, 1 October–31 December 1972, 1:11–12; Capt. David Francis and Maj. David Nelson, Project CHECO Report, Search and Rescue Operations in SEA, 1 April 1972–30 June 1973, 21–22, AFHRA.

57. History of the 56th SOW, July–December 1972, doc. A, 3A:21–24, AFHRA.

58. JRCC Log.

59. Hobson, *Vietnam Air Losses*.

60. JRCC Log; Mission Report, File K318.2411–6, 2 June–18 Dececember 1972, AFHRA.

61. JRCC Log; Mission Narrative Report, File K318.3712–5, pt. 3, AFHRA.

62. History of the 56th SOW, July–December 1972, doc. A, 3A:25–30, AFHRA.

63. Thompson, *To Hanoi and Back*, 258–259.

64. History of the 3rd ARRG, 1 October–31 December 1972, 3-1, AFHRA.

65. Col A. Picinich, Project CHECO Report, The F-III in Southeast Asia, September 1972–January 1973, HQ PACAF 21 February 1974, 50, AFHRA; Hyre and Benoit, *One-Eleven Down*, 94.

66. Jane Hamilton-Merritt, *Tragic Mountains: The Hmong, the Americans, and the Secret Wars for Laos, 1942–1992* (Bloomington: Indiana University Press, 1993), 298–299; French Smith File, Special Collections, McDermott Library, University of Texas, Dallas; JRCC Log; "Carroll, John Leonard," POW Network, accessed 18 October 2015, http://www.pownetwork.org/bios/c/c365.htm.

67. Hobson, *Vietnam Air Losses*, JRCC Log; Milam, "HC-7 Rescue 124, 10 Nov

1972," "Historical Documents Pertaining to Helicopter Combat Support Squadron Seven (HC-7)."

68. Hobson, *Vietnam Air Losses*, JRCC Log.

69. Hobson, *Vietnam Air Losses*, JRCC Log; Milam, "HC-7 Rescue 125, 11 Nov 1972," "Historical Documents Pertaining to Helicopter Combat Support Squadron Seven (HC-7)."

70. JRCC Log; "USAF Aircraft Losses, SEA," USAF Southeast Asia Review, 31 May 1974, Air Force Special Operations Command History Office, Hurlburt Field, Florida.

71. Brig. Gen. (ret) Dale Stovall, manuscript review comments, email to author, 2 July 2018.

72. Darrel Whitcomb, "New Sandys in Town: A-7s and Rescue Operations in Southeast Asia," *Air Power History* 62, no. 3 (Fall 2015): 34–41; Stovall, manuscript review comments, 2 July 2018.

73. Hobson, *Vietnam Air Losses*; Whitcomb, "New Sandys in Town," 34–41.

74. Whitcomb, "New Sandys in Town," 40–41.

75. Col. Jack Robinson, End-of-Tour Report, 18, AFHRA.

76. Whitcomb, "New Sandys in Town," 40–41.

77. Hartsook, *Air Power Helps Stop the Invasion and End the War, 1972*, 137–139.

78. Hobson, *Vietnam Air Losses*; JRCC Log; Mission Report, File K318.3912.5, pt. 3, AFHRA; Bill Anderson, email to author, 6 April 2020.

79. Hobson, *Vietnam Air Losses*; JRCC Log; Milam, "HC-7 Rescue 125, 20 Nov 1972," "Historical Documents Pertaining to Helicopter Combat Support Squadron Seven (HC-7)."

80. Col. A. Picinich, Project CHECO Report, The F-111 in Southeast Asia, September 1972–January 1973, HQ PACAF 21 February 1974, 57, AFHRA; Hyre and Benoit, *One-Eleven Down*, 95.

81. Hobson, *Vietnam Air Losses*; JRCC Log; Mission Report, File K318.3912-5, pt. 3, AFHRA.

82. Hobson, *Vietnam Air Losses*; JRCC Log; Mission Report, File K318.3412-5, pt. 3, AFHRA; Philip Chinnery, *Full Throttle: True Stories of Vietnam Air Combat Told by the Men Who Lived It* (New York: St. Martin's, 1988), 280–281.

83. Hobson, *Vietnam Air Losses*; JRCC Log; Lt. Col. (ret) Chris Cole, mail to author, 2 October 2018; Robert Martensen, email to author, 3 September 2019.

84. JRCC Log; Lt. Col. (ret) Lew Hatch, email to author, 25 July 2017.

85. JRCC Log.

86. Hartsook, *Airpower Helps Stop the Invasion and End the War, 1972*, 139–140.

87. Hobson, *Vietnam Air Losses*.

CHAPTER EIGHT. DECEMBER

1. Chris Hobson, *Vietnam Air Losses: United States Air Force, Navy, and Marine Corps Fixed-Wing Aircraft Losses in Southeast Asia, 1961–1973* (Hinkley, UK: Midland, 2001); JRCC Log, Air Force Historical Research Agency, Maxwell AFB, AL (hereafter AFHRA); personal recollections of the author.

2. James Chiles, "Air America's Black Helicopter," *Air and Space Magazine,*

March 2008, http://www.airspacemag.com/military-aviation/air-americas-black-helicopter-24960500/?all.

3. Chiles, "Air America's Black Helicopter."

4. JRCC Log.

5. Lt. Col. (ret) Lew Hatch, emails to author, 26, 27, 28 June 2018; Dr. Joe Leeker, *Air America in Laos*, pt. 2, manuscript, Air America Archives, University of Texas–Dallas, undated, 43–44.

6. Lt. Col. (ret) Chris Cole, email to author, 2 October 2018.

7. Stephen Randolph, in presentation, "Fighting While Negotiating: Force and Diplomacy in the Vietnam War," George C. Marshall Conference Center, Washington, DC, 30 September 2010, https://history.state.gov/conferences/2010-southeast-asia/fighting-while-negotiating; E. H. Hartsook, *Air Power Helps Stop the Invasion and End the War, 1972* (Washington, DC: Office of Air Force History, 1978), 141–143.

8. *Nghe An: History of the Resistance War against the Americans to Save the Nation (1954–1975)* (Hanoi, Vietnam: People's Army Publishing House, 1995), 262–269, trans. Merle Pribbenow.

9. Hobson, *Vietnam Air Losses*; History of the 354th TFW, October–December 1972, vol. 3, doc. 45, 11, AFHRA; "Acosta, Hector Michael," POW Network, accessed 31 July 2017, http://www.pownetwork.org/bios/a/a079.htm; Sandy pilot debriefs, provided by Jack Trimble (Desoto 03Bravo) to author, 25 July 2017; Lt. Col. (ret) Hector Acosta, 2016 Freedom Flyer briefing, POW Symposium, video, YouTube, accessed 9 April 2018, https://www.youtube.com/watch?v=WC1MFmmwzTg.

10. Hartsook, *Air Power Helps Stop the Invasion and end the War, 1972*, 143–145.

11. Hartsook, *Air Power Helps Stop the Invasion and end the War, 1972*, 145–146.

12. Pete Camerota, interview by author, 19 August 2017, Elizabeth City, NC.

13. Marshall Michel III, *Operation Linebacker II 1972: The B-52s Are Sent to Hanoi* (Oxford, UK: Osprey, 2018), 45.

14. Hobson, *Vietnam Air Losses*; JRCC Log; Karl Eschmann, *Linebacker: The Untold Story of the Air Raids over North Vietnam* (New York: Ivy, 1989), 97; G. Ray Sullivan Jr., "It Was the Chance to Explore Further," Linebacker II 12/72, accessed 30 June 2017, http://www.linebacker2.com/-.php.

15. Col. A. Picinich, Project CHECO Report, The F-111 in Southeast Asia, September 1972–January 1973, HQ PACAF, 21 February 1974, 53, AFHRA; Steven Hyre and Lou Benoit, *One-Eleven Down: F-111 Crashes and Combat Losses* (Atglen, PA: Schiffer Military History, 2012), 96.

16. Hobson, *Vietnam Air Losses*; JRCC Log; Eschmann, *Linebacker*, 101–106; Sullivan, "It Was the Chance to Explore Further."

17. Hobson, *Vietnam Air Losses*; JRCC Log; Eschmann, *Linebacker*, 106; Sullivan, "It Was the Chance to Explore Further."

18. Lt. Col. (ret) Jerry Singleton, briefing to the Jolly Green Reunion, Fort Walton Beach, FL, 5 May 2018.

19. JRCC Log.

20. Hobson, *Vietnam Air Losses*; JRCC Log; Col. (ret) Rich Finn, Covey 270, email to author, 29 June 2017; Warren E. Fuller, email, 5 February 2011, http://www.vhpa.org/stories/Covey64ShootDown.pdf.

21. Hartsook, *Air Power Helps Stop the Invasion and End the War, 1972*, 148.

22. Hobson, *Vietnam Air Losses*.

23. Hobson, *Vietnam Air Losses*; JRCC Log; Eschmann, *Linebacker*, 116; Sullivan, "It Was the Chance to Explore Further."

24. Hobson, *Vietnam Air Losses*; JRCC Log; Eschmann, *Linebacker*, 116; Sullivan, "It Was the Chance to Explore Further."

25. Hobson, *Vietnam Air Losses*; JRCC Log; Eschmann, *Linebacker*, 120; Sullivan, "It Was the Chance to Explore Further."

26. Hobson, *Vietnam Air Losses*; JRCC Log.

27. Lt. Col. (ret) Paul Munninghoff, email to author, 17 March 2018. He was on this mission.

28. Hobson, *Vietnam Air Losses*; JRCC Log; Eschmann, *Linebacker*, 131–132; Sullivan, "It Was the Chance to Explore Further."

29. Hobson, *Vietnam Air Losses*; JRCC Log; Eschmann, *Linebacker*, 133; Sullivan, "It Was the Chance to Explore Further."

30. Hobson, *Vietnam Air Losses*; JRCC Log; Eschmann, *Linebacker*, 133; Sullivan, "It Was the Chance to Explore Further."

31. Eschmann, *Linebacker*, 134.

32. Hartsook, *Air Power Helps Stop the Invasion and End the War, 1972*, 148; Eschmann, *Linebacker*, 134–135.

33. JRCC Log.

34. Hobson, *Vietnam Air Losses*; JRCC Log: Mission narrative, File K318.3912-5, pt. 3, January–December 1972, AFHRA; Harrold Ownby, interview by author, 6 June 2017, Plano, TX ; Col. (ret) Jerry Shipman, manuscript review comments in email to author, 30 May 2018; Lt. Col. (ret) Lew Hatch, email to author, 3 July 2018.

35. Lt. Col. (ret) Lew Hatch, email to author, 3 July 2018.

36. Lt. Col. (ret) Joe Richardson, email to author, 28 May 2018.

37. Pete Camerota, interview by author, 19 August 2017, Elizabeth City, NC.

38. Hobson, *Vietnam Air Losses*; JRCC Log; Eschmann, *Linebacker*, 142–145; Sullivan, "It Was the Chance to Explore Further"; Philip Chinnery, *Full Throttle: True Stories of Vietnam Air Combat Told by the Men Who Lived It* (New York: St. Martin's, 1988), 285–287.

39. "Camerota, Peter Paul," POW Network, accessed 29 July 2017, http://www.pownetwork.org/bios/c/c164.htm.

40. Hobson, *Vietnam Air Losses*; JRCC Log; Eschmann, *Linebacker*, 145–147; Sullivan, "It Was the Chance to Explore Further."

41. Darrel Whitcomb, *On a Steel Horse I Ride: A History of the MH-53 Pave Low Helicopters in War and Peace* (Maxwell AFB, AL: Air University Press, 2012), 49–50, 94–96; Darrel Whitcomb, *Combat Search and Rescue in Desert Storm* (Maxwell AFB, AL: Air University Press, 2006), 16–17; Col. (ret) Jerry Shipman, email to author, 30 May 2018.

42. JRCC Log; Mission File 3912-5, pt. 3, AFHRA; History of the 354th TFW, 1 October–31 December 1972, 3:12, AFHRA.

43. Bob Hope as told to Pete Martin, "The Last Christmas Show," accessed 9 January 2019, http://www.geocities.ws/seavet72/LB2/lb2-bh.htm; Michel, *Operation Linebacker II 1972*, 73.

44. Hartsook, *Air Power Helps Stop the Invasion and End the War, 1972*, 150.

45. JRCC Log; Jon Couch, *The Jackal's Journey* (Draft manuscript, 2017), used

with permission, 16–20. In all of the logs and mission reports, "Jackel" is spelled with an *e*.

46. *A Number of Air Defense Battles during the Resistance War against the Americans to Save the Nation*, vol. 2 (Hanoi, Vietnam: People's Army Publishing House, 1994), 3–4, trans. Merle Pribbenow.

47. JRCC Log.

48. JRCC Log; Couch, *The Jackal's Journey*, 21–23.

49. Lt. Col. (ret) Lew Hatch, email to author, 3 July 2018.

50. Christopher Robbins, *The Ravens: The Men Who Flew in America's Secret War in Laos* (New York: Crown, 1987), 313–315.

51. Robbins, *The Ravens*, 313–315. JRCC Log.

52. *A Number of Air Defense Battles*, 7.

53. JRCC Log; Couch, *The Jackal's Journey*, 25–26; History of the 354th TFW, 1 October–31 December, 1972, 3:12–13.

54. Hobson, *Vietnam Air Losses*; JRCC Log; Ron Milam, "Historical Documents Pertaining to Helicopter Combat Support Squadron Seven (HC-7)" (Unpublished, undated), used with permission.

55. Hobson, *Vietnam Air Losses*; "Jackson, Paul Vernon 'Skip' III," POW Network, accessed 5 December 2015, http://pownetwork.org/bios/j/j353.htm; Chuck Hines, in *Cleared Hot: Forward Air Controller Stories from the Vietnam War: A Collection of Histories by US Air Force and Allied Forward Air Controllers from the Southeast Asia War, 1961–1975*, comp. Charlie Pocock, Bob Gorman, and Peter Condon (Fort Walton Beach, FL: Forward Air Controller Association, 2009), 2:64–65; History of the 354th Tactical Fighter Wing, October–December 1972, 1:24, AFHRA; JRCC Log.

56. Hobson, *Vietnam Air Losses*: JRCC Log.

57. JRCC Log; Charles Melson and Curtis Arnold, *U.S. Marines in Vietnam: The War That Would Not End* (Washington, DC: Headquarters, U.S. Marine Corps, 1991), 134.

58. *A Number of Air Defense Battles*, 7.

59. "Camerota, Peter Paul," POW Network; Pete Camerota, interview by author.

60. John Penney, email to Jack Trimble, provided to author by email, 29 July 2017.

61. JRCC Log; Couch, *The Jackal's Journey*, 28–32.

62. *A Number of Air Defense Battles*, 7.

63. JRCC Log; Hartsook, *Air Power Helps Stop the Invasion and End the War, 1972*, 153.

64. Hobson, *Vietnam Air Losses*; JRCC Log; Eschmann, *Linebacker*, 170–173.

65. Hobson, *Vietnam Air Losses*; JRCC Log; Eschmann, *Linebacker*, 164–166.

66. Michel, *Operation Linebacker II 1972*, 83–84.

67. Bill Anderson, email to author, 7 April 2020.

68. John Penney, email to Jack Trimble, provided to author by email, 29 July 2017.

69. *A Number of Air Defense Battles*, 8.

70. *A Number of Air Defense Battles*, 8.

71. Mission Debrief, Capt. Richard Shapiro, Mission File K318.3912–5, pt. 3, January–December 1972, AFHRA.

72. History of 3d ARRG, 1 October 1972–31 December 1972, AFHRA; Hobson, *Vietnam Air Losses*, JRCC Log; Capt. David Francis and Maj. David Nelson, Project CHECO Report, USAF SAR in SEA, 1 April 1972–30 June 1973, 48, AFHRA; Chuck Rouhier, email to author, 7 June 2017; Col. (ret) Jerry Shipman, email to author, 30 May 2018.

73. *A Number of Air Defense Battles*, 8.

74. Couch, *The Jackal's Journey*, 55–57.

75. Hobson, *Vietnam Air Losses*; JRCC Log; Eschmann, *Linebacker*, 182–183.

76. Hobson, *Vietnam Air Losses*; JRCC Log; Eschmann, *Linebacker*, 182–183.

77. John Penney, email to Jack Trimble, provided to author by email, 29 July 2017; John Morrissey, email to author, 3 August 2017.

78. Sherwood Cox, email to Jack Trimble, provided to author by email, 29 July 2017.

79. Jack Trimble, email to Sherwood Cox, provided to author by email, 29 July 2017.

80. John Penney, email to Jack Trimble, provided to author by email, 29 July 2017.

81. Hobson, *Vietnam Air Losses*; JRCC Log; Eschmann, *Linebacker*, 184–185.

82. Hobson, *Vietnam Air Losses*; JRCC Log; Eschmann, *Linebacker*, 184–185.

83. Michel, *Operation Linebacker II 1972*, 85.

84. JRCC Log.

85. Hobson, *Vietnam Air Losses*; JRCC Log.

86. Hartsook, *Air Power Helps Stop the Invasion and End the War, 1972*, 154; Michel, *Operation Linebacker II 1972*, 85.

87. JRCC Log.

88. JRCC Log; Couch, *The Jackal's Journey*, 61–62. History of the 354th TFW, 1 October–31 December, 1972, 3:12–13.

89. *A Number of Air Defense Battles*, 9.

90. "Camerota, Peter Paul," POW Network.

91. Pete Camerota, interview by author.

92. JRCC Log; Couch, *The Jackal's Journey*, 62.

93. Michel, *Operation Linebacker II 1972*, 85.

94. Michel, *Operation Linebacker II 1972*, 85.

95. Eschmann, *Linebacker*, 192–193.

96. Hartsook, *Air Power Helps Stop the Invasion and End the War, 1972*, 154–156.

97. Capt. Gordon Peterson and Capt. David Taylor, "Intelligence Support to Communications with US POWs in Vietnam," *Studies in Intelligence* 60, no. 1 (March 2016): 1–15.

98. Eschmann, *Linebacker*, 179; Rudy Zuberbuhler, phone interview by author, 20 August 2018.

99. JRCC Log.

100. JRCC Log; "Camerota, Peter Paul," POW Network; Pete Camerota, interview by author.

101. JRCC Log.

102. JRCC Log.

103. Hobson, *Vietnam Air Losses*.

104. Darrel Whitcomb, "Rescue—1972: A Year of Challenge for Rescue Forces in the Violent Skies of Southeast Asia," *Air Power History* 64, no. 2 (Summer 2017): 33–42.

105. Stanley Karnow, *Vietnam: A History* (New York: Penguin, 1983), 686.

CHAPTER NINE. THE EVADER

*Interview by author, August 18–19 2017, Elizabeth City, NC.

1. Pete Camerota, interview by author.

2. JRCC Log, Air Force Historical Research Agency, Maxwell AFB, AL.

3. Camerota, interview by author.

4. Camerota, interview by author.

CHAPTER TEN. IN REDUCTION

*Quoted in Lt. Col. LeRoy Lowe, Project CHECO Report, Search and Rescue Operations in SEA, January 1971–March 1972.

1. Chris Hobson, *Vietnam Air Losses: United States Air Force, Navy, and Marine Corps Fixed-Wing Aircraft Losses in Southeast Asia, 1961–1973* (Hinkley, UK: Midland, 2001).

2. "ARRS SEA Combat losses," 30 October 1972, 1 January 1965–31 December 1972, K300.3912–3; History of the 3rd ARRG, 1 October–31 December 1972, K318.222–3, Air Force Historical Research Agency, Maxwell AFB, AL (hereafter AFHRA).

3. George Galdorisi and Tom Phillips, *Leave No Man Behind: The Saga of Combat Search and Rescue* (Minneapolis, MN: Zenith, 2008), 449.

4. MACV History, January 1972–March 1973, 1:B-39, AFHRA.

5. USAF Southeast Asia Review, 31 May 1974, SEAR-22, Air Force Special Operations Command History Office, Hurlburt Field, FL.

6. Command History of Helicopter Combat Support Squadron Seven, 1 January–31 December 1972, 9, provided by Ron Milam.

7. "Search for Military Medal Recipients," The Wall of Valor Project, accessed 4 April 2017, http://valor.militarytimes.com/search.php?medal=1&service=&conflict=&term=&page=2.

8. U.S. Department of Defense, "U.S. Air Force Air Force Cross Recipients," accessed 1 October 2015, http://valor.defense.gov/Recipients/AirForceAirForce-CrossRecipients.aspx.

9. "Search for Military Medal Recipients," The Wall of Valor Project, accessed 4 April 2017, http://valor.militarytimes.com/search.php?medal=2.

10. "Search for Military Medal Recipients," The Wall of Valor Project, accessed 4 April 2017, http://valor.militarytimes.com/search.php?medal=12.

11. Capt. David Francis and Maj. David Nelson, Project CHECO Report, Search and Rescue Operations in SEA, 1 April 1972–30 June 1973, 31, AFHRA.

12. End-of-Tour Report, Col. Cecil Muirhead, 14 January 1972–9 January 1973,

and End-of-Tour Report, Col. Herbert Zehnder, 9 January 1973–15 December 1973, K318.2131, AFHRA.

13. Ron Milam, email to author, 25 July 2018.

14. James Chiles, "Air America's Black Helicopter" (quotes), accessed 27 June 2016, http://www.air-america.org/index.php/en/15-about-air-america/articles/45-air -america-s-black-helicopter.

15. Brig. Gen. (ret) Dale Stovall, manuscript review comments, email to author, 2 July 2018.

16. Brian Laslie, *The Air Force Way of War: U.S. Tactics and Training after Vietnam* (Lexington: University Press of Kentucky, 2015), 25.

17. Brig. Gen. (ret) Dale Stovall, manuscript review comments in email to author, 28 July 2018.

18. Pete Camerota, interview by author, NC, 18–19 August 2017, Elizabeth City.

19. Earl Tilford, *Search and Rescue in Southeast Asia* (Washington, DC: Office of Air Force History, 1980), 155.

20. "Paris Peace Accords," Wikisource, accessed 27 September 2015, https:// en.wikisource.org/wiki/Paris_Peace_Accords; Marshall Michel III, *The Eleven Days of Christmas* (San Francisco, CA; Encounter, 2002), 234; John Sherwood, *Fast Movers: Jet Pilots and the Vietnam Experience* (New York: Free Press, 1999), ii; Alexander Haig and Charles McCarry, *Inner Circles: How America Changed the World—A Memoir* (New York: Warner, 1992), 313.

POSTSCRIPT

1. Darrel D. Whitcomb, *On a Steel Horse I Ride: A History of the MH-53 Pave Low Helicopters in War And Peace* (Maxwell AFB, AL: Air University Press, 2012), 134, 153, 286, 453, 645.

2. "General David L. Goldfein," U.S. Air Force, July 2016, http://www.af.mil /AboutUs/Biographies/Display/tabid/225/Article/108013/lieutenant-general -david-l-goldfein.aspx.

BIBLIOGRAPHY

**AIR FORCE HISTORICAL RESEARCH AGENCY (AFHRA),
MAXWELL AFB, ALABAMA**
Unit Histories
Third Aerospace Rescue and Recovery Group
    1 October–31 December 1971 (includes Thirty-Seventh ARRS, Thirty-Ninth ARRS, Fortieth ARRS)
    1 January–31 March 1972 (includes Thirty-Seventh ARRS, Thirty-Ninth ARRS, Fortieth ARRS)
    1 April–31 June 1972 (includes Thirty-Seventh ARRS, Fortieth ARRS)
    1 July–30 September 1972
    1 October–31 December 1972
Seventh Air Force
    1 July 1971–30 June 1972
    1 July 1972–30 March 1973
Fortieth Aerospace Rescue and Recovery Squadron
    1 July–30 September 1972
Fifty-Sixth Aerospace Rescue and Recovery Squadron
    1 July–31 December 1972
Fifty-Sixth Special Operations Wing
    1 October–31 December 1971, vols. 1, 2, 3 (includes First SOS)
    1 January–31 March 1972, vols. 1, 2, 3 (includes First SOS and Twenty-Third TASS)
    1 April–30 June 1972, vols. 1, 2, 3 (includes First SOS and Twenty-Third TASS)
    1 July–31 December 1972, vols. 1, 2, 3 (includes First SOS and Twenty-Third TASS)
307th Strategic Wing
    1 October–31 December 1972, vols. 1, 2, 3, 4
354th Tactical Fighter Wing
    1 October–31 December 1972, vols. 1, 2, 3, 4
    1 January–31 March 1973, vol. 1
366th Tactical Fighter Wing
    1 January–30 March 1972, vol. 1 (includes Twentieth TASS)
    1 April–30 June 1972, vol. 1 (includes Twentieth TASS)
504th Tactical Air Support Group
    1 October–31 December 1971, vol. 2 (includes Twenty-Third TASS)
6498th Air Base Wing
    1 July–30 September 1972, vol. 1 (includes Twentieth TASS)
    1 October–31 December 1972, vol. 1 (includes Twentieth TASS)

Oral Histories/End of Tour Reports
Maj. Gen. Jack Bellamy, 15 August 1974
Brig. Gen. Richard Cross, 20 December 1972
Capt. Charles DeBellevue, 14 October 1972

Lt. Col. William Harris, 12 June 1971–1 June 1972
Lt. Col. Baylor Haynes, undated
Maj. Gen. Eugene Hudson, 20 April 1973
Lt. Col. Gabriel Kardong, undated
Capt. Richard Ritchie, 11–30 October 1972
Col. Jack Robinson, 17 June 1972
Col. Scott Smith, 31 May 1973
Lt. Col. Stephen Sutton, 29 March 1973
Col. Robert Wayne, 16 October 1973
Col. Herbert Zehnder, 15 December 1973

Documents

Project CHECO (Contemporary Historical Examination of Current Operations)
Southeast Asia Reports
Capt. Conn Anderson, USAF Search and Rescue in Southeast Asia,
1961–1966
Maj. Richard Durkee, USAF Search and Rescue, July 1966–November 1967
Capt. David Francis and Maj. David Nelson, Search and Rescue Operations
in SEA, 1 April 1972–30 June 1973
Maj. Calvin Johnson, Linebacker Operations, September–December 1972
Lt. Col. LeRoy Lowe, Search and Rescue Operations in SEA, 1 January
1971–31 March 1972
J. Loye, Maj. G. St. Clair, and Maj. L. Johnson, Lam Son 719, 30 January–24
March 1971
Walter Lynch, USAF Search and Rescue in SEA, 1 July 69–31 December 1970
Capt. David Mann, The 1972 Invasion of Military Region I: Fall of Quang
Tri and Defense of Hue
Capt. Charles Nicholson, The USAF Response to the Spring 1972 NVN
Offensive: Situation and Redeployment
Maj. James Overton, USAF Search and Rescue, November 1967–June 1969
Col. A. Picinich, The F-111 in Southeast Asia, September 1972–January 1973
M. Porter, Linebacker: Overview of the First 120 Days
Maj. Paul Ringenbach, Airlift to Besieged Areas, 7 April–31 August 1972
———. The Battle for An Loc, 5 April–26 June 1972
Joint Rescue Coordination Center (JRCC) Logs, January 1969–February 1973,
missions referenced by date.

TRANSLATIONS OF VIETNAMESE HISTORIES BY MERLE PRIBBENOW

Air Defense Service Chronology of Events, 1953–1998. Hanoi, Vietnam: People's
Publishing House, 2000.
*The Dome of Fire in the Skies over Hanoi: Commemorating the 40th Anniversary
of Our "Dien Bien Phu in the Air" Victory.* Vietnam: Information and Media
Publishing House, 2012.
*The Fighting on the Annamite Mountains—Ho Chi Minh Trail Battlefield during
the Resistance War against the Americans.* Hanoi, Vietnam: People's Army
Publishing House, 2008.

The Intelligence Officer and the Prisoner of War Pilots. Hanoi, Vietnam: People's
   Army Publishing House, 2009.
*A Number of Air Defense Battles during the Resistance War against the Americans to
   Save the Nation.* Vol. 2. Hanoi, Vietnam: People's Army Publishing House, 1994.
A Number of Battles Fought by the Air Force during the War against the Americans.
   Hanoi, Vietnam: People's Publishing House, 1996.
History of the Air Defense Missile Troops, 1965–2005. Hanoi, Vietnam: People's Army
   Publishing House, Hanoi, 2007.
History of the Air Defense Service. Vol. 2. Hanoi, Vietnam: People's Army
   Publishing House, Hanoi, 1993.
History of the Air Defense Service. Vol. 3. Hanoi, Vietnam: People's Army Publishing
   House, Hanoi, 1994.
History of the 367th Air Defense Division. Vol. 2. Hanoi, Vietnam: People's Army
   Publishing House, Hanoi, 1993.
History of the 230th Anti-Aircraft Artillery Regiment. Hanoi, Vietnam: People's Army
   Publishing House, 1998.
History of the 236th SAM Regiment. Hanoi, Vietnam: People's Army Publishing
   House, 2004.
History of the 276th Air Defense Missile Regiment. http://www.vnmilitaryhistory.net
   /index.php/topic,371.30.html. Reply #31, 15 August 2008.
*Nghe An: History of the Resistance War against the Americans to Save the Nation
   (1954–1975).* Hanoi, Vietnam: People's Army Publishing House, 1995.
Remembering Our Debt to the Martyrs of the People's Air Force of Vietnam. Hanoi,
   Vietnam: People's Army Publishing House, 2010.
*The Fighting on the Annamite Mountains—Ho Chi Minh Trail Battlefield during
   the Resistance War against the Americans.* Hanoi, Vietnam: People's Army
   Publishing House, 2008.
The Intelligence Officer and the Prisoner of War Pilots. Hanoi, Vietnam: People's
   Army Publishing House, 2009.

BOOKS
Air War Vietnam. Introduction by Drew Middleton. New York: Merrill, 1978.
Albery, William, Raymond Robb, and Lt. Col. Lee Anderson. *MH-53J/M
   PAVELOW II/IV Systems Engineering Case Study.* Wright-Patterson AFB, OH:
   Air Force Institute of Technology, 2010.
Andrade, Dale. *America's Last Vietnam Battle: Halting Hanoi's 1972 Easter Offensive.*
   Lawrence: University Press of Kansas, 2001.
Anthony, Victor, and Richard Sexton. *The War in Northern Laos.* Washington, DC:
   Center for Air Force History, 1993.
Bell, Don. *The Tiger FACs.* Denver, CO: Outskirts, 2014.
Berger, Carl. *The United States Air Force in Southeast Asia, 1961–1973.* Washington,
   DC: Office of Air Force History, 1977.
Boivin, Lt. Col. Richard, Maj. John Schmidt, and Maj. Paul Balfe. *PAVE LOW—
   Evaluation of a Terrain Following Radar System for the HH-53 Helicopter,*
   Technical report No. 73–11. Edwards AFB, CA: Air Force Systems Command,
   US Air Force, March 1973.

Cates, Allen. *Honor Denied: The Truth about Air America and the CIA.* Bloomington, IN: IUniverse LLC, 2011.

Chinnery, Philip. *Full Throttle: True Stories of Vietnam Air Combat Told by the Men Who Lived It.* New York: St. Martin's, 1988.

Churchill, Jan. *Classified Secret: Controlling Airstrikes in the Clandestine War in Laos.* Manhattan, KS: Sunflower University Press, 1999.

Clarke, Jeffrey. *United States Army in Vietnam Advice and Support: The Final Years, 1965–1973.* Washington, DC: Center for Military History, 1988.

Cleared Hot: Forward Air Controller Stories from the Vietnam War: A Collection of Histories by US Air Force and Allied Forward Air Controllers from the Southeast Asia War, 1961–1975. Compiled by Charlie Pocock, Bob Gorman, and Peter Condon. 3 vols. Fort Walton Beach, FL: Forward Air Controller Association, 2008–2016.

Cosmas, Graham. *MACV: The Joint Command in the Years of Withdrawal, 1968–1973.* Washington, DC: Center for Military History, 2007.

Couch, Jon. *Caged Heroes: American POW Experiences from the Revolutionary War to the Present.* Bloomington, IN: AuthorHouse, 2011.

Davidson, Phillip B. *Vietnam at War: The History, 1946–1975.* New York: Oxford University Press, 1991.

Dockery, Kevin. *Operation Thunderhead.* New York: Berkley Caliber, 2008.

Dorland, Peter, and James Nanney. *Dust Off: Army Aeromedical Evacuation in Vietnam.* Washington, DC: Center of Military History, 1984.

Dorr, Robert. *Air War Hanoi.* New York: Blandford, 1988.

———. *Vietnam Air War Debrief.* Westport, CT: AIRtime, 1996.

———. *Vietnam MiG Killers.* Osceola, WI: Motorbooks International, 1988.

Drendel, Lou. *And Kill MiGs.* Warren, MI: Squadron/Signal, 1974.

Driscoll, Bill. *Peak Performance under Pressure.* Bloomington, IN: Triple Nickel, 2013.

Eschmann, Karl. *Linebacker: The Untold Story of the Air Raids over North Vietnam.* New York: Ivy, 1989.

Ethell, Jeffrey. *One Day in a Long War: May 10, 1972, Air War, North Vietnam.* New York: Random House, 1989.

Fails, Lt. Col. William. *Marines and Helicopters 1962–1973.* Washington, DC: History and Museums Division, Headquarters, USMC, 1978.

Fuller, John, and Helen Murphy. *The Raven Chronicles in Our Own Words from the Secret War in Laos.* Middletown, DE: Chronicles Project, 2016.

Galdorisi, George, and Tom Phillips. *Leave No Man Behind: The Saga of Combat Search and Rescue.* Minneapolis, MN: Zenith, 2008.

Gillespie, Robert. *Black Ops Vietnam: The Operational History of MACVSOG.* Annapolis, MD: Naval Institute, 2011.

Gilster, Herman. *The Air War in Southeast Asia: Case Studies and Selected Campaigns.* Maxwell AFB, AL: Air University Press, 1993.

Haig, Gen. Alexander, with Charles McCarry. *Inner Circles: How America Changed the World—A Memoir.* New York: Warner, 1992.

Hamilton-Merritt, Jane. *Tragic Mountains: The Hmong, the Americans, and the Secret Wars for Laos, 1942–1992.* Bloomington: Indiana University Press, 1993.

Harrington, Scott. *They Called It Naked Fanny.* Ashland, OR: Hellgate, 2016.

Hartsook, E. H. *Air Power Helps Stop the Invasion and End the War, 1972.* Washington, DC: Office of Air Force History, 1978.

Hobson, Chris. *Vietnam Air Losses: United States Air Force, Navy, and Marine Corps Fixed-Wing Aircraft Losses in Southeast Asia, 1961–1973.* Hinkley, UK: Midland, 2001.

Hofmann, Col. George R. Jr. *Operation Millpond: US Marines in Thailand, 1961.* Quantico, VA: History Division, United States Marine Corps, 2009.

Hyre, Steven, and Lou Benoit. *One-Eleven Down: F-111 Crashes and Combat Losses.* Atglen, PA: Schiffer Military History, 2012.

Karnow, Stanley. *Vietnam: A History.* New York: Penguin, 1983.

Kurlantzick, Joshua. *A Great Place to Have a War.* New York: Simon & Schuster Paperbacks, 2016.

Laslie, Brian. *The Air Force Way of War: U.S. Tactics and Training after Vietnam.* Lexington: University Press of Kentucky, 2015.

Lavalle, Maj. A. J. C. *Airpower and the 1972 Spring Invasion.* Washington, DC: Office of Air Force History, 1985.

Marolda, Edward. *By Sea, Air, and Land: An Illustrated History of the U.S. Navy and the War in Southeast Asia.* Washington, DC: Naval Historical Center, 1994.

Marshall, Phil. *Helicopter Rescues Vietnam.* Vols. 1–5. San Bernardino, CA: Self-published, 2016.

Mather, Paul. *M.I.A.: Accounting for the Missing in Southeast Asia.* Washington, DC: National Defense University Press, 1994.

McCrea, Michael. *U.S. Navy, Marine Corps, and Air Force Fixed-Wing Losses and Damage in Southeast Asia (1962–1973).* Arlington, VA: Center for Naval Analysis, 1976.

McKenna, Thomas. *Kontum: The Battle to Save South Vietnam.* Lexington: University Press of Kentucky, 2011.

Melson, Maj. Charles, and Lt. Col. Curtis Arnold. *U.S. Marines in Vietnam: The War That Would Not End.* Washington, DC: Headquarters, U.S. Marine Corps, 1991.

Michel, Marshall III. *Clashes: Air Combat over North Vietnam, 1965–1972.* Annapolis, MD: Naval Institute, 1997.

———. *The Eleven Days of Christmas.* San Francisco, CA: Encounter, 2002.

———. *Operation Linebacker II 1972: The B-52s Are Sent to Hanoi.* Oxford, UK: Osprey, 2018.

Newland, Claude G., James W. Reese, and Fellow Rustics, eds. *The Rustics: A Top Secret War in Cambodia, History of the Rustic Forward Air Controllers, 1970–1973.* Destin, FL: LuLu, 2001.

Norris, Tom, Mike Thornton, and Dick Couch. *By Honor Bound.* New York: St. Martin's, 2016.

O'Rourke, Kevin, and Joe Peters. *Taking Fire: Saving Captain Aikman: A Story of the Vietnam War.* Havertown, PA: Casemate, 2013.

Pararescue 50 Years Plus. Charlotte, NC: Fine, 1996.

Plaster, John. *SOG: A Photo History of the Secret Wars.* Boulder, CO: Paladin, 2000.

———. *SOG: The Secret Wars of America's Commandos in Vietnam.* New York: Simon & Schuster, 1998.

Price, Alfred. *History of U.S. Electronic Warfare.* London, UK: Macdonald and Jane's, 1977.

Randolph, Stephen. *Powerful and Brutal Weapons: Nixon, Kissinger, and the Easter Offensive.* Cambridge, MA: Harvard University Press, 2007.

Rawlins, Lt. Col. Eugene, and Maj. William Sambito. *Marines and Helicopters 1946–1962.* Washington, DC: History and Museums Division, Headquarters, USMC, 1976.

Reeder, William. *Through the Valley: My Captivity in Vietnam.* Annapolis, MD: Naval Institute Press, 2016.

Reynolds, Roger. *Inside Operation Linebacker. Two USAF Project CHECO Reports: Linebacker: Overview of the First 120 Days, 27; Linebacker: September–December 1972.* West Chester, OH: Nafziger Collection, 2017.

Ridnouer, Col. (ret) Dennis. *The Vietnam Air War: First Person.* Charleston, SC: CreateSpace, 2016.

———. *The Vietnam Air War: From the Cockpit.* Charleston, SC: CreateSpace, 2017.

Robbins, Christopher. *Air America.* New York: Avon, 1979.

———. *The Ravens: The Men Who Flew in America's Secret War in Laos.* New York: Crown, 1987.

Rock, Col. (ret) Edward. *First In, Last Out: Stories by the Wild Weasels.* Bloomington, IN: AuthorHouse, 2005.

Sander, Robert. *Invasion of Laos, 1971: Lam Son 719.* Norman: University of Oklahoma Press, 2014.

Sherwood, John. *Fast Movers: Jet Pilots and the Vietnam Experience.* New York: Free Press, 1999.

Stoffey, Col. Robert. *Fighting to Leave: The Final Years of America's War in Vietnam, 1972–1973.* Minneapolis, MN: Zenith, 2008.

Thompson, Wayne. *To Hanoi and Back: The U.S. Air Force and North Vietnam, 1966–1973.* Washington, DC: Smithsonian Institution Press, 2000.

Tilford, Earl. *Search and Rescue in Southeast Asia , 1961–1975.* Washington, DC: Office of Air Force History, 1980.

———. *Setup: What the Air Force Did in Vietnam and Why.* Maxwell AFB, AL: Air University Press, 1991.

Trest, Warren, *Air Commando One: Heinie Aderholt and America's Secret Air Wars.* Washington, DC: Smithsonian Institution Press, 2000.

Turley, Col. (ret) Gerald, *The Easter Offensive: The Last American Advisors, Vietnam, 1972.* Annapolis, MD: Naval Institute Press, 1985.

Uhlig, Frank Jr. *Vietnam: The Naval Story.* Annapolis, MD: Naval Institute Press, 1986.

Van Etten, Ben. "Rescue," Terry Turner File, Air America Files, Eugene McDermott Library, University of Texas, Dallas, n.d.

Whitcomb, Darrel. *Call Sign—Dustoff: A History of U.S. Army Aeromedical Evacuation from Conception to Hurricane Katrina.* Frederick, MD: Borden Institute Press, 2011.

———. *Combat Search and Rescue in Desert Storm.* Maxwell AFB, AL: Air University Press, 2006.

———. *On a Steel Horse I Ride: A History of the MH-53 Pave Low Helicopters in War and Peace.* Maxwell AFB, AL: Air University Press, 2012.

———. *The Rescue of Bat 21.* Annapolis, MD: Naval Institute Press, 1998.

Willbanks, James. *The Battle of An Loc.* Bloomington: Indiana University Press, 2005.

Yarborough, Tom. *Da Nang Diary: A Forward Air Controller's Gunsight View of Flying with SOG.* Philadelphia: Casemate, 2018.

ARTICLES

Curry, Ken. "My Miracle Day." *Friends Journal* (Spring 2017): 5–7.

Geffen, Theo van. "U.S. Mini-air War against North Vietnam: Protective Reaction Strikes, 1968-1972." *Air Power History* 66, no. 2 (Summer 2019): 31–44.

Glines, C. V. "The Son Tay Raid." *Air Force Magazine* 78, no. 11 (November 1995): n.p.

Jane, Maj. Gen. (ret) Randy. "The Last Prop Fighter Sandys, Hobos, Fireflies, Zorros, and Spads." *Air and Space Power Journal* 31, no. 2 (Summer 2017): 82–90.

Latham, Brig. Gen. (ret) James. "Prairie Fire FAC, Fighter Pilot, POW." *Drop* (Summer 2018): 35–42.

Morgan, Mark. "The Story of HC-7/CSAR: Orphans of the 7th Fleet." *Hook, Journal of Carrier Aviation* (Fall 1998): 32–41.

Peterson, Capt. (ret) Gordon, and Capt. (ret) Michael Slattery. "Spence Dry: A SEAL's Story." *Proceedings* 131, no. 7 (July 2005). https://www.usni.org/magazines/proceedings/2005/july/spence-dry-seals-story.

Peterson, Capt. (ret) Gordon, and David Taylor. "Intelligence Support to Communications with US POWs in Vietnam." *Studies in Intelligence* 60, no. 1 (March 2016): 1–15.

Schlight, Col. (ret) John. "A War Too Long: Part I." *Air Power History* 62, no. 2 (Summer 2015): 28–49.

Whitcomb, Col. (ret) Darrel. "'Bar Napkin Tactics,' Tactical Leadership in Southeast Asia." *Air Power History* 61, no. 4 (Winter 2014): 26–33.

———. "Flying the First Mission of Desert Storm." *Air Power History* 59, no. 1 (Spring 2012): 4–11.

———. "New Sandys in Town: A-7s in Rescue Operations in Southeast Asia." *Air Power History* 62, no. 3 (Fall 2015): 34–41.

———. "Pave Nail: There at the Beginning of the Precision Weapons Revolution." *Air Power History* 58, no. 1 (Spring 2011): 14–27.

———. "Rescue—1972: a Year of Challenge for Rescue Forces in the Violent Skies of Southeast Asia." *Air Power History* 64, no. 2 (Summer 2017): 33–42.

———. "Rescue Operations during Linebacker II." *Air Power History* 65, no. 2 (Summer 2018): 31–44.

Whitcomb, Col. (ret) Darrel, and Col. (ret) Forrest Marion. "Team Sport, Combat Search and Rescue over Serbia, 1999." *Air Power History* 61, no. 3 (Fall 2014): 28–37.

NARRATIVES/MANUSCRIPTS

Andrews, Col. (ret) William. "To Fly and Fight: The Experience of American Airmen in Southeast Asia." Doctoral thesis, George Mason University, Fairfax, VA, 2011.

Couch, Jon. *The Jackal's Journey*. Draft manuscript, 2017. Used with permission.

Crowe, Cdr. (USCG) Joseph. After Action Report, Coast Guard—Air Force Exchange, May 1971–May 1972. Provided by family.

Haynes, Col. (ret) Baylor. Jolly Green 2002 Reunion, Baylor Haynes Seminar, 4 May 2002. Unpublished. Copy from the Jolly Greens Association.

Milam, Ron. "Historical Documents Pertaining to Helicopter Combat Support Squadron Seven (HC-7)." Unpublished, undated. Used with permission.

Plunkett, Howard, "F-105 SEA Losses—1972." Unpublished, n.d. Used with permission.

INDEX

operations, 29; at Son Tay, 31, 34–35, 120, 206; statistics on, 29, 45, 76, 113, 144, 248, 290, 295

prisoners of war. *See* POWs

Quang Tri, South Vietnam: and Nguyen Hue offensive, 78–87, 88–90, 98–100, 113; NVA offensive at, 38, 78–79, 114–116; SARs in area of, 81–86, 87–88, 93–94, 113, 116–117, 118–119, 127–128, 145, 225, 276, 297; South Vietnamese capture of, 127–128, 165, 221–222; US air operations at, 79, 107, 113, 114–115, 116–118, 127–128, 129, 136, 139, 160, 186, 187–190, 193, 225, 233, 258, 276

Queen. *See* OL-A (Operating Location Alpha, Son Tra)

QU-22s, 92, 104–105, 171, 207, 208, 232

Radcliffe, Ron, 65, 99, 318n41
RA-5s, 170, 274, 286
Ramsbottom, W., 130
Ramsey, William, 197
Randall, Robert, 196
Rash 31 SAR, 246, 247 (photo)
Ratzlaff, Brian, 212–213
Raven 11 SAR, 58–59, 76
Raven FACs: and A-7 concerns, 249–250; in Laos, 48, 52, 56–59, 76, 174–175, 219, 236–237, 249–250, 262–264, 268, 271–273, 272 (photo), 275; Laotian FACs trained by, 268; losses of, 76, 271, 275
Raven 52 SAR, 56–58, 57 (photo)
Raven 40 SAR, 271–273
Raven Jet 314 SAR, 237
Raven 20 SAR, 236–237
Red Baron 752 SAR, 221
Red Crown, 62, 124, 176, 182, 197–198, 202, 279
Red River, 147, 150, 151, 153–154
Reeder, Bill, 131–132
Reich, Bill, 126
Rescue Combat Air Patrol (RESCAP), 140
rescue coordination centers (RCCs), 5, 22, 147, 183, 194–195, 196–197, 268, 290. *See also* OL-A (Operating Location Alpha, Son Tra); OL-B (Operation Location Bravo, Udorn)
rescue statistics, 29, 45, 76, 113, 144–145, 248, 290–291, 295–297
RF-4s, 40, 93, 195, 227–228, 236, 238, 249, 292; downing of, 204–205; as "Fast Facs," 121; loran navigational system and, 61, 217; NVA air defenses and need for, 121; and

RF-8s, 6, 173–174, 197; and RF-4Cs, 26, 32, 55, 254; at Udorn, 104, 200–202, 218, 253–254, 284–285
RF-101s, 6, 11
Riess, Chuck, 275
Ringwood, Paul, 174
Ripley, John, 81
Ritchie, Steve, 147, 182
Robb, Warren, 218
Robbin, Jay, 298 (photo)
Roberson, Danny, 192
Robertson, Leonard, 186–187
Robinson, Jack, 42, 144, 161–162
Robinson, Paul, 194
Rocket Ridge, 111, 130–131, 132
Rockriver 100 SAR, 203
Rolls, Karl, 228–229
Rosebeary, Mike, 191
Ross, R., 129
Rowe, Bruce, 64
Royal Laotian forces, 6, 52
Russell, Don, 252
Rutledge, Jimmie, 211
Ryan, John, 21, 71

Sabre 74 SAR, 206
Sabre 73 SAR, 234
Sabre 26 SAR, 229
SAC (Strategic Air Command), 43–44, 101, 122, 255, 260, 261–262, 292
Saigon, South Vietnam: JRCC at, 82, 83, 134, 147; in NVA attack plan, 53, 138, 139, 252; SARCC/JSARCC at, 5, 13, 19; Tan Son Nhut Air Base at, 252; US embassy in, 49
Sandys. *See* A-1s
SARCC (Search and Rescue Coordination Center), 5–6, 13. *See also* JRCC (Joint Rescue Coordination Center); JSARCC (Joint Search and Rescue Coordination Center)
Saunders, Alan, 6
Savannakhet, Laos, 67, 70, 74–75, 92, 105
Scarlet 03 SAR, 264–266, 266 (photo), 276–277, 286–288, 289–290
Schibler, Mark, 140, 141 (photo), 220–221
Schuyler, Philip, 143
Schwertfeger, Bill, 62–63
Scorpion 85 SAR (7 October), 225
Scorpion 85 SAR (31 July), 194
Scorpion 115 SAR, 99
Scott, Jackson, 117, 161
Scott, Randy, 62–63, 157, 178, 204, 207